T0317714

ENVISIONING DEMOCRACY

Envisioning Democracy

New Essays after Sheldon Wolin's
Political Thought

EDITED BY TERRY MALEY AND JOHN R. WALLACH

UNIVERSITY OF TORONTO PRESS
Toronto Buffalo London

ISBN 978-1-4875-6560-2 (cloth)
ISBN 978-1-4875-5404-0 (EPUB)
ISBN 978-1-4875-6913-6 (PDF)

Library and Archives Canada Cataloguing in Publication
Title: Envisioning democracy : new essays after Sheldon Wolin's political thought /
    edited by Terry Maley and John R. Wallach.
Names: Maley, Terry, editor. | Wallach, John R., editor. | Wolin, Sheldon S., honoree.
Description: Includes bibliographical references and index.
Identifiers: Canadiana (print) 20220396752 | Canadiana (ebook) 20220396809 |
    ISBN 9781487565602 (cloth) | ISBN 9781487569136 (PDF) |
    ISBN 9781487554040 (EPUB)
Subjects: LCSH: Democracy. | LCSH: Political science.
Classification: LCC JC423 .E58 2023 | DDC 321.8 – dc23

We wish to acknowledge the land on which the University of Toronto Press operates. This land is the traditional territory of the Wendat, the Anishnaabeg, the Haudenosaunee, the Métis, and the Mississaugas of the Credit First Nation.

University of Toronto Press acknowledges the financial support of the Government of Canada, the Canada Council for the Arts, and the Ontario Arts Council, an agency of the Government of Ontario, for its publishing activities.

Canada Council   Conseil des Arts
for the Arts   du Canada

ONTARIO ARTS COUNCIL
CONSEIL DES ARTS DE L'ONTARIO
an Ontario government agency
un organisme du gouvernement de l'Ontario

Funded by the   Financé par le
Government   gouvernement
of Canada   du Canada

Contents

ENVISIONING DEMOCRACY

Introduction

Over the last century, democracy has become a term of political praise. But that was not always so, and it is now seen from a myriad of angles, making the meaning of "democracy" today seem empty or opaque. But democracy is too important to be left to vague references to "our democracy." We seek here to elucidate and enrich its meaning as public-spirited scholars, in the wake of the political thought of Sheldon S. Wolin (1922–2015), one of America's most illuminating theorists of democracy.

Ancient Greeks originated the term to characterize direct authoritative power by adult male citizens in a city-state of around 350,000 persons (including women, slaves, and resident-foreigners), most of whom opposed the pretensions and privileges of oligarchy. It is now used statically to refer to the political orders of states where thousands of politicians govern millions of citizens. In our era democracy not only begs definition; it harbours fragility. Sustaining it requires certain dispositions of its citizens and appropriate egalitarian institutions of governance. So, what can we cogently mean by "democracy," and how does that relate to its usages today and its possible future? More particularly, what is the dynamic of democracy in societies that belong to an interdependent world marked by growing inequality within and between states, many of whose citizens endorse autocratic leaders and movements that seem to sabotage the general welfare? These central questions cannot be answered in the abstract; they must address the real world of democracy as a political phenomenon interacting with economic, cultural, and intellectual life.

Sheldon Wolin's political thought encouraged this kind of thinking. In the following collection of essays, scholars inspired by Wolin's political visions take on the challenges facing democracy today, critically accounting for its historical conditions, theoretical elements, and practical impediments. Of late, democracy has been discussed in countless books, journals, other organs of public opinion, and social media. But its interpretation has been overwhelmed by the immediacy of political events, the spectacle of elections, the medallions of rights, populisms, liberalism, or narrow discursive conventions. Our collection of essays seeks to transcend such confines in promoting both knowledge of and care for democracy. For even if "democracy" is awkward as a term of political art, no other one encapsulates the potential power of common peoples. Moreover, threats to democracy now come from across the political spectrum – these days, particularly from the right's attacks on both the public realm and society's middle and lower classes, the political power of which make possible the form and substance of democracy.

The legacy of Wolin's work offers another layer of context. In *Politics and Vision: Continuity and Innovation in Western Political Thought* (1960), Wolin revived political theory when it was being dominated by behaviouralism as well as an historical empirical and linguistic analysis. His unique book indicated how the tradition of Western political thought can provide intellectual and cultural resources to help think about politics critically without reifying past prejudices. Aspects of that tradition have been extensively criticized by feminist, postcolonial, critical race, postmodern, political-economy, and poststructuralist writings since the 1980s, but Wolin's vision of political theory as a vocation has endured. Indeed, it has assumed special relevance amid new challenges posed to the political realm by authoritarian, madcap rulers, as well as COVID-19. New communications and social media technologies, and economic policies informed by neoliberalism, threaten to overwhelm political theory as well as the critical thinking cultivated by the liberal arts, humanities, and the critical social sciences.

In *Politics and Vision*, Wolin not only interpreted central texts and topics in the Western tradition of political thought. He also argued that retrieving its intellectual, philosophical, cultural, and political resources was necessary in conceiving politics that valued citizenship as a form or way of life. His notions of the political and democracy rejected not only behaviouralist methods for understanding politics but also Schumpeter's cramped view of democracy, sometimes echoed by the American political scientist Robert A. Dahl in the post–Second World War era, that authorized rule by competing elites. In the 1960s and 1970s, the Canadian political theorist C.B. Macpherson, as well as a growing number of scholars and commentators since then, have confirmed Wolin's critique, coming to regard the plural-elite "model" and the actual institutional arrangements of liberal democracy as inadequate means for fulfilling democracy's potential for enhancing personal development, political freedom, and egalitarian self-governance. We believe, as Wolin did, that democracy's ability to develop individual capacities, as argued by John Stuart Mill and John Dewey, has been undermined by the power of corporate capital and markets to exploit individuality and infiltrate the minds of citizens – facilitated now by capacities to surveil and punish deployed by bureaucratic, technocratic, and militarized states.

After *Politics and Vision,* and his involvement as a professor at the University of California Berkeley in the Free Speech Movement of the mid-1960s and the university's harsh debates about social science, Wolin began to address an even wider array of thinkers and issues. He wrote about Leo Strauss and the politics of interpretation; political theory as a vocation (and later, invocation); the limits of Max Weber's attempts to launch a modern social science; Hannah Arendt's views of politics and democracy; John Rawls's theory of political liberalism; and the absence of engagement with the real world of democracy by some of the Frankfurt School critical theorists, such as Horkheimer and Adorno. Wolin also began to focus less on the potentiality of the political as such than on the beleaguered condition of contemporary democracy. In 1980, he attracted funding (withdrawn three years later) to produce the intellectually and politically innovative journal, *democracy: a journal of political renewal and radical change* (1981–3), which vigorously responded to the "Reagan Revolution" and Thatcherism. Subsequently, Wolin focused more directly on democracy and political thought in the context of the American republic, notably in a collection of essays, *The Presence of the Past,* published in the wake of the bicentennial of the American Constitution. In 1996, Wolin's article, "Fugitive Democracy," appeared. It staked out a unique perspective on democracy, motivated significantly by his conception of the modern state as "superpower." In *Tocqueville between Two Worlds* (2001), Wolin offered a unique reading of Tocqueville's concerns about the growing powers of capitalism, modern science and technology, and the bureaucratic state in relation to the activity of political theory.

This shift in his work clearly articulated a standpoint that was different from Rawls's "political liberalism," models of deliberative democracy inspired by Madison and Habermas in the 1990s, as well as Foucault and postmodernisms.[1] With Wolin having retired from teaching in 1987, the new millennium saw two collections of scholarly essays that engaged many features of his work. In an expanded edition of *Politics and Vision* (2004 – nearly double the size of the first edition with new chapters on Marx, Nietzsche, Dewey, and twentieth-century liberalism), Wolin characteristically connected his interpretations to current political concerns and theoretical discourses. In his final book, *Democracy Incorporated,* published when he was eighty-six, Wolin delineated the deep dimensions of democracy's current malaise and noted the rough road ahead if democracy is to become full and strong.

In the current context, the post-war "models" of liberal democracy (about which Macpherson wrote in the 1970s) are being critically challenged from "the left" as well as from "the right." New political fissures have complicated collective landscapes, spurred by the expansionism of corporate economies, resentful nationalisms, and the manipulations of the media made possible by digital platforms. Meanwhile, worldwide protests attempt to thwart impending environmental disasters, while post-colonial movements, resurgent feminisms (Me-Too), Black Lives Matter, Idle No More and Land Back in Canada, the Landless peasant movements in Latin America, and others fight for dignity and recognition, and economic and social justice, against resistance from established elites and political parties promoting authoritarian capitalism in liberal democracies in the Global North and South. How shall we address them, given their complexity and histories, in ways that honour politics and democracy? In his last book, *Democracy Incorporated* (2008), Wolin asked: "What causes a democracy to change into some non- or anti-democratic system, and what kind of system is democracy likely to change into?"[2] By asking these questions we may gain a good sense of what is to be done.

The essays presented here, in their discussions of democracy, move on from Wolin's questions and concerns. Neither Wolin's works nor previous discussions of it are simply templates for this volume's writers.[3] Rather, they are touchstones. We engage Wolin's legacy and move beyond it in thinking through what democracy can mean now and in the future. For despite his significant influence on political theorists since the 1960s in terms of political theory and democratic thought, Wolin's intellectual contributions have been under-appreciated. Yet Wolin's thought is now undergoing something of a revival, amid the contemporary crises of and confusion about how to foster social-democracy in the wake of liberal democracy. These essays are not uncritical of Wolin's thought; rather, they reflect his intellectual influence and political care for democracy and independently build on it. Some contributors have worked with Wolin as undergraduate and/or graduate students, including co-editor John Wallach, while Terry Maley introduced Wolin to a French political theory audience at a 2015 conference in Paris and hosted a conference on Wolin's work at York University in 2016. Wolin valued independent, critical thinking above all else, and the contributors honour this value by taking his work as points of reference for their new essays.

Democracy as a political order has been regularly contested as a kind of power and term of discourse. As democracy slowly emerged in Athens under the thin frame of the Solonian polis, its advocates had to battle against aristocrats and ruling elites. Once a democratic order became ascendant in Athens in the wake of Kleisthenes's constitutional reforms (508–7 BCE), democratic Athenians battled *with* the oligarchic Spartans against the autocratic Persians on behalf of Hellenic independence.[4] Athenians then acquired an empire, which caused fear in Sparta and among independent city-states. In 431 BCE, war broke out between the Athenians and the Spartans, as the former had extended imperial control over other *poleis*. As the war turned against the Athenians, they suffered two brief oligarchic coups (in 411 and 404) but then restored their democracy which, after the second, stabilized and endured for eighty years before Macedonians took control of Athenian politics in 323 BCE.

Although the Roman republic and Florentine city-state had democratic elements, neither found it apt to call themselves democracies. "Democracy" did not appear in political parlance and practice again until the English Civil War in the 1640s, in the American War for Independence a little more than a century later, and then during the French Revolution, when French revolutionaries used it to denote their aspirations. But despite the introduction of democracy as a term of political rhetoric, it never signified a widely practised or valorized politics.[5] By the time democracy was publicly used to signify an actual political order, in the American republic in the early 1800s, it already had been overtaken by an expansive, representative republic that understood the *demos* as a multitude of enterprising individuals more than as a coherent political force. The shortcomings of what came to be known as "liberal democracies" radically disappointed Marx, who saw this kind of democracy as only able to reflect social and class conflict. This catalysed Marx's vision of communism as the transcending of "bourgeois" democracy.[6] From the late nineteenth century until the mid-twentieth century, democracy has been linked to a fungible ideology called "liberalism," with which John Dewey notably took issue throughout his work (despite some affinities).

In the second half of the twentieth century, the status of democracy changed again, under the impress of the American state. After agitation for universal suffrage, women's and trade union rights, and its rhetorical use to promote opposition to mid-century fascism, democracy emerged in the post–Second World War era as *the* normative gold standard by which states and politics were to be judged – thereby losing much of its historical edge as a critique of oligarchical power. In what was then known as the First World, it was regarded as an elite-led, or "plural-elite model" of democracy in which citizens became subjects or mere consumers whose primary options involved choosing among political programs proposed by elites in nominally competitive electoral systems. Over the last forty years, however, that model and its theoretical justifications, practices, and institutions have been intensely scrutinized and widely opposed – both by the right, which also has regarded democracy fearfully, and by the left, which began to see both "liberal" and "conservative" political parties as agents of the few rather than of the many. The Achilles' heel of democracy as the tyranny of the *majority* (Madison, Constant, Tocqueville, J.S. Mill) became a political order that authorized tyrannies of political *minorities*.

The term "democracy" is used indiscriminately today to refer to massive political orders heavily indebted to the demands of capital and the security of powerful states. Those who resist these tendencies are increasingly taking to the streets, as the only way to influence government. This chaos of meaning, generated amid the myriad of links between political orders contrived via globalization, calls for imaginative reinterpretations. Wonder abounds about what, and if, democracy of any kind can have a practical presence in the twenty-first century without being hijacked by political forces inimical to its commitments to freedom, equality, mutuality, and political agency for all citizens. Even so, the reasons for the emergence of democracy long ago still press upon us today, including resistance to the unjust arrogation of power by a few over the well-being of the many – wherever the many can act as a political force.

Democracy today presupposes consent via the ballot box. We regard that activity along with its corollary institutions as necessary yet insufficient conditions of democratic possibility. The volume's contributors tend to view democracy as an oppositional force, an interpretive ethos and discourse that acknowledges the extant realities of political power while transcending them by way of critical analysis, historical understanding, informed imagination, and political action. In the wake of Dewey and Wolin, we believe that to sustain itself democracy must always break existing political forms.[7] The intellectual perspectives, political subjects, and educational contributions of this volume, therefore, shift the discourse of democracy away from its function as a rhetorical mechanism for enlisting ordinary citizens to support leaders who too often betray them. It is not that we don't recognize the need for leadership; we are simply following a long tradition of ethical and political thought that advises critical scepticism about what results from the conjunction of governmental authority and its investment with power by some version of the people – especially if demotic concerns have been marginalized.

This collection of essays is dedicated to envisioning democracy and beyond, primarily in two dimensions – democracy and political theory, democracy as a political practice, as well as inter-connections between them. In theoretical terms, we understand democracy as the substantive political power of non-wealthy majorities in various societies. This includes not only the right of representation, but people's right and capacity to exercise that power actively in determining priorities of the collectivity, in the transparent design and implementation of policies, and having a meaningful say in how public resources are distributed – i.e., greater substantive equality, closer monitoring and regulation of elites, and avenues for various kinds of participation and decision-making for all members of the community. The contributors do not employ "democracy" as a signifier for contemporary states, even though most countries and many different kinds of politics now claim to be democratic. Also, people who identify with democracy as a value can oppose projects or policies that are designed to produce greater equality and serve democratic ends (more progressive taxation, or more funding for public schools or public health care). Contested views (and theories) of democracy, views of democracy from above and below, today and historically, contain their own tensions. The term democracy has included differing ideas of equality (broader or more inclusive), liberty (individual vs. collective), power (who has it and why), participation, the relation of citizens to and within the economy, and various inequalities (based on race, gender, class, disability, and others) among citizens and between citizens and non-citizens. Many views and models of democracy, and their institutional manifestations from Madison to today (like those in Schumpeter's post–Second World War plural-elite model or democracy from above) have had structural inequities built into them. These legacies of past inequalities persist within contemporary liberal democracy's institutional forms today. Witness how the arcane rules of the US Senate have been used to great effect to either pass unpopular legislation (large tax cuts for the wealthy) or to undermine and block popular bills from being signed into law (Obamacare, more robust voting rights legislation). Thus, envisioning democracy is not exhausted by what is presented as "democratic" by elites with deep pockets, in the mainstream media or social media, or in existing institutional arrangements.

Instead, the contributors to the volume embrace the plain meaning of democracy. And even as they recognize that the notion of a *demos* is partly anachronistic in the twenty-first century (because of its Athenian residue and the realities of huge, complex modern states and the globalized economy), they believe in democracy as humanity's best political hope. This volume, in short, renews a dialogue about politics and democracy among political theorists, social scientists, journalists, and untitled citizens that evokes and engages Wolin's political and democratic thought.

Section I – Wolin and Democratic Theory: Ancient Roots, Modern Issues

John R. Wallach's piece opens our collection with "Interpreting Democracy in Undemocratic Societies." All of the Framers of the US Constitution condemned democracy. They saw democracy as an inadequate model because of its inability to control the "majority factions" which they believed plagued political life – in small or large societies. Nonetheless, the American republic has come to be called a democracy – along with many other capitalist, highly developed states in the West and less economically developed states in Asia, Africa, and Latin America, which only can be called democracy with a wink and a nod. As a result, the task of interpreting "democracy" within societies that radically constrain popular political power puzzles. It has become exponentially more problematic with the rise of authoritarian populisms; the bizarre, troubling presidency of Donald Trump as the chief executive of American "democracy" and his continuing sway over the Republican party, and the appropriation of democracy as an agent for protecting minority factions rather than promoting demotic participation and interests. In this light, what does democratic criticism mean? Have we become entrenched in a post-democratic era? Whether or not that's so, what does it mean now to use democracy as a term of art to authorize or criticize political actions sanctioned by the people and their legislators?

This question is not new. Plato responded to Athenian democracy and political life with a theory of justice; Rousseau addressed the problems of failing *ancien regimes* by generating a theory that only could become practical in the hands of a hypothetical lawgiver; Marx folded democracy into communism, and Mill thought that "true" democracy could become manifest with institutionalizing structures that honoured "competence" in public bureaucracies and legislatures while managing the British Empire. None of their answers, however, can gain traction now. Yet using good democracy to criticize bad democracy (*pace* Dewey, Sheldon Wolin, and James Tully) sometimes begs the question. For those who still believe in the virtuous political potential of the *demos*, whether in the United States, the United Kingdom, the European Union, Asia, Africa, or Latin America, we need new angles for tapping that potential while keeping track of the political ethics of actual citizens and the political choices they have at their disposal. Wallach's chapter addresses the epistemological and practical obstacles that face "democracy" as a tool of political criticism in the present so as to enhance democratic politics in the future.

Ingrid Creppell's chapter, "Aristotle on Enmity: Ideology, Somatic Justice, and Emotions," goes beyond Wolin's perspective on Aristotle in *Politics and Vision*. Wolin read Aristotle's approach to compromise and mediation in a conflictual but vibrant political community. Creppell highlights Aristotle's treatment of searing, domestic political conflict (*stasis*). We not only differ, we sometimes find ourselves locked in irresolvable enmity. When and why does this happen? Aristotle explains the emergence and coherence of such a mindset. His *Politics* describes ways in which political communities struggle and fracture into destructive *stasis* or faction. While scholarship on Aristotle has recognized the realistic as well as teleological dimensions of his work, Creppell draws insights from Aristotle for addressing contemporary political conflict. She finds that Aristotle argued justice to be the fundamental reasoning behind enmity and reconstructs his distinction between two conceptions of (non-ideal) justice: ideological justice pertaining to the regime and somatic justice pertaining to living in the city. Emotions tied to justice operate through both levels of political justice. The distinction between ideological and somatic expressions of justice enables us to understand Aristotle's observation that enmity is about "big things" but must be filtered through both abstract ideas and individual embodied experiences. Fittingly, Creppell argues that enmity remains, for Aristotle, an action-disposition aimed at some good and coherent from a political-moral point of view.

Jason Frank's chapter, "Sheldon Wolin and Democratic 'Theory,'" explores the complicated and often contradictory relationship between democracy and "theory" in Wolin's work, with a particular focus on why democratic theory, as currently practised, does not grasp the experience and practice of democratic politics. A democratic theorist worthy of the name cannot proclaim epistemic authority and presume to make a one-time "gift to the demos" (as Wolin put it in his review of Rawls's *Political Liberalism)*, neglecting the central democratic importance of the formative collective struggle to achieve equal rights by the people themselves. For Wolin, political theory's focus on rules and norms, procedures and principles, organization and institutional form exists in sustained tension with democracy's egalitarian protest of the reduction of politics to rule, its transgressive opposition to norms and forms, and to the institutionalization and routinization of political action. Political theory's typical tendency towards abstraction and propositional authority is itself at odds with the historically embedded and power-sensitive conception of democracy Wolin emphasized. This poses a genuine challenge for seriously critical democratic thought.

Democracy always bears the mark of its diverse and localized origins and struggles, so the problem of identifying a tradition of theoretical reflection on democracy is not only a problem of content but also of theoretical form. Frank's chapter poses the central question "What form could a genuinely *democratic* theory possibly take?" Frank's discussion draws its answer – and its inspiration – from the scattered suggestions found across the full range of Wolin's work – from such early seminal work as "Political Theory as a Vocation" to his essays for *democracy*, from his writing on the student movements to his essays on "fugitive democracy" and the ancient Greeks. Across his diverse body of writing, Wolin challenged not only self-congratulatory contemporary understandings of democracy but also the self-congratulatory expectations of the tasks and goals of democratic theory.

Section II – Memory and Myth in Wolin and Beyond

Terence Ball, in his chapter "Wolin on Myth: A Kind of Refutation and Reform," notes that he and his teacher, Sheldon Wolin, agreed on many things, but that Wolin's views on the role and reality of myth in the modern (or perhaps postmodern) world were not among them. He argued that modern myths are manufactured by marketers and others seeking to "evoke the archaic" in a postmythic world. Ball argues that this is generally true. But there is a single important exception to this rule: the so-called myth of Adam examined by R.W.B. Lewis, among others. This is the myth that likens Americans to Adam and America to the garden he inhabited before being cast out. Ball argues that the myth of Adam, if genuine, would be pervasive in places one would not expect. Ball's chapter examines three of these: the physicist Gerard O'Neill in his *The*

High Frontier; the postmodernist philosopher Richard Rorty in *Contingency, Irony, and Solidarity*; and John Rawls in *A Theory of Justice*. These case studies suggest the possibility that *mythic presuppositions* underlie many significant political theories.

In "Collective Memory and the Settler-Colonial Politics of Reconciliation in Canada," Calvin Z.L. Lincez critically analyses the politics of reconciliation in settler-colonial contexts with a focus on Canada's Truth and Reconciliation Commission and Indian Residential Schools. The politics of reconciliation might be generally defined as a way for nation-states to publicly acknowledge the legacies of past wrongs in societies that are deeply divided by histories of state-sponsored violence, atrocity, and historic injustice. Originating in societies undergoing a transition from authoritarianism to democracy, the politics of reconciliation has recently migrated to the older and more settled democracies of the "Global North." Here, it has been enlisted to address an array of issues in different historical and political contexts. Lincez's chapter theorizes this theme in liberal-democratic states that were founded as settler-colonies through processes of Indigenous erasure and dispossession. An increasing number of settler-states have turned to the politics of reconciliation in an effort to facilitate a transformative renewal of their political relationships with Indigenous peoples. Lincez asks: Can the politics of reconciliation contribute to and perhaps even make possible conditions under which Indigenous-settler relations might be reconstructed on foundations that are more just? Might it help bring about the advent of a framework of coexistence that is conducive to the independent flourishing of Indigenous social and political forms? Or does the politics of reconciliation merely serve as an occasion for consolidating the legitimacy of the sovereignty of the settler-state over Indigenous peoples and thereby foreclose the possibility of Indigenous self-determination? In exploring these questions, Lincez challenges the idea that the liberal-democratic politics of reconciliation in its present form can facilitate a transformative renewal of the historical relationship between Indigenous peoples and the state. Drawing from Wolin's critique of the relationship between collective memory, democracy, and justice, as well as contemporary Indigenous theories and critiques of decolonization, settler-colonialism and the liberal politics of recognition, Lincez argues that the politics of reconciliation in liberal-democratic, settler-colonial contexts such as Canada ought to be conceived not as an occasion for a liberating renewal of Indigenous–state relations but instead as operating according to a logic that consolidates the legitimacy of the settler-state through forms of selective social amnesia that work to undermine Indigenous struggles for decolonization and self-determination that are directed against a coercively imposed structure of domination whose historical trajectory has yet to be interrupted.

Section III – Democracy and Political Education:
Wolin and Contemporary Interlocutors

Stephen Esquith's chapter is titled "Real Democratic Political Education." Esquith begins by noting that in his short programmatic book *Philosophy and Real Politics*, Raymond Geuss contrasts realist political theory with idealist applied ethics. Geuss advocates realist political theory because it better understands institutions and actual human motivations; is more historically informed; more effectively orients its readers towards action; treats politics as a craft and an art, not a science; and provides its readers with innovative concepts that can change structures of power. Idealist applied ethics, according to Geuss, is much less capable of educating citizens to improve existing structures of power. Esquith's chapter explores this contrast between political realism and ethical idealism through the theory and practice of democratic political education, a central concern of Wolin's. Wolin shared Geuss's strong antipathy towards applied ethics.

Included among the questions Esquith addresses are: Is Wolin's critique of "managed democracy and the spectre of inverted totalitarianism" in *Democracy Incorporated* a realist political theory in Geuss's sense? Does Wolin provide a better understanding of contemporary structures of power than alternative applied ethicists who have addressed issues such as immigration and inequality? And do Wolin's earlier essays on myth, power, and political commentary provide a theoretical ground for *Democracy Incorporated*? One serious objection to Geuss's critique of applied ethics is that his preferred conception of realist theory lacks a coherent normative ground. Esquith asks: What is the normative ground of Wolin's critique of "managed democracy"? Does Wolin's conception of "fugitive democracy" provide an adequate normative ground for political education in theory and in practice? The chapter concludes with some recommendations that might strengthen the normative ground of a democratic conception of political education in theory and guide it in practice.

Lucy Cane, in her chapter "Wolin and Said on Political Education, Vision, and Intellectual Tradition," critically explores Wolin's understanding of the relationship between political theory and political education by bringing his work into conversation with literary and cultural critic Edward Said. Wolin and Said both criticize academic specialization and profess a commitment to granting students agency. Both thinkers are also driven by an aspiration to offer broad, holistic perspectives on the world that maintain an emancipatory horizon. Finally, they share an abiding interest in studying the Western canon and are critical of some recent, "postmodern" theoretical trends. Nevertheless, Cane argues that Said looked sceptically on the potential chauvinism of epic political theory as Wolin defined it. Over time, Wolin too distanced himself from some of his epic aspirations. Wolin comes to realize that a radically democratic theory must be more multifaceted and consciously incomplete than epic political theories of the past. Accordingly, in his later work, Wolin aspires to a holistic perspective only in a tentative and diagnostic sense, by advancing an overarching diagnosis of "inverted totalitarianism." Wolin and Said thus reach relatively similar conclusions about how to balance the value of a holistic perspective with an awareness of the potential chauvinism of totalizing theory. More significant differences remain between the two thinkers regarding how they approach canonical intellectual traditions. While Said does defend his interest in the Western canon, he is always more critical than Wolin of the imperialist global contexts and the inadequacies of such intellectual traditions. Accordingly, Said has a far more expansive view of the archives that non-specialist academics ought to engage. Cane argues that a Wolinian approach to political theory could be brought closer to Wolin's own ideal of political education through an appreciation of Said's notions of counterpoint, exile, and worldliness. If so, that approach could look forward more inclusively as well as it looks back creatively.

Section IV – Thinking with and beyond Wolin: Current Democratic Practices

Iain Webb, in "Democracy between Reactionary Tribalism and the Megastate," argues that as he witnessed the institutions of liberal democracy become more vestigial and democracy itself increasingly moribund, Wolin looked to the cultural and social churn of postmodernity as the crucible of what remained of democratic hopes. This was in spite of his insistent problematizing of postmodern social theory and the tendencies he identified within it towards a pathological insularity and exclusivity. It was liable to be captured, as Robert Antonio has argued, by those on the far-right seeking to assert and maintain racial hierarchies that postmodern social theory initially challenged. The recent history of far-right groups in the UK and Italy illustrate dangers that Wolin and Antonio identified. Webb argues that the success, or lack thereof, of groups within the current wave of radical right-wing populism hinged on their ability to strategically embrace precisely what Wolin recognized as the vital element of the postmodern, centrifugal groups that carried his hopes for democracy. In sum, successful groups are able to sublate crude biological racism and xenophobia into a postmodern assertion of "difference" and "plurality" that rails against the universalizing and homogenizing logic of neoliberal democracy even as it maintains a conception of the political radically bound up with notions of ethnicity, culture, and race. The challenge, then, is in the balancing of inclusivity with the forming of such proximate bonds of association. The chapter examines the possibilities for such a balancing in the formation of a kind of political subject intimated in Wolin's work but which is undermined by a neo-liberal order corrosive of the demos in its production of an aggregate mass of individual capital accumulators.

In "The Historical Fate of Fugitive Democracy," Terry Maley notes that late in his career (2004) Wolin talked, improbably and controversially at the time, about a new form of power in the United States called "inverted totalitarianism." Wolin was concerned about what was happening to the democracy under circumstances in which capitalist dominance was being consolidated and becoming culturally totalizing under a new, neoliberal form of governance. In *Democracy Incorporated* (2008), Wolin asked two provocative questions that could not be more relevant today, Maley argues, in the age of Trumpism: "What causes a democracy to change into some non-or anti-democratic system, and what kind of system is democracy likely to change into?" (xii).

In his later work, Wolin explored the tension between the increasing power of the modern institutions of the state and capitalism and the diminished power of the demos under conditions of growing inequality and diminished citizenship. Already in the mid-1990s Wolin argued that democracy had become "fugitive," that genuine democratic involvement in public, common causes was only fleetingly possible in late modern liberal democracies, more locally and outside of the state. This argument "pre-figured" the horizontalism of the anti-statist and anti-capitalist social movements in the 2000s. The state had essentially been captured by a tightly interwoven plutocracy of wealth and power. In this way Wolin's later work continued and went beyond the critique of the Schumpetarian plural-elite model of liberal democracy developed by C.B. Macpherson and others in the 1960s and 1970s.

Maley assesses these key ideas from Wolin and brings them into conversation with recent discussions in political theory about what democracy means after forty years of the neoliberal "counterrevolution" in the Global North. In his re-assessment of Wolin's two questions, Maley engages Jeffrey Green's work on plebiscitary, "ocular" democracy and liberal democracy's inherent "shadow of unfairness"; the writing of Martijn Konings on neoliberal rationality, risk, and affect; and John Keane's view of "phantom democracies" in *The New Despotism*. Maley argues that against the backdrop of these recent discussions, Wolin's views of "fugitive democracy" and "inverted totalitarianism" were prescient – necessary but also insufficient, prefiguring the current tensions between a fragmented demos and the crisis-prone nature of neoliberalism. Wolin's critique of inverted totalitarianism remains relevant today in an era of growing authoritarianism. But we also need to rethink Wolin's separation of fugitive democratic moments from the institutional powers of the state. Maley suggests that with the forces unleashed by Trump and populism, a dual democratic strategy is necessary. Wolin's demos needs to keep organizing and protesting in the movements, but they also need to engage with state power, and can't leave it to the new authoritarians. In response to Wolin's two questions, Maley argues that democratic institutions weakened by neoliberalism need to be defended against authoritarians. But they also need to be significantly transformed from within so as to become more welcoming to democratic protests.

Romand Coles and Lia Haro's chapter is titled "Transformative Sanctuary: Rethinking Fugitive Democracy and Black Fugitivity with Frontline Communities in the Underground Railroad." This carefully titled chapter transposes Wolin's theoretical term "fugitive democracy" into a name for a practical experience – particularly those provided by Black communities located in the sanctuaries in the Underground Railroad. As Coles and Haro argued, these sanctuaries not only provided refuges – escapes from a terrible past – but seedbeds for alternative futures that would fuel new kinds of democracy not fully imagined in Wolin's work. Their piece is particularly relevant now as millions of human beings continue to move from politically, economically, or ecologically hostile homes in search of better lives. How can their destinations not only admit them as petitioners but embrace them as potential citizens able to expand and enrich the meaning of democracy in their new political communities? Coles and Haro find lessons from the practical experiences of Black abolitionist communities along the Underground Railroad, especially in Massachusetts, while also finding intellectual sources in Frederick Douglass and Jacques Derrida.

Andrew Biro, in "Visioning Limits or Unlimited Vision? The Vocation of Political Theory in the Anthropocene," notes that there is increasing consensus among geologists that human impacts are reshaping planetary systems to the extent that the current epoch ought to be labelled the Anthropocene. While its precise contours and political salience remain contested, this "Age of Man" is widely seen as – at least potentially – catastrophic for both human and non-human life, and as posing unprecedented political challenges. Although environmental issues do not figure prominently in Wolin's writings, the dilemmas of the Anthropocene highlight in stark terms some of the political tensions which were a central focus of his work. Of particular concern in this chapter is the tension between the limits necessary for democratic community and the need for expansive and imaginative political vision. An overview of Wolin's thinking on these issues reveals important resonances with the political dilemmas of the Anthropocene, including the question of the activity of the political theorist.

Altogether, these essays indicate the vitality of critical democratic thought addressing the difficulties facing democracy in contemporary societies. Inspired by but unbound to Sheldon Wolin's work in political theory, they indicate many of the major political questions of our time, along with some fertile conditions for democratic change.

NOTES

1 See Simone Chambers, "Deliberative Democratic Theory," *Annual Review of Political Science*, 6 (2003), 307–26; Mark E. Warren, Review of *Politics and Vision: Continuity and Innovation in Western Political Thought*, expanded ed., *Political Theory*, Vol. 34, No. 5 (2006), 667–73; and Fred Dallmayr's "Democracy and Multiculturalism," in *Democracy and Difference: Contesting the Boundaries of the Political*, ed. Seyla Benhabib (Princeton, NJ: Princeton University Press, 1996), 278–94. Dallmayr's discussion in this well-known article focuses on Wolin's ambivalent relationship to post-structural thought and Wolin's concerns about the possible relationship between "postmodern" forms of social, cultural, and economic fragmentation, and post-structuralist critiques of foundations in Western political theory. In their own co-edited book on Wolin's thought, William Connolly and Aryeh Botwinick wondered if Wolin had not, at times, moved onto post-structural terrain in his discussion of "fugitive democracy" and elsewhere. See the Introduction to Botwinick and Connolly, *Democracy and Vision: Sheldon Wolin and the Vicissitudes of the Political* (Princeton, NJ: Princeton University Press, 2001). Students of Connolly and Ernesto Laclau have published a collection on radical democracy (Lars Tonder and Lasse Thomassen, *Radical Democracy: Politics between Abundance and Lack* [Manchester: University of Manchester Press, 2014]), arguing that radical democracy should now become a distinct subfield of political theory. They were arguing against the predominance of deliberative democratic theory referred to above in the 2003 article by Simone Chambers – cited at the beginning of this note.

2 See Sheldon S. Wolin, *Democracy Incorporated: Managed Democracy and the Specter of Inverted Totalitarianism* (Princeton, NJ: Princeton University Press, 2008), xii.

3 See Jason A. Frank and John Tambornino, eds., *Vocations of Political Theory* (Minneapolis: University of Minnesota Press, 2000), oriented by Wolin's pivotal 1969 essay, and Botwinick and Connolly, eds., *Democracy and Vision*, which stemmed from a conference honouring Wolin's work. See also "Critical Exchange: Sheldon Wolin's Theoretical Practice" over Wolin's political thought in *Contemporary Political Theory*, No. 16 (2017), 65–115. That exchange focused more on Wolin as a "theorist." The focus of our collection is more substantive, about "envisioning democracy."

4 Scholars identify different times for the emergence of democracy in Athens. See Kurt A. Raaflaub, Josiah Ober, and Robert W. Wallace, *Origins of Athenian Democracy* (Berkeley: University of California Press, 2007).

5 See John Dunn, *Democracy: A History* (New York: Atlantic Monthly Press, 2005); Paul Cartledge, *Democracy: A Life* (New York: Oxford University Press, 2017); and John R. Wallach, *Democracy and Goodness: A Historicist Political Theory* (Cambridge: Cambridge University Press, 2018).

6 See, for example, Karl Marx, *The German Ideology* and (with Friedrich Engels) *The Communist Manifesto*, in *The Marx-Engels Reader*, 2nd ed., ed. Robert C. Tucker (New York: W.W. Norton, 1978), 161 and Part II, respectively.

7 See John Dewey, "To Form Itself, the Public Has to Break Existing Political Forms,"
   in *The Public and Its Problems: An Essay in Political Inquiry*, ed. Melvin L. Rodgers
   (Athens: Ohio University Press, 2016 [1927]), 81. Cf. Sheldon S. Wolin, "Norm and
   Form: The Constitutionalizing of Democracy," in *Fugitive Democracy: And Other
   Essays*, ed. Nicholas Xenos (Princeton, NJ: Princeton University Press, 2016 [1994]);
   and Wolin, "Political Theory as a Vocation," *American Political Science Review*,
   Vol. 63, No. 4 (December 1969), 1062–82.

SECTION 1

Wolin and Democratic Theory: Ancient Roots, Modern Issues

1 Interpreting Democracy in Undemocratic Societies

JOHN R. WALLACH

The cure for the ills of democracy is more democracy.[1]

Introduction

If we think of democracy as a political order in which major social freedoms and legal equality belong to virtually all adult citizens of heterogeneous identities, and if they, in turn, regularly exercise significant, authoritative power in the public realm, we know that democracy has never existed.[2] Besides, democracies always have an outside – those aspects of society within their borders and political life beyond their boundaries over which the democracy has little control – even as their course is continually in play. And democratic "insiders" typically treat their outsiders inequitably (*sometimes* as a way of sustaining freedom), if they are within the reach of democratic sovereignty, and unfairly if they are beyond the reach of their democratic sovereignty. Moreover, democracies comprise imperfect human beings. In other words, democracies always are at least partially unjust.[3]

We can say that democracy as a just political order is an idea whose practical time has never come, a *logos* (words, argument) with practical pretensions that has no wholly defensible embodiment in *ergon* (deeds, action). Instead, it is realized (like justice) in the manner of a second-best or best practicable political order – whether in ancient Athenian democracy, where women were excluded from political participation and slavery was accepted as a fact of life, or in modern "democracies," where the extension of the franchise is accompanied by minimal exercise of political power by the "sovereign" people because of its sublimation into the powers of the state and economy. Indeed, while modern liberal republics have been a force for democratic political progress since the Enlightenment, they tend to enhance the legal authority of individual rights more than the power of the *demos*. (Whether or not liberal democracy can generate social democracy in the near future, as many want, remains to be seen.) By extension, democracy as a political order is not coterminous with justice, even if it may be the best available or possible political order. Thus, by recognizing that democracy as a political form always has been connected to social hierarchies in discourse and practice that significantly constrain democratic power and justice, we acknowledge that democracy always interacts with undemocratic and unjust political conditions. In this respect, democracies always struggle with their own democratic characteristics – an activity that evinces the hermeneutic process of this essay's epigraph.

The consternation that marks the democratic project tends to be overlooked in current public discourse, preoccupied by conflicts facing democratic citizens. Today, we name most contemporary political orders that presuppose limited freedoms and equalities, aspirations and conditions as democracies. Whether or not social, economic, and political equality ought to be extended is a matter of public debate. But apart from the dominant wing of the current Republican Party (or Anti-Democratic Party) in the United States, those that disdain democracy embrace it for rhetorical cover. For most Americans, the United States is "our democracy." The result contributes to a lack of understanding of the practical terrain for democratic discourse about social policy and foreign policies. It leads to politically obtuse analyses of actual politics, which is troublesome amid new anxiety about "democracy" generated by growing socio-economic inequalities, political authoritarianism, systemic racism and sexism in American culture and institutions, and, more generally, globalization.[4] If democracies are to enhance their features as just political orders, their undemocratic and unjust features need to be understood. But then how do we understand democracy as a persuasive force of justice in undemocratic societies marked by many unjust and undemocratic contexts?

When John Dewey reiterated the "old saying" that "the cure for the ills of democracy is more democracy," he meant that democracy as a "social idea" and "way of life" may not be fully actualized but has the resources for correcting the problems of democratically rooted government, aka "political democracy."[5] In so doing, Dewey averred optimism about the possibilities of political education (broadly understood) for enabling a democratic society to become both more democratic and better – more so than did Jean-Jacques Rousseau 165 years earlier, John Stuart Mill in his account of "true [virtuous, representative] democracy" in Victorian England, or Saul Alinsky in the post–Second World War era when he formulated "rules for radicals" engaged in practical efforts at democratic persuasion.[6] Dewey drew on an idea of democratic potential that would enable but not inherently determine a better democratic actuality. Some would say his idea of democratic potential is an ideological myth. Even if it may be, rather, a noble myth for making democratic societies more democratic, it calls for interpretation.

We should acknowledge that democracy, *pace* its literal meaning as *demos* plus *kratos*, is primarily a form of political power. It is partly but not wholly an ethical form of life – partly, because the *demos* is an ethical force in politics, but not wholly because a *demos* may act wrongly or imperfectly. Despite its political virtues relative to other political formations, democracy requires ethical supplementation to bridge the gap that emerges whenever democracies or democrats act. (Even the politics of "democratic justice" divides in practice and has done so since ancient Greece when justice [*to dikaion*] was understood to cut through contention and improve extant political orders.) The minority needs to be kept in the political game because the *demos* qua group or political hegemon errs, and minorities in a democracy have political dignity and rights. As a result, politically coherent democratic action in *logos* and *ergon* entails an ethical perspective that includes the majority but reaches out to minorities – potentially protecting minorities against a domineering majority – adhering to, without being wholly controlled by, a rule of law or constitutionalism.[7] Laws surely constrain the exercise of democratic political power, but every democracy and democratic movement acknowledges the productive role of some legal constraints in sustaining democracy as a political community.[8] That said, given that democracy in *ergon* departs from its horizon in *logos*, a perpetual gap separates democracy as a political power and justice as an ethical horizon of political action.[9]

Sheldon Wolin illuminated a version of the potentially democratic but actually undemocratic character of today's Western (and particularly American) societies that self-identify their political form as democratic in his essays on the American political order from the 1980s and his conceptions of "fugitive democracy" and "inverted totalitarianism" articulated in the 1990s and 2000s – most of which had as their "other" either American liberalism or neoliberalism. But while Dewey's treatment is too breezy and Alinksy's is theoretically incomplete, Wolin's invaluable contributions to democratic thought arguably are insufficient for the task that he held dear, namely linking the diverse, historically rooted sensibilities of citizens in nominally democratic societies to a more politically vibrant and egalitarian vision of what he called "social democracy."[10]

Identifying more viable trajectories between extant and better democracies remains a challenge for democratic theory and practice. I briefly take on this challenge at the end of this essay when discussing the issue of democratic persuasion. Between here and there, I address the disconnect between democracy as a *logos* and democracy as an *ergon*, or the interpretation of democracy in and for undemocratic societies, in relation to three historical debates: (1) the differences between ancient and modern democracy, (2) the optimism of Dewey's progressivism amid undemocratic growths of American political power and capital, and (3) the debate since the 1960s between liberal and radical democracy. Each concerned Wolin at important moments of his career as a political theorist. My only departure from his perspective explicitly acknowledges that the interpretation and promotion of democracy presupposes a dialogue between the inside and outside of democracy as a powerful, desirable, and imperfect form of political life – a dialogue that infuses democracy at every moment of political choice.[11] The aim of this essay is to fortify "democracy" as a meaningful, critical term in public discourse. I use the aforementioned historical backgrounds to foreground elements of cogent democratic persuasion that could help to reduce harmfully undemocratic qualities of democratic societies.

From Ancient to Modern/Twenty-First-Century Democracy

The "outside" of ancient democracy informed its origins and operation. Athenian democracy emerged out of the aristocratic social orders that historically had marked ancient Greek life. And during the three centuries that preceded Athenian democracy, a tradition of critical and public discourse always had chastened that power, from the (partially or mostly) imagined poems of Homer to the more historically grounded texts of Herodotus and Thucydides. But the "outside" in ancient Greek *poleis* was hard to define. At the birth of *demokratia*, the power of the *demos* as collectively determined in the *polis* was limited by the "laws" (*nomoi*) of the polis, but there was no formal check on demotic interpretations of those laws – as illustrated in the case in the legal trial and conviction of Socrates.[12] Insofar as these *nomoi* were themselves only valid as interpreted by the male citizens whom they regulated (along with others), no firm boundary separated culture, economics, and politics in ancient democracies. Solon, the "lawgiver" for the Athenian *polis,* understood that justice regarding the distribution of private wealth operated differently than public political distributions of honour and privilege that might be democratically advantageous, and he was revered by democrats and quasi-democrats alike until the Macedonians acquired control of Athens in 323 BCE.

Ancient democracy has vouchsafed features of the idea of democracy that have not been gainsaid since, namely regard for the freedom and equality of all citizens who are legally and politically entitled to shape the character of the collectivity in which they live. Apart from the enormous gap in historical experience and the significantly different practical conditions that enabled ancient and modern democracy to thrive, the dramatic difference between them stems from the direct character of ancient democracy, which enabled all (adult, male) citizens to exercise direct power in shaping judicial, administrative, and overarching political decisions through public deliberation, voting, and the exercise of their rights to free public speech.[13] The differences between this kind of democracy and modern democracy have been oft noted but warrant reiteration here. First, the power of ancient democratic citizens is not exercised by modern democratic citizens, as their polity only came to be called democratic when the citizens' power was delegated to representatives – the actual conduits of legislative power. In Athens, elections were associated with oligarchies and only used in democracies to elevate individuals to offices that required special expertise – such as general or comptroller. Secondly, the domain of public activity in which citizens might act was significantly different in both its numerical size and temporal character. In contrast to a polity of ~350,000, in which women-citizens had no political rights and political participation was enabled by slavery, modern democracies include tens – if not hundreds – of millions of citizens, even though it was only until the twentieth century that women gained the vote and the legal remnants of chattel slavery disappeared. To be sure, we cannot restore the conditions of the relatively homogeneous citizen-state of ancient Athens, but these marks of the most important first democracy ought not to be erased from our democratic imagination.

Of equal importance, as noted by Benjamin Constant observing early nineteenth-century France and Robert Dahl analysing twentieth-century America, citizens' primary concerns are economic rather than political, so they are less likely to care about or participate in politics – which, indeed, calls into question the ethical and intellectual meaning of the vote.[14] Tocqueville raised concerns about this phenomenon in *Democracy in America*, when he praised by contrast "the art of association" – more or less the equivalent of the ancient Greek political art – that he saw cultivated in New England town meetings.[15] But none of these differences between ancient and modern *politics* touches upon the relationship between ancient and modern political *competence* manifested in the practice of politics and presupposed in Athenian democracy. Although Socrates, Plato, and Aristotle questioned its philosophical and practical adequacy, they did not actively seek to transform the Athenian polity. So what did ancient political competence consist of? Mostly a capacity for the regular exercise of effective, non-technical political judgment by "all" citizens. Political competence resulted from regular practice, not specialized expertise. This aspect of Athenian democracy encourages proponents of democracy on the left and strikes democracy's opponents on the right as politically dangerous.

When eulogizing the Athenians' democratic *politeia* (according to Thucydides), Pericles noted the uniquely different character of *political* art, skill, or competence from the kinds of knowledge manifested in specialized forms of life. For Pericles, there was the intelligent judgment of the Athenian citizen, expertise in which differed from the kinds of knowledge and skill he acquired in his work life. It might be utilized forty times per year in the Assembly, daily if selected by lot for the Council, and more regularly if the citizen self-nominated (and was randomly chosen) to be a juror on an Athenian court. That skill was to be enhanced and directed, but not managed, by leadership (of his sort). In virtually all of his dialogues, Plato, a radical critic but no political enemy of democracy *per se*, never equated the form and content of *political* skill with that of other skills. Good citizenship and leadership did not manifest superior competence that indicated a general form of the skills displayed in particular kinds of technical work and professional activity. Rather, citizenship and leadership were skilled dispositions different in *kind* from other sorts of competences – known in ancient Greek as *technai* – and utilized regularly.[16] Similarly, Aristotle famously noted how a skill in judgment displayed by the many (so long as they had not been corrupted) was particularly suited to political life and could not be replaced by a few persons of means, knowledge, or ethics.[17] Machiavelli, who rejected the ethical component to political activity prized by the ancients, nonetheless felt impelled to characterize the unique character of political *virtu*, which entailed possession of a uniquely powerful ability and skill. For the ancients, therefore, there was no notion of omnicompetence possessed by citizens or leaders. Indeed, the Protagorean myth of the origins of the human race told of how human beings could not be saved by the exercise of a myriad of *technai*; they needed a distinctive art and virtue of political activity if the human race was to survive. And insofar as there is a distinctively ancient character of the public, it consists of its integral connection to sustaining a "commons" (*koinon*) or "community" (*koinonia*). The outside of such a community was the *oikos*, the space for women and slaves, and dialogue between the inside and outside was mostly reserved to lawsuits against citizens for mistreatment of slaves and dramatic inclusion of women and slaves as significant, fully human beings in both tragedies and comedies.

The slow integration of ideas of human equality from the near east to Western thought, coupled with the legal isolation of economics and caste by capitalist states, the constitutional separation of religion from state power, and political unrest (*inter alia*) made possible the birth of modern representative democracy. That political order in the early modern era witnessed constant tussles between ordinary citizens (e.g., the Levellers, Antifederalists) and the state (e.g., Leviathan, Publius). Whereas segregation and subordination constituted the limitations of ancient, direct democracy, a different kind of gap between the potential and ideals of democracy emerged in modern, representative democracy, one which undermined – even as it also made possible – the literal aspirations for many of ethical and practical democracy. For now, despite the rhetoric of popular sovereignty, political power lies in the hands of elected representatives who, more often than not, use elections as means for transcending, resisting, or even betraying, their electoral warrant. (In the United States, see the differences between the campaign platforms and official conduct of Woodrow Wilson, FDR, LBJ, Richard M. Nixon, Ronald Reagan, Bill Clinton, George W. Bush, and Donald J. Trump – allowing for the different political conditions under which they were elected and served – not to mention the members of Congress who regularly defy public opinion not because they exhibit Madisonian virtue or Millian expertise but because of their hubris or self-subordination to big money and lobbyists.) In addition, we have seen the coupling of liberal, representative democracy to an economic ethic and practice that diminishes the value and power of public life.[18] Insofar as democratic freedom and equality are laudable, we face the difficult question of what to do to close the gap between coherent versions of these political ideas in *logos* and *ergon*, in ways that benefit political orders and avoid generating new forms of domination, when individuals supposedly have what they want. Debates now occur outside the ambit of liberal freedom and equality – in terms of race, class, religion, and gender – even as they were supposedly rendered unproblematic in the liberal revolutions of the late eighteenth and early nineteenth centuries. These debates have not been satisfactory when cast in the language of liberal individualism, for the antagonists either deny the major significance of these differences, leaving public interaction to resolve them, or reify the cause of outsiders in terms that call into question the meaning of the political equality they seek – which helps to explain the foundering of affirmative action and identity politics. Interpreting democracy in undemocratic liberal societies according to liberal principles has not been successful in fostering democratization.

The Progressive Democracy of John Dewey

Insofar as the Athenians (and every other political group until the twentieth century) did not seriously envision extending the full rights and privileges of citizenship to adult women or economically ordering their society without slavery or imperial domination, visions of revolutionary achievements of public happiness rooted in the egalitarian dimensions of ancient democracy belong to the realm of fantasy or marginal political opposition. Furthermore, the elevation of ideals of *mutual* respect have disabused us of notions that monological practices of reason can both constitute democracy and generate the common good. John Dewey recognized much of what was needed to be done in thought and action to foster democracy in modernity. (Wolin wrote favourably about Dewey in the enlarged edition of *Politics and Vision*.) An optimistic pragmatist and political theorist of the left from the first half of the twentieth century, he, without relying on philosophical certainties or ethical verities, believed in the potential for generating democratic progress out of the material of a barely democratic society suffused with many anti-democratic elements. The following interprets Dewey's attempts to democratize democracy as an effort to envision politics as education and to rebut the influential journalist and political theorist Walter Lippmann. He did so by defining and valorizing the need for a healthy and vigorous "public" – understood as a political agent more than a place – so as to counteract the depleting effects of corporate, political, and ethical currents of privatization. For Dewey, an intelligible notion of democracy "as a way of life" was itself ethical, imbued with the potential to transform extant, relatively democratic political orders in better and more democratic directions.[19] As we shall see, he tended to minimize the obstacles in American politics and society that had to be overcome for his pragmatic democracy to become practical, a catalyst for genuine democratization – a problem that arguably remains with us still unless the antidemocratic features of capitalism, sexism, and racism and the obstacles to mutual care disappear from American political life. But let's first note what he was up against.

For Lippmann, the public realm is real, but its comprehension by "the public" is illusory and dangerous – almost a null set. His reasons stem from the enlargement in number of the public and the exponentially greater complexity of the issues that matter to them. The result, he claims, is that any contemporary notion of the people as authoritative political actors depends on them assuming the role of "omnicompetent individuals" – an impossible task that hence discredits the political judgment of citizens.[20] Apart from his dour view of human nature, a basic problem with Lippmann's analysis, not directly combated by Dewey, is that the very notion of the omnicompetent citizen (as generated by Lippmann) is itself a conceptual illusion and ideological distraction, one borne from an overly dramatic differentiation between ancient (or an idealized picture of Jeffersonian) democracy and modern democracy.

Lippmann harboured no hope that ancient or early modern political competence could be developed in modernity. The reasons include the size of modern polities, the privatistic orientation of citizens, and the domination of the public realm by the filters of "stereotypes." These are not always invidious, but they easily can distort the ears, eyes, and minds of citizens. This is because – and here's where Lippmann's pessimism about democracy becomes apparent – ordinary citizens are primarily emotive, with their intellects narrowly framed by their personal lives. They are naturally much less able to filter out the distortions produced by stereotypes than social science "experts" who, from their abstract perches, can do the integrative analysis needed for understanding modern political life. In this way, Lippmann's experts could provide the impetus for dispelling political illusions and improving modern democracies (without making them more democratic). The illusory character of *Lippmann's* conceptual outlook appears when he tries to replace democratic political judgment with a class of technocratic experts knowledgeable about the new fashions of so-called objective social science.[21] That group would look at the world "objectively" and "realistically" without being misled by the imagery that suffuses contemporary public life, thereby producing public knowledge to guide public opinion and, hence, perfect a "realistic" democracy. The idea never got off the ground as an official political phenomenon, although one could say that a network of individuals in the higher reaches of American political, economic, legal, and academic institutions could be said to perform that function – often without the beneficent perspective Lippmann envisions them having.

Intellectual experts in the EPA and CDC surely produce useful social and political knowledge. But such knowledge is insufficient for producing insight into the political leadership that ought to guide public policy even as the value of each agency has been blunted by the Trump administration and Trumpism. The value of each agency during the Trump administration was blunted by presidential directives. Not only is such expert knowledge an inadequate stand-in for political knowledge; so is the capacity that would acquire it. But the real illusion stems from Lippmann's own conception. Like Pericles, Plato, and Aristotle, Lippmann disdained the political judgment of oligarchs. But could his experts provide the kind of *political* knowledge for which he yearned? They would need to. For Lippmann degrades not only the political judgment of citizens but also politicians who depend on tapping the public's ignorance for their own purposes as well as news-gathering organizations that are just as prone to stereotypical rendering of current events for credulous citizens.[22] So he imagines a group whose knowledge can inform in a non-partisan way the top-down leadership that modern democracies require. But the theoretical and practical coherence of such a group is itself incoherent. Lippmann himself may have admitted this privately when commenting in his newspaper columns on the lack of realism and knowledge informing the American pursuit of war in Vietnam by "the best and the brightest."[23] Dewey argued this point against Lippmann in *The Public and Its Problems*, where he searched for a "public" that was in "eclipse."

Dewey's most systematic work of democratic theory in fact was *The Public and Its Problems*.[24] Published in 1927, its foils are Walter Lippmann's *Public Opinion* (1922) and *The Phantom Public* (1925), which have little good to say about the public or democracy (although they don't abandon all democratic hope). *Contra* Lippmann, Dewey claims that there is such a thing as a politically constructive "democratic public," but he shares Lippmann's doubts about its efficacy – albeit for different reasons. Dewey's "public" has lots of problems; indeed, it is in "eclipse." Of the six chapters in *The Public and Its Problems*, only Chapter III discusses democracy directly, and that chapter's last sentence is, "The democratic public is largely inchoate and disorganized."[25] Two of the six chapters in Dewey's book include "search" in their titles; "discovery" appears in another title, and the last chapter begins with "problem." It is not a book that effuses confidence in democracy. Dewey fully recognizes that his conception of democracy presents an intellectual challenge in his context. It entails political education of a certain kind that had no one and nothing to carry its banner during the second half of his long life. That the Depression is around the corner of the publication of *Public* suggests that his anxieties were well placed. But the value of the work stems from its assumption that "we are in this together" in theory, if not in practice, which makes possible a thorough-going societal education in democracy, how to find a better democracy within the currents of contemporary democracy without resorting to the shibboleths of liberal individualism. This optimistic process of improvement reflects both the attractive and limited character of Dewey's democratic theory. Each feature appears in his account of "the public" that challenges Lippmann's dour, "realistic" account of the public.

For Dewey, the "public" exists but must be searched for. How does that work? Dewey understands "the public" in relation to "the private." But importantly, he doesn't reify the makeup of each or the boundaries between them. Both are aleatory phenomena; as such, they are not immediately subject to common criticisms of "the public" as capitalist or racist or sexist. The difference between the public and the private entails a difference between what is encased and isolated around an individual or group and that which is accessible to "all," potentially affecting the experience of "all" in society. In this respect, Dewey has modernized the difference between the ancient Greek realms of the *oikos* and *polis or idioten* and *demosion* or *koinon*, or, more literally in ancient Rome, between the *res privata* and the *res publica*. Whereas ancient politics was not supposed to concern the "private" realm, leaving the subordinate status of women and slaves untouched, for Dewey, easily could become matters of public concern. The oxygen of politics comes from anywhere and anyplace, from interactions among any and all citizens. For matters that may seem to originate in the lives of individuals actually may involve the public and common concerns once they seriously engage the lives of others. These need to be addressed and cared for by the *demos* even if the *demos* does not originally understand its relevance to their lives. Generating that care and intellectually appreciating the significance of such indirect consequences is the object of democratic education.

Dewey's vision of democratic education offers a clear alternative to Lippmann's dismay, if not disgust, with the public as a political agent amid twentieth-century society. But to what extent does it meet the demands of politically beneficial democratization? While Dewey rejected any fixed practical content for the public realm or public activities, he defined its generic purview by identifying its perennial "function," operating between the individual as agent and the state as a governmental power. Activities that belonged to the *private* realm involved direct interactions between individuals or groups and their consequences, the *public* realm entailed the *indirect* consequences of human relationships: "The public consists of all those who are affected by the indirect consequences of transactions to such an extent that it is deemed necessary to have those consequences systematically cared for."[26] The fact that the public enacts itself by addressing phenomena not directly connected to participants requires that the public care about common experiences and be cared for by representatives, official or unofficial – those occupying determinate or indeterminate office, i.e., public officials or ordinary citizens, which Dewey collectively identifies as the *Populus*.[27] An attentive "public" and a strong public realm makes it possible for democracy to cure its own ills. Today, a democratic public would require the means to oppose the self-serving claims of private capital to manage the distribution of public goods. Imagine what would be needed to yield a democratic takeover of the fossil fuel industries and forestall ecological suicide. But what does the constitution of the public realm by "indirect consequences systematically cared for" mean and entail – especially when the behaviour of citizens is being transformed regularly by algorithmic technologies and "surveillance capitalism"?[28] Pandemics have killed or hospitalized hundreds of thousands of persons, most fatally for those already suffering injustice; dozens of police killings have been captured on video; world wars have ended the lives of millions. These have created publics, but they have not led to democratic results.

Dewey's attention to "consequences" stems from his aversion to philosophical and political ideas that have no anchors in history or political practice and that often have been "explained" in terms of unseen "causes." Dewey's attention to consequences relates to his deeply held view that one's account of social reality had to stem from observable phenomena of practical interest – not from appealing pies in the sky. In this regard, Dewey has listened to Machiavelli, the first theorist of political consequentialism. About four hundred years later, Max Weber drew on Machiavelli's legacy when he famously noted that politics not only had to reflect an ethics of "ultimate ends" or "conviction" but also an ethics of "responsibility" or "consequences."[29] Dewey surely read Machiavelli's *The Prince* but may not have read Weber's essay. In any event, Dewey's conception of democracy was inherently ethical – at both the beginning and end of his career of writing – but not because he marginalized the political significance of raw power and inequality in shaping the conduct of citizens.[30] Dewey believed that democracy possessed the greatest political capacity to enhance human potential, and he believed that potential – *contra* Hobbes – to be positive and entwined with intelligently comprehending opportunities for cooperation. Dewey took for granted the value of "freedom" and "equality" but always wanted to know how these ideas could be practically realized. So his political consequentialism depends on a presumptively favourable attitude towards freedom and equality as constitutive features of human potential. But that still leaves open the question of how "indirect consequences" – whether "beneficial" or "harmful" ("good" or "evil") in their effects on agents or their relations – function in his conception of "the public" that makes possible democratic action and cures the "ailments" of democracy.

The meaning of such consequences tends to reflect Dewey's optimistic, pragmatic vison of a political future shaped by an educated public, one not egregiously divided by social, economic, religious, or racial/ethnic conflicts that prevent such education from taking hold.

Conflicts among the consequences of practical action generate the need for representatives who have the capacity to address them. These representatives and the state in which they function are "good" insofar as they care for the public's interests and minimize conflict.[31] Dewey subsequently translates "conflicts" into his terminology of "consequences" and "obstacles" that need re-formations. But will political representatives allow their actions to be harnessed by public goods? Here the limits of Dewey's consequentialism appear, for in focusing attention solely on "observable phenomena" and abjuring the search for "causes," Dewey prevents interpretation and appreciation of the roots of the conflicts. To be sure, this kind of "research" can lead to articulating flimsy ideas, "ghosts in the machine," or diffuse ideologies (e.g., "neoliberalism") that democratic agency presumptively abjures, but it also can lead to better means of understanding *why* political individuals act the way they do along with the beneficial and harmful character of consequences of their actions and *how* they ought to be addressed.

Radical vs. Liberal Democracy

As understood in the United States, the idea of radical democracy primarily emerged in political movements of the 1960s and as a critique of liberal democracy, principally understood as John Rawls's political theory – first fully articulated in *A Theory of Justice* (1971) and then partly revised in *Political Liberalism* (1993–6). This theory of liberal democracy honours the principles of freedom and equality for all citizens but provides minimal political empowerment of ordinary citizens. Its principal aim is to protect against the kind of intolerance evidenced in the religious wars of sixteenth- and seventeenth-century Europe and the legal discrimination against African Americans in the United States, as identified and outlawed in the 1950s and 1960s. The kind of structural racism reflected in police brutality against African Americans in recent years (but also throughout American history) and blue-collar *ressentiment* of the last decade manifest dimensions of public life that Rawls's theoretical perspective cannot address (other than as being despicable). In addition, it legitimates welfare rights for citizens via "the difference principle," which accepts social and economic inequality at the margin and only if it helps "the worst off." Political participation by ordinary citizens was a preference, not a constituent, of Rawls's liberal democracy, as political power was mostly located in the hands of representatives.

Sheldon Wolin's extensive review of *Political Liberalism* levelled an extensive critique of Rawls's theory for being (even if unintentionally) an ideological cover for American capitalism and political elitism.[32] Democracy could only be just if it shed its liberal moorings and reflected democracy radically, all the way down. Yet, in an article entitled "Fugitive Democracy," also published in 1996, Wolin argued that the practical expression of demotic power which enacted an egalitarian and participatory conception of "the political" only could be episodic and rare.[33] It was unclear whether Wolin ever thought it had been actualized institutionally (unless the radically imperfect, albeit fulsomely democratic, Athenian *polis* of the fifth and fourth centuries counted as its foundational incarnation). Nonetheless, democracy only could be genuine if it was "radical," that is, generated by opposition to all institutions that inhibited the *demos* as a political agent. The substance of the contemporary *demos* to which he appealed was iterated rather than fully defined. It may have stemmed from the Athenian notion of the *demos* as a socio-economic and political class of low- and middle-income citizens who provided the material basis for Athenian politics (unimaginable as a material class now) and typically carried the day in political institutions against oligarchic, aristocratic opponents from 462–323 BCE. But what could it foster in the political life of the twenty-first century, other than the obvious inclusion of women, illegality of slavery, and the empowerment of downtrodden races, genders, and ethnicities? This relatively sketchy argument was significantly fleshed out by Wolin with respect to the "contemporary" (2008) American political order in *Democracy Incorporated: Managed Democracy and the Specter of Inverted Totalitarianism*.[34] Not yet a household term (although it was invented in 1938), "neoliberalism" was mentioned but not discussed in Wolin's book. (It had not yet been popularized.) Yet he could have used it to shine a light on the predominant ideology that has reigned since the late 1970s in Western institutions and political life – and opposed the glimmers of substantive democracy – displayed in the democratic civil and political protests of the 1960s and early-mid 1970s.[35] The inevitable question raised by the book's argument (a question of which Wolin must have been aware) was, "If it is so difficult to identify an actual *demos* in the American (or any other) political order, is 'democracy' in a 'genuine' sense much more than a figment of theoretical imagination?" One hears sceptical echoes of Dewey's mantra that the cure for the ills of democracy is more democracy. Two different conceptions of democracies are at work in Dewey's and Wolin's formulations, but how are they related? In short, how does one interpret democracy in an undemocratic society – without being ideological in a narrow-minded or question-begging way, especially if most citizens regard their society as democratic as they do in the twenty-first century? The question highlights the argument between liberal and radical democrats.

These are difficult questions to answer. For if liberal democracy is fair game for those who argue against its toleration of severe inequalities in social, economic, and political power – first spelled out by Karl Marx in 1843 – what does "radical democracy" actually mean or connote?[36] Marx pointed out that the etymological root of "radical" is *radix*, and for Marx that root was "man himself." But what does "radical democracy" mean – even with the root expanded to include women as well as men (something that Marx may have envisioned)? Marx initially idealized the elimination of conflict between civil society and the state, in which "the shoemaker" is a representative. But he left this radically democratic image behind when he started to illuminate the power and exploitation of capitalism – with the result that, for him, "democracy" either was transcended by communism (in *The Communist Manifesto*) or functioned only for two turbulent months (in the Paris Commune).[37] But the modern *demos* is not an economic class in modernity. Moreover (as previously stated), democracy primarily expresses a form of power, not ethical virtue (at least not automatically), and there is no unchangeable substance of democratic politics other than prohibition against self-destruction. Finally, to reiterate this essay's opening, democracy always has an "outside." Yet such an outside seems to be foreclosed by the notion of "radical democracy" – lest it become totalistic. Wolin's radical democracy obviously isn't "totalitarian" (although the neologism "totalitarian democracy" was coined by right-wing post-war theorists to tar Rousseau and leftists), but then how do we define its limits?[38] How might taking on board the idea of fugitive, radical democracy cure the ills of "our democracy"? Does Wolin want to trim our sails, recast our hopes, or consign democracy to the realm of political utopias?

"Democracy" signifies power of, by, and for the *demos* or people – with both indicating the legally empowered citizenry of a political order (not all society). *Liberal democracy* defines that power primarily in terms of the capacities of legally equal individuals to exercise state-protected rights, leaving the degree to which power accrues to the people to individuals and groups playing politics and economics. *Radical democracy* critiques the inequalities accepted by liberal democracy without requiring mathematical equalities. Instead, its standards resemble those of Rousseau and Marx – with Rousseau counselling that a social contract society must have a distribution of property in which everyone has something and none too much and Marx projecting the ideal of "from each according to their ability, to each according to his needs." More particularly in terms of the power of the *demos* or people, radical democrats seek a relatively egalitarian distribution of *political* power as a condition of human flourishing and a preventative check on the power of hierarchical economic, social, and political arrangements.[39] For radical democrats, no aspect of society is necessarily irrelevant for enhancing or inhibiting democracy, and each should be considering in fostering a democratic project. The boundaries separating the public and private as understood by liberals are artificial and invidious – which doesn't mean that every aspect of life needs or ought to be politicized. Apart from the dangers such politicization would involve, that would stifle the energies of individuality that fuel the free exercise of democratic citizenship.

The democratic mantras of liberal and radical democrats have come under stress in our era of globalization and increased migration because of economic and cultural displacement as well as political harassment. Globalization has tended to hollow out the middle class in Europe and North America, and the resulting *ressentiment* among significant portions of the lower and middle classes has encouraged them to lash out at immigrants and let loose their racism and sexism. Just as the German SDP chose solidarity with Germany vs. European workers at the onset of the First World War in 1914, many citizens in advanced-capitalist Western countries over the past decade have doubled down on nationalism rather than humanitarianism. Figuring out how best to enhance the well-being of a liberal or radical *demos* in this situation has bedevilled political thinkers and politicians of good will – especially because the only alternative agenda – viz., human rights – does not speak coherently at a practical level to democratic sensibilities.[40] The best arguments for the progressive left in the United States (e.g., those of Bernie Sanders and Elizabeth Warren) have focused on economic inequality. But they have not yet eliminated the suspicions among citizens that government cannot be a spearhead of social justice, a view (promoted by millions of corporate dollars) that motivate opposition to Medicare for All, the Green New Deal, and more egalitarian tax and social structures. Maybe that will change. But for the time being the *demos* in most societies has trouble incorporating radical democracy into its way of life.

Democratic Persuasion

The task of convincingly and politically persuading citizens in modern republics in ways that benefit them as *democratic* citizens is not one that ever can be definitively completed.[41] Democratic persuasion entails tools of persuasion (means, skills, competence) and the goals for which that persuasion is linked (ends, values, egalitarian vitality). The markers for those means and ends vary in time, as do the makeup of democratic citizens themselves, creating the need to adapt to these changes. It presupposes the virtue and debilities of the *demos*. Democratic persuasion must assume different forms amid the demands of changing contexts and varying obstacles, but it requires politically relevant knowledge and competences, non-authoritarian ethical goods, and practical power. While these were interwoven almost seamlessly in the stratified political communities of antiquity, they did not always generate the best possible outcomes. And the fabric of ancient democracies was rent by historical changes that overcame the integrity of the *polis*. The diverse, demographically huge, capital-driven, and privatized societies of modernity enlarge and complicate the challenge of interpreting and promoting democracy in undemocratic societies. Democracies do not fully control their own destinies. Crises of democracy may come from above, via authoritarians, or below, via protest, yet because the fault lines around which the crises build stem from deeper societal rifts that often transcend democracy, the tools of persuasion are often not up to the tasks of democratization. At the same time, alternative strategies of violence or authoritarian force have not proved to be assets of greater democracy. Words and non-ideal deeds informed by historical understanding and reasonable hope have to be the principal ingredients for bringing about democratic goals.

The task of healing social wounds is attempted in highly constrained ways by politicians seeking votes on the hustings. Apart from the corrupting effect of money on their democratic legitimacy, elections may tap the sentiments of not much more than half the adult population and promote electoral strategies that, at least in the United States, mostly attend to "swing states," not the needs of individuals. In addition, they need to be sensitive to the uptake of their campaign rhetoric by their opponents and the media – even if the role of the media can be overstated.[42] They need to address public unhappiness without irritating familiar features of social and economic life which citizens want to retain – often over and against tropes promoted by corporate media. Thus, advocates for Medicare for All have to deal with their program being framed by opponents as "taking away your health insurance" without mentioning that citizens would be *given* guaranteed health insurance for life. In every event, however, the activity of democratic persuasion entails listening. As proponents of democratic education from Jefferson to Dewey to Saul Alinsky have emphasized, its successful practice involves dialogue across differences – not hectoring from the left, centre, or right – and it faces potent obstacles that question the utility of democratic persuasion. How do you change the views of individuals whose political perspectives are best characterized by mean epithets and harsh comedy?

Sometimes, persuasion can be understood solely as a discursive and sociological style, whether in antiquity or modernity. It also can be understood in terms of the effects of major political experiences (such as enduring war upon one's soil or massive losses of soldier-citizens and civilians) and proposals for structural changes that would bolster the public realm (such as public transit, national health coverage, and a globally green transformation of the production and distribution of energy). In any event, democratic persuasion as a means must connect with practical dispositions for democratic ends – lest it become a tool of demagogues. How can this be done without being either autocratic, moralistic, or powerless? How do we transform undemocratic divides into basic political equality and the celebration of differences? How can we understand political knowledge as a tool of democratic persuasion? These questions (to which there can be no propositional answer) lead me to return to Plato's attempt to address major dimensions of these questions. Plato criticized (often unfairly) the failures of Athenian democracy on behalf of a knowledgeable view of social justice, but he also was concerned about the drawbacks of uneducated democracy – concerns that naturally engage anyone who would interpret and foster better democracies today, especially amid the emotive discourse that colours our political conversations.

Plato unsympathetically addressed the problem of democratic persuasion when he sublimated his sorrow at the Athenians' judicial vote in 399 BCE that found Socrates guilty (by a margin of 3:2 out of 501 votes cast) of "corrupting the young" and "not believing in the gods of the city but other strange divinities." How could a democratic citizenry supposedly endowed with virtuous political judgment find guilty the most virtuous man of his day? Plato plumbs this issue in an illuminating way – although he does not "solve" it – in his dialogue, *Gorgias*, most likely written ten to fifteen years after Socrates's death. There, Plato's Socrates engages Gorgias, a Sophist from Leontini who taught rhetoric (for a fee) in the Greek world, probably coming to Athens in 427 BCE to make money by enhancing the power and skill of Athenians whose words were deeds in the Assembly, Council, and Courts (probably tutoring the demagogue Cleon in the bargain). Plato's Socrates also engages Polus, a student of Gorgias, and Callicles, a smart, power-hungry (and perhaps fictional) citizen. These characters present different ways of using rhetoric to persuade Athenian citizens to acquire speaking skills in order to enhance their political power.

The dialogue begins with Plato's Socrates asking Gorgias to define his art. After a few false starts, Gorgias does so in a way that has rhetoric offer skill for citizens who speak to their fellow citizens gathered in the collective settings of Athenian political institutions. Plato's Socrates and Gorgias do not understand the *demos* as a congerie of citizens, as it tends to be understood today, but as a coherent political actor.[43] Gorgias presupposes that they will use the skill justly, even though it is not rooted in any substantive knowledge of the subject of his persuasive skill. His rhetoric produces persuasion without knowledge. Socrates points out the incoherence of this project, insofar as Gorgias presupposes the justice of his skill while nothing in the skill itself enables its student to use the skill justly (453e–61a). Flummoxed, Gorgias gives over the defence of rhetoric to his student, Polus, who proceeds to associate the effectiveness of rhetoric with the ability to use words to acquire power. Again, Plato's Socrates takes issue with this formulation, linking power to the need for rhetoric as a *techne* that exhibits and promotes knowledge (*episteme*), not arbitrary preferences. If this doesn't occur, holders of power may use their possession unjustly, thereby hurting themselves. Polus responds by saying that harm will be visited on others and the harm to oneself is insignificant. Plato's Socrates takes issue with *this* notion and claims (as the historical Socrates seems to have done, in fact) that no one harms another willingly because it is worse to do harm than to suffer harm

(461b–81b). At this point, Callicles (for whom there is no known historical corollary) jumps into the argument with a lengthy address that affirms that only sissies believe this Socratic view; it won't get you anywhere in society. You will be hauled into court and found guilty when innocent. (Virtually all readers of the dialogue would understand the reference to the historical Socrates.) Plato's Socrates obviously has to respond and does so, but only by pleading the virtues of political moderation that (he claims) were not practised by the greatest generals of Athens but are practised by himself (to no avail for preserving his life). Thus, Plato reasonably articulates a tension between a democratic public with imperfect political knowledge and a philosophical sensibility that has insufficient support in the world of practical politics – thus between philosophy and politics.

The dialogue does not suggest – and only could do so for us anachronistically – that Plato or the historical Socrates opposed free public speech for Athenian citizens. But it does note that such freedom can be used unjustly and effectively through either ignorance or greed for personal power. How does one practise political persuasion for democratic citizens without pandering to their ignorance or presupposing one's virtue? As with many readers' responses to Plato's quandaries, critical commentators and political practice have not offered adequate or definitive responses. Rather, they have noted the emotional and epistemological dimensions of moderate (not middle-of-the-road) political judgment and the problems of putting too much power in the hands of tyrannical individuals or oligarchic elites *or* banking too much on the basic goodness of the citizenry. Insofar as Athenian democracy was direct, Plato did not address current ways in which practical-structural dimensions of power in civil society and political representation may inhibit democracy or prospects of persuasion. But he revealed the tensions between spotless political ethics and the force of power, the injurious effects of which are scrawled across the body and memory of Socrates.

The question of democratic persuasion has two other dimensions that Plato noted but defined too rigidly – namely, persuasion that generates unjustified belief and persuasion that generates true belief (or conviction rooted in knowledge, cf. *Gorgias*, 454c). The division is not as clear-cut as Plato would have it. And yet the distinction must hold at some level, lest the division between really fake news and realistic news disappears. The issue is not as obviously resolved as some would have it – by asserting, say, the truth of the *New York Times* vs. the patently politicized news of Fox. For the *New York Times* has its own journalistic and economic agendas. But (the vetted) *Times* reporters endeavour to be truthful and to promote informed and constructive public discourse, which counts for a great deal. Unfettered efforts to achieve accuracy and sincerity in the effort to report "what happened" may be the best we can hope for in human beings' quest for truth (which is not to say that we don't need a plurality of "real news" outlets).[44] With regard to democratic persuasion, however, the task not only includes reliance on our best efforts to understand what has happened in today's public life, buffeted as we are by "news" from countless directions; it entails interest in persuading the person in need of persuasion about what ought to be – for example, (possibly) from less democratic, ignorant, and unjust to more just, knowledgeable, and democratic sensibilities. The activity of persuasion operates between what the individual citizen intellectually knows and ethically believes on the one hand and what social knowledge and ethical belief plausibly entails for, let's say, a healthy democracy. It does not depend on a "concept of truth" so much as it relies on the preservation of public realms that link citizens and make possible the expression of their political claims as part of a *demos* that cares about and acknowledges their differences.[45] Sometimes this can be practically achieved; at others, it can only be theoretically envisioned. The task involves perceiving what can generate movement towards greater democracy (interpreting democracy) and goodness in walks of life that lack them (harmfully divisive and undemocratic societies).

Within this area are material realities involving power and ethical ideals that aspire to goodness, crystallized via political processes in the extant but ever-changing identities and judgments of individuals and institutions. A myriad of factors incline individuals to accept one or another set of beliefs and perspectives about politics and democracy. These are individuated and studied by pollsters of religion, economic class, education, gender/sexual orientation, race, urban vs. rural, and so on. None may be determinative in the last instance – in the manner that class and occupational position amid the means of production were for Marx – but none ought to be ignored or bracketed. Instead, they ought to be considered in terms of their human being and effective power. At the same time, however, apart from the connections fostered by the social media and Zoom, we are faced with the increasing dedication of individuals' mental attention to what they see on flickering hand-held screens and other streaming devices (ruining the apolitical, technological fantasies of pioneers of the internet that it would automatically promote knowledge and beneficent human connections across social divides). As many have noted, this has simultaneously produced echo chambers for individuals – "The Daily Me" – and eviscerated public realms that previously provided opportunities for individuals to interact deliberatively across their differences. The new availability and accessibility to information about the world is coupled with less understanding of the world. This makes the creation of public platforms on which democratic persuasion can occur increasingly difficult. But social media obviously foster political connections as well, from the Arab Spring to the Black Lives Matter and Me-Too movements. And while the ability of extremists to post rants has increased exponentially in the digital era, it remains unclear exactly what is their unique role in forming political judgments.[46] After all, the Ku Klux Klan did not need Zello.

To what extent has the internet generated qualitatively different political divides than those which previously resulted from socio-economically entrenched privileges and inequalities? Surely one's political preferences are shaped by what one understands to be "reality," and that may be intentionally distorted by the economic and political sources of its digital depiction. But to what extent do they modify ideological dispositions already shaped by race, class, religion, gender, and discourses of governmentality? To what extent does the gravitational pull of visual technologies explain the formation of *political* preferences? The practical effects of three-dimensional political protests illustrate the limits of online political education – if not political education more generally. Here, it's worth recalling Marx's dispiriting comment in *The German Ideology* that modern "democracy" can do no more than mediate social conflicts.[47] That democracy did not merely do that in ancient Athens was probably because it economically could oust oligarchical rule and constantly had to fight against its return; it had a transformative agenda. Can contemporary democracy acquire a similarly transformative agenda?

The only answer to these questions about the role of media or other institutional venues for public discourse in determining the challenge of democratic persuasion today is to look, see, and critically evaluate. Be a good friend, citizen, reporter, journalist, social scientist, and political theorist. Note and address inequalities of political power and their undesirable roots. But how these and other interpretive discourses interact is itself important for democratic persuasion. Reporters and journalists attempt to account for "what happened" on a daily or monthly basis. Their reportage is enhanced by their practical and educational backgrounds, but it is still constrained by their particular objects of study. Murders, disastrous fires, and ravaging floods sell more papers than investigative journalism. As a result, unless their background enables them to be particularly imaginative, their work does not reach far beyond conventional understandings or, if it does, it is quickly overwhelmed by contemporary prejudices. Social scientists are constrained by their embrace of data as constituents of social truth, and political theorists are constrained by their relative ignorance of how democratic politics operates "on the ground." Ideally, the work of reporters, social scientists, and political theorists would complement each other and engender political and democratic persuasion. But this may be an ideal that only functions as a distracting illusion.

The task of democratic persuasion is not necessarily to *make* citizens more democratic in their political perspectives. As mentioned before, we all emerge from the undemocratic conditions of our birth and live in undemocratic societies. *Making* a citizen more democratic does not *necessarily* make them better as citizens or human beings. It depends on the democracy they are encouraged to embrace, in either words or deeds. But *if* the democracy is amenable to their participation, citizens (in general) ought to be encouraged to take part in public life wherever it becomes manifest – in their neighbourhoods, localities, social groups, governmental regions, if only to become more knowledgeable about, and responsive to, the power they experience. This is needed so that the political dimension – how "politics interests them" – is personally experienced and actively transformed into what Tocqueville called the art of association. The result empowers them as democratic citizens, even as it does not guarantee democratic (let alone good democratic) choices. It moves undemocratic sensibilities to becoming more democratic, without stipulating a single pathway. After all, democratic choices cannot and should not be guaranteed.

The principal task of democratic persuasion is to provide citizens the intellectual and practical *means* for making good political choices. In this regard, we may have to draw on our own resources, as Dewey stated, in order to define the path forward negatively, since the promised land cannot be discerned. Yet such democratic education may go beyond the limits of democracy, if only negatively – i.e., *against* arrogance, myopia, ignorance, cruelty, and the practical forces that foster them – so as to help envision how to exercise our human and political rights and how to enhance our human and political capacities. These homilies, unprofessional remedies that midwife us towards "big, structural change" may be the best democracies have on to make sure that life prospects are not distorted by ethical, discursive, and practical environments that impair demotic agency. There is no single, rational method or theoretical approach for producing this democratic result, and we must acknowledge both the constitutive and deformative effects of power. But if we can be pointed in a beneficent direction, that may be enough. Of course, we cannot know whether it is, but we should know that there is no time to lose for thinking and acting democratically. Democracies must draw on every available resource if they are to become what they would be, if they are to interpret and heal themselves.

NOTES

Many thanks to Terry Maley for his very helpful comments on a previous version of this essay.

1 John Dewey refers to this "old saying" in *The Public and Its Problems* (Chicago: Swallow Press, 1946 [1927]), 144, cf. 146.

2 After writing this sentence, I came upon Astra Taylor's interesting, recent book *Democracy May Not Exist but You'll Miss It When It's Gone* (New York: Metropolitan Books/Henry Holt and Company, 2019).

3 This was so even when *demokratia* said what it meant – namely, a political order in which the *demos* (made up of citizens registered in officially recognized demes) practically exercised the predominance of political power.

4 This paper assumes that all of the marginalized groups that have recently received widespread attention belong to, and constitute, the *demos*. This does not make the demos agonistic, but it is likely to be raucous in coming up with a political program. So a further assumption is that all members of the *demos* are united by an eagerness to combat unjust inequalities and to work together to reduce them – because "we are all in this together." What I mean by "we" is the demos within various nation-states, supplemented by the "we" of the United Nations General Assembly, along with systematically marginalized groups. And I endorse the "we" as the best political agent – served by leaders – because (a) it experiences most severely the material inequalities that need to be ameliorated, and (b) its position is most likely (given the available alternatives) to promote a disposition that will serve the common good (understood as a projection of claims fostered under conditions of freedom and good will onto a public, shared forum).

5 John Dewey, *The Public and Its Problems* (Chicago: The Swallow Press, 1946 [1927]), 143–6. Cf. John Dewey, *The Public and Its Problems: An Essay in Political Inquiry*, ed. with intro. by Melvin L. Rogers (Athens, OH: The Swallow Press/Ohio University Press, 2016), 171–4. (All subsequent references to *The Public and Its Problems* pertain to the Rogers edition.) Dewey's interlocutor and opponent here was Walter Lippmann, who had argued that the cure for the ailments of democracy was a kind of political expertise that was unavailable to most citizens. See his *Public Opinion* (New York: The Free Press, 1922/1997) and *The Phantom Public* (New York: Harcourt, Brace, 1925).

6 Rousseau believed that radical political change required the intervention of a lawgiver for enabling a society to shed its vices and develop its virtues. See Rousseau, *The Social Contract*, II.7. See John Stuart Mill's *Considerations of Representative Democracy*, Ch. VII. Alinsky preached non-violence as a *sine qua non* of political organizing but emphasized that even democratic organizing would involve conflict and confrontation. See Saul Alinsky, *Rules for Radicals: A Pragmatic Primer for Realistic Radicals* (New York: Vintage Books, 1972 [1971]), 3–23, *passim*. (Raymond Geuss reminded me of Alinsky's relevance for understanding democratic practice and persuasion.) Dewey does not systematically address conflict in his theory of democracy or the public. For confirmation and qualification of this bald statement, see Melvin Rogers's introduction to *The Public and Its Problems* (*supra*), 13–16.

7 Sheldon Wolin pointed out how democracy as a "form" restricts democracy as an activity. See his "Norm and Form: The Constitutionalizing of Democracy," in *Athenian Political Thought and the Reconstruction of American Democracy*, ed. P. Euben, J.R. Wallach, and J. Ober (Ithaca, NY: Cornell University Press, 1994), 29–58. In drawing on ancient Greek political thought and practice in this essay, Wolin illustrates his debt to them. Wolin was a principal teacher of mine.

8 That said, it is important to note that fears of a "tyrannical majority" usually are misplaced, as such majorities typically operate at the level of representation – e.g., the US Senate in recent years – than activities of a *demos*. The Athenian *demos* was

remarkably fair for its approximately 150 years in charge of the Athenian *politeia* – especially its utilization of an amnesty after the rule of The Thirty, which even Plato praised. And it always advocated fidelity to the law. Wolin articulated and took issue with the conflict between democracy and constitutional form in "Norm and Form" (republished in *Fugitive Democracy*).

9 For a roughly compatible conception of the relationship between democracy and justice from a "realist" perspective, see Ian Shapiro, *Democratic Justice* (New Haven, CT: Yale University Press, 1999) and *Politics against Domination* (Cambridge, MA: Harvard University Press, 2016).

10 Wolin used this formulation to articulate his constructive vision of better contemporary manifestations of democracy. See his Foreword to *Fugitive Democracy and Other Essays*, x–xi.

11 John R. Wallach, *Democracy and Goodness: A Historicist Political Theory* (Cambridge: Cambridge University Press, 2018), Ch. 1.

12 The raw political judgments authorized by the Assembly were, after 415 BCE – the Sicilian Expedition – partly vetted by the *graphe paranomon*. It penalized those who proposed what later were deemed to be illegal decrees. This screening process was enhanced after the institution of the *Nomothetai* in 403 BCE (with the revision of the Athenian laws. *Nomothetai* were a group of citizens randomly selected from eligible judges (*dikastai*) who were themselves randomly selected from a self-selected roster of citizens.

13 On the limits of comparative discussions of ancient and modern democracy and political thought due to not accounting fully for their different historical situations, see my "Deconstructing the Ancients/Moderns Trope: Historical Reception in Political Theory," *Polis*, Vol. 33, No. 2 (2016), 265–90.

14 Benjamin Constant, "Liberty of the Ancients Compared to the Moderns" (1819), in Constant, *Political Writings*, ed. Biancamaria Fontana (Cambridge: Cambridge University Press, 1988); Robert A. Dahl, *Who Governs?* (New Haven, CT: Yale University Press, 1961). These arguments are supplemented by Albert O. Hirschman's sociological observations of the inability of modern citizens to sustain attention to the public realm for any extensive period of time, thus rotating between public and private interests. See his *Shifting Involvements: Private Interest and Public Action* (Princeton, NJ: Princeton University Press, 1982).

15 Alexis de Tocqueville, *Democracy in America*, ed. J.P. Mayer & trans. George Lawrence (New York: Anchor/Doubleday, 1969), Pt. I, Ch. II, XII.

16 These points are made over the course of a lengthy interpretation of Plato's political thought, namely, John R. Wallach, *The Platonic Political Art: A Study of Critical Reason and Democracy* (University Park: The Pennsylvania State University Press, 2001).

17 Aristotle, *Politics*, III.xi.

18 This phenomenon nowadays goes by the shorthand ideological term "neoliberalism." For roots of this phenomenon, see Wolin, *Politics and Vision*, Ch. X and *Democracy Incorporated*. For complementary treatments, the books cited in n. 34, *infra*.

19 Apart from the previous reference to this idea in *The Public and Its Problems* (fn.
    1), see Dewey's book from his late period (1939), *Freedom and Culture* (New York:
    G.P. Putnam's Sons, 1939), and his famed, subsequently published article "Creative
    Democracy: The Task Before Us" (1939), which is readily accessible in his *Later
    Works*, Vol. 14 (Carbondale: Southern Illinois University Press, 1988), 224–30.

20 Joseph Schumpeter's critique of the "classical theory of democracy" on behalf
    of an elitist theory that reduces democracy to competition among elites echoes
    Lippmann's critique. See his *Capitalism, Socialism and Democracy* (New York:
    Harper & Row, 1942–50).

21 See Lippmann, *Public Opinion*, 233–8.

22 Lippmann, *Public Opinion*, 201–30.

23 See David Halberstam, *The Best and the Brightest* (New York: Random House, 1972).

24 His previous analyses of democracy were not systematic – namely, "The Ethics of
    Democracy" (1888), which was a review of Henry Maine's *Popular Government*
    (1888), and *Democracy and Education: An Introduction to the Philosophy of Education*
    (1916), which focuses more on education as a social process than democracy as
    a political phenomenon. When *The Public and Its Problems* was reissued in 1946,
    Dewey's writes a postscript stating that since the book's publication twenty years ago
    a new problematic for the public has emerged, namely international relationships
    and the conflict between "democracy" (i.e., NATO) and "totalitarianism" (i.e., Soviet
    Russia). This statement reveals how pre-war discussions of democracy would be
    eclipsed by concern for protecting the new American empire.

25 Dewey, *The Public and Its Problems*, 143. This sentence falls at the end of the
    chapter's last paragraph, which goes as follows: "The same forces which have
    brought about the forms of democratic government, general suffrage, executives
    and legislators chosen by majority vote, have also brought about conditions which
    halt the social and humane ideals that demand the utilization of government as the
    genuine instrumentality of an inclusive and fraternally associated public. 'The new
    of human relationships' has no political agencies worthy of it."

26 Dewey, *The Public and Its Problems*, 69.

27 Dewey's next sentences follow up the one just quoted and complete the
    paragraph: "Officials are those who look out for and take care of the interests
    thus affected. Since those who are indirectly affected are not direct participants
    in the transactions in question, it is necessary that certain persons be set apart
    to represent them, and see to it that their interests are conserved and protected.
    The buildings, property, funds, and other physical resources involved in the
    performance of this office are *res publica*, the common-wealth. The public as far as
    organized by means of officials and material agencies to care for the extensive and
    enduring indirect consequences of transactions between persons is the *Populus*."

28 See Astra Taylor, *The People's Platform: Taking Back Power and Culture in the
    Digital Age* (New York: Picador, 2014); Shoshana Zuboff, *The Age of Surveillance
    Capitalism: The Fight for a Human Future at the New Frontier of Power* (New

York: Public Affairs, 2019). Here is Zuboff's definition of "surveillance capitalism" provided as an epitaph of her long book. "1. A new economic order that claims human experience as free raw material for hidden commercial practices of extraction, prediction, and sales; 2. A parasitic economic logic in which the production of goods and services is subordinated to a new global architecture of behavioral modification; 3. A rogue mutation of capitalism marked by concentrations of wealth, knowledge, and power unprecedented in human history; 4. The foundational framework of a surveillance economy; 5. As significant a threat to human nature in the twenty-first century as industrial capitalism was the natural world in the nineteenth and twentieth; 6. The origin of a new instrumentarian power that asserts dominance over society and presents startling challenges to market democracy; 7. A movement that aims to impose a new collective order based on total certainty; 8. An expropriation of critical human rights that is best understood as a coup from above: an overthrow of the people's sovereignty." Of course, one can get too enthralled by a theory and overstate its significance (especially #7). But Zuboff is on to something that many others have noted in other ways, the result of a pervasive and increasing digitalization of human behaviour and its exploitation and management by behemoth, centralized, private corporations and governments.

29 See Max Weber, "Politics as a Profession and Vocation" (*Politik als Beruf*), in his *Political Writings*, ed. Peter Lassman and Ronald Speirs (Cambridge: Cambridge University Press, 1994), 309–69.

30 See Dewey's review essay on Sir Henry Maine's, *Popular Government*, and his well-known essay, "Creative Democracy: The Task Before Us," published in 1888 and 1939, respectively. (See notes 5 and 6, *supra*).

31 *The Public and Its Problems*, 116. *Nota bene*: "When the public adopts special measures to see to it that the *conflict* [between 'political' and 'non-political' aims, acts, roles – my italics] is minimized and that the representative function overrides the private one, political institutions are termed representative."

32 See Sheldon S. Wolin, "The Liberal/Democratic Divide: On Rawls' Political Liberalism," *Political Theory*, Vol. 24, No. 1 (Feb. 1996), 97–119.

33 Wolin initially delivered this piece at a 1994 conference at Yale University (that included Jurgen Habermas). It was first published in a collection edited by Seyla Benhabib, entitled *Deliberative Democracy: Contesting the Boundaries of the Political* (Princeton, NJ: Princeton University Press, 1996). It has been republished recently, along with many other articles by Wolin, in a volume entitled *Fugitive Democracy and Other Essays*, ed. Nicholas Xenos (Princeton, NJ: Princeton University Press, 2016).

34 See Sheldon S. Wolin, *Democracy Incorporated: Managed Democracy and the Specter of Inverted Totalitarianism* (Princeton, NJ: Princeton University Press, 2008).

35 See these critiques of neoliberalism, cast from different perspectives: David Harvey, *A Brief History of Neoliberalism* (Oxford: Oxford University Press, 2005);

Colin Crouch, *The Strange Non-Death of Neoliberalism* (Cambridge: Polity Press, 2011); and Wendy Brown, *Undoing the Demos: Neoliberalism's Stealth Revolution* (New York: Zone Books, 2015) and *In the Ruins of Neoliberalism: The Rise of Antidemocratic Politics in the West* (New York: Columbia University Press, 2019).

36 See Part I of Marx's essay "On the Jewish Question."

37 Marx's shoemaker metaphor appears in his 1843 *Critique of Hegel's Philosophy of Right*. The *Communist Manifesto* appeared in February 1848, and his favourable remarks on the Paris Commune as a democratic society were published in 1871.

38 The oxymoronic notion of totalitarian democracy was coined by right-wing liberals in the post-war (Second World War) era to tar Rousseau and leftists.

39 One issue that interestingly does not divide liberal and radical democrats is that of free speech. Rights-oriented and power-oriented democrats may well differ on the question of whether there ought to be more regulation of social media and other kinds of "free speech." See how both arguments are finessed by Cass R. Sunstein, in *#republic: Divided Democracy in the Digital Age* (Princeton, NJ: Princeton University Press, 2017), with an afterword by the author (2018). This question will be addressed extensively in a different article/book chapter. For the earliest argument for how free speech ought not to be understood simply in terms of the "marketplace of ideas" if it is to promote civic education and cogent democracy, see Alexander Meiklejohn, *Free Speech and Its Relation to Self-Government* (New York: Harper & Brothers, 1948).

40 See Ch. 6 of my *Democracy and Goodness*.

41 See the useful attempt to "save" persuasion by Bryan Garsten, *Saving Persuasion: A Defence of Rhetoric and Judgment* (Cambridge, MA: Harvard University Press, 2009). It should be noted in our context, however, that the book is mostly concerned about rationalism in the history of political thought and avoids addressing in sustained ways what can be read as democratic vs. anti-democratic attributes of persuasion.

42 Surely it is this concern that has made Elizabeth Warren discuss "total costs" going down for "the middle class" (whatever that is) rather than noting that taxes for parts of the middle class probably would go up. The media and her opponents would lambast her with sound-bites for advocating raising taxes on the middle class without talking about the benefits (e.g., no premiums for private insurance companies). Bernie Sanders is more forthright and less enamoured with the prospects of conventional politics. Partly because of these and related constraints, Joe Biden's presidency has not heeded widespread calls for political change that would generate more egalitarian and reconstructive benefits on behalf of Americans of every walk of life along with the natural environment.

43 Here is an instance of how Plato, the source of Gorgias's voice (which may or may not be historically faithful) combines anti-democratic comments. The *demos* as a public may or may not act *en masse* in various societies; Socrates encouraged

Athenians to act as political individuals. But Plato writes the *demos* as a mass actor, not as an infinite number of statistical niches, as in many contemporary "scientific" and journalistic accounts of the *demos*.

44 See Bernard Williams, *Truth and Truthfulness: An Essay in Genealogy* (Princeton, NJ: Princeton University Press, 2002).

45 Critiques of "the concept of truth" have been lodged by philosophers and political theorists from Nietzsche to Foucault, Rawls, and Williams. One or another of these critiques is presupposed by the contributors to *Truth and Democracy*, ed. Jeremy Elkins and Andrew Norris (Philadelphia: University of Pennsylvania Press, 2012).

46 Need it be said, there probably would be no President Trump without Twitter, but Twitter is hardly sufficient to explain the victories of President Trump or the political communities that have utilized it to forge their bonds. We cannot know what would have happened without Twitter, but the outrage ignited by the murder of George Floyd stemmed more from a widely seen video than any online shout-outs.

47 Robert C. Tucker, ed., *The Marx-Engels Reader*, 2nd ed. (New York: Norton, 1978), 161.

2 Aristotle on Enmity: Ideology, Somatic Justice, and Emotions

INGRID CREPPELL

In a recent book attacking democratic politics, Jason Brennan writes: "One of the repugnant features of democracy is that it transforms ... people into threats to my well-being. My fellow citizens exercise power over me in risky and incompetent ways. This makes them my civic enemies."[1] For Brennan, we already begin as "ignorant, irrational, misinformed nationalists,"[2] but democracy adds an especially dangerous catalyst. By drawing us into debates and policymaking about big political issues, about which we have emotions but not knowledge, we come to "have grounds to hate one another."[3] Even if one does not agree with Brennan's dramatic distrust of his fellow citizens, his description of political conflict rings true. Amid the passions of illiberal democracy, resurgent authoritarian strongmen and Trumpist America, we need to understand better than we do political conflict and its roots. In this essay, I turn to Aristotle's explanation of enmity as an endemic aspect of political life, focusing on its relationship to his conception of justice. This essay explores the interplay of justice and enmity, with an eye to its relevance for us, in the spirit of Sheldon Wolin's readings of the history of Western political thought.[4] Wolin had contrasted Plato's insertion of immutable truth at the foundations of political order (a viewpoint Brennan would no doubt applaud) to Aristotle's insistence on the inescapable reality of variation and diversity of perspectives, and the condition of political life as "fraught with change, accident and contingency."[5] This should not be lamented, nor should we try to overcome it. Wolin's Aristotle theorized forms of compromise and mediation in conflictual but vibrant political community. My reading of Aristotle goes much further in the direction of Aristotle's focus on conflict. We not only differ, we sometimes find ourselves locked in irresolvable enmity. But unlike Brennan's depiction of hopelessly flawed political psyches, Aristotle explains the coherence of such a mindset from a political-moral point of view.

To smooth our road from the present to the past, I propose a preliminary, working definition of enmity: political enmity is an action-oriented mindset with intent to harm another based on justifying ideas, beliefs, and intense emotion, connected to collective public matters. This definition describes what I will search for in Aristotle's analysis of conflict in order to delineate his approach to its causes. Enmity as a definitive mindset comes into existence at particular times. Thus, we cannot explain it by invoking the existence of righteous mentalities, group tribalism, a vague sensation or attitude of hostility, or a universal, aggressive instinct. Aristotle grapples with the hardness and shadings of conflict in both ordinary and extreme politics, and gives us tools for understanding and perhaps alleviating the worst of enmity today.

In addressing these phenomena, Aristotle could be said to have been addressing *agonism* in Athenian society [Greek *agon* = contest or conflict], a feature of its political life spawned by its numerous arenas for collective interaction (e.g., sports, drama, politics).[6] Aristotle was responding to a culture of agonism undergoing change, so the question of enmity's occurrence in time would merit curiosity and theoretical elaboration. In the final lines of the *Politics* V.12, he criticizes Plato's Socrates, who he claims argued in the *Republic* that revolutions happen because "nothing is lasting, but everything undergoes revolution over a certain cycle" (*Pol.* 1316a5).[7] On the contrary, they happen for reasons and those reasons are not reducible to greed or the appetite for power, as if some natural agonism explained hostility as a temporal phenomenon. Enmity should not be treated as a natural or an invariant code.

I

Aristotle argued that enmity emerged at specific occasions when people perceived and felt particular aspects of their political world to be coming apart and transgressing expectations. The context for their judgments was a conception of justice. He may be understood to have distinguished among kinds of political justice: a reason-based ideology, a form of "somatic justice" grounding perceptions and sensations of injustice, and justice embedded in emotions. For Aristotle, justice anchors people's perceptions and their monitoring of events and changes in the world. I will refer to an aspect of monitoring as somatic in that it connotes a body's experience (often indirect but still palpable) of political embodiment. Aristotle's theory of enmity therefore grows out of the conception of politics as an endeavour striving towards the good of a common existence but subject to the forces of partiality and intense emotion. The ideal purpose of a just community itself becomes the embodied grounds for generating enmity as an emotionally charged action-orientation, even as it also makes possible political friendship.

To begin, we need to examine Aristotle's treatment of faction in *Politics*, Book V. The problem of faction or *stasis* preoccupied ancient Greeks: Socrates states in *The Republic*, "Then when Greeks fight with barbarians and barbarians with Greeks, we'll assert they are at war [*polemos*] and are enemies by nature, and this hatred [*echthran*] must be called war; while when Greeks do any such thing to Greeks, we'll say that they are by nature friends, but in this case Greece is sick and factious, and this kind of hatred must be called faction [*stasin*]" (V 470c, 1968, 150).

The word "*stasis*" has been translated as factionalism or partisan conflict in general, civil discord, strife, sedition, revolution, and civil war. The central idea is the internal disruption of a community through group animosity.[8] Scholarly debate revolves around whether Aristotle's use of the concept means (a) a general tendency or proneness towards conflict and discord of individuals and groups, (b) a particular type of "diseased" condition of the political body, or (c) a specific type of conflictual action/activity using forceful means and intended to achieve transformational change.[9] I use the third conception. Aristotle is "investigating the things from which both factional conflicts and revolutions affecting regimes arise." Thus, "one must first grasp their beginning points and causes" (*Pol.* 1302a17ff). In V.2 Aristotle outlines his method: "One should grasp what condition men are in when they engage in factional conflict; for the sake of what they do so; and thirdly, what the beginning points are of political disturbances and of factional conflicts among one another" (1302a20–3). One temptation would be to define enmity as "the condition men are in when they engage in factional conflict" (*Pol.* 1302a21), but though this first element is foundational for explaining how factional conflict depends upon an enemy mindset,[10] to develop the full potential of Aristotle's analysis, we need to expand on that initial disposition. Aristotle does not directly use the terminology of enmity (*échthra*, *polemos*) when discussing faction because he reserves those terms for other types of conflict (personal enmity and war), but his description of the factional frame of mind provides the basis of an enmity conception.

Aristotle begins and ends Book V asserting that people are inflamed against others based on judgments about justice and fairness. In the opening paragraphs he sets out this position: "All regimes … have … a certain sort of justice, but in an unqualified sense they are in error. [W]hen either group does not take part in the regime on the basis of the conception it happens to have, they engage in factional conflict" (1301a27–40). The final sentences reinforce the claim: "men engage in factional conflict and effect revolution in regimes if they have no part in the prerogatives or if they are treated unjustly or arrogantly" (1316b22–3). These general statements refer to different ways persons perceive justice, injustice, and wrong actions. The power of the justice motivation lies at the core of Aristotle's approach.[11] Other theories might centre on order, security, and belonging in a group, or causes of glory and power. How should we understand the argument that justice acts as the basic motivation of people driven to faction?

II

One may be *moved by* justice and enmity at multiple levels. The three primary locations of enemy formation are reasoned ideologies of the just regime, perceptions of injustice in a city, and emotions of hostility. No one of these locations can fully explain enmity's consolidation. For purposes of this paper, I will focus on ideology and somatic (in)justice.

A. Ideologies of Justice

Justice inspires antipathy by means of ideology. Although the term is a product of nineteenth-century Europe, we can employ it here as a matrix of ideas held by a group of people about the basic functioning of politics and society. It carries explicit claims about how things do and ought to work and serves as a (quasi-) holistic vision of policy and action.[12] Aristotle treats the motive of justice, in part, as an ideology, a view "biased" by the point of view of the holders, but this is not a mere veneer of justification. Groups make abstract and encompassing claims – they give reasons – about the right regime's order. He elaborates a specific political form of thinking, seeing, and feeling tied to justice claims. An ideology of justice disposes people to be in the *condition men are in* when they engage in factional conflict.

CLAIMS ABOUT THE JUST REGIME: THE POWER OF REASON
At the start of Book V Aristotle notes:

> [The power of the] *demos* … arose as a result of those who are equal in any respect supposing they are equal simply … and oligarchy arose as a result of those who are unequal in some one respect conceiving themselves to be wholly unequal.… Then the former *claim to merit* taking part in all things equally on the grounds that they are equal, while the latter seek to aggrandize themselves on the grounds that they are unequal, since "greater" is something unequal.… And it is *for this reason* that, *when either group does not take part in the regime on the basis of the conception it happens to have,* they engage in factional conflict. (*Pol.* 1301a27–40; emphasis added)

In this opening, Aristotle asserts the central role of *claims about the just regime* leading to factional conflict, but before he elaborates, he insists on the reason-based nature of ideological justice.

The subject matter is a big one: the nature of the regime. A regime [*politeia*] is "a certain arrangement of those who inhabit the city" (*Pol.* 1274b38); it is "an arrangement of a city with respect to its offices, particularly the one that has authority over all matters" (*Pol.* 1278b9–10). It entails the institutionalization of power and order in a political community – the foundational rules about ordering rule. Claims about justice support partisan positions of power and contribute to factional enmity. But this cannot account for his observations, which centre on the substance of diverging abstract conceptions of justice. Aristotle emphasizes that people apply reason to considering their place in this encompassing order: *all agree regarding justice and proportionate equality.*[13]

Claims of justice rest upon some form of equality. Aristotle states, "The political good is justice.... Justice is held by all to be a certain equality" (*Pol.* 1282b17–23). Both the ideal notion of political justice and the "erroneous" shadow incarnations held by people striving to gauge and act on some defensible basis in a real world rest on equality as a standard for reasoning about the right distribution of offices. Aristotle emphasizes: "Equality is twofold: one sort is numerical, the other according to merit.... Now while there is *agreement that justice in an unqualified sense is according to merit*, there are differences, as was said before: some consider themselves to be equal generally if they are equal in some respect, while others claim to merit all things unequally if they are unequal in some respect" (*Pol.* 1301b30–9; emphasis added). A group's conception of its standing vis-à-vis others and the justice due to it in regard to rule based on an objective standard of equality determines how it will argue for the just regime. Democratic groups argue for a *principle of free-birth* and oligarchic groups a *principle of superiority.*

People arguing politically think in generalizable, abstract terms, though they protect and advance their own positions. The fact of protecting/advancing one's own position does not delete the impulse and need of reason.[14] Aristotle accepted that argumentation in a world of public communication, despite its inevitable bias, would be held passionately because of groups' claims to legitimacy, not simply to self-serving ends. Each side's general ideas of justice fuel its sense of standing and action-claims. Abstractness here is intrinsically coupled with normative rightness. It is not just a set of arms-length ideas. Aristotle portrays political disputants as feeling they have *a right to have ideas about justice.*[15] Thus, reason and general abstract ideas provide a purchase on the normativity of ideology: substantive claims about justice inherently involve the passions of citizens to assert public rightness in political arenas.

CLAIMS ABOUT THE JUST REGIME: THE ERROR OF REASON

Aristotle explains that *when either group does not take part in the regime on the basis of the conception it happens to have,* it will engage in factional conflict. Groups mobilized by ideology cannot help but be partial, but error of reasoning not partiality per se paves the way to enmity: "in an unqualified sense they are in error." What is their error? They generalize but they stop generalizing too soon. "In oligarchies ... the many engage in factional conflict on the grounds that they are done an injustice because they do not partake of equal things in spite of being equal. In democracies the notables engage in factional conflict because they partake of equal things although they are not equal" (*Pol.* 1303b4–8). Here both sides perceive the damage they will or do suffer in a "partially" constructed regime: the poor in oligarchies reject the principle of superiority. The wealthy in democracies reject the principle of free birth. Aristotle shows both to be in error because they hold up as a general principle what is rather a generalization from a partial point of view: "they judge badly with respect to what concerns themselves" (Pol. 1280a21) while simultaneously believing they are "speaking of justice simply" (Pol. 1280a23). Partiality becomes a source of enmity not because it is partial and materialist but because it claims to be complete (the whole truth) – they believe they are *speaking of justice simply* when they are not. Error consists in ideological hubris bringing on blindness to one's inherent partiality. When people fail to achieve an additional level of more capacious reasoning, they act on the basis of the partial, yet fuelled by a sense of being impartial, thinking they are taking a view of the whole, which generates the righteous, sharpening, and impassioned power of reason as a generalized logic. Still, the partial and erroneous nature of their conceptions does not undermine the authenticity of actors' claims based on justificatory beliefs.

FROM REASON TO ENMITY

I have laid out Aristotle's stark delineation between two versions of an ideology of the just regime, which ground factional ideas and basic forms of rule. A polarized situation of people aligned in parties wielding alternative truths would seem to make enmity endemic to political life. Aristotle might appear to view political society as strictly a détente where the forces in precarious balance bide their time ready for upheaval should opportunity present itself – in effect an ongoing state of war by other means. But he rejects agonistic détente as an adequate account of a stable polity, even the flawed incarnations of political systems of the real world. Indeed, he observes that any regime established on the basis of an absolutist version of either democracy or oligarchy will be unstable: "to have everywhere an arrangement that is based only on one or the other of these sorts of equality is a poor thing. This is evident from the result: none of these sorts of regimes is lasting" (*Pol.* 1302a3–5).[16] The ideological basis of factional division found in partisan political parties obtains in many ongoing systems without breakdown into the kind of revolutionary faction at issue in Book V. If Aristotle is not reducing his argument to a clash of ideas or a mere clash of powers, how should we read his observations on the role of ideologies of justice in the formation of the enemy mindset? I have already indicated some elements of the transformation into enmity.

Ideological reasoning plays a determinative (but not sufficient) role because it is essential to the way citizens interact with one another in a public sphere. Abstract ideals of justice provide tools at hand for resolving public chaos and can be a basis for igniting it. There are multiple powers embedded in claims of justice: they clarify/simplify, impassion, and coordinate. People will hold on to generalizable, abstract reasoning about complex, typically muddled ideas regarding social order; that reasoning can become sharpened into a simplified call to arms. The ideals invest a normativity of right, which may become righteous emotion. For political groups, especially non-elite people, these claims also carry the additional validation of social standing through the legitimacy of arguing over equality. Justice claims contain sources of power and also an inherent competitive stance. Those who hold diverging conceptions face each other vying over the right interpretations, over righteous passion, and over claims for group power. They also face each other over the space in-between them – over the same thing – the regime and its order. The clarifying, impassioning, and coordinating powers of ideology are intertwined. Any society in which ideas circulate in public must sustain itself despite the tension built into those contentious ideas. In "normal" political contestation, the sides fight for their version of rule, but in a loose way, holding it as an ideal type, a beacon to guide political thinking and the direction of policy, but still in balance with the other side(s). Their partiality is contained, in balance with a view and feeling towards being part of a whole. Looser political contestation depends on a tacit agreement to sustain argumentation through public disputation. To be able to do that, each side accepts that it falls short of its pure ideology of justice; no side can win the eternal battle for predominance in their ongoing interaction.

A dynamic of enmity may be precipitated when people purposely seek to stir up instability and confusion in order to force simplified alignments in zero-sum, categorically antithetical directions. The intertwined power within claims of justice then becomes an accelerator to enmity because the stakes are raised. Unqualified ideological purity sets in motion all the empowerments. Some situations may be highly vulnerable to being stirred up, disrupting the tacit background modes of acceptance. People move towards more enmity orientations of simplified clarity, passion, and status coordination. In addition, in conditions of public fluidity, when people feel compelled to assert more rigid versions of their claims to rule, a logic of enmity comes about because the perception of one's options and one's intensified rightness lead to a mirroring effect: each side views the other as uncompromising or as *expecting the other side to have no choice* but to be uncompromising, as it feels it must become. Both sides expect a move towards hardened dichotomous versions of their ideologies, which in theory denies the legitimacy of the other side's partaking of rule. To deploy purely abstract reasoning indicates an emotional extreme rejecting the other's right to exist as a political being.

I read the core of Aristotle's observation – all regimes of this kind have, then, a certain sort of *justice, but in an unqualified sense they are in error. And it is for this reason that, when either group does not take part in the regime on the basis of the conception it happens to have, they engage in factional conflict* – in the following way: (a) when people become unqualifying in their political thinking, feeling, and acting, they harden into a categorical position on political justice, taking an all-or-nothing position, which (for Aristotle) must be politically erroneous because the destruction of a regime of complex order can never constitute a mode of justice; and (b) when either group finds itself caught in the recriminating purity cycle, both (either) see themselves as erased from the other's regime. Each side projects onto its competitor its own need for lock-down. In situations of apparent disruption to the tacit rules of exchange, political actors harden definitions of themselves solely via ideology, to force political order towards a singular solution and thereby a threat of mutual destruction. It seems to be built into the ideological incarnation of justice that to insist on it alone is to court destruction of a human political order.

Aristotle begins with the ideology of justice because he seeks to demonstrate the reason-based thinking of those who move into civil war. It is tempting to ascribe enmity to bad character, a collective disease, or an inevitable cycle of disintegration, but to explain human behaviour in those terms condemns politics to an occult fate. Politically active persons do and must think, reason, and care about big issues. Thus, reason-based ideology directly plays a role in self-destruction. At the end of Book V, Aristotle juxtaposes Plato's theory of regime change in the *Republic* against his own. Plato told a story about forms of injustice in which regimes devolve because men fail to be educated in the virtues and honourable desires. All ruling parties eventually become corrupted through obsession with property. Aristotle sharply objects that the motivation to bring about a change of revolutionary scope cannot fundamentally be materialistic. "It is also odd to suppose that there is a revolution in the direction of oligarchy because those holding the offices are greedy and involved in money-making, and not because those who are very pre-eminent by the fact of their property suppose it is not just for those possessing nothing to have a share in the city equal to that of the possessors" (1316a38–1316b2). We can see how this kind of public engagement through ideas will necessarily happen. We must reason about the big issues in a public politics, and our reasoning will be erroneous when it is prosecuted solely in a categorical and therefore incomplete way. Ideological politics is both essential and dangerous. Yet, episodes of enmity do not only result from arguments over regime form.

B. Injustice in the City: Alienation and Betrayal

We not only live in regimes, we live in cities. Aristotle does not sharply distinguish these two constitutive contexts, but I would argue doing so is necessary if we want to make sense of his treatment of enemy mindsets. People living in cities think and feel in response to a regime (*politeia*) and to a city (*polis*); these perceptions and emotions are not identical. People indeed react to their political worlds through abstract ideas, but also through the felt experience of living in a city of which one is part of a whole. Collective life brings shared benefits – sustenance and well-being, security and status recognition. When they perceive access to the benefits of collective life threatened, people feel betrayed or become alienated and may move towards enmity against those who appear to destroy the wholeness of the city and its goods.

In *Politics*, V.2, Aristotle outlines his method of investigating factions: to recall, he states, "One should grasp what condition men are in when they engage in factional conflict; for the sake of what they do so; and thirdly, what the beginning points are of political disturbances and of factional conflicts among one another" (1302a20–3). Taken together, these three angles help us understand occurrences of faction, he argues. We've already discussed the first; now I shall discuss the second and third. Aristotle spells out these two further components as follows:

> As for the things over which they engage in factional conflict, these are profit and honor and their opposites (for they may engage in factional conflict in cities in order to avoid dishonor or punishment either for themselves or for their friends). (*Pol.* 1302a33–4)
>
> The causes and beginning points of the changes through which they come to be in a state of the sort spoken of and concerning the things mentioned are in one sense seven in number, but in another sense more. Of these, two are the same as the ones spoken of, though not in the same way. For men are stirred up against one another by profit and by honor – not in order to acquire them for themselves, as was said earlier, but because they see others aggrandizing themselves (whether justly or unjustly) with respect to these things. They are stirred up further by arrogance, by fear, by preeminence, by contempt, by disproportionate growth, and further, though in another manner, by electioneering, by underestimation, by [neglect of] small things, and by dissimilarity. (1302a35–b1–4)

The most general cause or driving force behind enmity is political justice, which I've interpreted as ideologies of justice and perceptions of somatic (in) justice. Justice exists and is perceived in indirect ways for people living in a city. The second two angles from which Aristotle explores faction (profit and honour, and background conditions) are tied to the issue of the more indirect perceptions of somatic (in)justice. Aristotle's tripartite approach establishes the primacy of the question of distributive justice: "The general cause of men being in a certain condition with respect to revolution[:] … they aim at equality" (1302a24–6). Excessive desire for equality and inequality (the equality of the unequal) are not shaped solely relative to a logic of ideas about a regime's organization of rule. They are also linked to a more flexible standard of measure for a balanced life in the city, to which I now turn.

THINGS OF THE CITY

Aristotle refers to profit and honour in their first role as things over which men strive and for the sake of which they pursue faction. Many interpreters have taken this to mean that Aristotle's theory boils down to an indictment of people's avaricious and arrogant drives. David O'Connor, for instance, notes: "both honor and wealth are competitive goods, what Aristotle calls 'things people fight over' (*perimacheta*).... Both by nature are ordered toward (and hence limited by) the life of virtuous activity. But *when they are pursued as ends themselves, this natural limit gives way to an insatiable desire that leads to injustice and ultimately to civil conflict (stasis)*" (O'Connor 1991, 153; emphasis added).[17] In most treatments of faction as a result of profit/honour, the transition from normal to abnormal striving is submerged within a process dynamic, where the tipping point from a state of civil order to one of civil *stasis* occurs beyond observation and explanation. The fetishism of the external goods line of argument stresses the having and striving for external marks as the key to differential value. If so, Aristotle should argue that a world where external goods could not be fought over and sought in grasping, competitive ways would alleviate the causes of faction. In *Politics* Book II, he considers arguments for the abolition of private property made from such premises: snuff out sources of material inequality and greed and envy will have no soil to grow from. However, entirely getting rid of private property may actually enhance factionalism rather than avoid it (cf. *Pol.* 1263a16–21), he insists.

I read the importance of seeking competitive goods in a different light. Profit and honour always exert intense concern and comparison in a city's political and social life. They grip people because they contain the outer signifiers of intersubjective assessments of one another. In the desiring and having of profit and honour, people desire and need others' comparative witnessing of approval, a proof of their rank and validation. To have acquired much profit and honour testifies to one's superiority (in some form) within a world of mutual valuation and assessment. We should not focus on the extent of people striving for such external goods as the primary cause of faction. The motor to strive is always on, Aristotle holds. In *Politics* II, he observes "the wickedness of human beings is insatiable: at first the two *obol* allowance was adequate, but now that this is something traditional, they always ask for more, and go on doing so without limit. For the nature of desire is without limit, and it is with a view to satisfying this that the many live" (*Pol.* 1267b1–5). Something else takes place in the dynamic of seeking profit and honour that will lead to groups acting to destroy an ongoing political community. A feeling and idea of justice and the perception of an unjust balance of external goods leads to calamity. People become enraged because of injustice, not because others have more wealth or more honour *per se*: "For it is when those who are in office behave arrogantly and aggrandize themselves that men engage in factional conflict – both against one another and against the regimes which provide them license to do so" (*Pol.* 1302b6–10) and "For it is on account of injustice, fear, and contempt that the ruled in many cases attack.... Though arrogance is of many sorts, each of them gives rise to anger; and most of those who are angry attack for the sake of revenge, rather than preeminence" (*Pol.* 1311a25–38), revenge driven by a sensation of unjust treatment rather than the simple fact of a difference in rank (pre-eminence).

To see the role played by the pursuit of profit and honour in the genesis of faction, we need to tie this activity to perceptions of injustice. The pursuit of these external goods happens within a context of others doing the same thing. People perceive and feel aspects of the relationship between their own situation and that of others. Is that comparative relationship out of kilter? Is it going in an expected or an alarming direction? The sensation and perception of a discrepancy in basic parameters of the relative dynamic between groups and persons will alert people to something happening. If the expectation of acceptable behaviour and another actor's arrogance or greed appears hugely divergent, then people may feel drastic measures are necessary. Aristotle emphasizes that perceptions of justice are elemental to factional breakdown, not the incessant striving for profit and honour.

When Aristotle writes, "the things over which they engage in factional conflict, these are profit and honor and their opposites," he does not mean they engage in faction to amass more profit/honour in absolute or relative terms because they have become corrupt and out of control. But such desires become extreme, tending towards faction, because of the perceived betrayal of justice. People turn towards enmity and are willing to overturn the prevailing order when they believe stakes are profound, not out of normal competitiveness – "it is over great things that men engage in factional conflict." A perception of injustice becomes more amped up and acute when people view the change in pursuit of or the distribution of profit/honour to be unacceptable and provocative. When will this happen? To answer, we must step back briefly to think about how people perceive justice at the level of the city.

LIVING IN THE CITY

Living in a city rests upon a tacit but relatively fixed expectation about people's commitment to a common project. When enmity arises as a response to living in the city, persons and groups view the attitudes of contenders as deviating from the commitment to the life of the city. Because Aristotle holds that commitment to the city glues the city together, if they clash about their commitments, this will foster suspicion, anger, and fear about basic embodiment. How so?

First, the city includes the organizational means to attain self-sufficiency "for the sake of living," but it goes beyond survival to create the possibility that people live well (*Pol.* 1252b28–30) by orienting themselves towards "a good life," that is a life of attempting to achieve virtue. Thus, and secondly, a city contains an elevating purpose, pushing people beyond rudimentary and purely self-oriented activities. Third, and at its heart, the city is a type of political community composed of citizens who share in public deliberation, decision-making, and rule (*Pol.* 1275b19–21); they are capable of ordering power and sharing it. A political community offers conditions for self-sufficient life, aspirations towards a good life, and the achievement of self-rule (see also *Pol.* 1328b3–23).

This list of qualities, however, does not fully capture the unique kind of collectivity embodied in a city. At the opening of the *Politics*, Aristotle describes the city's unity: "Since we see that every city is some sort of community, and that every community is constituted for the sake of some good ... the community that is most authoritative of all and embraces all the others does so particularly, and aims at the most authoritative good of all. This is what is called the city or the political community" (*Pol.* 1252a5–7). Key to citizens' aiming at the most authoritative good, however, is that this aim is carried forward by persons and groups that are different: "For no community comes into existence out of two doctors but rather out of a doctor and a farmer and, in general, out of those who are different and not equal. But these [differing types] must be equalized" (*Nicomachean Ethics*, 1133a16–18). The city, distinct from other human orderings such as large nations; empires; or tribal, clan-based entities, offers an ideal scope and form for unifying different people into a political community. The authoritative good of city life connects individual goods and the common good (material and ideal). The city structures physical survival and needs through collective provision and security, and ideational, emotional well-being and needs through ideas and collective justice. It is a honing of differences into a unified entity, not through natural harmonization but forged through political methods of dispute and agreement in a public space. City life is hard, but people need and want it; it provides the arena in which they can work and see themselves through the tension between individual and collective goals. In this way, the city develops its diverse citizens, and citizens forge the city.

For this to work, people must be committed to the project of a city. Aristotle portrays the attitude of commitment to the city in his discussion of political friendship. However, his description is ambiguous.[18] On the one hand, the bond constituting the city appears as *affection* among groups and people for their political project of a common life. The city as a "community [*koinonia*] involves the element of affection [*philikon*] – enemies do not wish to have even a journey in common" (*Pol.* 1295b24–5). An ethos of friendliness also must be sustained: "For we suppose friendship [*philia*] to be the greatest of good things for cities, for in this way they would least of all engage in factional conflict [*stasiazoien*]" (*Pol.* 1262b8–9); "friendship holds cities together and.... For like-mindedness seems to resemble friendship, and lawgivers aim at this especially and drive out discord because it especially produces hatred. When people are friends, they have no need of justice, but when they are just, they do need friendship in addition" (*NE* 1155a23–8). These passages seem to underscore the need for a kind of moral care and emotional concern – even if it does not reach the level of intimate individual friendship. Aristotle clearly holds that some emotional involvement must be present among participants in the city, for not only the good but also the very perpetuation of the city. But what is the nature of that affection? I have already noted the extent to which relationships among citizens are filled with tension, competition, and friction, and class conflict often seems on the verge of open class war.

Aristotle also allows political friendship to be more practical and pragmatic. In this light, friendship consists in *rational agreement* on mutual advantage among groups and persons who disagree about many other things: "cities are like-minded whenever people are of the same judgment concerning what is advantageous, choose the same things, and do what has been resolved in common" (*NE* 1167a27–9); "Like-mindedness ... appears to be political friendship ... for it concerns advantageous things" (*NE* 1167b3).

Thus, Aristotle entertains two attitudes that may exhibit political friendship. One derives from affection and a sense of community, the other from a sense of shared interests and mutual advantage. How do they contribute to his theory of enmity?

(a) Civil Affection and Whole/Parts Thinking and Feeling. We can think of political bonding as *civil affection*. This notion combines Aristotle's emphasis on a mentality of like-mindedness about political matters and an ethos of emotion-based friendliness and affection. Without trying to precisely integrate the two endpoints, I propose the following interpretation of Aristotle's civil bond of friendship. People living in a city (a) desire to live in *that* city and therefore hold affection for the city as a whole; and they (b) accept their own and others' parts within the city as necessary to the ongoing project of living together in this particular political body. Civil affection pertains directly to the city as a holistic project, and it arises indirectly from the contributing parts accepting and acknowledging one another because everyone forges the collective project (which each part directly desires and cares for). Thus, the nature of civil affection does not require direct sensations of intimate bonding between subgroups in the city, nor does it depend on desiring to be blended into one unified identity. Rather, all accept that common life depends on their collective work and on the contributions of people and groups who are different: they share work and caring for the whole and share an acknowledgment of each person's and group's work.

The claim that members of the city must *care for the whole* operates as a defining idea for Aristotle's theory of politics. In Book II of the *Politics* he reinforces the importance of support for the common endeavour: "If a regime is going to be preserved, all the parts of the city must wish it to exist and continue on the same basis" (*Pol.* 1270b21–3).[19] This idea should be paired with the second prong of civil affection friendship: that concern for the whole remains emotionally powerful side by side with recognition of the involvement of diverse parts. The fact of difference does not undercut one's commitment to the whole. Difference is acknowledged alongside direct emotional investment in the community. Civil affection that includes both an orientation towards the whole and parts depends on whole/parts thinking and feeling. We cannot understand the logic of Aristotle's theory of enmity without this notion of whole/parts. Here we can begin to put together the building blocks of a conception of somatic justice.

What is whole/parts thinking and feeling? It is rarely an exact mental state. We can conceive it as the need and capacity to carry in one's mental map a picture of an encompassing phenomenon with component elements constituting it. We require whole/part maps to make sense of the complex world and politics we live in, which demand opinions, judgment, decisions, and action. Not that we deploy it as a blueprint, but it helps to situate and simplify the kaleidoscope of phenomena. A person or group holds a picture in a more and less explicit and clear way, depending on circumstances and the need to deploy it for cognitive and emotional purposes. For instance, people may hold a general picture of the world and global political relations and with this, a picture of the role of their own country. They may carry a view of class, race, or ethnic balance vis-à-vis a political-social order. Whole/parts thinking and feeling are necessary for political-cultural-social minds to make sense of the bewildering buzz of the world and exigencies of action.

Aristotle's discussion of the city as a compound whole made up of parts pervades his writings on politics.[20] Though Aristotle develops his political philosophy to provide the legislator with knowledge to construct and administer a stable, virtuous, and just city, the language of wholes, parts, and compounds is not solely a theoretical toolkit for describing the most practical or best constitutions. He considers people's perceptions and responses to their worlds as also deeply shaped by whole/parts thinking and feeling. The "parts" – conscious persons and politicized groups – see and feel their connections in a larger context of comparison, measuring, and judgment.

Take, for example, Aristotle's descriptions of citizens' capacities for such assessment in many of his analyses: property, the division of labour, the ethos of sharing in rule, and customary notions of proportionality and equity, as well as the principle of justice as giving persons their due. In a key passage he notes: "the city is in its nature a sort of aggregation" (*Pol.* 1261a18), a *multitude* whose "consonance" cannot be reduced to a "unison" (*Pol.* 1264b35–6). "[T]he city is made up not only of a number of human beings, but also of those differing in kind: a city does not arise from persons who are similar…. [T]hose from whom a unity should arise differ in kind. It is thus reciprocal equality that preserves cities…. This is necessarily the case even among persons who are free and equal, for all cannot rule at the same time" (*Pol.* 1261a23–34). The ability to engage in practices of reciprocal equality and to take turns ruling requires a mental map of the workings of a whole and its parts. People care about the city and its just operations, and they know it requires diverse contributions. Thus, the political consciousness undergirding city life depends upon an ability to see the whole, to see and accept one's part in this whole, and to appraise and judge others' parts in that whole of which one is a part. In addition, however, people – "differing in kind" – engage each other about the most important things, which also divide them and over which they fight.

So, then, what does it mean for citizens to view the workings of the city as a whole? Political groups react to their political world using ideas about the right institutional rules, that is, the reason-based ideology of regimes discussed earlier, but they also hold a more general perception about how the elements of a city fit together. This distinction will aid in clarifying faction and in constructing a theory of enmity.

(b) Civil Affection and Fixing Expectations. Civil affection should not be viewed as keeping the city together through a flow of either emotionality or rationality. The consequence of civil affection, which binds the city in a complex mode of interaction and awareness, is that expectations are established. Expectations about each other comprise an ethical "pact" of sorts, different from a pragmatic alliance. People make something like an ethical pact, which sustains their common life. This pact has a public emotional-ethical structure buried in its ethos. The emotional-ethical structure is embedded in whole/part thinking; it holds that (a) everyone should desire to live in and continue to support the city as a whole, and (b) each part should accept others' parts within the city as being necessary to the ongoing project of living together in this distinct political body. Again, what is expected will not be an emotional submersion in unified oneness. Aristotle criticizes Socrates: "it is impossible for [the city] to be happy as a whole unless most people, or all or some of its parts, are happy. For happiness is not the same kind of thing as evenness" (*Pol.* 1264b17–20).[21]

Perhaps we can conceive it this way: a city needs "hard" structures of institutions and laws to give it a strong framework within which political life becomes stable and can flourish over time. But it also needs the less tangible ethos of civil affection to carry on. However, this less tangible ethos cannot be too evanescent, or it will fail to exert a causal force in the maintenance of the city. In order to conceptualize the way in which an ethos of civil affection acquires a fixedness, we can think about it as these expectations forming the emotional-ethical terms of a tacit public pact, alongside the more apparently concrete constitutional and ideological structures. Civil affection of the parts establishes an informal but quasi-fixed set of expectations. The differences between the groups, which inevitably generate inequality, are balanced by their recognized role in the whole, and the collective commitment to everyone's common life. For less prominent persons and groups, the pact installs a presumption of validation in the eyes of others.[22] And for the more powerful, their role is justified and protected through demonstrating action for the good of the collectivity. Certainly, to accept the other's necessary role does not thereby make them one's intimate friend or social equal. The political bond is mediated by a notion of just place within a whole. Nevertheless, a kind of justice sensation attaches to the acknowledgment of diversity within a whole, without which one's own life would not be possible. People accept a particular place vis-à-vis others because they seek to live here, and in so doing everyone's agreement establishes expectations of just due. Political friendship then is more than rational calculated advantage, and yet less than emotional-ethical unison. The like-mindedness of civil affection includes (a) care for the city's collective existence and (b) acceptance of everyone's diverse part in the shared enterprise.

The cooperative spirit/ethos knitting together an amalgam of different parts establishes informal political justice. I will call the quasi-fixed rubric of expectations erecting informal political justice "somatic justice," as in the justice of a political body. The word somatic means "of or relating to the (or a) body; bodily, corporeal" (OED). The value of this formulation is that it brings out how something intangible and indirect like an ethos of friendship anchors itself in a type of political-psychological concreteness – through expectations of justice, justice that is neither only distributive justice nor only justice as a virtue of character, but justice as a way of thinking and feeling about the person and group's connectedness in a living, embodied political community. The kind of justice paired with friendship in politics is somatic justice: it is the will of all members, individuals, and people divided into parts, desiring to live together in this particular whole, acknowledging that desire, and committing to protect its whole embodied political being, as so constituted.

STUFF HAPPENS, OR PERCEIVING INJUSTICE IN THE CITY

In every society, there will be conflict, tension, and competition – over profit and honour, and at some points about the overarching terms of constitutional order. Events jar the prevailing arrangements and accommodations. Competition and conflict can be sustained within a flexible enough bond of connection to keep factional disintegration at bay. When a city is working well or well enough, the commitment to the whole and everyone's part seem to operate in the background, and people pursue their lives and goals, expecting to do so in a context of collective order. People do not need continually to test out the limits of the whole or the durability of each other's commitments.

Why would people be moved towards enmity that puts them on a path to destruction of the city with all its benefits? Aristotle argues for the centrality of justice in the genesis of enmity. Somatic justice serves as the tacit framework according to which perceptions and judgments respond to things happening. It anchors people's monitoring of events and political change. There needs to be an implicit justice-expectation at the city level, not just the regime level, such that responsiveness to justice and injustice takes place under both. People perceive injustice as deviation from both care for the city as a whole and recognition of its diverse, embodied parts.

We can now turn back to *Politics* Book V to continue unpacking Aristotle's analysis of faction. A notion of somatic justice, defined as the quasi-fixed expectations about the whole and parts of a community and civil affection, provides a necessary perspective for analysis. As noted previously, Aristotle lays out three angles from which to explain factionalism: "what condition men are in when they engage in factional conflict; for the sake of what they do so; and thirdly, what the beginning points are of political disturbances" (*Pol.* 1302a17–23). The "condition or mindset men are in" emerges as a reaction to challenges to somatic justice; these challenges stem from competition over profit and honour and other "beginning points" that can incline people to feel and to see their situation vis-à-vis others in a new and negative light. Recall the important passage:

> For men are stirred up against one another by profit and by honor – not in order to acquire them for themselves, as was said earlier, but because they see others aggrandizing themselves (whether justly or unjustly) with respect to these things. They are stirred up further by arrogance, by fear, by preeminence, by contempt, by disproportionate growth, and further, though in another manner, by electioneering, by underestimation, by [neglect of] small things, and by dissimilarity. (*Pol.* 1302a35–1302b1–4)

This third type of beginning point comprises things out of the ordinary, happenings felt and seen that set people on a trajectory of disturbance. A couple of examples give us an idea of this line of thought. When regimes experience "disproportionate growth," citizens may become suspicious, fearful, or angry:

> Revolutions in regimes also occur through disproportionate growth of a part. A body is composed of parts which must increase in proportion if a balance is to be maintained, and if this does not happen it perishes – for example, when a foot is four yards long and the rest of the body two feet high; and sometimes too it may be altered to the shape of another animal, if the increase is not only quantitative but qualitative and contrary to proportion. So too is a city composed of parts; and frequently an increase in one of them is overlooked – for example, the multitude of the poor in democracies and polities. Sometimes this happens also through chance occurrences. At Tarentum, for example, a democracy replaced a polity when many of the notables were defeated and killed by the Iapygians shortly after the Persian War. (*Pol.* 1302b35–1303a5)

Or "those who come to be a cause of power's being acquired, whether private individuals, offices, tribes, or generally a part or multitude of any sort, give rise to factional conflict. For either those who envy their being honored initiate factional conflict or they themselves are unwilling to remain on an equal footing on account of their preeminence" (*Pol.* 1304a34–8). Diverse passages display the variety of ways whole/parts somatic justice can be experienced as under attack, leading to the perception of something wrong in the background of informal justice due to disequilibrium. These interpretations of happenings jar expectations. Where before the workings of the city had carried on as relatively balanced, now disturbed citizens and members of the polis see and feel events or processes as dislodging the ongoing arrangement. Aristotle portrays people as hermeneuticists of somatic justice over a stretch of political time.[23]

Enmity will arise spurred by perceptions of injustice: (a) when some significant part of the whole feels its role to be denied or destroyed, (b) when the city is felt and believed to be betrayed directly, or (c) when the intactness of the city is viewed as no longer possible. In the final logic (c), people may not believe a group intentionally attacks it, but will perceive this group to be making the city's ongoing life as a whole impossible. If we circle back to the three "things from which both factional conflicts and revolutions affecting regimes arise," we see that the mindset of enmity cannot be explained solely by the more ideologically worked-up "state of mind" men are in or the automaticity of pursuing profit/ wealth and honour. People become prone to enmity when they feel expectations betrayed or fear destruction through what has taken place in a city.

I have developed a notion of somatic justice in order to conceptualize the kind of relationship between persons and groups in a city, which Aristotle describes as subject to breakdown. For Aristotle, enmity is propelled by sensations of imbalance, betrayal, disproportion, and arrogance. To speak of somatic injustice provides a way to pinpoint a palpable experience of an endangered project of city life. If somatic justice exists as a customary or tacit order of *a desire for going along together*, precisely when and how will "perceptions" of injustice of the somatic sort take place? Here we would need to investigate Aristotle's conception of emotions as integral to our nature as political animals.

In concluding, I will merely indicate this further component of Aristotle's rich treatment of enmity.

Conclusion: Emotion and Time

My analysis of Aristotle's explanation of factionalism emphasized his focus on ideas about justice and perceptions of injustice. The distinction between justice at the level of the regime versus the city helps to make sense of some of the complex aspects of his observations. My argument is not that Aristotle himself used this distinction in the study of factionalism, but his depiction of informal and normative modes of combining diverse people and groups into a community must be relevant for understanding when enmity will arise and break it apart. There is no city subject to factionalism unless there is a city that contains sufficient civil affection to be a city. And there is no city without the regime that orders rule. The project of achieving political order through a constitution depends upon the pre-existing body of a people struggling simultaneously through informal means to knit itself together. The city of need that sustains somatic justice requires the regime's explicit constitution of political order. Justice undergirds a people's ongoing collective life through institutions of rule and through somatic expectations and civil affection. When the people's state of mind locks into civil combat they are catalysed by major assaults on ideas and expectations about living together. A theory of enmity cannot, however, be reduced to an account of ideological bifurcation or the notion of a transgression or betrayal of somatic justice.

When Aristotle describes the genesis of faction, he does so with reference to intense emotions. To feel anger at being dishonoured, treated with contempt, arrogance, shame, to fear or hate other groups who unravel one's implicit conceptions of the city's order or who are different and dislocating – these emotions continually arise in his discussion of politics. Two features of Aristotle's theory of emotion help explain the tie between emotions, justice, and enmity in time.[24] Emotions contain thought or cognition, thus their reaction to the world is inherently an interpretive one. They are not reasonless outbursts but relate to our perception and interpretation of what is taking place. And Aristotle insists that the essence of emotions is motion; their very nature consists in movement within the self (Rhet 1369b33–1370a11). Thus, an impetus to carry forward the motion of emotion creates a mindset towards outer action. We feel we must respond.

Experiencing strong emotion relative to public happenings constitutes an event in itself, which people must deal with. We see or feel changes in the world and our reactions generate a double layer of significance: the perceived phenomena out there and the raw event of the emotion in one's self. The turbulence of emotion puts pressure on those having it to act. If emotion is tied to something of great importance – ideals of the just regime and betrayal of somatic justice – then we can see how its intensity and scope of application would exert itself politically. Defining emotion as motion in the self helps us understand its role in enmity. Thus, emotions act as barometers of change in the world and are events in themselves – demanding that persons take public action.

To answer the question when and why a mindset of enmity (a will to harm another) emerges, our answer must go beyond ideologies, beliefs, and events and pay attention to the emotionality of reaction at a particular moment in time. The *when-ness* of enmity cannot be an objective condition but can only be revealed by people discovering through the medium of emotion that they must prove what and who they are, through owning that moment in time. The defining mindset of action, therefore, does not arise simply in order *to be* a self vis-à-vis the other. People already feel themselves *to be* but are in the process of dissolution or of (re)constitution when the possibility of enmity confronts them. They are taking the emotional turmoil in themselves, caused by ideas and betrayed expectation, and directing it against the forces they believe antithetical to themselves. Emotions act not just as the medium carrying forward and propelling enmity. They provide people with a heightened awareness of their existence in time. To feel anger and hatred – two essential justice-inflected emotions – is to be confronted with one's own disruption. Intense emotions raise the stakes of ideological difference and of expectations of somatic justice, because the urgency of mobilized emotion demands a group consolidate who it is vis-à-vis another.

Aristotle offers a strong answer to enmity's genesis, yet this genesis remains intriguing. Ancient Athens was an intensely emotional public space. It was also a political realm in which rhetoric, argument, and a culture of logical deliberation flourished. In this space of public performance and argumentation over policy, honour, and recognition, equilibriums of ideological and somatic justice maintained a functioning and flourishing polity. Vigorous public debate and emotions were prevalent features, so their mere existence cannot answer the dynamic of enmity. Aristotle's work gives an explanation of how the hardening of a political mindset grows out of active citizen's ideational and embodied response to a world that changes in dramatic and unexpected ways. When will the confluence of ideas and emotions towards enmity emerge from a complicated, agonistic political culture? I have suggested the factors a justice-based theory of enmity must take into consideration, using Aristotle as a launching pad.

Can Aristotle offer a perspective on contemporary American society? Wolin found in Aristotle the original model for political science as an art responsive to the tensions, striving, and potentiality of a world in which "plans, aspirations, and claims of its members are in conflict" (2004, 55). Embedded in Aristotle's constructive art was a penetrating, timeless account of elements in the enemy mindset. The unusually emotional condition of our current body politic echoes features of Aristotelian *stasis*. We fear implied ideological extremes, even as some of us promote them. We expect and suspect each other's commitments to the "nation," "republic," or "Constitution." People commit to the destructive and costly work of enmity when the encompassing goods of politics are on the line: "Factional conflicts arise, then, not over small things but from small things – it is over great things that men engage in factional conflict" (*Pol.* 1303b18). Enmity is the *struggle for a world* that no longer exists or does not yet exist but that moves the actors to claim their standing based on justice in a world of time, order, and significance. Enmity is not only destructive but seeks to achieve a positive goal. Every action aims at some good, Aristotle insisted, and oddly, that is so even with enmity.

NOTES

1 Jason Brennan, *Against Democracy* (Princeton, NJ: Princeton University Press, 2016), 245.
2 Brennan, ibid., 19.
3 Brennan, ibid., 7.
4 Sheldon S. Wolin, *Politics and Vision: Continuity and Innovation in Western Political Thought*, expanded ed. (Princeton, NJ: Princeton University Press, 2004 [1960]), esp. 53–60, 63–4, and *passim*.
5 Wolin, ibid., 55.
6 It may be useful to distinguish my project from the contemporary political theory of agonism – the influential normative, critical, and explanatory theories which argue that conflicts among ways of life, ethical perspectives, basic policy goals, and so forth are unavoidable. The most prominent theorists of normative agonism are Chantal Mouffe, Bonnie Honig, and William Connolly. See Mouffe, *The Return of the Political* (1993), *The Democratic Paradox* (2000), *On the Political* (2005), *Agonistics* (2013); Honig, *Political Theory and the Displacement of Politics* (1993); and Connolly, *Identity/Difference: Democratic Negotiations of Political Paradox* (1991) and *The Ethos of Pluralization* (1995). I agree with normative agonism regarding the necessarily conflictual dimensions of political life, but find its explanatory project inadequate. How and when does unacceptable enmity – hard, harm-seeking, forceful, and often violent antagonism – arise? Normative agonists do not have an answer. I discuss these and related theories of conflict in my larger project on philosophers' approaches to explaining political enmity. I show how, in addition to Aristotle, Hobbes, Schmitt, and Arendt directly confront the phenomenon of political enmity, often in tacit conversation with thinkers preceding them, and that each focuses on a different but unique political purpose in the genesis of group antagonism: justice, truth, freedom, and identity, respectively. While all of them accept enmity as a defining action-orientation for political standing, Aristotle, Hobbes, and Arendt would reject Carl Schmitt's notion that destructive enmity defines the "high point" of politics; see Schmitt, *The Concept of the Political* (1996), 67.
7 I use the Carnes Lord translation, *Aristotle's Politics*, 2nd ed. (Chicago: The University of Chicago Press, 2013), unless otherwise noted.
8 On the subject of conflict and *stasis*, I have used the following: Andrew T. Alwine, *Enmity and Feuding in Classical Athens* (Austin: University of Texas Press, 2015); Mary Blundell, *Helping Friends and Harming Enemies* (Cambridge: Cambridge University Press, 1989); Patrick Coby, "Aristotle's Three Cities and the Problem of Faction," *The Journal of Politics*, Vol. 50, No. 4 (Nov. 1988), 896–919; David Cohen, *Law, Violence, and Community in Classical Athens* (Cambridge: Cambridge University Press, 1995); Kostas Kalimtzis, *Aristotle on Political Enmity and Disease, An Inquiry into Stasis* (Albany, NY: State University of New York Press, 2000);

David Keyt, *Aristotle Politics*, Books V and VI (Oxford: Clarendon Press, 1999); Lynette G. Mitchell and P.J. Rhodes, "Friends and Enemies in Athenian Politics," *Greece & Rome*, Vol. 43, No. 1 (Apr. 1996), 11–30; Ronald Polansky, "Aristotle on Political Change," in *A Companion to Aristotle's Politics*, ed. David Keyt and Fred D. Miller Jr. (Oxford: Blackwell, 1991), 323–45; Arlene W. Saxonhouse, "Aristotle on the Corruption of Regimes: Resentment and Justice," in *Aristotle's Politics, A Critical Guide*, ed. Thornton Lockwood and Thanassis Samaras (Cambridge: Cambridge University Press, 2015), 184–203; Steven Skultety, "Delimiting Aristotle's Conception of *Stasis* in the Politics." *Phronesis* 54 (2009), 346–70; Ronald Weed, *Aristotle on Stasis: A Moral Psychology of Political Conflict* (Berlin: Logos Verlag, 2007); and Bernard Yack, *The Problems of a Political Animal* (Berkeley: University of California Press, 1993).

9 See Polansky (1991) for a discussion of translation difficulties regarding Aristotle's terms for "change" in general (*metabolē*) and "stasis" in particular. See also Ernest Barker, *The Politics of Aristotle* (Oxford: Oxford University Press, 1977), 204n1; and Keyt (1999), 66. Steven Skultety argues for the third approach (c), insisting Aristotle intends "a very precise political phenomenon" – a type of action and event (Skultety 2009, 348 and 357).

10 I will sometimes refer to "faction" or "factional conflict" as the mindset of enmity. This should be taken as shorthand; faction, factional conflict, and factionalism (all locutions for the term *stasis*) consist in collective action ready to engage in confronting and harming another. This behavioral disposition is presumed to carry a mindset of enmity, but the behavioral phenomenon and the mental disposition/ mindset are theoretically two different phenomena. My definition of enmity includes an action orientation, thus is entwined with a behavioral disposition. Nevertheless, we can attempt to disentangle them for purposes of trying to grasp the formation of this complex phenomena.

11 Polansky notes: "the closest he gets to a single explanation is the remarkable emphasis on the role of virtue or justice" (Polansky 1991, 336). Skultety highlights the motive of justice by emphasizing: "when agents actually engage in stasis, they are motivated by a sense of injustice" (Skultety 2009, 358–9).

12 See Michael Freeden's definition in *Ideology* (Oxford: Oxford University Press, 2003), 32.

13 The reality of the ancient Greek world rendered women and slaves outside the orbit of political standing. We should acknowledge Aristotle's view that women and slaves were naturally incapable of exercising the type of reason necessary for political participation, which justified their exclusion.

14 See Yack (1993), 221–3, for discussion along these lines.

15 See Stephen Halliwell's stress on the duality in Aristotle's philosophical and social scientific methods in "The Challenge of Rhetoric to Political and Ethical Theory in Aristotle" in *Essays on Aristotle's Rhetoric*, ed. Amélie Oksenberg Rorty (Berkeley: University of California Press, 1996), 180.

16 He solves this problem by arguing for a form of mixed regime: "once the first and initial error is committed [an arrangement based simply on one or other type], it is impossible not to encounter some ill in the end. Hence numerical equality should be used in some cases, and in others equality according to merit" (*Pol.* 1302a6–14). See also his discussion in *Politics* III.9 where he rejects contingent compacts as sufficient for justice in a city.

17 David K. O'Connor, "The Aetiology of Justice," in *Essays on the Foundations of Aristotelian Political Science*, ed. Carnes Lord and David K. O'Connor (Berkeley: University of California Press, 1991), 136–64.

18 I cannot engage here the large literature on Aristotle on friendship except to present a view of friendship as a component of his theory of enmity.

19 Reeve points out that this principle of "every part of the city-state must want it to exist and to remain as it is" can be found in various forms throughout the *Politics*. See *Politics*, trans. C.D.C. Reeve (Indianapolis: Hackett, 1998), 52, fn. 109. See also Wolin describing Aristotle's emphasis on difference as necessary to the whole of a political community: "the nature of the political association was that of a self-sufficient whole, and this end of self-sufficiency was possible only through diverse contributions" (2004, 53).

20 See, for instance, R.G. Mulgan, *Aristotle's Political Theory* (Oxford: Clarendon Press, 1977), "The Whole and Its Parts," 28–35.

21 In the *Nicomachean Ethics*, he had described like-mindedness (*homonoia*) in this way: "For to be like-minded is not for each to have the same thing in mind, whatever it may be, but to have it in mind in the same way – for example, when both the demos and the decent have it in mind for the best persons to rule – since in this way what they aim at comes to pass for everyone" (NE 1167a34–1167b2). Expectations are built by observing one another commit to the city and to sustain one's role in the city's enterprise. Diverse people then can be unified insofar as they share expectations about each other's commitment to their community. Aristotle insists Socrates's basic premise – "for the city to be as far as possible entirely one" (1261a15) – was a mistake. To become increasingly one renders a city not a city at all, but a sort of household. We can reduce singularity even further to the level of an individual human being, he writes. But a city is not a family or a person. See *Politics* 1261b16 and 1261b31–2. I use *Aristotle's Nicomachean Ethics*, trans. Robert C. Bartlett and Susan D. Collins (Chicago: University of Chicago Press, 2011).

22 Josiah Ober explores a form of mutual recognition through difference among classes in democratic Athens in his *Mass and Elite in Democratic Athens* (Princeton, NJ: Princeton University Press, 1989).

23 Other examples can be found in (*Pol.* 1303a25–7) on the "dissimilarity of stock" (immigration or colonizing incompatibility) over "any chance period of time" and the perennial example of persons gaining office who "behave arrogantly and aggrandize themselves" (*Pol.* 1302b6–14).

24 See Aristotle's *Rhetoric*, Book II, where he presents seven pairs of emotions: anger/
gentleness; friendliness/enmity (hate); fear/confidence; shame/shamelessness;
kindness/unkindness; pity/indignation; envy/emulation. Cf. Robert C. Solomon,
What Is an Emotion? (Oxford: Oxford University Press, 2003), 5; on the originality
of Aristotle on emotion, see W.W. Fortenbaugh, *Aristotle on Emotion* (London:
Duckworth, 2002), 9–12. For the *Rhetoric*, I use *The Complete Works of Aristotle*,
ed. Jonathan Barnes (Princeton, NJ: Princeton University Press, 1984).

3 Sheldon Wolin and Democratic "Theory"

JASON FRANK

Should the democrat be suspicious of the theorist, especially when the latter professes to be a "democratic theorist"?

          – Sheldon Wolin, *Fugitive Democracy: And Other Essays*

"The idea of democracy," Sheldon Wolin once wrote, "comes to us … primarily through hostile interpreters. The politics of the demos has not been lost to memory but is preserved, though half-buried, in the political theories of democracy's critics."[1] Democracy, as Wolin came to understand it, has had very few theoretically articulate advocates in the canon of Western political thought, but the contours of democratic experience have nonetheless left discernable traces in canonical texts that can be reconstructed by scholars hoping to illuminate the hidden – and perhaps repressed – memory of the "politics of the demos" for critical political orientation in the present day.

Taking this claim seriously means that reconstructing a tradition of theoretical reflection on democracy – a tradition of democratic theory – requires a distinctive kind of interpretive work excavating what lay "half-buried" in the writing of democracy's theoretically articulate critics. For Wolin, studying the history of democratic theory entails identifying how democratic experience is both articulated within and obscured by the "continuity of preoccupations" that defines the canon of political theory itself; it demands that we become a particular kind of reader.[2]

This hermeneutic enterprise is further complicated by the problem of theoretical form, by the fact that what we have too often come to expect of political theory – its primary aims and its means for achieving them – exists in a deep tension with the diffuse experimentalism of democratic practice. This tension came into focus as a central concern of Wolin's later work as he made his "journey from liberalism to democracy," but he had long reflected on the complex and dynamic relationship between theory and politics, beginning with *Politics and Vision.*[3] Building on Thomas Kuhn's work on paradigm shifts in the philosophy of science, Wolin's evolving reflections on political theory coming out of his own experience at Berkeley in the 1960s often turned on the ways theory enframes the political world in a certain way, rendering certain kinds of actions and dynamics legible, and leaving others hidden or obscure: encouraging certain forms of politics and discouraging others.[4]

Political theories, and especially what Wolin would come to call "epic" political theories, inaugurate "a new way of looking at the world, which includes a new set of concepts, as well as new cognitive *and* normative standards."[5] Theories delineate the horizon of political possibility, guide the forms of action that can be taken, and therefore shape the political world to correspond to their own "repicturization" of it. Political theory is always entangled with the demands of "political education," always a central concern of Wolin's and other members of the "Berkeley School," and it often fails in educating citizens for the demands of democracy.

Wolin came to see the relationship between theory and democratic politics as particularly fraught the more he came to associate democracy with "the political" itself – so closely related as to be "almost synonymous" – and the more suspicious he grew of the sovereign claims of the epic theorist he once championed.[6] A democratic theorist worthy of the name cannot proclaim epistemic authority and presume to make a one-time "gift to the demos," as Wolin put it in his famous review of Rawls's *Political Liberalism*, neglecting the central democratic importance of the formative collective struggle to achieve equal rights by the people themselves.[7] To attend to the needs of democracy would require doing political theory otherwise.

For Wolin, political theory's usual focus on rules and norms, procedures and principles, organization and institutional form, exists in sustained tension with democracy's egalitarian protest of the reduction of politics to rule, its inefficient decentralizations of power, its transgressive opposition to norms and forms, and to the institutionalization and routinization of political action. Political theory's tendency towards abstraction is itself at odds with the historically embedded and power-sensitive conception of democracy Wolin emphasized. Political theory "typically advances by generalizations," he would write. "We classify and categorize, we simplify and we quantify ... we regularize phenomenon so that we can subsume them under general statements or hypotheses. In the very form of our theory we duplicate the modern administrative outlook which seeks to fit individual cases under general rules and abhors exceptions as a scientist does anomalies."[8]

Democracy always bears the mark of its diverse and localized origins and struggles, so the problem of identifying a unitary tradition of theoretical reflection on democracy is not only a problem of content but of theoretical form. What form could a *democratic* democratic theory – a radical democratic theory – possibly take? Is it "possible to theorize democracy without resorting to anti- or undemocratic impositions," Wolin asked, and to envision a different way of thinking "the relationship between political theorizing and democratic politics?"[9] These questions are posed in different ways in scattered suggestions found across the full range of Wolin's work – from such seminal work as "Political Theory as a Vocation" to his essays for *democracy*, from his writing on the student movement to his essays on the "fugitive democracy" of the ancient Greeks – although he never provided a sustained metatheoretical answer to them. Wolin offered exemplary instances of ways of doing *democratic* democratic theory rather than programmatic statements or rules.

Across his diverse body of writing, Wolin challenged not only self-congratulatory contemporary understandings of democracy and its supposed triumph but also the self-congratulatory expectations of the tasks and goals of democratic theory. From his early critiques of positivism, behavioralism, and methodism in political science, Wolin exposed the political content of seemingly neutral theoretical forms, revealing their quiet implications in modern forms of state and corporate power – what he would eventually come to call "Superpower" – inimical to democracy. Political theory has too often worked in the service of the generalization and abstraction that facilitates the power of control; it has been "a form of knowledge that could freely construct its objects and their relations."[10] A radical democratic theory, by contrast, would be a form of theoretical inquiry attendant to the transgressive, radically egalitarian, historically situated, and power-laden dimensions of democracy itself. It could not remain democratic if it was premised on an attempt to transcend those defining traits.

Wolin's efforts to identify instances of this tension between theory and politics more broadly, and theory and democratic politics in particular, and to trace its historical emergence, were varied and wide ranging. For example, this question plays an important role in Wolin's understanding of the debates over constitutional ratification in the United States and of his assessment of the Anti-Federalists' failure to provide a counter "theory" to the Federalist "new science of politics" and the aggregative, routinized, homogenous, and sovereign vision of politics it implied.[11] Wolin's sustained engagement with Tocqueville, and beyond him Montesquieu, were also focused on these questions and allowed him to explore them in great textual detail. The issue "central in Tocqueville's formulation of his ideas," Wolin wrote in *Between Two Worlds*, was "whether theorists would assume the task of normalizing the appearance and presence of [modernity's] huge powers, preserving their impressive and triumphal character while rendering them familiar and, above all, demonstrating their manageability, or whether the powers would be revealed to have certain unsettling and unnatural qualities that portended a continuous discontinuity in the human condition."[12]

Wolin's "journey from liberalism to democracy" occurred during his period of political activism in the 1960s, which infused these theoretical reflections with political urgency, but it was in his remarkable writing during the 1980s – for the journal *democracy,* which he edited, and on early American political thought, anthologized in *The Presence of the Past* – where he began to most fully develop these themes.[13] In his writing on American politics in the age of Reagan, and in his simultaneous engagement with early American political thought, Wolin came to view radical democracy (as opposed to democratic theory) as a distinctive kind of tradition, one that distinguished it in content from the reigning ideological paradigms of liberalism and civic republicanism but that also, and this has to be emphasized, led to a very different understanding of what constitutes a political tradition in the first place. This is an aspect of Wolin's work that has yet to be fully recognized and developed. It was a view of political tradition that contrasted sharply with the reigning scholarly paradigms of post–linguistic turn historiography associated with the Cambridge School and that was focused on formative experience and popular practice rather than theoretical articulation or ideological expression (in this, Wolin might have been quietly drawing from Arendt's *On Revolution*). As far as I know, Wolin left no clear methodological statement on these questions – perhaps unsurprising, considering his dismal view of "method" – but a highly distinctive view of radical democracy as a tradition can nonetheless be pieced together from his key writings from the period. As with the question of what a democratic democratic theory might be, he engaged this question through the examples he pursued, rather than the explicit criteria he declared.

In the first essay he wrote for *democracy* – entitled "The People's Two Bodies" – Wolin offered an early indication of what this refigured sense of democratic tradition might mean, at least in the United States. In America, Wolin argued, the people have always had two bodies. One of these imagined forms emerged from the politically active collectivity enacted by the Revolution, a collective being who would "not just participate in politics, but would join in actually creating a new political identity, to "institute," "alter," or "abolish" government, to lay a "foundation" and to organize power."[14] Wolin called this the body politic. The other dominant collective imaginary, which Wolin dubbed the political economy, was theorized in the Federalist "new science of politics" and enshrined in the US Constitution. It was defined by a passive form of sovereign legitimation of the state, the depoliticizing disaggregation of the collective agent into individual consumers, and the conversion of the collective deliberation over matters of common concern into sublimated regulations of an impersonal market. Long before contemporary political theorists focused attention on neoliberalism's dissolution of the demos, Wolin had indicated the democratic costs of imagining and institutionalizing political subjectivity along economic lines.[15]

Wolin's increasingly trenchant critique of liberalism, already forcefully articulated in the *New York Review of Books* essays he co-authored with John

Schaar in the 1960s, takes on a new force in these writings, emphasizing liberalism's myriad forms of depoliticization and of the imaginary and institutional disaggregation of the collectivity that it entails.[16] Wolin's understanding of democracy assumed a more definite outline in opposition to liberalism over the course of these writings. One of the most striking aspects of this developing understanding of democracy was Wolin's focus on the collective actor as both agent and object of action. This oddly self-referential dynamic of demotic agency and power is already there in "The People's Two Bodies" and remains constant across these writings and beyond to the radical democratic works of the 1990s focused on ancient Greece – "Norm and Form: The Constitutionalizing of Democracy," "Fugitive Democracy," and "Transgression, Equality, Voice."[17]

Many commentators have emphasized the discontinuities in Wolin's turn to ancient Greek democracy, as he came to take a more radical "fugitive" view of democratic action. Nick Xenos, for example, distinguishes two periods of Wolin's engagement with democracy: his writing for the journal *democracy* and work on early American political thought in the 1980s, on the one hand, and his turn to ancient Greek democracy during the 1990s, on the other. Wolin, however, emphasized theoretical continuities over the discontinuities in his work on democracy from these periods, and for good reason. The continuities between them bring out what is most distinctive in his conception of democracy itself.

The focus on the collective actor working on and enabling its own emergence, for example, and the practical creation of demotic power remains constant across these later works. "The continual self-fashioning of the demos," he writes, is self-referential "because it aims to transforms the political system in order to enable itself to emerge, to make possible a new collective actor, collective in nature."[18] Even as late as *Democracy Inc.* Wolin would write that "the survival and flourishing of democracy in the first instance depends upon the people's changing themselves, sloughing off their political passivity and acquiring the lost characteristics of the demos ... To become democratic – to embrace political freedom under threat on so many sides in the modern world – is to change one's self, to learn how to act collectively, as a demos."[19]

These are provocative formulations, figuring the demos as both actor and acted upon, agent and subject. It is also notable that in these descriptions of demotic emergence, Wolin does not engage with the theoretical language of representational claims, performativity, and dynamics of popular identification through antagonistic lines of inclusion and exclusion (friend and enemy). Wolin did not envision democratic enactment through the framework of agonistic claims of popular authorization.[20] Wolin shared the agonistic critique of liberal strategies of depoliticization, "in which the meaning and scope of politics is to be "settled" beforehand, that is, before conflict and controversy among social groups and the alignment of classes is recognized," but with an emphasis on the world-making dimensions of democratic contention itself and on the recovery of a lost and newly empowered collectivity.[21]

At a time when radical democratic theory was very closely, if not exclusively, associated with anti-foundational agonism and the unending disagreements of a deep democratic pluralism, Wolin rejected the Schmittian undertones of these approaches, whether explicitly declared or more ambivalently expressed, and provocatively defined "the political" as an egalitarian recovery of collective commonality out of a "an expression of the idea that a free society composed of diversities can nonetheless enjoy moments of commonality when, through public deliberations, collective power is used to promote or protect the wellbeing of the collectivity."[22]

Wolin's arguments about demotic power taking its own emergence as its political goal has also led to some rather striking misinterpretations of his work as being too preoccupied with the ruptural and transgressive quality of democracy, even dangerously aestheticizing action in the celebration of the revolutionary emergence of demotic power. "There are no limits," as George Kateb writes along these lines, "to Wolin's praise of limitlessness."[23] Wolin's detailed response to Kateb's charge of "demotic rage," and his aestheticized embrace of "wildness," in a letter now available to researchers in his archive at Berkeley's Bancroft Library, offers perhaps the clearest articulation of Wolin's rejection of the oversimplification of this common "ruptural" interpretation of his later work on democracy. The letter also clearly demonstrates Wolin's own understanding of the continuity between the "two periods" of deepened reflection on the meaning of democracy mentioned by Xenos.

Reading Wolin's work from the 1980s and 1990s alongside other radical democratic theory from the period – whether the agonistic populism of Ernesto Laclau and Chantal Mouffe, the deep pluralism of William Connolly, or the resurgent theories of popular constituent power, like Antonio Negri's – what is most striking is not the neo-Schmittian themes of existential antagonism on the one hand or the extraordinary or revolutionary enactments of constituent against constituted power on the other, so much as Wolin's distinctive combination of the extraordinary and the ordinary, the revolutionary and the quotidian. In these writings democracy's antagonism to the "state," "unum," "Superpower," can sometimes appear in the form of insurgent praxis and sometimes as organizing for better schools and safe drinking water. Democracy, Wolin writes, "lives in the ebb-and-flow of everyday activities, responsibilities, and relationships."[24]

Nowhere is this productive tension between the insurgent event and quotidian practice more clearly elaborated than in another famous essay from *democracy*, appropriately titled "What Revolutionary Action Means Today." In this essay, Wolin called for a renewed and radicalized conception of citizenship, "a fuller and wider notion of being whose politicalness will be expressed not in one or two modes of activity – voting or protesting – but in many."[25] Wolin argued this fuller practice of citizenship was revolutionary in the context of consolidating Superpower and that its radicalism was defined, in part, by its inhibitions of the seemingly limitless powers of technological, economic, and scientific progress: the "new Trinitarianism" of capital, state bureaucracy, and science.[26]

In contrast to other prominent theorists of radical democracy, Wolin's key words in this essay and other works from the period were deeply conservative: "inheritance," "birthright," "tending," "remembrance," and "renewal." Wolin occasionally had positive things to say about Thomas Paine, but I think he hated the famously Promethean dictum of *Common Sense* – "We have it in our power to begin the world over again" – as much as Ronald Reagan loved it. Wolin clearly saw how the American embrace of futurity and radical independence helped construct the founding myth of the New World as nature's nation, "fresh land seemingly without limits or boundaries and innocent of past inequities."[27] Wolin feared the despotism of constant innovation and change more than he did the despotism of tradition.[28]

Wolin's revolutionary citizens did not treat tradition, inheritance, and birthright as so many heteronomic fetters to overcome, as a "nightmare which weighs upon the brain of the living," but as crucial sources of democratic power and renewal. "The role of the citizenry was to tend and defend the values and practices of a democratic civic life," he writes in one typical formulation.[29] "Democratic power depends on an historical accumulation of dispositions." Wolin argued that democrats had to disenthrall themselves of their dangerous fantasies of sovereign autonomy. "Transgressive, changeable, and forgetful man is heteronomous man," Wolin wrote, "the subject of a variety of laws. He is by nature not the malleable object of a single and sovereign lawmaker. Instead, he is the object of multiple claims and the subject of multiple constitutions."[30] Wolin not only urged readers to think democracy beyond the state, but beyond the conceptual traps of their commitment to popular sovereignty. Radical democracy is a tradition for Wolin, but it is one that contrasts with, rather than springs from, modern theories of popular sovereignty (here, too, the parallels with Arendt's *On Revolution* are suggestive).

Not one constitution, but many. Not one single line of authoritative inheritance, but multiple and sometimes conflicting birthrights. Wolin's essays on early American political thought from the 1980s are remarkable, in part, for the prominent scholarly preoccupations they do not engage. Wolin is not primarily preoccupied with traditions of political discourse or with tracing the continuities and discontinuities of different theoretical paradigms or ideologies. He has very little to say about the historiographical debates between defenders of liberal consensus or the republican revival, and what he does say is mostly critical. Of the new civic republicans Wolin insightfully argues: "their categories serve to obscure questions of power and authority and to sever political activity from specific localities, thereby producing the abstract category participation."[31] The republican revivalists' focus on a tradition of political thought abstracted from social conflicts and power struggles "has the effect of muting the tensions between republicanism, with its strong historical attractions to elitism, and democracy, with its irreducibly populist strain."[32] Wolin presciently anticipated criticisms of the republican revival in political theory that would come to dominate critical discussions two decades later.[33]

Wolin sought democratic resources in America – sources of renewal – that were not reducible to an isolated tradition of political thought, discourse, or ideology, but rather drew from practical repertoires of political action and association. In this, as in so much else, he followed Tocqueville. Wolin did not seek to recover radical democracy as another tradition of political discourse alongside liberalism and republicanism, but to reveal it as a tradition of a different kind. Wolin had been a student of Louis Hartz, and one of Wolin's most provocative engagements with the debates between liberals and civic republicans was a distinctive and revealing criticism of the Hartz thesis. Wolin's objection to the liberal consensus paradigm was not primarily that it neglected alternative political discourses that thrived beyond the parameters of Lockean liberalism. His criticism was more fundamental: that there had been "feudalism" in America. Rather than construing feudalism as part of the old regime the American revolutionaries fought against, Wolin figured it as the local and decentralized political culture that they fought to preserve. For Wolin, feudalism had a very different meaning in the colonial American context. He describes it as the "system in which inheritance, with its implicit historicity, is the master notion."[34] Feudalism "serves as a metaphor for historicized politics," "a politics that over time inevitably produces inherited privileges and unequal powers. The result is a social space crowded with prior claims to unequal ownership and status and the transformation of a manifold of injustices (unlawful conquests and forcible seizures) from the dim past into vested rights of the present."[35] Drawing on the work of Tocqueville and Montesquieu, Wolin figures feudalism as the archaic resource of renewal for a political culture that is democratic, participatory, localist, and overall, more egalitarian than elitist in ideology (although one could certainly argue with this latter claim).

Wolin's attempt to locate radical democratic resources of renewal in this archaic remnant was also an attempt to give "feudalism" a theoretical articulation it never had. "It did not gel into a coherent theory," Wolin writes, primarily because there was no available theoretical language to give adequate expression to a distinctive blend of ideas that seemed at once progressive and at the same time regressive in the sense of emphasizing values of place and locality."[36] Here, too, he highlights the tensions between theoretical form and democratic practice. Wolin acknowledged that these living archaisms have not always been radically egalitarian, emancipatory, or inclusive; they have not always been political movements of the left. "Religious fundamentalism, 'moralism,' and racial, religious, and ethnic prejudices," he writes, "belong to the same historical culture as traditions of local self-government, decentralized politics, participatory democracy."[37] Any attempt to assess Wolin's legacy for radical democratic theorizing – and for conceptualizing a distinctive radical democratic tradition – must confront these arguments directly.

This American archaism and odd feudalism was one of Wolin's sources of democratic renewal, but it was not the only one. He would also turn to the pamphlets of the English Civil War, the writings of the Old Oligarch, the surprising and fugitive appearances of democracy in the margins of the traditions of Western political theory mentioned above. Xenos is right to say that Wolin attempted to articulate for us in theory what was essential to the "experience of democracy."[38] The incredible body of work Wolin left behind will be a continued source of provocation and inspiration for democratic theorists and democratic actors. Wolin argued that "democracy has never produced its own word-smiths."[39] This is an exaggeration, but it is an exaggeration that reveals an important truth; it is what Theodor Adorno once called a true exaggeration. Wolin's work powerfully demonstrates the truth of that exaggeration while also being its most eloquent refutation.

NOTES

1 Sheldon S. Wolin, "Norm and Form: The Constitutionalizing of Democracy," in *Athenian Political Thought and the Reconstruction of American Democracy*, ed. J.P. Euben and J. Wallach (Ithaca, NY: Cornell University Press, 1994), 55.

2 Sheldon S. Wolin, *Politics and Vision: Continuity and Innovation in Western Political Thought*, expanded ed. (Princeton, NJ: Princeton University Press, 2004), 1.

3 See Nicholas Xenos, "Momentary Democracy," in *Democracy and Vision: Sheldon Wolin and the Vicissitudes of the Political*, ed. A. Botwinick and W.E. Connolly (Princeton, NJ: Princeton University Press, 2001).

4 See Sheldon S. Wolin, "Paradigms and Political Theories," in *Politics and Experience: Essays Presented to Michael Oakeshott*, ed. P. King and B.C. Parekh. (Cambridge: Cambridge University Press, 1968).

5 Sheldon S. Wolin, "Political Theory as a Vocation," *American Political Science Review*, Vol. 63, No. 4 (1969), 1062–82, 1078.

6 Sheldon S. Wolin, "Hannah Arendt: Democracy and the Political," in *Hannah Arendt: Critical Essays*, ed. L.P. Hinchman and S.K. Hinchman (Albany: State University of New York Press, 1994): 289–306, 290; and J. Wiley, "Sheldon Wolin on Theory and the Political," *Polity*, Vol. 38, No. 2 (2006), 211–34.

7 Sheldon S. Wolin, "The Liberal-Democratic Divide: On Rawls's Political Liberalism," *Political Theory*, Vol. 24, No. 1 (1996b), 97–119, 98.

8   Sheldon S. Wolin, *The Presence of the Past: Essays on the State and the Constitution* (Baltimore: Johns Hopkins University Press, 1989), 136.

9   See Sheldon S. Wolin, "The Liberal-Democratic Divide," op. cit., 1996.

10   See Sheldon S. Wolin, *Tocqueville between Two Worlds: The Making of a Political and Theoretical Life* (Princeton, NJ: Princeton University Press, 2003), 21.

11   Sheldon S. Wolin, *The Presence of the Past*, op. cit., 136.

12   See Sheldon S. Wolin, *Tocqueville between Two Worlds*, op. cit., 133.

13   See Sheldon S. Wolin, *Politics and Vision*, xv.

14   See Sheldon S. Wolin, "The People's Two Bodies," *democracy*, Vol. 1, No. 1 (1980), 11–17, 15.

15   See Wendy Brown, *Undoing the Demos: Neoliberalism's Stealth Revolution* (Cambridge, MA: Zone Books/MIT Press, 2015).

16   See Sheldon S. Wolin and John Schaar, *The Berkeley Rebellion and Beyond: Essays on Politics & Education in the Technological Society* (New York: New York Review of Books, 1970).

17   See Sheldon S. Wolin, "Norm and Form: The Constitutionalizing of Democracy," op. cit., 1994; "Fugitive Democracy," op. cit., 1996; and "Transgression, Equality, Voice," op. cit., 1996.

18   See Sheldon S. Wolin, "Transgression, Equality, Voice," in *Demokratia: A Conversation on Democracies, Ancient and Modern*, ed. J. Ober and C. Hedrick (Princeton, NJ: Princeton University Press, 1996), 64.

19   See Sheldon S. Wolin, *Democracy Inc.: Managed Democracy and the Specter of Inverted Totalitarianism* (Princeton, NJ: Princeton University Press, 2008), 289.

20   See Jason Frank, *Constituent Moments: Enacting the People in Postrevolutionary America* (Durham, NC: Duke University Press, 2010).

21   See Sheldon S. Wolin, "The Liberal-Democratic Divide," op. cit., 1996, 99.

22   See Sheldon S. Wolin, "Fugitive Democracy," op. cit., 1996, 31.

23   See George Kateb, "Wolin as Critic of Democracy," in *Democracy and Vision: Sheldon Wolin and the Vicissitudes of the Political*, ed. A. Botwinick and W.E. Connolly (Princeton, NJ: Princeton University Press, 2001), 39–57, 55.

24   See Sheldon S. Wolin, *Politics and Vision*, op. cit., 2004, 604.

25   See Sheldon S. Wolin, "What Revolutionary Action Means Today," *democracy*, Vol. 2, No. 4 (1982), 17–28, 27.

26   See Sheldon S. Wolin, "From Progress to Modernization: The Conservative Turn," *democracy*, Vol. 3, No. 3 (1983), 9–21.

27   See Sheldon S. Wolin, *The Presence of the Past*, op. cit., 1989, 75.

28   See David McIvor, "The Politics of Speed: Connolly, Wolin, and the Prospects for Citizenship in an Accelerated Polity," *Polity*, Vol. 43, No. 1 (2011), 58–83.

29   See Sheldon S. Wolin, *Politics and Vision*, op. cit., 2004, 598.

30   See Sheldon S. Wolin, *The Presence of the Past*, op. cit., 1989, 105.

31   Ibid., 5.

32   Ibid.

33 See John McCormick, *Machiavellian Democracy* (Cambridge: Cambridge University Press, 2011).
34 See Sheldon S. Wolin, *The Presence of the Past*, op. cit., 1989, 74.
35 Ibid., 75.
36 Ibid., 132.
37 Ibid., 79.
38 See Nicholas Xenos, "Momentary Democracy," op. cit., 2001, 36.
39 See Sheldon S. Wolin, "Transgression, Equality, Voice," op. cit. 1996, 84.

SECTION 2

Memory and Myth in Wolin and Beyond

4 Wolin on Myth: A Critique

TERENCE BALL

Introduction

Contrary to a modern conceit, the "politics of identity" – to use a still-fashionable phrase – is not a new variety of politics but is almost as old as politics itself. The ancient Greeks distinguished themselves from foreigners or "barbarians" (so called because their languages sounded to Greek ears like nonsensical yammering: "bar bar bar"). In Athens, women and slaves and metics (resident aliens) lacked the requisite identity – that of free male native-born Athenian – to be citizens. (Distinguished as he was, Aristotle, as a metic, could not participate in the affairs of the polis whose praises he sang.) The politics of identity (or "identity/difference") is now, and always has been, about inclusion and exclusion, about belonging and being cast out or aside.[1]

Or, to put the point in the terms of the now somewhat dated "communitarian-liberal" debate, the politics of identity is about defining and claiming membership in a community of one or another sort. All communities are "imagined communities" in that they are maintained and legitimated by their members' shared self-images, images that shape and make possible their interpretations of who they are and where and to whom they belong.[2] These, more than any articulate theory or doctrine, determine the shape and mark the boundaries of a community, giving its members a sense of belonging and of shared identity. Humans are self-interpreting animals whose sense of self and identity depend in important ways on the communities to which they belong and with which they identify.[3]

In late eighteenth- and early nineteenth-century America there developed a new way of identifying oneself and interpreting one's relation to one's community. Americans claimed to belong to a nation composed not only of individuals but of individualists – or "rugged individualists," in Herbert Hoover's later phrase. America was said to be not only a new nation but a new type of nation, and Americans a new type of people. America was, in short, a new kind of community – a non-communitarian community, as it were, populated by a new kind of individual.

"What, then, is the American, this new man?" asked Crevecoeur towards the end of the eighteenth century.[4] It is a question asked many times since, and in any number of idioms and accents. But it is at bottom a question, or rather a series of questions, about individual and collective identity: Who am I? Where do I come from? Who are my people and what is my relationship with them? How am I related and what do I owe to those who are, and are not, my people? These questions have been posed, if not answered to everyone's satisfaction, by almost any American writer one cares to name. No one can claim that the riddle of American identity has been solved or doubt that this terrain is anything but hotly contested.

My aim here is to look at one way of framing these questions about American identity, as a means of shedding some light on the (im)possibility of re-imagining a different kind of national community. I want to examine the claim that there is, or once was, a native American mythology – a myth already presupposed in Crevecoeur's question. The American, according to this myth, is a "new (kind of) man," the likes of whom has not been seen before, except perhaps in the biblical account of creation. The "American Adam" is innocent and uncorrupted, as was Adam before the Fall, living without Eve (and therefore free from sin and temptation) in the Eden of the New World.[5] This is an early and recurring expression of the Americans' self-identification as innocents, bereft of ideology and imperial ambition, of American "uniqueness," and the other markers by which Americans would come to define themselves to each other and to the rest of the world. And, arguably, this self-definition and sense of identity persists even today.

Anyone who wishes to make, much less sustain, such a claim must of course recognize that America is today largely, though by no means exclusively, a secular, modern, and presumably post-mythic culture. Most Americans, when asked who they are and how they see themselves, are not likely to answer – very readily anyway – in mythic, much less "Adamic" terms. I want nevertheless to suggest that this myth, or something like it, supplies the scaffolding or framework within which otherwise puzzling odds and ends come together and make a certain kind of sense. If this myth be present, and as pervasive as I believe it to be, then we must begin by asking just where this cultural equivalent of the Loch Ness Monster is to be found in a modern (or perhaps postmodern) and presumably post-mythic culture.

The creators and practitioners of the genre now known as "American studies" long ago taught us to look to literature and other forms of popular culture for the traces and themes of a native American mythology. And, as R.W.B. Lewis, Leo Marx, and Henry Nash Smith have shown, such themes and traces abound in highbrow and lowbrow literature, in nineteenth-century dime novels and modern detective stories, in Hollywood movies and Madison Avenue ads.[6] But in its search for an American mythology this interpretive genre encounters a singular difficulty. For one of the characteristics of a genuine mythology – as distinguished from the ersatz contrivances that are quite consciously created for political purposes or literary effect – is its pervasiveness in all a society's thought-forms, whether literary and artistic or philosophical and scientific.[7] Moreover, a genuine myth, as Marcel Detienne maintains, is a mode of thought that does not know its name and is unaware of its status as myth.[8]

It is the un-self-conscious quality of myths and those who hold them, said Sheldon Wolin, that shows modern or postmodern "myths" to be nothing of the kind. The postmodern era is characterized by the proliferation of ersatz myths – in movies, literature, art, advertising and other forms of popular culture – and the absence of any genuine ones. And among postmodern societies, America has gone further than most. What in postmodern America passes for mythic themes "are more in the nature of post-mythic strategies than direct expressions of myth. They are evocations of the archaic in the midst of a modernizing society which, by its own self-understanding, is committed to the systematic extirpation of mythical thought. They are mythmaking self-conscious of itself, aware that it is engaged in a premeditated act of fabrication. There is, consequently, an irreducible element of alienation that accompanies contemporary mythologizing."[9]

My aim here is to agree with one part of Wolin's diagnosis and to disagree with another. While it is certainly true that art, literature, movies (e.g., Star Wars), and other modern media are wont to employ post-mythic strategies and even to concoct ersatz myths, it is less certain that genuinely mythical themes are altogether absent from other aspects of contemporary American culture. I want to suggest that several surviving features of an American mythology are to be found in some rather unlikely and heretofore unsuspected places. In the domains of academic analytical philosophy, in futurology, and in certain postmodernist political visions we can, I believe, find quite un-self-conscious expressions and articulations of mythic themes. Since so sweeping a claim cannot be substantiated here, I shall confine myself to three recent works in these genres. The texts I have chosen to examine might at first sight appear to be rather unpromising candidates – John Rawls's *A Theory of Justice*, Gerard O'Neill's *The High Frontier*, and Richard Rorty's *Contingency, Irony, and Solidarity*. The first is by a distinguished American philosopher, the second by an eminent physicist and futurologist, and the third by a prominent postmodern thinker. Despite their very different subject matters, all are alike in drawing upon, and being more fully intelligible in light of, the same native myth, the myth of Adam in the Edenic garden of the New World.

My plan is to begin by briefly saying what I mean by myth generally, and by a native American mythology in particular. I shall then take a fresh look at several foundational features of Rawls's theory of justice, claiming that much of its intelligibility, and even perhaps its persuasiveness, derives from several mythic features implicit in the imagery of his argument. I then go on to examine O'Neill's proposals for the colonizing of space. His highly technical vision of the American future is, I believe, fraught with mythic presuppositions and Adamic imagery. So too, I contend, is Richard Rorty's vision of a postmodern culture consisting of the self-creating contingency-embracing individuals whom he calls "strong poets." Finally, I shall conclude by connecting the pervasiveness of the Adamic myth to some of the difficulties encountered in contemporary debates among political theorists about "identity" and "community."

The Myth of Adam

"A myth," says Mark Schorer in his luminous study of Blake, "is a large, controlling image that gives philosophical meaning to the facts of ordinary life; that is, has organizing value for experience." Myths, in other words, "are the instruments by which we continually struggle to make our experience intelligible to ourselves.... Without such images, experience is chaotic, fragmentary, and merely phenomenal." Not even the most rational thinker among us is immune to the appeals of myth, thus understood. "Rational belief," Schorer continues, "is secondary. We habitually tend to overlook the fact that as human beings we are rational creatures not first of all but last of all, and that civilization emerged only yesterday from a primitive past that is at least relatively timeless. Belief organizes experience not because it is rational but because all belief depends on a controlling imagery, and rational belief is the formalization of that imagery."[10] I shall suggest a little later on that two paradigms of rational belief – analytical philosophy, and science turned into technology and applied to particular problems – can to some extent be understood as formalizations and articulations of mythic themes and images. And much the same can be said of the "postmodern" mode of thinking that is critical of both.

However illuminating and suggestive, Schorer's characterization of myth is deficient in one important respect. It is simply not true that "experience" and our "interpretation" of it are two separable things. On the contrary, as modern post-positivist philosophers of science and hermeneutically minded literary critics remind us, experience without interpretation is impossible; indeed, it is not experience at all. All experience – artistic, literary, moral, religious, scientific, political, or otherwise – is (in Gadamer's phrase) "always already" interpreted or "pre-interpreted"; even the barest, most unvarnished scientific observation, for example, is "theory-laden."[11] Far from being two separable things, experience and interpretation constitute a single indivisible whole. Thus, for example, devout Christians do not have experiences upon which they subsequently superimpose a "Christian" interpretation or structure of meaning;

rather, they have Christian experiences.[12] Nor, for that matter, do scientists make observations upon which they then place a "scientific" interpretation; rather, they make scientific observations.[13] Much the same is true of the activity of political, literary, artistic, and social-scientific interpretation.[14]

For our present purposes, the most important difference between a philosophical or scientific theory and a myth is that the former tend to be more self-conscious and tentatively held than the latter. A theory can accordingly be more readily (and rationally) criticized than a myth, if only because the latter often supplies the symbolic frame of reference in terms of which the former assumes a socially shared meaning – so, at any rate, I shall suggest shortly in connection with Rawls's theory of justice. We may say of theories what Leslie Stephen said of doctrines: "The doctrines which men ostensibly hold do not become operative upon their conduct until they have generated an imaginative symbolism."[15] To disinter such symbolic frames and to trace them to their source is somewhat akin to what Foucault called "archeology" and later, and in a somewhat different (and decidedly Nietzschean) version, "genealogy."[16] This, indeed, is just the sort of inquiry in which students of American culture have long been engaged.

In attempting to discover and to sketch the "outlines of a native American mythology," R.W.B. Lewis's *The American Adam* (1955) proved to be one of a select band of books that have decisively influenced the course of American literary criticism and, more generally, the methodology of American studies. Lewis did for high-brow literature what Henry Nash Smith (in *Virgin Land*) had earlier done for popular pulp literature and political oratory, and what Leo Marx (in *The Machine in the Garden*) was later to do for the anomalies afflicting both: namely, to disinter and examine the half-submerged ideals and imagery in terms of which Americans tended to think of themselves as a people possessing a distinctive national character and culture.

That ideal and its constitutive imagery can be roughly recounted in this way. America was – and at its best still is – a pastoral nation, a veritable Eden in the New World. The scene of perpetual rebirth and rejuvenation, this pastoral paradise is permanently without a past. The American, the "new man" of whom Crevecoeur wrote, can be compared to Adam before the Fall. The American Adam thus represented "a radically new personality, the hero of a new adventure: an individual emancipated from history, happily bereft of ancestry, untouched and undefiled by the usual inheritances of family and race; an individual standing alone, self-reliant and self-propelling, ready to confront whatever awaited him with the aid of his own unique and inherent resources."[17]

Clint Eastwood and the Marlboro Man (and his Camel-smoking counterpart) are merely the latter-day Hollywood and Madison Avenue versions of a venerable myth, the myth of the American Adam. (It goes without saying that the imagery is deeply and indelibly gendered.)

Although the imagery is biblical, the context of its invocation is identifiably and distinctly American. The Americans were the first people to make a "case against the past." What Lewis's lawyerly turn of phrase obscures is that the case was not a well-constructed and articulated argument but, myth that it was, an interlacing structure of sentiment, symbol, and feeling. The Adamic myth's most memorable expressions are, arguably, literary (as when, in Cooper's narrative, Natty Bumppo, reversing the direction of time itself, traverses the distance from old age to ageless youth). But its most self-conscious and articulate expressions are, pace Lewis, political. Here Paine is perhaps a more representative spokesman than Jefferson.[18]

Besides being a pamphleteer and propagandist, Thomas Paine was among the earliest and most adept articulators of the Adamic myth and its political implications. "The case and circumstances of America," wrote Paine, "present themselves as in the beginning of a world." America is "the only spot ... where the principles of universal reformation could begin." To make such a beginning Americans must think and act as if they were the first people ever to think. This stricture he duly applies to himself. In thinking and writing about politics, he assures us, "I followed exactly what my heart dictated. I neither read books, nor studied other people's opinions. I thought for myself."[19] As Adam turns philosopher, new truths emerge as in the clear light of morning. Heretofore hidden from view, the eternally valid principles of justice are at last accessible to the pastless, present-minded American. Finally freed from "the errors of tradition," Americans can see that "The wrong which began a thousand years ago is as much a wrong as if it began to-day." And, he adds, "the right which originates today, is as much a right as if it had the sanction of a thousand years. Time with respect to principles is an eternal NOW."[20] Once emancipated from the prejudices of the past, we will finally be free to consult and to be guided by Reason alone: "The present age will hereafter merit to be called the Age of Reason, and the present generation will appear to the future as the Adam of a new world."[21]

Whether we turn to Paine or to Jefferson, to Crevecoeur or Cooper – or even to Adam's nemeses Melville and Hawthorne – we are struck by the omnipresence of Adam in the Garden of the New World. To students of American cultural history this is, of course, a familiar story. Less familiar, perhaps, is the tale concerning the continued presence of Adam in some unsuspected places, including modern American analytical philosophy.

Rawls in Eden

Published in 1971 to a chorus of critical praise, John Rawls's *A Theory of Justice* continues even now to excite scholarly controversy. Despite the defects duly noted by its critics, *A Theory of Justice* is a monumental work, and all the more remarkable because it was written in an age in which "normative" or "prescriptive" political philosophy was presumed to be dead and buried.[22] If nothing else, Rawls has proved that the genre is still vital and very much alive. Without wishing to detract from Rawls's achievement, I should like to inquire into the sources of his theory's appeal, at least some of which seems to lie less in its theoretical argumentation than in its imagery and symbolism. And its very imagery, it seems to me, is inescapably mythic, drawing less upon its ostensible philosophic forerunners than upon the symbolic resources of a native American mythology.

Rawls, rightly enough in some sense, saw himself as the inheritor of the social contract tradition. Like Hobbes, Locke, and Rousseau, he begins with his own version of a pre-civil state of nature, which he calls "the original position." This *Gedanken* experiment he quite clearly regards as a moral and methodological fiction meant to make a point about objectivity and impartiality.[23] More originally still – and utterly unlike any of his philosophical predecessors – Rawls imagines that people placed in the original position suffer from a kind of meta-ethical amnesia. For, once situated behind an imaginary "veil of ignorance," they do not know who they are or where they have come from, or to what race, sex, or generation they belong, what their talents and/or handicaps are, and so on. Thus, deprived of all contingent and particular features of their personalities, social status, and situation, such disinterested hypothetical choosers are therefore presumably equipped to arrive at, and to articulate, general and impartial principles of justice.[24] The first, and primary, principle is that extending equal liberty to all individuals takes precedence over other values, including human happiness. The second stipulates that inequalities are justifiable only insofar as they work to everyone's advantage and are attached to offices or positions open to all.[25] The two principles of justice at which Rawls's ideal choosers arrive are of less interest here than is the situation and circumstance under which he has them make their imaginary choice. In the technical terms favoured by modern mathematically minded game theorists, the situation in which Rawls places his hypothetical choosers is an N-person, non-zero-sum cooperative bargaining game in which players make choices on the basis of incomplete information about their respective positions. The logical and mathematical properties of this game-theorist's fantasy interest me less than its mythic possibilities.

The conventional interpretation of Rawls's theory is, so to speak, Eurocentric. Rawls's rational choosers are presumed to be ideal Rousseauian citizens solicitous only of the General Will, or Kantian moral agents, making ethical choices not from any particularistic "phenomenal" perspective but from the wholly disinterested "noumenal" vantage point of the perfectly rational person. There is much to recommend this way of reading Rawls. It is the perspective adopted by almost all of his defenders and critics.[26] Indeed, it is the position adopted by Rawls himself.[27] I want to suggest that there exists a second, more distinctive – and more identifiably "American" – and indeed mythical – perspective from which Rawls's theory of justice may be read and understood.

Like Paine's Adamic American, Rawls's hypothetical choosers are placed "as in the beginning of a world." Unencumbered by the past, by tradition, or by the memory of previous practices, they alone are able to articulate, for the first time, truly universal principles of justice. Having been tainted by tradition, particularity and partiality (sexual, racial, class, generational, or otherwise), earlier principles and theories of justice were clearly deficient. These old theories and principles can now be criticized, discredited, and set aside. Situated behind the veil of ignorance, Rawls's rational choosers choose not for themselves alone but for all of mankind and for all time.[28] Like Paine, Rawls thinks that principles of justice discovered by disinterested Reason are eternally valid: "This standpoint ... enables us to be impartial, even between persons who are not contemporaries but who belong to many generations. Thus to see our place in society from the perspective of this position is to see it *sub specie aeternitatis*: it is to regard the human situation not only from all social but also from all temporal points of view."[29] Or, as Paine put it, "Time with respect to principles is an eternal NOW."[30] A well-honed historical sensibility, derived from diligent study of the past, is therefore philosophically irrelevant. History, as Henry Ford said, is bunk.

Stripped of a past and of all particularity, Rawls's hypothetical choosers are, in effect, amnesiacal orphans. They are orphans, indeed, in much the same sense that Billy Budd is. Melville's Adamic antihero was also without a past, uncertain of his parentage (though distinctly European and quite possibly aristocratic), and – as his very name suggests – perpetually alive with the spring-like possibility of rebirth and renewal. But Billy Budd suffered from a singular defect – a stammer which soon proved to be a fatal flaw. His failure to communicate in the clinch – when confronted with the absolute evil represented by the "serpentine" Claggart – leads to his literal death and symbolic crucifixion.[31]

A far cry from Rawls's theory of justice, surely; but not so far as one might think. For both are, after all, concerned with justice and injustice. And it is a grievous and malign act of injustice that renders Billy Budd mute. Moreover, Billy Budd's inability to communicate, just when it is most important that he do so, shares several features of the imaginary situation in which Rawls places his ideally rational choosers. For, being ignorant of their particular circumstances, they are incapable of communicating anything about them. Thus they too are mute about their individual interests and idiosyncrasies. Billy Budd and Rawls's rational choosers are solitary figures, unable (because of ignorance, isolation, or impediment of speech) to communicate to others anything about their respective circumstances or situation. The upshot, unsurprisingly, is that the solitary individual is in all cases thrown back upon his own resources. Unable to rely upon others, each relies solely upon himself.

Several "communitarian" critics have suggested that Rawls's theory of justice is deficient inasmuch as it is predicated upon a peculiarly narrow and unsatisfactory conception of human selfhood and moral agency. This, says Michael

Sandel, is the vision of a solitary "unencumbered self."[32] Unencumbered by enduring connections to other similar selves, and even to its own past, this paragon of Emersonian self-reliance is, so to speak, at home in the homeless condition that Rawls calls the original position. Indeed, according to Rawls, it is only in this position that valid principles of justice can be chosen. Only individuals unencumbered by the past, by history, by memory, or by tradition are capable of rationally and disinterestedly choosing such principles. Sandel suggests, quite rightly I believe, that the theory is flawed because no rationally or humanly satisfactory self can ever be wholly unencumbered in the way that Rawls's hypothetical choosers are assumed to be. But having disagreed with Rawls's argument and his conclusions, Sandel goes on to trace his vision of moral agency, autonomy, and self-sufficiency to the same philosophical parentage that Rawls claims. Liberalism in general, and Kant in particular, Sandel says, are the culprits. It is this Kantian conception of selfhood and moral agency that we now need to transcend.[33]

Perhaps. But is it not equally plausible to suggest that Rawls's theory of justice has even deeper roots in a quite un-self-consciously held native American mythology, the myth of Adam, and that whatever appeal it possesses might owe as much to Paine or Emerson as to Kant? And, if so, does it not then follow that extricating ourselves from its confines is likely to be an even more difficult and onerous task, raising as it does questions about our very identity – about who we are as a people, where we have come from, and what we can hope to achieve and to be?

I shall conclude by answering these questions in the affirmative. But first I want to turn to a second, and seemingly very different, author and text.

O'Neill in Space

The breaking out of narrowing confines has long been a hallmark of the Adamic myth. Crevecoeur's farmer, Cooper's Natty Bumppo, and Twain's Huck Finn are all alike in taking their leave, heading for the frontier or the territories, leaving their pasts behind, and seeking their freedom and their fortunes in the open space of the West. The actual physical frontier having been closed, according to Frederick Jackson Turner's reckoning, shortly before the end of the nineteenth century, Americans had no new places to go, no new space to conquer. Only when they ran out of space, said Hegel earlier in that same century, would the Americans then confront their past and become a people with a genuinely historical consciousness.[34] As Richard Hofstadter observed:

> Time is the basic dimension of history, but the basic dimension of the American imagination is space.... What Americans have lacked in a sense of time they have tried to make up by an enlarged sense of space. Their thoughts tend not to run

backward into an antiquity they do not know but rather outward into a larger geographical theater of action, the theater not of the past but of the future.... For Americans, uprooted from many soils and stemming from many ancestries and thrust into the open natural environment of the new continent, the very possibility of freedom quickly became associated with the presence of empty space, and also with the freedom to move, to get away from the physical proximity of others, to escape from society itself into the innocence of nature.[35]

This ahistorical and "spatial" sensibility is a fundamental feature of the American Adam. He is, as Lewis reminds us, a hero not in time but in space.[36] His two-fold freedom – freedom from the past, and the freedom to move in and through space – is deeply ingrained, as only myths can be, in our national consciousness (and perhaps even more deeply etched in our shared subconscious). The first of these freedoms is exemplified in the situation in which Rawls places his ideally rational choosers. The second, I want to suggest, is to be found in Gerard O'Neill's vision of the American future.

O'Neill is no arm-chair visionary. A distinguished physicist, O'Neill left his post at Princeton to head his own Geostar Corporation and for some time served as a consultant for the National Aeronautics and Space Administration (NASA). He claims not to write science fiction, a genre in which he professes not to be greatly interested; nor does he wish to spin out utopian schemes. He insists that his proposals for "space habitats" require no suspension of credulity or any leap of literary imagination. All are predicated upon presently existing scientific and technological capabilities.[37] It is now technically possible for human beings to create, to live and work within, and to travel between, space habitats. With a wealth of technical detail, O'Neill described the construction of such "space colonies." Large, slowly rotating stations in space, several miles in diameter and constructed of lunar material, could house hundreds, even thousands, of people. Fascinating though they are, the technical details do not concern me here. I am more interested in O'Neill's vision and, so it seems to me, its essentially mythical imagery and rationale.

In effect, the whole mythic message of O'Neill's *The High Frontier* is that Turner and Hegel were mistaken. The geographic and physical frontier of the American West may well be closed forever. But for Americans the *idea* of the frontier is not, and never will be, dead or passé. And this is not an idea that exists exclusively in the historical past – an abomination for Adam – but in a present perpetually alive with possibilities for self-assertion and exploration. The "high frontier" of outer space is in its very nature infinitely open, presenting an unlimited horizon of limitless possibility, of renewal, regeneration, and rebirth. Americans need never confront the closure and finitude of the "steady state" society and an economy of scarcity.[38] That being the case, they are forever able to strike out, in Huck Finn fashion, for the territories, thereby thumbing their noses at Aunt Sally – and Hegel – and anyone else who wants to "civilize" us by restricting our freedom.

One is understandably tempted to think that colonies in outer space would be the very antithesis of the agrarian ideal. The pastoral paradise that was Eden before the Fall – and America afterwards – could scarcely be imagined to exist in an environment so utterly "unnatural" and so dependent for its existence upon technology and engineering expertise. After all, the machine in the garden, as Leo Marx reminds us, was seen as an anomaly in the Eden of the New World.[39] True enough. But O'Neill's extraterrestrial Eden turns Marx upon his head (if I may be forgiven for saying what an earlier Marx once said about Hegel). In effect – and apparently quite unconsciously – O'Neill gives us The Garden in the Machine. The controlled climate, seasons, sunlight, and water supply make the space station an ideal environment for farming.[40] Crops can be grown year-round. There are no pests or insects to destroy the crops. But there are birds to charm the space colonists with their songs, and beautiful butterflies for the birds to eat. Better still, "there need not be mosquitoes – or cockroaches, or rats." Nor need there be pollution, poverty, or unemployment.[41]

In an imaginary "letter from space," a newly emigrated colonist describes the New World to a friend still living on earth: "It's a comfortable life here. Fresh vegetables and fruit are in season all the time.... We grow avocados and papayas in our own garden, and never need to use insecticide sprays. Of course, we like being able to get a suntan without ever being bitten by a mosquito."[42] In a later editorial aside, O'Neill adds: "how delightful would be a summertime world of forests without mosquitoes!" Space colonists "can take along the useful bees while leaving behind wasps and hornets."[43] There are, moreover, no volcanic eruptions, floods, earthquakes, hurricanes, typhoons, or tornadoes.[44] Made even better than the original by Yankee ingenuity, this is an Eden without wasps.

Even as pains and dangers are minimized, pleasures are maximized. Clothing could be light, or perhaps discarded altogether. And in this Edenic habitat human existence could be eroticized as never before. "Can one imagine a better location for a honeymoon hotel," O'Neill asks, "than the zero-gravity region of a space community?"[45] Evidently not, for he later returns to the topic. In another letter from space, a mother writes – rather more rapturously than most mothers, one suspects – to her daughter back on earth:

> [Your father and I went] to the Floating Island Hotel for our weekend. Most of the hotel, like the lobby and restaurants – and the showers – are at one-tenth gravity, but those bedrooms! My dear, it's just indescribable. Of course, you could watch TV or listen to music if you want, but really, as Dad says, those rooms are designed for just one thing. I can't imagine you [and your husband] not getting along well together, but if you ever have a problem ... bring him up here for a second

honeymoon! You may never want to go back. Now that we've found out what it's
like, I can tell you it's going to be a lot harder for us to leave![46]

Little wonder, then, that this couple confide in another letter that they are "more
likely to move farther out [into space] than to go back [to Earth]."[47]

Life in this demi-paradise is made possible by an escape from a darkening Old
World – not Europe this time, but the planet Earth itself – and an earthbound
state of mind that O'Neill describes as "planetary chauvinism" and "the planetary hang-up."[48] Over-populated, its atmosphere poisoned, its air and water
polluted, its inhabitants perpetually warring over increasingly scarce resources,
the planet Earth is, at the end of the twentieth century, a place unfit for human
habitation, still less for adventure and exploration. Nothing is left save to escape
from an earthbound past into an idyllic future in the endless vastness of space.[49]

As Lewis describes it, "the American myth saw life and history as just beginning. It described the world as starting up again under fresh initiative, in a
divinely granted second chance for the human race, after the first chance
had been so disastrously fumbled in the darkening Old World."[50] No longer
Europe, but the entire planet Earth, must now be abandoned. The Adams of the
twenty-first century abandon their planetary past and light out for the timeless
territory of space, there to tend their celestial Garden. Only in space, O'Neill
maintains, can mankind attain immortality. While we remain on the earth, he
warns, we are an endangered species, vulnerable to slow poisoning or to sudden
nuclear annihilation. Once dispersed through the galaxy, however, the human
species will become unkillable.[51] Space promises to conquer time and mortality itself. It is the medium of perpetual rebirth and regeneration. O'Neill's is a
vision at once hopeful and bleakly pessimistic – and, if I am right, deeply and
genuinely mythic in its imagery and its appeal.

Rorty in Bloom

My third and final illustration of the claim that the Adamic myth is to be found
today in unlikely places is Richard *Rorty's Contingency, Irony, and Solidarity*.
The following précis does scant justice to a book that is at once ingenious and
(intentionally?) irritating, and replete with brilliant re-readings of familiar
texts. I have, I hope, given Rorty his due in another place.[52] Here I want to
redescribe Rorty's project, and in a way that he might have found uncongenial
and unrepresentative of his intentions. But, as a postmodern thinker who holds
that readers may read and interpret texts without regard to authorial intention,
he could have no grounds for complaint or objection.

Rorty described himself as a "postmodern bourgeois liberal." He is "postmodern" in that he holds that "modernity" generally – and "the Enlightenment
project" of emancipating men and women through reasoned criticism and the

rational reform of social and political institutions in particular – has failed, leaving us in what Jean-Francois Lyotard calls "the postmodern condition."[53] This condition is characterized by a thoroughgoing scepticism as regards claims to truth or even to the validity of arguments advanced in support of such claims. Rorty was "bourgeois" in the sense that he accepted without dissent the institutions of the society in which he lived, that is, a capitalist or free-market or (in Marx's term) "bourgeois" society. And, not least, Rorty was "liberal" in that he saw society (or at any rate this society) as populated by self-interested individuals who aspired towards autonomy even as they eschewed cruelty towards other similarly situated selves. Whether one could be all three at once and without contradiction – a possibility raised by Rorty's critics – does not concern me here.[54] I am interested, instead, in the "Adamic" assumptions and implications of Rorty's picture of a postmodern American society.

His is indeed a "picture" rather than a theory or a sustained and systematic argument. A distinguished "analytical" philosopher turned postmodern renegade, Rorty later eschewed the very idea of reasoned argument and analysis. He favoured instead the essentially rhetorical and aesthetic strategy of redescribing the familiar world in new, unfamiliar, and more "attractive" ways, so as to persuade people, not by argument – as a philosopher might do – but by painting a new and attractive picture of a possible world.[55] It is worth noting, as students of myth remind us, that this non- or anti-argumentative mode of presentation and persuasion is a key feature of mythic thinking.[56] So we might without undue distortion read Rorty as a postmodern myth-maker and his vision of a liberal society as an attractive postmodernist myth.

Following Rorty's own method, I propose not to advance an argument, but to paint a picture. I want, that is, to redescribe his project in an alternative vocabulary and imagery – the idiom and the image of the American Adam. I shall suggest that Rorty is a thoroughly "American" thinker in that his idiom and imagery is identifiably Adamic. This is not, of course, how Rorty described his project and his stance as a "postmodern bourgeois liberal." Both come out of his encounters with thinkers who are, in the dismissive multicultural phrase, dead white European males.[57] He makes repeated reference and expresses debts to Derrida, Foucault, Nietzsche, Nabokov, Orwell, and Oakeshott. And if Rorty owes anything to any American thinker, it is – by his own oft-stated admission – to Dewey and, to a lesser degree, to Harold Bloom.

Rorty borrows Bloom's notion of the "strong poet" – the arch-individualist who creates but is not created, who wills into existence the world in which he (yes, he is identifiably male) lives alone and unencumbered. The strong poet is, in Bloom's and Rorty's descriptions, driven by "the anxiety of influence," the fear that his thoughts and language might be borrowed or derivative, that he might be beholden or indebted to anyone, ancestor or contemporary, for anything. Capable even of "giving birth to [him]self," the strong poet is the unencumbered self par excellence.[58] "In my view," Rorty writes, "an ideally liberal polity would be one whose culture hero is Bloom's 'strong poet.'"[59]

Now many things might be said about Bloom's and Rorty's vision of the strong poet driven by the anxiety of influence. One might say, with Wendell Berry, that Bloom's is "an adolescent critical theory."[60] Or one might simply note that the vision is unoriginal and old-hat, at least in America. (Paine, for one, articulated the anxiety of influence in terms only slightly different from, and hardly less adamant than, Bloom's.) Oddly, Bloom seems not at all anxious about (or even aware of) having been influenced by at least one earlier European thinker. His (and Rorty's) idea of the "strong poet" is almost palpably Nietzschian, and arguably another (and nicer) name for Nietzsche's *Übermensch*.

Ostensibly European sources aside, I want to suggest that the image of the strong poet driven by the anxiety of influence has an even older, and more distinctly American, ancestry. In America the anxiety that one might be beholden to or influenced by an ancestor or predecessor is hardly a new notion. Bloom's (and Rorty's) anxiety of influence can be found in the Adamic aspirations and boasts of Paine, Crevecoeur, and Emerson. Paine wished to think thoughts and speaks words that no one had ever thought or spoken before. So did Crevecoeur's new man. And so too did Emerson, who imagined a self-creating individual without ancestors, free of the dead weight of the past, and unencumbered even by the burden of friendship.

If Bloom gives us (as Berry says) an adolescent theory of criticism, Rorty gives us an adolescent theory of politics. Rorty's vision of a society whose culture hero is the unencumbered postmodern bourgeois-liberal strong poet animated by anxiety about being beholden or answerable to others is not only an adolescent vision – it is nothing less than our Adamic myth, our picture of ourselves in relation to others, past, present, and future. It is a profoundly anti-communitarian vision with a long history and deep cultural roots. Until and unless we recognize this, the communitarian critique of liberal individualism will deal only in surfaces and appearances.

Identity and Community

I began by suggesting that a genuine mythology is apt to appear not only in the art and literature of a culture but in virtually all of the thought-forms through which its aspirations, hopes, and fears are conceived and communicated. It may well be true that our national literature, as Lewis lamented many years ago, has lost much of its mythic richness, resonance, and vigour. But this does not mean that American culture has been denuded of all mythic traces and themes. It may mean merely that these have to be searched for elsewhere. Perhaps, then, Weber and Wolin are mistaken in suggesting that science and technology, and the increasing rationalization of everyday existence, necessarily entails the thoroughgoing "disenchantment" (*Entzauberung*) of the social world. Far from being wholly abandoned or outgrown or somehow transcended, myths may instead be transferred from traditional symbolic spheres – religion, art, and literature, for example – to newer, nontraditional spheres such as science, analytical philosophy, and postmodern criticism. Such, at any rate – *pace* Wolin – appears to have been the fate of the myth of Adam in America.

But Adam's fate need not be ours. We need not accept or acquiesce in the thoughtways of our peers or predecessors. If they have shown nothing else, communitarian critics of liberal individualism have at least called attention to the faults and flaws of Adamic individualism – of the ideal of an "unencumbered self" shorn of all connection with others – and to the need to critically reconsider, and perchance replace, this flawed ideal of individual (and, by implication, collective) conduct.[61] We Americans have, like Huck Finn, too often tried to escape to the territory to the west – a frontier more of myth and mind than of matter – in order to evade responsibility and avoid growing up. As Wendell Berry observes, "Huckleberry Finn fails in failing to imagine a responsible, adult community life." And this, he adds, is not the failure, in fiction, of a particular author or his character, but "of our life, so far, as a society."[62]

We appear to be left in a modern, or perhaps a postmodern, version of limbo. On the one hand are those who, knowingly or not, celebrate our Adamic condition as disconnected individuals, without memory, bereft of history and ancestors, autonomous and self-creating Adams or strong poets. On the other hand, however, are those who see "us" as having no national or collective identity, Adamic or otherwise. Each of us must base his or her identity on a particular facet or feature which we share with some and which, no less importantly, distinguishes or divides us from others. According to the adherents and champions of "identity politics," one must act not as a citizen or an American per se, but as one who is female or male, gay or straight, Black or Native American or Hispanic (etc.). This view of identity would appear, at first sight, to be the antithesis of Adam: one's history and identity, far from being forgotten, are as indelible as a tattoo; one cannot escape from one's group past, which is ever-present. One's community, and the identity one adopts and on which one acts, are inherited conditions: one is born a woman or Black or gay; and, just as one had no choice in who, or what, one was born, one is not wholly free to choose (much less invent) one's personal or political identity. Against the Adamic vision of the unencumbered self, identity politics presents an alternative vision of the eminently encumbered self, a socially situated self bearing the burdens of one's group's past as a badge of identity.

In one sense, then, the current concern with "identity" represents the apotheosis of the Adamic myth. Does the emphasis on identity then supply a corrective to the excessive individualism of that venerable myth? I want to conclude by suggesting that it does not. The current preoccupation with identity merely grasps the other horn of a continuing national dilemma.

The champions of Adamic individualism and the proponents of identity/difference are agreed on one crucial point: both eschew citizenship and, with it, "community" in any broader and more inclusive sense. Each is alike in grasping one horn of a persistent American dilemma. On the one side are those who wish to belong to a community of one – an unencumbered sovereign self or a "majority of one," in Thoreau's phrase.[63] On the other are those who wish to belong to a small and select community based on gender, or race, or sexual orientation. But – and this is the important point – both are alike in denying the possibility of communality, of shared sympathy (and antipathy), of common joys and sorrows. Each is, in Tocqueville's sense, shut up in the solitude of their own heart, individual or group.[64] But neither heart is, so to speak, a civic heart. From a political point of view such an identity is partial, partisan, and even, one might say, prejudiced. Such prejudice, properly understood, need not be a bad thing. After all, our prejudices, as Gadamer reminds us, provide a place to begin or to stand, not to stay.

The problem with modern (or perhaps postmodern) "identity politics" is that while it supplies some with a place to stand initially, it provides no one a place to stay. Its ersatz rootedness ratifies our rootlessness and celebrates our partialities. The politics of identity offers, as it were, a homeless shelter rather than a home. And this is because identity politics, like Adamic individualism, offers no sustainable civic vision, no wider view of political possibilities for the community of which we might yet be full members and citizens.

In this I would hope that my teacher Sheldon Wolin might have agreed.

NOTES

1 William E. Connolly, *Identity/Difference: Democratic Negotiations of Political Paradox* (Ithaca, NY: Cornell University Press, 1991). The now hotly contested phrase, "politics of identity," was coined by the Cohambee River Collective of Black feminists in their 1977 manifesto. It has been something of a political lightning rod ever since.

2 Benedict Anderson, *Imagined Communities: Reflections on the Origin and Spread of Nationalism* (London: Verso, 1991).

3 Charles Taylor, "The Liberal-Communitarian Debate," in *Liberalism and the Moral Life*, ed. Nancy L. Rosenblum (Cambridge, MA: Harvard University Press, 1989); Charles Taylor, et. al., *Multiculturalism and "The Politics of Recognition"* (Princeton, NJ: Princeton University Press, 1992).

4 Hector St. John de Crevecoeur, *Letters from an American Farmer* (New York, [1782]/1963), 63.

5 R.W.B. Lewis, *The American Adam* (Chicago: University of Chicago Press, 1955).

6 Ibid.; Leo Marx, *The Machine in the Garden: Technology and the Pastoral Idea in America* (Oxford: Oxford University Press, 1964); Henry Nash Smith, *Virgin Land:*

The American West as Symbol and Myth (Cambridge, MA: Harvard University Press, 1950).

7 See, e.g., Wendell C. Beane and William G. Doty, *Myths, Rites, Symbols: A Mircea Eliade Reader,* Vol. 1 (New York: Harper & Row, 1976), 2–7.

8 Marcel Detienne, "Rethinking Mythology," in *Between Belief and Transgression: Structuralist Essays in Religion, History, and Myth,* ed. Michel Izard and Pierre Smith, trans. John Leavitt (Chicago: University of Chicago Press, 1982), 43–5.

9 Sheldon Wolin, "Postmodern Politics and the Absence of Myth," *Social Research,* 52 (1985), 217. Although my focus here is on this essay, Wolin has written extensively and elsewhere about myth. See *The Presence of the Past: Essays on the State and the Constitution* (Baltimore: Johns Hopkins University Press, 1989), 17–18, 23, 144–5; *Democracy Incorporated: Managed Democracy and the Spectre of Inverted Totalitarianism* (Princeton, NJ: Princeton University Press, 2008), ch. 1, "Myth in the Making"; *Tocqueville between Two Worlds: The Making of a Political and Theoretical Life* (Princeton, NJ: Princeton University Press, 2001), ch. VII, "Myth and Political Impressionism."

10 Mark Schorer, *William Blake: The Politics of Vision* (New York: Vintage, 1959), 25–6.

11 See, e.g., Hans-Georg Gadamer, *Philosophical Hermeneutics,* ed. and trans. David E. Linge (Berkeley: University of California Press, 1976), 64. The phrase "always already" (*immer schon*) originates with Heidegger and has, in spirit if not in letter, been adopted by a number of post-positivist philosophers of science. Cf. Norwood Russell Hanson, *Patterns of Discovery: An Inquiry into the Conceptual Foundations of Science* (Cambridge: Cambridge University Press, 1958); Harold I. Brown, *Perception, Theory and Commitment: The New Philosophy of Science* (Chicago: University of Chicago Press, 1979), chs. 6 and 7. See, further, Stanley Fish, *Is There a Text in This Class? The Authority of Interpretive Communities* (Cambridge, MA: Harvard University Press, 1980).

12 See S. Fish, op. cit. 269–72.

13 Stephen Toulmin, "The Construal of Reality: Criticism in Modern and Postmodern Science," *Critical Inquiry,* 9 (1982), 93–111.

14 Hans-Georg Gadamer, *Truth and Method* (New York, 1980), 431–47.

15 Quoted in Schorer, *William Blake,* 25.

16 Michel Foucault, *The Archaeology of Knowledge* (New York: HarperCollins, 1976), Part IV; "Nietzsche, Genealogy, History," in *Language, Counter-Memory, Practice* (Ithaca, NY: Cornell University Press, 1977), 139–64.

17 R.W.B. Lewis, *American Adam;* cf. Charles L. Sanford, *The Quest for Paradise* (Urbana: University of Illinois Press, 1961).

18 *Pace* Lewis, *American Adam,* 15–19.

19 Paine, *The Rights of Man* (Garden City, NY: Doubleday, 1973), 455.

20 Paine, "Dissertation on First Principles of Government" (1795); quoted in Mason Drukman, *Community and Purpose in America: An Analysis of American Political Theory* (New York: McGraw-Hill, 1971), 62.

21 Paine, op. cit., 505.

22 *Vide* Norman Daniels, ed., *Reading Rawls: Critical Studies on Rawls' "A Theory of Justice"* (New York: Basic Books, 1975); Brian Barry, *The Liberal Theory of Justice* (Oxford: Oxford University Press, 1973); and Robert Paul Wolff, *Understanding Rawls: A Reconstruction and Critique of "A Theory of Justice"* (Princeton, NJ: Princeton University Press, 1977).

23 John Rawls, *A Theory of Justice* (Cambridge, MA: Harvard University Press, 1971), ch. 3. For an in-depth examination of the author and the book, see Andrius Galisanka, *John Rawls: The Path to A Theory of Justice* (Cambridge, MA: Harvard University Press, 2019).

24 Ibid., 136–50.

25 Ibid., 60.

26 See, e.g., R.P. Wolff, op. cit., Part III.

27 See J. Rawls, *A Theory of Justice*, sections 3, 40.

28 Ibid., 137, 289–93.

29 Ibid., 587. Rawls subsequently eschewed such universalist claims: see his *Political Liberalism* (Cambridge, MA: Harvard University Press, 1993).

30 See note 20, above.

31 Herman Melville, *Billy Budd*, in *Four Short Novels* (New York: Bantam Books, 1959), esp. 207–8, 246.

32 Michael J. Sandel, "The Procedural Republic and the Unencumbered Self," *Political Theory*, 12 (1984), 81–96; and his *Liberalism and the Limits of Justice* (Cambridge: Cambridge University Press, 1982). Cf. John H. Schaar, *Legitimacy in the Modern State* (New Brunswick: Transaction Publishers, 1981), ch. 7.

33 Sandel, op. cit., 175–83.

34 G.W.F. Hegel, *Lectures on The Philosophy of History* (New York: Dover, 1956), 85–6. Cf. George Armstrong Kelley, "Hegel's America," *Philosophy & Public Affairs*, 1 (1972), 3–36.

35 Richard Hofstadter, *The Progressive Historians: Turner, Beard, Parrington* (New York: Alfred A. Knopf, 1969), 5–6.

36 R.W.B. Lewis, *American Adam*, ch. 5.

37 Gerard K. O'Neill, *The High Frontier* (New York: Bantam Books, 1978), 116. See also the lavishly illustrated volume by T.A. Heppenheimer, *Colonies in Space* (New York: Warner, 1978).

38 Ibid., ch. 2. The idea that small is *not* beautiful and that the "steady state" economy is abhorrent recurs throughout O'Neill's work. See, e.g., his *2081: A Hopeful View of the Human Future* (New York: Simon & Schuster, 1981). O'Neill's ethic of economic growth mirrors one of the distinguishing features of the American national character: see David M. Potter, *People of Plenty: Economic Abundance and the American Character* (Chicago: University of Chicago Press, 1954), part II.

39 L. Marx, op. cit., 4.

40 G. O'Neill, *The High Frontier*, 51, 71–8, 118–20.

41 Ibid., 221.

42 Ibid., 9.

43 Ibid., 49.

44 Ibid., 112.

45 Ibid., 97.

46 Ibid., 214–15.

47 Ibid., 10.

48 Ibid., 35, 50.

49 Ibid., 234. For a powerful but unintended antidote to O'Neill's ersatz Eden in space, see Hannah Arendt, "The Conquest of Space and the Stature of Man," *Between Past and Future: Eight Exercises in Political Thought* (New York: Viking Press, 1968), 265–80.

50 R.W.B. Lewis, *The American Adam*, 5.

51 See G. O'Neill, *2081*.

52 Richard Rorty, *Contingency, Irony and Solidarity* (Cambridge: Cambridge University Press, 1989). See my review-essay, *History of the Human Sciences*, 3 (1990), 101–4.

53 Cf. Jean-Francois Lyotard, *The Postmodern Condition: A Report on Knowledge* (Minneapolis: University of Minnesota Press, 1984).

54 See the symposium on Rorty's *Contingency* in *History of the Human Sciences* (*supra*, note 52).

55 Rorty, op. cit. (1989), 9.

56 On the non-discursive or "pictoral" character of myth, see *supra*, notes 7, 8, 10.

57 It strikes me as curious that many critics of the "canon" of works by "dead white European males" are at the same time apt to be extravagant admirers of Nietzsche, Heidegger, Lacan, Foucault, de Man, and Derrida.

58 Harold Bloom, *Anxiety of Influence: A Theory of Poetry* (New York: Oxford University Press, 1973). On "giving birth to himself," see Bloom, *Agon* (New York: Oxford University Press, 1982), 43–4. R. Rorty, *Contingency*, 29.

59 Ibid., 53.

60 Wendell Berry, *What Are People For?* (London: Trafalgar Square, 1991), 165.

61 *Vide* Sandel, *Liberalism*; Alasdair MacIntyre, *After Virtue: A Study in Moral Theory* (Notre Dame, IN: University of Notre Dame Press, 1981); Robert N. Bellah, Richard Madsen, William M. Sullivan, Ann Swidler, and Steven M. Tipton, eds., *Habits of the Heart: Individualism and Commitment in American Life* (Berkeley: University of California Press, 1985); Taylor, "Liberal-Communitarian Debate."

62 W. Berry, op. cit., 77.

63 H. Thoreau, "Civil Disobedience," in *Selected Writings* (New York: Liberal Arts Press, 1952), 19.

64 A. Tocqueville, *Democracy in America*, op. cit. II, ii, ch. 2.

5 Collective Memory and the Settler-Colonial Politics of Reconciliation in Canada

CALVIN Z.L. LINCEZ

Introduction: Transformation, the State, and Collective Memory

The politics of reconciliation has become a prominent feature of the political landscape of Indigenous politics in Canada. While the term itself has been a feature of this landscape for some time, its recent rise to prominence is largely a result of the demands for justice by survivors of Canada's Indian Residential School system. Under this system, several generations of Indigenous children were removed from their families and communities and placed in state-sanctioned, church-operated boarding schools. Their purpose: disrupting connections to Indigenous language, culture, and ways of life with the ultimate aim of total assimilation into Euro-Canadian, Christian culture. The last Indian Residential School in Canada closed in 1996, and it was later discovered that this project of enlightened erasure was overshadowed by a dark truth: conditions of life for Indigenous children under these instruments of genocide[1] were almost ubiquitously marked by extreme and repulsive forms of violence, degradation, and abuse. With the legal system straining under the weight of the sheer number of cases being brought before the courts, the Canadian state was forced to act in response to the survivors' demands for justice and begin the work of confronting this dark chapter in its own history of state-sponsored violence against Indigenous peoples. It did so by embarking on a project of reconciliation marked by the advent of Canada's Truth and Reconciliation Commission on Indian Residential Schools (IRS TRC).

What follows is only in part a critical assessment of the state's capacity to facilitate any sort of fundamental change in the settler-colonial relationship that defines the common experience of Indigenous peoples in established liberal-democracies that were founded as settler colonies. It might also be read as a collection or assemblage of arguments developed by Indigenous and non-Indigenous critical thinkers, which strongly suggest that the liberal, settler state is structurally predisposed in such a way so as to be rendered incapable of facilitating what I will refer to as political reconciliation's *transformative potential*. In elaborating on this claim I wish to highlight three background claims that orient the analysis.

The first has to do with how political reconciliation's transformative potential gets defined. The politics of reconciliation is both a theory and a practice that might be generally understood as a way for nation-states to publicly acknowledge, address, and deal with legacies of past wrongs in societies that are deeply divided by histories of state-sponsored violence, atrocity, and historic injustice.[2] It might be said of the politics of reconciliation that it is called into being to manage societal and political transformation peacefully, that is, in a way that does not lead the society in question into further bloodshed. While the contemporary politics of reconciliation has, since its inception in the post-1989 era, been adopted in and adapted to a range of different historical and political contexts, perhaps the only assumption that most commentators agree upon and that remains constant across all of its instantiations and interpretations is that the politics of reconciliation tends to understand itself as a phenomenon whose purpose it is to address injustice and to do so in a way that either contributes towards or makes possible some sort of fundamental political change that is capable of generating conditions that ensure non-repetition of the sorts of collective wrongs that the politics of reconciliation is subsequently called upon to address. However, beyond the argument that the politics of reconciliation exists in part because of a capacity to contribute towards and even make possible political and social transformation, there is no settled consensus concerning how change is to be facilitated, the end or ends towards which processes whose purpose it is to facilitate change are aiming and the theories that make sense of the relationship between the two. Stated somewhat differently, no settled consensus exists about what exactly constitutes political reconciliation's transformative potential, which is another way of saying that there are a number of ways that this promise gets interpreted and defined.[3]

In what follows, I suggest that much of what goes into defining political reconciliation's transformative potential depends on the historical-political context in which reconciliatory processes unfold. For countries such as Canada that have officially declared a desire to reconcile with Indigenous peoples, the relevant historical-political context is *settler-colonialism*. Briefly, settler-colonialism might be defined, following Patrick Wolfe and Glen Sean Coulthard, as "a structure rather than an event"[4] whose defining trait consists of the establishment of a relationship between settlers and Indigenous peoples where, "power – in this case, interrelated discursive and nondiscursive facets of economic, gendered, racial, and state power – has been structured into a relatively secure or sedimented set of hierarchical social relations that continue to facilitate the *dispossession* of Indigenous peoples of their lands and self-determining authority."[5] Stated somewhat differently, settler-colonialism might be defined as a coercively imposed, territorially acquisitive and autonomy-denying structure of domination whose historical trajectory has yet to be interrupted and that tends to justify itself on the basis of a political imaginary that conceives of Indigenous peoples as beings who are destined to disappear over time (if not physically then as distinct cultures and politically independent peoples). This foundational assumption, in turn, justifies policies designed to re-constitute Indigenous peoples as organically related (naturalized) and politically subordinate national sub-populations *of* the multicultural settler societies that have been and continue to be constructed over them. In what follows, settler-colonialism, so defined, will act as the backdrop against which political reconciliation's transformative potential will be defined and interpreted. This essay will consider the relationship between two interpretations of political reconciliation's transformative potential in settler democracies such as Canada.[6]

The first might be defined as the mainstream, liberal form, and while there is no single, monolithic form of liberalism, I characterize this approach to interpreting political reconciliation's transformative potential in terms of a capacity to facilitate a sense of belonging by addressing the "enduring effects" and "lingering inequalities" of structures of exclusion and discrimination that are generally conceived of as having already been "historically superseded."[7] Here, political reconciliation's transformative potential tends to be conceived in terms of a capacity to act as a *supplement* to the liberal politics of recognition in the search for less "difference-blind" models of democracy and the advent of a political environment where the heirs of those who suffered under the "historically superseded" structures of domination, exclusion, and oppression can, politically speaking, feel at home in the liberal-democratic nation-state.[8] Recent critiques by Indigenous scholars of mainstream liberal approaches, however, suggest that efforts to theorize and institute more inclusive forms of citizenship as a response to Indigenous justice claims does not facilitate a break with the policies of the past but instead reproduces the structures of domination that these approaches purport to transcend in more subtle ways.[9] Critical Indigenous scholars, such as Taiaiake Alfred, Glen Sean Coulthard, and Leanne Simpson, have argued that mainstream ways of conceiving and addressing the painful legacies of past violence in established settler democracies are grounded upon presuppositions that situate settler-colonialism firmly in the past, resulting in an overall approach that "ignores or downplays" the *enduring* structural dimensions of settler-colonialism and the ongoing forms of violence, misrecognition, dispossession, assimilation, and domination that these structures produce and are predicated upon.[10] In what follows, I adopt the Indigenous approach and argue that political reconciliation's transformative potential in settler-colonial contexts ought to be identified with *decolonization*.

I will provisionally define three elements or conditions of decolonization in the context of the politics of reconciliation in settler-colonial contexts such as

Canada as the inclusion of Indigenous peoples as agents and architects in and of the process of reconciliation, the advent of a social and political environment that is not only less hostile to Indigenous normativities but that is also less hostile to Indigenous bodies – especially female bodies, LGBTQ bodies, and the bodies of Indigenous youth – and, finally, the creation of a political relationship or framework of coexistence that would be conducive to the independent flourishing of Indigenous social and political forms (i.e., something like the advent of a "nation-to-nation" or treaty relationship, where "treaty relationship" is understood normatively in terms of the *Gus-Wen-Tah*, or Two-Row Wampum, and the related image of the two vessels).[11] Defining political reconciliation's transformative potential in this way is, in one sense, an extension to settler-colonial contexts of a definition that typically gets reserved strictly for what are often referred to as "transitional societies." The transformative potential of the politics of reconciliation in transitional societies tends to be defined as a capacity to interrupt the historical trajectory of authoritarian or despotic political regimes and not only contribute to but in some cases make possible a liberating transformation in the basic political structure of society. South Africa's transition from apartheid is often taken as a paradigmatic case, illustrating political reconciliation's transformative potential as it plays out in transitional contexts. Identifying political reconciliation's transformative potential with a transformation in the basic political structure of authoritarian regimes may seem incongruent when applied to a liberal-democratic regime. This argument is in part grounded on the claim that while settler-colonial societies such as Canada promote conditions of freedom for Canadians they can and often do get experienced by Indigenous peoples in a way that is best described as authoritarian. Here, one need not look much further than Canada's *Indian Act*, which has been described as a "controversial and intrusive piece of federal legislation" that has "governed almost all aspects of Aboriginal life, from the nature of band governance and land tenure systems to restrictions on Aboriginal cultural practices," and, perhaps most crucially, *membership* via its authority to determine who does and who does not count as a "status Indian" in Canada.[12] Drawing from Sheldon Wolin, political reconciliation's transformative and decolonizing potential might therefore be said to entail a process of collective self-transformation aimed at the rectification of collective injustice and which is realized in the "wholesale transgression of inherited"[13] settler-colonial forms and the advent of post-settler-colonial forms of commonality defined by conditions where Indigenous peoples might once again constitute themselves as politically free peoples.

The second claim that I wish to focus on has to do with an attempt to *adapt* one of the central elements of Yellowknives Dene scholar Glen Sean Coulthard's critique of the liberal politics of recognition to the politics of reconciliation in settler-colonial contexts such as Canada.[14] In his seminal work, *Red Skin,*

White Masks, Coulthard argues that the transformative promise associated with the liberal politics of recognition in settler-colonial contexts gets undercut in various ways by the predominance of the *state* in collective decision-making processes. Here, Coulthard focuses on the "dialect of recognition theorized in Hegel's master/slave narrative," which is relevant because it often serves as a justification or background assumption in prominent liberal formulations of the politics of recognition.[15] Charles Taylor, for instance, develops a theory of recognition based on the assumption that the end-point of the dialectic of recognition will be "an era of peaceful coexistence grounded on the Hegelian ideal of *reciprocity*."[16] Drawing from Frantz Fanon, Coulthard argues that the ideal end point of the master/slave dialectic is undercut in various ways by the nature of the unequal relationship between the colonizer and colonized – i.e., the colonial master does not need or depend upon the recognition of the colonized – and the state which, in its role as mediator, undermines the dialectical progression towards a condition of reciprocity because it "continues to be structurally committed to maintain – through force, fraud, and more recently, so-called 'negotiations' – ongoing state access to the land and resources that contradictorily provide the material and spiritual sustenance of Indigenous societies on the one hand, and the foundation of colonial state-formation, settlement, and capitalist development on the other."[17] In what follows, I aim to build on Coulthard's critique of the state by applying it to the politics of reconciliation. My primary focus, however, will be on the nature of the logic of the *collective memory* of the state, which will act as a lens for considering the question of whether the liberal-democratic settler-state can serve as an instrument of justice and as an agent capable of realizing political reconciliation's transformative potential.

Collective memory is central to the realization of political reconciliation's transformative potential in no small part because what the collectivity recollects and what it forgets will determine both the injustices that get addressed and the nature of the transformation that ensues. Collective memory might be conceived of, moreover, as a collective faculty that operates through *representations* of the past and whose inherent plasticity[18] renders it susceptible to the imposition of form. Among other things, this means that powerful collective entities such as the state can employ the faculty of collective memory as a means of selectively shaping history into a narrative that grounds the construction of national identity in a way that is palatable and has meaning for those who are destined to be "exalted" as national subjects (here, white, upper-class, male citizens have historically served as a prototype for the ideal national subject).[19] Stated somewhat differently, I argue that the state employs the faculty of collective memory to *re-present* history *ideologically*, where ideology might be defined, following Cornelius Castoriadis, as "a set of ideas that relate to a reality not in order to shed light on it and to change it, but in order to veil it and to justify it in the imaginary, which permits people to say one thing and do another, to appear as other than they are."[20] It is largely through selective omissions and disavowals in the narrative of which collective memory is the author that the state can cleanse or sanitize the story of the nation of its darker aspects and facilitate the production of idealized yet one-sided forms of political identity. The one-sided narrative works to naturalize the legitimacy of the settler-state for settler subjects while simultaneously obscuring or distorting the atrocities and despotic forms of rule that constitute both the foundations and ongoing condition for nation- and state-building in North America. The liberal settler state might therefore be viewed as having a vested interest in the content and form of collective memory as a means of producing the narrative that underwrites the identity of a national subject for whom the settler state possesses legitimacy as sovereign and that will – as a result of the constitutive influence that the state's collective memory exerts on political subjectivity – experience difficulty in comprehending the nature of the justice claims of Indigenous peoples or, perhaps at its worst, that will view those claims as a nonproblem.

In what follows, my basic argument is that the logic and structure of the state's collective memory both facilitates and emerges from a politics of reconciliation that prevents the Canadian state from making good on the promise of decolonization. Stated somewhat differently, I argue that the transformative potential of the politics of reconciliation cannot be realized under conditions where the state exercises a monopoly over collective decision-making processes and that this is in no small part due to the logic of the collective memory of the state. This logic reveals the settler-state to be *structurally predisposed* to bring about a form of post-settler-colonial commonality that is diametrically opposed to decolonization. The decolonizing potential of the politics of reconciliation is undermined by a form of collective memory that reflects, reinforces, and generates a structural predisposition towards facilitating a version of post-settler-colonial commonality that can be referred to, following Elizabeth Strakosch, as "colonial completion." Colonial completion refers to a condition where the dissolution of the colonial status of the settler-state occurs via the "erasure of Indigenous political independence."[21] I argue that the central means employed by the settler state to undermine political reconciliation's decolonizing potential from the standpoint of the topic of collective memory is *selective social amnesia*.

This essay proceeds as follows. The first section employs Sheldon Wolin's theory, analysis, and critique of collective memory in the context of the politics of unresolved historic injustice to, first, examine the nature of the generative roots of the amnesiac tendencies of the modern state and, second, to identify a tension that marks the political-mnemonic terrain of Indigenous politics in settler democracies. The second section employs the radical Indigenous thought of Glen Sean Coulthard in an effort to explore how the Canadian state negotiates this tension in a way that facilitates colonial completion. The concluding section very briefly explores two contrasting models or forms of political reconciliation and also very briefly reflects on the relationship between democracy and decolonization in settler-colonial contexts.

Social Amnesia and the Contradictory Terrain of
Collective Memory in Settler-Societies

In his essay "Injustice and Collective Memory," Wolin develops a theory of social amnesia through a critique of the modern forces of nationalism, liberalism, and capitalism. Wolin's account of collective memory in contemporary liberal democracies begins with an analysis of the politics of collective memory as it plays out at the level of the nation. Here, Wolin examines some of the paradoxes and peculiarities of the politics of national collective memory as they play out in several case studies from which he draws a set of conclusions about the nature of the relationship between collective memory and the politics of unresolved historic injustice.[22] The first conclusion that Wolin draws about this relationship is that national collective memory differs, for instance, from individual memory in the sense that it is less of an involuntary affair and more of a *selective and strategic undertaking.* Here, Wolin argues that the collective memory of the nation is not so much a witness to injustice but instead ought to be conceived of as an "accomplice of injustice, forgetting or remembering, whichever is the more convenient."[23] Wolin argues that the nation will tend to publicly recall or memorialize some things – such as "heroic deeds or shaping events" – while at the same time it will tend to want to suppress "memories of collective injustice."[24] This tendency leads Wolin to the claim that one of the central paradoxes of collective memory in established democracies is that while the nation *wants* to forget great historical wrongs, they are not "actually forgotten" by the nation but are instead allowed to remain "publicly un-recalled."[25] The nation-state leaves certain collective wrongs publicly un-recalled, in part because of the discomfort associated with an awareness of "corporate complicity," in part because of a concern over national self-image and perhaps most importantly because of the threat that processes associated with recollecting historical injustices pose to the artifice of national unity. Wolin, however, is interested in an explanation of the logic of the collective memory of the liberal state that goes beyond what national "expediency or oversight or blocked recollection" might suggest.[26] For Wolin, the analysis and critique of the peculiarities and paradoxes of the politics of memory at the level of the nation reveals the contours of deeper, underlying processes. The transition between these two levels of analysis is facilitated by Wolin with the question of "how forgetfulness is established as a condition, perhaps even a precondition, of a certain form of society."[27] By "form of society," Wolin is referring to the "characteristic ways in which" a society's "hegemonic powers are constituted" while forgetfulness is defined as the establishment of a "context where the self must renounce some part of itself or of its own experience if it wants to be accepted into political society."[28] Wolin, in other words, is arguing that established liberal-democracies constitute power in a form where "the act of reconstituting the self into a civic self, forgetting becomes a rite of passage and as such a condition of membership."[29] This leads Wolin to an analysis of liberalism and capitalism and the constitutive influence they each exert on the relationship between collective memory and the policies, politics, and practices of the "post-mnemonic" modern state.

Wolin's critique of liberalism is articulated through an analysis of Western social contract theory. Here, Wolin focuses on the early-modern political thought of Thomas Hobbes and John Locke in part because of continuities between their own thought and contemporary liberal political thinkers such as John Rawls and Robert Nozick and in part because of continuities with "recent practices" in Anglo-American liberal-democratic politics.[30] Wolin is quick to stipulate that his focus on the works of Hobbes and Locke is not due to the fact that their theories provide "accurate descriptions of the actual constitution of contemporary society" but instead "because they enable us to glimpse some of the inarticulate premises in the political practices and processes of our society."[31] Wolin's critique of the political-mnemonic tendencies of liberalism revolves around an analysis of the politics surrounding the transition from the pre-political state of nature to political society with a focus on how social contract theorists employ the concept of *equality* in a way that promotes and justifies inequality. Here, Wolin notes that in order for the promise that each individual must make to be "acceptable to the other promisers," the contracting individuals must universally conform to a version of equality that ignores difference. Social contract theorists, from Hobbes to Rawls, interpret and rely on a version of equality that might be construed as an equality of sameness and satisfy the condition of equality that is required for the transition to political society by positing a blank, universal individual as the basic contracting unit in their respective political theories of the social contract. Wolin notes, however, that in order to achieve an equality of sameness, social contract theorists require that some of the promisers must "agree to forget" certain matters.[32] The purpose of the social contract, from the standpoint of the relationship between collective memory and collective wrongs, is therefore "not so much on what the self promises but on what the self has to forget about itself."[33] For Wolin, this dimension of the social contract entails a focus not on rights that are retained and rights that are lost but rather on the "question of the identities" of the promisers. Here, social contract theory is interpreted not as dealing fundamentally with the question of individuals understood as abstract "bearers of rights" and "rational subjects" but as the "bearers of particularized identities" or, bearers whose identity is premised on characteristics such as "race, color, gender, community, or creed."[34] Acknowledging the identity of individuals is crucial for Wolin because it is this very identity that often serves as an occasion for the perpetration of collective wrongs by other contracting parties. Ignoring the identity of individuals introduces an element of *incoherence* in the conception of equality underlying social contract theory because what "can it mean to say that for the moment I must forget that I am a person of color or a woman so that I may think about the basic conditions of a just society, when for me what matters most is how that difference will be treated?"[35]

The "trick" for social contract theorists, Wolin argues, is to trade "equality for remembrance" and thus facilitate a situation where "equality serves the ends of inequality."[36] In order to achieve this, social contract theorists "enlisted memory," which was "told that it had to forget the social categories that were the marks of inequality."[37] The social contract, in other words, establishes a context that requires individuals to agree to temporarily suspend the memory of collective wrongs associated with their experience as bearers of particularized identities so that political society might "start afresh without inherited resentments."[38] Wolin notes, however, that forgetting does not eliminate inequalities, which are resumed, but with an important change – society can now legitimately justify the "equal protection of inequalities."[39] In this way, equality is conceived of in social contract theory not as an "ideal that is necessarily at war with power (because power presupposes inequality)" but a "fiction" that served "to legitimate power."[40] Wolin thus concludes that the "individual who contracts or covenants" is "an artifact, a constructed being whose attributes appear as unconditioned by the kind of resentments at past offenses which were and are the notorious accompaniments to the categories of gender, etc."[41] The upshot of Wolin's analysis is that social amnesia is *built into the foundations of liberalism* and remains in play as a pattern or tendency of the modern state.

The third force that Wolin examines is capitalism. Here, Wolin argues that, together with liberalism, capitalism helped to constitute a distinct political formation, or "system of political economy," which had "profound effects upon collective memory and notions of collective injustice."[42] The emergence of the economy as an "autonomous entity" resulted in the advent of a totalizing, hybrid system of power where the economy "is at once autonomous and determinative of all other social and political relationships."[43] In order to achieve the social amnesia that seventeenth-century social contract theorists only glimpsed, the universal, blank individual was, over the course of the nineteenth century, inscribed with a deep economic structure. The rise of "political-economy" thus facilitated a tacit redefinition of political subjectivity in economic terms and contributed to a restructuring of the conditions of membership in liberal societies. Wolin attempts to demonstrate the effects that political economy had in terms of its redefinition of political membership and the effects this in turn had on collective memory and the capacity for liberal societies to acknowledge and address injustice in a substantive way through a brief account of the rise of capitalism. According to Wolin, the "close collaboration between science, industry, and the state" that began in the seventeenth century acquired a crystallized form by the end of the nineteenth century and "resulted in forms of power which produced a series of technological revolutions that dramatically altered the human capacity for collective memory."[44] The new system of political-economy

> drew men, women, and children from the country-side and gathered them into cities of strangers; old skills and crafts had to be forgotten and new ones acquired; the rhythms of the factory replaced those of the natural seasons; tradition and custom as arbiters of existence gave way to rational calculation of utility. The pace of change grew ever more intense, and survival came to depend upon rapid adaptation. Those who traveled fastest and farthest were those who traveled with the least baggage inherited from the past. Memory was transformed into nostalgia, the longing for that which had once been but could be no more.[45]

Under these conditions, the individual must accept the *denial* of what Wolin refers to as the "narrative structure of justice." Here, the story associated with the claim of, for example, the recently unemployed factory worker is denied "not by a counter narrative but by a demonstration of the costs and benefits involved in the decision to relocate."[46] As Wolin notes, this does not constitute an act of injustice from the standpoint of the rationality of political-economy and while political-economy does nevertheless routinely produce injustice it remains devoid of "conceptions of collective injustice of the kind" that exist in traditional or "mnemonic" societies.[47] Liberalism, capitalism, and nationalism coalesce in the modern state which is established, following the social contract, as the primary agent responsible for dispensing justice and is conceived of as a sort of neutral arbiter of objective norms. In actuality, according to Wolin, this neutrality is undermined by the fact that the state is the servant and protector of that which forms the basis of national power, namely, the economy.

The constitutive tendency towards social amnesia that is a built-in feature of Western political modernity is countered by another tendency that is implied yet not explicitly developed in Wolin's theory and analysis of collective memory. Here, Wolin's theory highlights the "searing experiences of those for whom social categories have symbolized social wounds," social wounds that are, moreover, described by Wolin as the "ineradicable marks of inequality."[48] I interpret Wolin's remarks as suggesting that the liberal state's establishment of a context where "the self must renounce some part of itself or of its own experience" in order to be accepted into political society as being opposed by a context where those "who still carry the marks of the original wrong," cannot forget. Grievances and resentments associated with the unresolved injustices of the past, in other words, are also not actually forgotten by those who suffered the injustice. The tenacity of the memory of historic injustice is reinforced not only by the fact that in many cases the causes or generative roots of injustice are allowed to remain intact but also by the fact that, as Wolin notes, efforts to suppress recollection of the collective misdeeds of the past can only serve to contribute to "the accumulation of resentments without settling sharp disputes."[49] Wolin's theory, analysis, and critique of collective memory might be interpreted as pointing to a form, or forms, of collective *counter*memory. The space is not available to go into great detail about the nature of the logic of the *counter*memory of peoples and groups that are denied justice for collective wrongs as a condition of political membership, except to say the following. First, Wolin's analysis suggests that the transition to political society does not eliminate inequalities but only generates the appearance of equality. This means, in part, that those whose characteristics serve as an occasion for harm by the society of which they are a part might be said to suffer from the imposition and subsequent encasement in a structure of domination and oppression. Second, due to this fact, the logic of the *counter*memory of those who are denied justice as a condition of their membership/incarceration in society might be conceived of as a form of *fugitive memory*. One of the central characteristics of fugitive memory is the enduring durability of the collective memory not only of collective wrongs but also, in some cases, of the circumstances that might render the advent of conditions of actual equality a historical possibility. In the case of Indigenous peoples, the collective memory of actual equality is bound up with the collective memory of the autonomous Indigenous subject and the objective conditions under which this subject is rendered possible, i.e., the re-emergence of the treaty relationship. The logic of the collective memory of Indigenous peoples might be conceived of as a fugitive form of *counter*memory because the absence of justice generates both an impulse towards struggles for freedom from confinement in a coercively imposed structure of domination and an impulse towards the recovery of lost yet not forgotten forms of commonality based on actual equality (more on this below).

The political-mnemonic terrain of Indigenous politics in settler democracies such as Canada is therefore marked by a tension, perhaps even a contradiction, between, on the one hand, a society with a constitutive impulse towards forgetting historic and ongoing injustice as a condition of membership and, on the other hand, traumatic experiences that ought not, and perhaps even cannot, simply be forgotten. The liberal-democratic settler-state, in other words, is under a constitutive impulse that places intense pressure on Indigenous peoples to forget that which cannot be forgotten. Stated somewhat differently, the logic that underpins the fugitive memory of Indigenous peoples suggests that the outcome sought after by the liberal settler state in its dealings with Indigenous peoples – i.e., that Indigenous peoples forget themselves as free peoples and incorporate as subordinate and organically related elements in and of the conquering collectivity – is a highly unlikely outcome of the politics of reconciliation. The question remains, however, of how the settler state goes about managing this tension in its own favour. I begin to explore the question of how the Canadian state negotiates this tension in a way that facilitates colonial completion by turning to Glen Sean Coulthard's critique of the liberal politics of recognition.

From (Mis)Recognition to Misremembering and Back Again

For Coulthard, liberal democratic contexts such as Canada maintain settler-colonialism by relying not only on the "coercive authority of the settler state" but also, and perhaps more importantly, on what Coulthard refers to as the "productive character of colonial power," which is defined as the capacity for the liberal state to subtly reproduce structures of domination by producing "forms of life that make settler-colonialism's constitutive hierarchies seem natural."[50] The settler state achieves this through "delegated exchanges of political recognition" from the colonizer to the colonized that are designed to facilitate and secure a sense of allegiance to "circumscribed, master-sanctioned forms" of life – forms of life, moreover, that tend to be "structurally determined by and in the interests of the colonizer." The liberal politics of recognition is conceived by Coulthard as a theory and a practice that works to reproduce structures of domination and dispossession *through freedom*. Here, it might be said that the state misrecognizes in the act of recognition through forms of accommodation that grant, for example, the right to collective self-determination but in a political and economic form that simultaneously denies collective self-determination. In Canada, this process occurs, in part, through "self-government negotiations." "Self-government negotiations" might be conceived of as a state-driven, paternalistic process whereby Indigenous peoples are required by the state to demonstrate a capacity to enact certain pre-determined political standards the nature and proper performance of which is determined and strictly monitored by state authorities. It is a process that might be conceived of, in part, as sharing affinities with John Stuart Mill's version of normative developmentalism and, more specifically, his notion of government by "leading-strings" or "parental despotism," which is a form of enlightened despotism whereby a colonial master is burdened with the responsibility of expediting the political development of conquered, non-European peoples through the imposition of a political-pedagogical structure designed to "educate" and re-constitute colonized peoples in accordance with liberal political norms understood as an element of a wider – i.e., universal – process of civilizational development.[51] One of the key differences is that liberalism has since then made space for variations in those norms in the sense that it acknowledges that different cultures may interpret and enact liberal norms in different ways. This, however, simply means that, in Gerald Kernerman's felicitous phrase, Indigenous peoples are granted the right to be "liberal in their own communitarian way."[52] Coulthard thus rejects the liberal politics of recognition and the transformative promise that it invokes because it leaves untouched the generative roots of the structures that generate the ideologies that naturalize colonial hierarchies and facilitate the production of Indigenous "subjects of empire" who willingly become "instruments of their own dispossession."[53] Stated somewhat differently, to the extent that the Canadian state "remains structurally committed to the dispossession of Indigenous peoples of our lands and self-determining authority," liberal models of recognition not only do not facilitate a liberating transformation of Indigenous–state relations but instead work to reproduce the subjective and objective conditions of colonial power in more subtle ways.[54]

Nishnaabe political theorist Dale Turner argues that the subtle logic of domination at play in mainstream versions of the politics of recognition and reconciliation is facilitated by substituting political self-determination for cultural self-determination and then guaranteeing cultural self-determination as a right within the constitutional framework of Canadian law. This substitution in turn acts as the basis for a renewal of the project of assimilating Indigenous peoples into mainstream Canadian society via their reconstitution as formally equal individuals with special group rights. There is, however, a "profound difference between treating individual Indians equally, and treating *with* Indians as equal nations."[55] The state, in other words, misrecognizes Indigenous struggles for self-determination by "locating their source in the context of Aboriginal cultures – in their 'Aboriginality' – and not in the political context of Indigenous nationhood."[56] Stated somewhat differently, following Jakeet Singh, the state-driven politics of recognition operates "through the separation and prioritization of the political (understood in liberal-democratic terms) over the cultural," whereas radical Indigenous approaches do not "prioritize the search for meta-normative or universal principles upon which a state could appropriately manage cultural diversity from above."[57] Radical Indigenous approaches tend to conceive of the "political and the cultural as inseparable" and instead seek "to build from the ground up cultures of politics that embrace deep, irreducible pluralism."[58] For Coulthard, the danger inherent in the liberal politics of recognition in part consists of the subtle ways in which the state can entice "colonized populations" to internalize the "derogatory images imposed on them by their colonial master." Here, "derogatory images" might be interpreted as referring, in part, to the imposition and internalization of an image of Indigenous peoples as beings who are not and perhaps never existed historically as politically free peoples. The image of the autonomous Indigenous subject and the objective conditions that might be conducive to its re-emergence – for example, a renewal of a nation-to-nation, treaty-based relationship – gets replaced by the imposition of an image of Indigenous peoples not as free peoples but as culturally distinct yet organically related and politically subordinate social groups for whom it has become natural for their individual and collective fates to be determined externally by what is tantamount to a hostile and demeaning logic. In addition, it is important to note that the burden of change tends to be placed squarely on the colonized who are expected to adopt *as their own* the basic political forms and identities of the colonizing society. In this way, the settler-state employs the politics of recognition as means of co-optation that strives to get Indigenous peoples to "buy into" the Canadian social contract via processes that place intense pressure to identify delegated forms of (un)freedom with freedom itself and thereby facilitate the onset and consolidation of a sense of allegiance to the settler-state, which in turn grounds the settler-state's legitimacy *for* Indigenous peoples.

I believe that a similar logic of co-optation is at work in the sphere of collective memory at the level of the state in relation to Canada's politics of reconciliation. I believe that by its exclusive focus on residential schools and on the individual survivors of residential schools, Canada's IRS TRC is not only situating settler-colonialism in a past that is selectively forgotten but also reducing and thereby obscuring the entirety of settler-colonialism to what is reconceived of as a sort of temporally circumscribed, misguided state policy – as opposed to an endemic characteristic and ever-present possibility inhering in a distinct set of hierarchically structured relations whose historical trajectory has yet to be interrupted – directed at what is also reconceived of as a sort of victimized national sub-population – as opposed to independent peoples whose autonomy and self-determining authority is denied via the coercive imposition of a structure of domination. As Wolin notes, "by its silence, collective memory will have signified the limits of justice."[59] In this case, selective social amnesia, or the act of publicly recalling a *part of the story in a way that eclipses the whole story*, casts a veil over the violent origins of Canada and supports the one-sided ideological narrative of the Canadian nation-state as tolerant, diverse, and originary. The state thus negotiates the tension between its own built-in amnesiac tendencies and the fugitive memory of Indigenous peoples by not only misremembering in the act of remembering but also by remembering *for* Indigenous peoples and doing so in a way that expands the scope of the collective memory of the nation-state – i.e., by admitting the Residential School System as an element of the historical national narrative – but simultaneously contracts the terrain of collective memory as a whole – i.e., by omitting from the narrative the genocidal practices and the coercive imposition of a structure of domination that are conditions for nation- and state-building in North America. This undermines political reconciliation's decolonizing potential because, as Courtney Jung notes, in order for political reconciliation to act as a transformative force it must encompass the *whole terrain* of history, including the whole of the "collective and cultural harms" that populate this terrain.[60] The politics of reconciliation must, in other words, address a larger segment of history and "open up broader debates on historic injustice" because the Indian Residential School system does not constitute an "aberration of government policy."[61] The state's narrow focus "draws a line through history" that enables the settler-state to absolve itself of the guilt associated with one particular instance of state-sponsored violence and move on without addressing either the generative roots of the problem or the plethora of harms against Indigenous peoples that served as conditions for the advent of settler democracies in North America. Furthermore, as Nishnaabeg theorist Leanne Simpson notes, such a selectively narrow definition of historic injustice can work to undermine further struggles for decolonization in the sense that the state's admission of guilt combined with an official apology and compensation for survivors signifies the onset of a post-reconciliation era where there is no longer a legitimate basis for Indigenous struggles for freedom and decolonization. If in the "eyes of liberalism" this historical wrong has been "righted" then the "historic situation has been remedied" and Indigenous–state relations become co-opted in the sense that it facilitates the perception among Canadians that we now live in an era of post-reconciliation where "Indigenous peoples no longer have a legitimate source of contention."[62]

Wolin argues that the nature of the logic of the collective memory of the modern state might indicate a situation where justice no longer figures as the organizing principle of collective life, which in turn gets replaced by a concern for the management of risk and social discipline.[63] One of the central ways that the state manages the risk posed by the fugitive memory of Indigenous peoples and simultaneously disciplines Indigenous peoples to settler-colonial hierarchies is through their tendency to be misrecognized by the state in the context of the politics of reconciliation as *victims*. The primary means by which this identity gets imposed upon Indigenous peoples is via the medicalization of political reconciliation's transformative potential. Stated somewhat differently, the construction of Indigenous peoples as victims and of the state as saviour allows the state to reconceive political reconciliation's transformative potential as something like a state-sponsored therapeutic, self-help program. In *Therapeutic Nations*, Dian Million suggests that Canada's IRS TRC entwines Indigenous self-determination with a "state-determined biopolitical" program for "emotional and psychological self-care" that results in the transformation of Indigenous peoples into administered subjects "of a humanitarian project" as opposed to "subjects of their polities negotiating for political empowerment."[64] Jenny Edkins argues, in a similar vein, that the "normalisation and medicalization" of trauma and victimhood is a way of managing the risk posed by the potential politicization of survivors. Here, the state "helps" survivors to "recover" by allowing them to "verbalise and narrate what has happened to them" and by providing "counselling" but not so that they may re-acquire political agency but instead to facilitate their reinsertion into structures of power.[65] If this process of normalization "fails, then the status of victim of post-traumatic stress disorder serves to render the survivor more or less harmless to exist-ing power structures."[66] In this way, the challenge to existing power structures posed by the potential radicalization of survivors is neutralized, while the bear-ers of those memories are simultaneously disciplined to social hierarchies. Political theorist Andrew Schaap argues that reliance on metaphors of "heal-ing and settlement" is a way of managing the "risk of politics," which Schaap defines agonistically as the possibility that "the community is not inevitable" and that some conflicts may be irreconcilable.[67] Here, the risk of politics is managed by placing "plurality in the service of a higher unity: a nation to be redeemed, a society to be healed, a truth to be settled."[68] Casting the politics of reconciliation in these terms not only "diminishes the representational space in which the terms of reconciliation itself might be contested" but also establishes conditions where the "collective memory on which community is supposed to depend requires a selective forgetting of that which might call into question the commonness of the past."[69]

These critiques suggest the outlines of a model of political reconciliation that invokes political reconciliation's transformative promise but in a way that simultaneously undermines the conditions of justice and the promise of change in the basic political structure of settler-colonial nation-states. In the next sec-tion I will attempt to sketch the outlines of two contrasting models of political reconciliation, which will in turn serve as a context for a very brief reflection on the relationship between democracy, decolonization, and collective memory in settler-colonial contexts.

Conclusion: Democracy, Decolonization, and Collective Memory

The first model of political reconciliation is the mainstream form that the poli-tics of reconciliation tends to assume in established democracies and it might be referred to as "reconciliation from above." I argue that this model of political reconciliation might be conceived of as a form that is constitutively shaped by the model of democracy that tends to hold sway in settler-colonial contexts, namely, what democratic theorists often refer to as the "realist-elitist" model of democracy. While critics of this model have noted its top-down, institutional-ized, proceduralist, aggregative, and capitalist tendencies, I wish to focus *primar-ily*, though not exclusively, on what critics have identified as, on the one hand, its tendency to concentrate collective decision-making power in the hands of state-sanctioned political, bureaucratic, and academic elites and experts and, on the other hand, the political passiveness among ordinary citizens that it both generates and presupposes as a condition of normal politics. Stated somewhat differently, insofar as the politics of reconciliation tends to be constituted in a way that reflects tendencies inherent in the realist-elitist model of democracy, it results in a situation where bureaucratic and political elites with the support of legal and academic experts exercise an effective monopoly on collective decision-making processes as they pertain to both Indigenous peoples and ordinary citizens. There are at least two dimensions of this feature of the realist-elitist model of democracy that undermines the transformative and decolonizing potential of the politics of reconciliation. First, following Simpson, Canada's IRS TRC undermines decolonization to the extent that it locks Indigenous peoples into a position of victimhood that denies agency, decision-making power, and the "power to decide restorative measures."[70] Denying Indigenous peoples an active role as architects in and of the process of reconciliation both pre-supposes and facilitates a political environment that is hostile to Indigenous normativities and that reaffirms settler-colonialism's constitutive hierarchies. The second way that these tendencies undermine the political reconciliation's transformative potential has to do with Simpson's claim that the decolonizing potential of political reconciliation is bound up with its capacity to re-educate ordinary Canadian citizens. For Simpson, "treaties are not just for governments, they are for the citizens as well" and, given the highly institutionalized nature of processes associated with the politics of reconciliation and the distance that is thus generated from the everyday political experience of ordinary citizens, Simpson wonders "how we can reconcile when the majority of Canadians do not understand the historic or contemporary injustice of dispossession and occupation, particularly when the state has expressed its unwillingness to make any adjustments to the unjust relationship."[71]

"Reconciliation from below," on the other hand, is a version of political reconciliation where agency is relocated with Indigenous peoples and ordinary citizens acting outside of the institutionalized, state-centric boundaries of what counts as normal politics under the realist-elitist model of democracy. I begin to sketch the conceptual outlines of the decolonizing potential of reconciliation from below by turning to Coulthard's use of the Fanonian-inspired notion of "strategic de-subjectification." For Coulthard, strategic de-subjectification refers to strategies that a colonized people employ for the purpose of decolonization at the level of the subject and is formulated in part as a response to the state's capacity to facilitate the internalization by Indigenous peoples of an imprisoning self-image that works to constitute Indigenous peoples as "subjects of empire" and thereby render them amenable to the reproduction of settler-colonial hierarchies. Coulthard argues in this regard that while processes of colonization are totalizing, they are not total and that the colonized "are often able to turn internalized forms" of imperial (mis)recognition into "expressions of self-empowerment" through a process of reclamation involving the revitalization of non-contemporaneous modes of being.[72] The colonized, in other words, can undermine processes that aim to facilitate their constitution as subjects with ideological attachments to imperial forms through a process that com-prises two "movements": a "turning away" from the "assimilative reformism" of state recognition accompanied by a "turn inwards," which is defined as processes involving "the reclamation and revitalization of precolonial social relations and cultural traditions."[73] Here, it is important to note two things. First, Coulthard conceives of the turn inwards not as a literal "return to the past" but as a *critical* turn that seeks to recapture "values, principles and other cultural elements that are best suited to the larger contemporary political and economic reality."[74] Second, for Coulthard, processes of decolonization at the level of the subject are inextricably linked to forms of resistance that aim to facilitate objective political change. Coulthard politicizes the process of cultural reclamation by connecting it to political practices of on-the-ground, or grassroots, political action that occur outside of the boundaries of what counts as normal politics under the modern state.

I argue that while Coulthard tends to apply this concept in relation to the ways in which Indigenous resurgence can act as a force of Indigenous liberation, I believe that it is equally important to theorize the conditions for the strategic de-subjectification of settler-colonial subjectivities. There are two dimensions of this problem that I wish to highlight. First, the urgency of theorizing such conditions is suggested by Mohawk scholar Taiaiake Alfred, whose critique of the politics of reconciliation revolves around the claim that political reconciliation's transformative potential is undermined by the widespread existence among settler majorities of what he refers to as the "colonial mentality." The colonial mentality remains "alive at the core" of the collective identity of Canadians, and as such it continues to "frame, animate, shape and constrain all thinking in Canadian political circles on the problems and solutions of the relationship between Indigenous peoples and the state, and on the multiple crises being endured by Indigenous women, children and men."[75] The widespread existence of the hostile attitudes, behaviours, and beliefs that define the "colonial mentality" makes for conditions where Indigenous peoples are, "still living in a relationship framed in colonial terms; the language we use today has changed over the years but the perspective is still straight out of the seventeenth century. Newcomer people in this land, their governments and the powerful interests that have dominion in this society still see a need for the Original People to be in a certain place (out of the way of development), to be defined in a certain way (aspiring to be just like the rest of us), and to be prevented from doing certain things (living the ways of their ancestors)."[76]

The second dimension that I wish to highlight is the argument that radical democratic theory might contribute to decolonization through its capacity to act as a resource for theorizing the strategic de-subjectification of settler subjectivities. This claim is grounded on three further claims. First, I interpret Simpson's claim that "treaties are not just for government, they are for the citizens as well," as suggesting that the transformative and decolonizing potential of the politics of reconciliation is undermined under conditions where political, bureaucratic, and academic elites usurp the collective decision-making power of the *demos*. Realizing political reconciliation's transformative potential, in other words, depends on the advent of a more radically democratic constitution of the *political* in settler-colonial societies. Second, Corntassel, Dhamoon, and Snelgrove argue that Indigenous struggles for decolonization and self-determination "cannot occur in isolation" and that decolonization requires a "collective conversation and mobilization" that is premised on "the possibility of settlers being transformed through anti-colonial resistance."[77] The third claim is associated with Little and Maddison's argument that the issue of *demographic scale*[78] is a crucial dimension of decolonization because "the attitudes of the non-indigenous majority to indigenous claims is a hugely significant political factor" that shapes and conditions any attempt to facilitate decolonizing transformations.[79] I interpret these claims as suggesting that there is, if not a necessary then at least a crucial, role for radical democratic theories and practices as a moment in processes of decolonization in the sense that decolonization depends, in part, on a capacity for settlers to engage with Indigenous politics and in a way that facilitates a de-imperializing de-subjectification of settler subjectivities.

I believe, moreover, that Wolin's radical democratic definition of the *political* resonates with Indigenous struggles for decolonization and collective self-determination. If democracy is defined, following Wolin, as moments of collective self-determination and collective self-transformation that are motivated by the resentments associated with the memory of unresolved collective wrongs, and if, moreover, decolonization is defined by a collective self-transformation that is motivated, in part, by the pursuit of justice for past wrongs and that results in the advent of conditions that are conducive to Indigenous self-determination, then radical democratic action can, in principle, contribute to decolonization if the *demos* were to adopt as their own a desire to rectify the injustices of settler-colonialism through acts of collective self-transformation aimed at the "wholesale transgression of inherited" settler-colonial forms. Here, it is important to note that I am not suggesting that the burden of change is the sole responsibility of settlers. What I am suggesting is that due to issues of scale and other concerns, decolonization might be construed as a *mutually transformative decolonial-democratic process* that crucially depends upon the capacity for settlers to embark on a parallel process of de-subjectification, which might be defined, in part, as the transformation of the *demos* from being complicit with settler-colonial structures and histories of domination to being allies in the struggle against injustice. I believe that situations where Indigenous forms of on-the-ground political action and resistance result in broad-based alliances involving a multiplicity of diverse actors might serve as one context for the strategic de-subjectification of settler-subjectivities. The transformative potential of such alliances in part lies in their capacity to *re-educate the collective memory* of ordinary citizens. Stated somewhat differently, the transformative and decolonizing potential of the politics of reconciliation might realize itself in on-the-ground alliances where Indigenous peoples and settlers re-constitute themselves as political agents and that the educative potential of such grassroots alliances might contribute to the renewal of forms of collective memory that counter the effects of selective social amnesia and help facilitate the rejection by settler subjects of the hostile attitudes, behaviours, and beliefs that justify and sustain settler-colonial hierarchies. Here, a crucial source of alternatives to the contemporary settler-colonial relationship lies in the past, or more specifically, a renewed orientation to the past as a potential source of the de-subjectification of settler subjectivity. The past might act as a source of new political imaginaries and contribute to the realization of political reconciliation's decolonial-democratic potential in at least two ways.

First, a renewed orientation towards the past might facilitate an expansion of the terrain of the collective memory of settlers to include what Michael Mann refers to as the "dark side of democracy"[80] and, more specifically, the recognition that nation- and state-building processes in settler-colonial contexts such as Canada are predicated upon genocidal practices and the imposition of a structure of domination upon Indigenous peoples. Disavowing foundational moments that do not reinforce the positive self-image that the nation-state jealously guards is a central means of not only naturalizing the settler-colonial relationship but also of undermining the capacity for such recollections to act as a source of resentment and, by extension, the possibility of transformative political action in the present. The crucial importance of recollecting foundational injustices is suggested by Kevin Bruyneel, who argues, following Giorgio Agamben, that foundational moments are not "once and for all" historical events that are "cemented in [linear] time" but instead ought to be conceived of as "continually operative," that is, as moments that are "perpetually and necessarily reinscribed in the present through the discourse, practices, and mnemonics of state sovereignty and white settler nationalism."[81] The story of the (settler) nation-state is not, in other words, "written in sequential chapters but rather in texts that fold on top and through each other like a palimpsest in which, most notably, founding moments continually reoccur in the present, not the past."[82] Here, Bruyneel notes that in "politics, time is a structuring force that shapes collective and individual identities, subjectivities, and imaginaries."[83] The de-politicizing effects of certain temporal structures is evident "in sweeping historical narratives, such as those a nation tells itself about its founding moment and subsequent arc of development, an arc that almost always legitimizes the status of the contemporary social and political order."[84] If, in other words, political time is a "construct, not a natural entity" and if, moreover, temporal structures are an "inescapable organizing element of a cohesive social and political order," then, Bruyneel suggests, it is necessary to conceive of the "unstructuring of temporalities that serve to preserve injustices, such as those that too seamlessly distance past injustices from the present," as a crucial dimension of change. Educating collective memory to become cognizant of the injustices of the past might help to facilitate an understanding of Indigenous justice claims and fuel the sort of resentment that motivates acts of collective self-transformation that undo injustice in the present.

Second, a renewed orientation towards the past might also contribute to new understandings not only of Indigenous peoples but of the nature of the historical relationship between Indigenous peoples and newcomers in North America. It might, in other words, contribute to the widespread acceptance of historical counter-narratives that in turn might ground the emergence of alternative frameworks or patterns of coexistence. Robert A. Williams Jr., for instance, in his analysis of early modern treaties and patterns of cooperation between Indigenous peoples and Newcomers, argues that the founding of North America did not occur as the single-handed act of expansion-oriented European colonizers on a civilizing mission, but rather emerged as a mutually constituted process. Here, Williams quotes Francis Jennings, who suggested that "Indian *cooperation* was the prime requisite for European penetration and colonization of the North American continent."[85] As Williams notes, "cooperation" is not a concept that "the American public imagination usually calls up from its collective memory to describe Indian-white relations" in the narrativization of nation- and state-building in America.[86] The habitual ways in which the mainstream founding myths construct the relationship between Indigenous peoples and Newcomers have made it difficult for contemporary settlers to conceive of "these two different groups of peoples sharing the identity of interests necessary to make any sort of intercultural cooperation possible during any period of our history."[87] It is thus the case that the sorts of narratives that the collective memory of the state constructs work to obscure "the historical significance of the Indian's important role in facilitating these patterns of accommodation in the early colonial settlement of North America."[88] And yet, it is alternative origin stories such as these that Indigenous peoples often turn to in their search for an alternative and more just relationship. The stories, in other words, that "can be generated from a countermythology of Indian-white relations" can serve as an alternative account of origins, one which might facilitate the sort of identities that are required in order to build a "workable social order" in which Indigenous peoples might constitute themselves autonomously.[89] Counter-narratives of this sort which are based on actual evidence allows for a remembering of origins and a re-imagining of North America "as an extended story of cultural group negotiations in selected areas of intercultural cooperation" which might in turn act as the basis for a shared sense of destiny that does not presuppose political and national homogeneity.[90] This in turn could nourish the possibility of post-settler-colonial imaginaries and forms of commonality in the present where nation- and state-building is conceived of as a mutually constitutive process as opposed to a set of circumstances where the freedom of settlers requires and depends upon the historical and ongoing subjugation of Indigenous peoples.

NOTES

1 The UN Genocide Convention defines genocide as: "Acts committed with intent to destroy, in whole or in part, a national, ethnical, racial or religious group, such as, including the following: (a) Killing member of the group; (b) Causing serious bodily or mental harm to members of the group; (c) Deliberately inflicting on the group conditions of life calculated to bring about its physical destruction in whole or in part; (d) Imposing measures intended to prevent births within the group; (e) Forcibly transferring children of the group to another group." In their commentary, Benvenuto, Woolford, and Hinton quote both Canadian Treaty Commissioner Duncan Campbell Scott, who, in his capacity as a residential school administrator, proclaimed, "Our objective is … to get rid of the Indian problem," as well as the American superintendent of the Carlisle Indian Industrial School, Richard Henry Pratt, who stated that the aim of the industrial school system was to "kill the Indian in him, and save the man." Andrew Woolford, Jeff Benvenuto, and Alexander Laban Hinton, eds., *Colonial Genocide in Indigenous North America* (Durham, NC: Duke University Press, 2014), 3.

2 Alexander Keller-Hirsch, "Fugitive Reconciliation: The Agonistics of Respect, Resentment and Responsibility in Post-Conflict Society," *Contemporary Political Theory*, Vol. 10, No. 2 (2011), 167; Adrian Little and Sarah Maddison, "Reconciliation, Transformation, Struggle: An Introduction," *International Political Science Review*, Vol. 38, No. 2 (2017), 145–54; Glen Sean Coulthard, *Red Skin, White Masks: Rejecting the Colonial Politics of Recognition* (Minneapolis: University of Minnesota Press, 2014); Andrew Schaap, *Political Reconciliation* (New York: Routledge, 2005).

3 The literature on political reconciliation and interpretations of its transformative potential is vast. For accounts of various interpretations of political reconciliation's transformative potential from the standpoint of democratic theory, political theory, legal theory, settler-colonial theory, and critical Indigenous theory, see essays contained in Will Kymlicka and Bashir Bashir, eds., *The Politics of Reconciliation in Multicultural Societies* (Oxford: Oxford University Press, 2012); Alexander Keller Hirsch, ed., *Theorizing Post-Conflict Reconciliation* (New York: Routledge, 2012); Patrick Macklem and Douglas Sanderson, eds., *From Recognition to Reconciliation* (Toronto: University of Toronto Press, 2016); Sarah Maddison, Tom Clark, and Ravi de Costa, eds., *The Limits of Settler Colonial Reconciliation* (Singapore: Springer Nature, 2016); and Michael Asch, John Borrows, and James Tully, eds., *Resurgence and Reconciliation* (Toronto: University of Toronto Press, 2018).

4 Patrick Wolfe, "Settler Colonialism and the Elimination of the Native," *Journal of Genocide Research*, Vol. 8, No. 4 (2006), 390.

5 Coulthard, *Red Skin, White Masks*, 7.
6 The term "settler democracy" is borrowed from Michael Mann's seminal study on the relationship between liberal democracy and genocide, *The Dark Side of Democracy* (New York: Cambridge University Press, 2005).
7 Will Kymlicka and Bashir Bashir, "Introduction," in *The Politics of Reconciliation in Multicultural Societies*, ed. Will Kymlicka and Bashir Bashir (Oxford: Oxford University Press, 2012), 1–3.
8 Ibid. See also Bashir Bashir, "Accommodating Historically Oppressed Social Groups: Deliberative Democracy and the Politics of Reconciliation," in *The Politics of Reconciliation in Multicultural Societies*, ed. Will Kymlicka and Bashir Bashir (Oxford: Oxford University Press, 2012), 48–69.
9 Glen Sean Coulthard, "Subjects of Empire: Indigenous Peoples and the 'Politics of Recognition' in Canada." *Contemporary Political Theory*, 6 (2005), 438. See also Michael Elliott, "Participatory Parity and Indigenous Decolonization Struggles," *Constellations*, Vol. 23, No. 3 (2016), 413–24.
10 Coulthard, *Red Skin, White Masks*, 12.
11 I justify my appropriation of this imagery in the following way. The *Gus-Wen-Tah* and its related image originate with the Haudenosaunee. I do not have personal experience with the story of the *Gus-Wen-Tah* and do not possess authentic, first-hand knowledge or the right to act as an authority in relation to this Indigenous concept of how to go about structuring international relations. The *Gus-Wen-Tah* and its related imagery has, however, taken on a life of its own outside of the traditional territories, stories, and knowledge systems of the Haudenosaunee and has come to exercise a powerful hold on the political imaginary of Indigenous North America. This is the version of the *Gus-Wen-Tah* that I am here dealing with. The version that has come, in other words, to represent for many Indigenous peoples the meaning of the treaty relationship, or at least to serve as a widespread heuristic device in attempts by Indigenous peoples across North America to ground explanations of and struggles for the sort of objective political relationship between Indigenous peoples and Newcomers that might be conducive to the independent flourishing of Indigenous social and political forms. Robert A. Williams Jr. describes the *Gus-Wen-Tah* and its related imagery in the following way: "The *Gus-Wen-Tah* is comprised of a bed of white wampum shell beads symbolizing the sacredness and purity of the treaty agreement between the two sides. Two parallel rows of purple wampum beads that extend down the length of the belt represent the separate paths traveled by the two sides on the same river. Each side travels in its own vessel: the Indians in a birch bark canoe, representing their laws, customs, and ways, and the whites in a ship, representing their laws, customs, and ways. In presenting the *Gus-Wen-Tah* to solemnize their treaties with the Western colonial powers, the Iroquois would explain its basic underlying vision of law and peace between different peoples as follows: 'We shall each travel the river together, side by side, but in our own boat. Neither of us will steer the other's

vessel'" (Robert A. Williams Jr., *Linking Arms Together* [New York: Routledge, 1999]), 4.

12 Ken Coates, "The Indian Act and the Future of Aboriginal Governance in Canada," *Research Paper for the National Centre for First Nations Governance* (May 2008), 1.

13 Sheldon Wolin, "Fugitive Democracy," in *Democracy and Difference*, ed. Seyla Benhabib (Princeton, NJ: Princeton University Press, 1996), 37.

14 Coulthard defines the politics of recognition in *Red Skin, White Masks* as having emerged as the predominant paradigm of state Indigenous policy in the late 1960s and early 1970s, replacing the previous paradigm defined by its reliance on naked force. The liberal politics of recognition is more specifically defined by Coulthard as consisting of a "now expansive range of recognition-based models of liberal pluralism that seek to reconcile Indigenous assertions of nationhood with settler-state sovereignty via the accommodation of Indigenous identity claims in some form of renewed legal and political relationship with the Canadian state" (3).

15 Here, Coulthard's critique focuses specifically on Charles Taylor's theory of recognition but argues that it also holds for other formulations, such as those theorized by Will Kymlicka, for instance (*Red Skin, White Masks*, 16).

16 Coulthard, "Subjects of Empire," 438–9.

17 Coulthard, *Red Skin, White Masks*, 7.

18 Its capacity to be moulded, to receive a shape, or to be made to assume a desired form.

19 Sunera Thobani, *Exalted Subjects: Studies in the Making of Race and Nation in Canada* (Toronto: University of Toronto Press, 2007), 8–9.

20 Cornelius Castoriadis, *The Imaginary Institution of Society* (Cambridge, MA: MIT Press, 1998), 11.

21 Elizabeth Strakosch, "Beyond Colonial Completion: Arendt, Settler Colonialism and the End of Politics," in *The Limits of Settler Colonial Reconciliation: Non-Indigenous People and the Responsibility to Engage*, ed. Sarah Maddison, Tom Clark, and Ravi de Costa (Singapore: Springer Nature, 2016), 15.

22 The three case studies Wolin analyses include Benedict Anderson's commentary on the work of Ernest Renan and more specifically "Renan's paradox," the politics of reparations associated the history of Black slavery in the United States and the internment of Japanese Americans during the Second World War (Wolin, 1989).

23 Sheldon Wolin, "Injustice and Collective Memory," in *The Presence of the Past: Essays on the State and the Constitution* (Baltimore: Johns Hopkins University Press, 1989), 34.

24 Ibid., 33.

25 Ibid., 34.

26 Ibid., 36.

27 Ibid., 45.

28 Ibid., 36.

29 Ibid., 36.

30 Ibid., 36.
31 Ibid., 36.
32 Ibid., 37.
33 Ibid., 37.
34 Ibid., 37.
35 Ibid., 38.
36 Ibid., 39.
37 Ibid., 39.
38 Ibid., 38.
39 Ibid., 38.
40 Ibid., 38.
41 Ibid., 38.
42 Ibid., 42.
43 Ibid., 42.
44 Ibid., 43.
45 Ibid., 43.
46 Ibid., 45.
47 Ibid., 44.
48 Ibid., 39.
49 Ibid., 38.
50 Coulthard, *Red Skin, White Masks*, 152.
51 John Stuart Mill, *Considerations on Representative Government* (New York: Cambridge University Press, 2010), 39–40.
52 Gerald Kernerman, *Multicultural Nationalism: Civilizing Difference, Constituting Community* (Vancouver: University of British Columbia Press, 2005), 8.
53 Coulthard, *Red Skin, White Masks*, 156.
54 Ibid., 151.
55 Dale Turner, "Indigenous Knowledge and the Reconciliation of Section 35(1)," in *From Recognition to Reconciliation: Essays on the Constitutional Entrenchment of Aboriginal & Treaty Rights*, ed. Patrick Macklem and Douglas Sanderson (Toronto: University of Toronto Press, 2019), 169.
56 Ibid., 171.
57 Jakeet Singh, "Recognition and Self-Determination: Approaches from Above and Below," in *Recognition versus Self-Determination: Dilemmas of Emancipatory Politics*, ed. Avigail Eisenberg, Jeremy Webber, Glen Coulthard, and Andrée Boisselle (Vancouver: University of British Columbia Press, 2014), 58–9.
58 Ibid., 58.
59 Wolin, "Injustice and Collective Memory," 35.
60 Courtney Jung, "Research Brief: Transitional Justice for Indigenous People in a Non-Transitional Society," *International Center for Transitional Justice* (October 2009), 2.
61 Ibid., 2.

62 Leanne Simpson, *Dancing on Our Turtle's Back: Stories of Nishnaabeg Re-Creation, Resurgence and a New Emergence* (Winnipeg: ARP Books, 2011), 22.

63 Wolin, "Injustice and Collective Memory," 42.

64 Dian Million, *Therapeutic Nations: Healing in an Age of Indigenous Human Rights* (Tucson: University of Arizona Press, 2013), 6.

65 Jenny Edkins, *Trauma and the Memory of Politics* (New York: Cambridge University Press, 2003), 9.

66 Ibid., 9.

67 Andrew Schaap, *Political Reconciliation* (New York: Routledge, 2005), 18.

68 Ibid.

69 Ibid.

70 Simpson, *Dancing on Our Turtle's Back*, 22–4.

71 Ibid., 21.

72 Coulthard, *Red Skin, White Masks*, 153.

73 Ibid., 154.

74 Ibid., 156–7.

75 Taiaiake Alfred, "For Indigenous Nations to Live, Colonial Mentalities Must Die," *Policy Options Politique*, 13 October 2017, https://policyoptions.irpp.org/magazines/october-2017/for-indigenous-nations-to-live-colonial-mentalities-must-die/.

76 Ibid.

77 Jeff Corntassel, Rita Kaur Dhamoon, and Corey Snelgrove, "Unsettling Settler Colonialism: The Discourse and Politics of Settlers, and Solidarity with Indigenous Nations," *Decolonization: Indigeneity, Education & Society*, Vol. 3, No. 2 (2014), 3.

78 Adrian Little and Sarah Maddison, "Reconciliation, Transformation, Struggle: An Introduction," *International Political Science Review*, Vol. 38, No. 2 (2017), 145–54. The issue of "demographic scale" is defined in terms of the relationship between majorities and minorities and how the shape of this relationship affects attempts to theorize political reconciliation's transformative potential. In settler-colonial contexts such as Canada and Australia, for instance, Indigenous peoples constitute roughly 4.9 per cent and 2.5 per cent of the total population, respectively (151). These "numbers" have a significant impact on the manner in which political reconciliation's transformative potential is theorized and put into practice. Among other things, it means that Indigenous struggles for decolonization and self-determination in the context of the politics of reconciliation ought to be conceived of differently than, for example, the struggles for freedom of Black peoples in South Africa in the context of the politics of reconciliation where those oppressed by the coercive imposition of a structure of domination constituted a majority, or roughly 80 per cent of the total population (151).

79 Ibid., 151.

80 Michael Mann, *The Dark Side of Democracy* (New York: Cambridge University Press, 2005).

81 Kevin Bruyneel, "The Trouble with Amnesia: Collective Memory and Colonial Injustice in the United States," in *Political Creativity: Reconfiguring Institutional Order and Change*, ed. Gerald Berk, Dennis C. Galvan, and Victoria Hattam (Philadelphia: University of Pennsylvania Press, 2013), 236–57, 240.
82 Ibid., 240–1.
83 Ibid., 236.
84 Ibid., 236.
85 Robert A. Willimas Jr., *Linking Arms Together* (New York: Routledge, 1999), 20.
86 Ibid.
87 Ibid.
88 Ibid., 21.
89 Ibid., 22.
90 Ibid., 27.

SECTION 3

Democracy and Political Education: Wolin and Contemporary Interlocutors

6 Realistic Political Education

STEPHEN L. ESQUITH

Introduction

In the United States the control over elections by corporate power in the name of freedom of speech has been judicially upheld. The privatization of public goods – from schools to native lands – is hailed as a sign of good management. The militarization of foreign policy is rationalized as the necessary response to global terrorism. The balance between separate branches of government has been discarded as gridlock in the name of national security. The norms of tolerance, mutual forbearance, and trust have been replaced unapologetically by pervasive lying, manipulation, distraction, propaganda, and "bullshit" in Harry Frankfurt's refined sense of that term.[1] This is our political reality today.

Former President Donald Trump and his equally unprecedented revolving cast of incompetents, sycophants, and enablers share much of the blame. However, the polarization of the political party system certainly preceded his electoral college majority. Corporate power and privatization have been as much a part of the neoliberal agenda as the neoconservative agenda. Sheldon Wolin saw this coming and labelled it "inverted totalitarianism."[2] The alternative, he argued, is a "fugitive" incarnation of the *demos*.

Contrary to some of the early critics of this formulation (i.e., inverted totalitarianism vs. fugitive democracy),[3] the "*demos*," according to Wolin, is "ordinary" in the sense that its concerns are the basic concerns of everyday life, not the false choices presented to it by a political party system that serves corporate interests. Its goal – "creating new patterns of commonality at any moment" – cannot be achieved in a moment, but the realization that such patterns are possible, that is, they can be imagined, can happen at any moment, and from there the long process of political education can continue.[4]

In this essay I approach fugitive democracy through the lens of political education. Political education was a recurring theme in Wolin's major theoretical work, beginning with the first edition of *Politics and Vision* in 1960, and it also informed his university teaching and his political commentary in *The Nation* and *The New York Review of Books* and his editorship of the journal *democracy*. Altogether they constitute, in theory and practice, a realistic political education for the *demos*.

Political Theory as Political Education

In *Politics and Vision*, Wolin summarized his understanding of the connection between what he called "the epic tradition" in political theory and political education. "In studying the writings of Plato, Locke, or Marx, we are in reality familiarizing ourselves with a fairly stable vocabulary and a set of categories that help to orient us towards a particular world, the world of political phenomena. But more than this, since the history of political philosophy is, as we shall see, an intellectual development wherein successive thinkers have added new dimensions to the analysis and understanding of politics, an inquiry into that development is not so much an antiquarian venture as a form of political education."[5] A capacity for re-orientation, innovation, and understanding are the intellectual virtues that political theory can cultivate, particularly around what Wolin famously called "the political," that is, those things that depend upon collective action and coercive power for the sake of a common good. Machiavelli's economy of violence and Hobbes's metaphysics of power, Wolin argued, are part of an "epic" tradition that addressed this task. So are the writings of Luther and Calvin, who are not typically thought of as political theorists but should be because of their reconstitution of the language of politics (community, membership, participation, and power).

The ancients were of particular interest to Wolin in this regard, and not only Plato and Aristotle. Thucydides's *History of the Peloponnesian Wars* was a cautionary tale for his contemporaries who, he feared, had not learned the tragic lessons of the imperial expansion of Athenian power. These lessons, according to Wolin, still hold. "In the US, from the beginning, there has been a persistent tension between the drive for expansion … and the struggle to devise new institutions for adapting the practices of democracy and its ethos of political commonality."[6] As he concludes in *Democracy Incorporated*, Wolin connects this "persistent tension" to Thucydides's reading of the "drive for expansion" and its consequences for American democracy.

> We might restate Thucydides: by its nature imperial conquest imposes a heavy, perhaps unbearable demands upon human rationality, not just upon virtue. There are too many unknowns, contingencies, unpredictable consequences as well as a vast sale on which things can go wrong. The kind of power that democracy brings to conquest has been formed in a local context and according to well-understood norms and traditions. In order to cope with the imperial

contingencies of foreign wars and occupation, democracy will alter its character, not only by assuming new behaviors abroad (e.g., ruthlessness, indifference to suffering, disregard of local norms, the inequalities in ruling a subject population) but also by operating on revised, power-expansive assumptions at home. It will, more often than not, try to manipulate the public rather than engage its members in deliberation. It will demand greater powers and broad discretion in their use ("state secrets"), a tighter control over society's resources, more summary methods of justice, and less patience for legalities, opposition, and clamors for socioeconomic reforms.[7]

The impact of imperial power on democracy's behaviour abroad and its character at home was particularly evident during the Vietnam War, and for that reason Thucydides's relevance has often been cited by critics of the war.[8] Wolin was one of these critics, during and after the war,[9] coining the phrase "the powerlessness of power" to describe the way in which imperial expansion can undermine power,[10] and he saw the same "tighter control" and "summary methods of justice" in the aftermath of September 11.

Another theorist who appreciated the value of classical Greek philosophy, literature, poetry, and drama for understanding the contemporary patterns and dynamics of power was Simone Weil, whose essay on the *Iliad* Wolin was fond of referencing. In "The *Iliad*, Poem of Might," Weil argued that power is intoxicating, not just an instrument for objectifying the Other. It blinds those who exercise it to the cruelty of their acts and to their own mortality.[11] However, despite these destructive effects of power, Weil also identified moments of moderation and sound political judgment in this epic tragedy. Encouraged by Priam, Achilles recognizes himself as a father who might lose a son in battle as Priam has, and he agrees to give Hector's body back to Priam and to suspend hostilities so that the body can be buried properly. Enemies occasionally can recognize a common bond and suspend hostilities.

In Weil's hands, the *Iliad* is more than a story of Achillean pride, tempered by a few exceptional moments of compassion. The "true hero," according to Weil, is power itself. Wolin might have us read the *Iliad* today, as Weil did during the darkest hours of the Second World War, so that we do not forget the dynamics of power and violence, especially when we are most confident that our cause is just and we are filled with righteous indignation. But we should also read it so that we can remember, as Priam and Achilles did, that there are things we hold in common, even in times of violent conflict. This is what it means to be realistic about political education. It is not the same as dividing the political world into the metaphysically real and unreal. Realistic political education is concerned with seeing opportunities for democratic political change in the constellations of power, as well as being concerned with the obstacles to greater democratic participation.

By calling for a renewed commitment to political theory as a vocation, Wolin hoped to invest political theory with its own heroic ethic in the way that Weber had invested the Protestant ethic. However, Wolin's call gradually became less confident and, I would argue, more realistic. Without entirely abandoning the goals of epic theory as political education, he was reluctant to invoke that term. His portrait of the epic theorist gave way to the political education of a protean *demos*, who unavoidably are a work in progress.[12] The *demos*'s struggle for greater inclusion must always result in new boundaries.[13] With new boundaries of inclusion come new lines of exclusion. To walk on this razor's edge, the *demos* must be prepared to handle unexpected alliances and adversaries. This means they must be realistic about what can and cannot be done at any given moment (not in a single moment), what they imagine they can accomplish, and with whom they may be able to accomplish it.

Realistic Political Education in Theory

Realistic political education is an education in the myriad forms of power, more specifically, an education in the unavoidable dilemmas facing citizens who participate in the generation of power, are changed by it, and still struggle to retain some control over its exercise. Power is not limited to state power. It runs through the various forms of private administration, family and gender relations, and the many other networks of civil society.

What do the *demos* need in order to generate and retain control over power when power can be so ubiquitous, seductive, and expansive, and their own lines of membership so fluid and contested? At the same time, what do the *demos* need in order to see what they can hold in common within this maelstrom of power relations? The answers to these questions in this section are theoretical, but they are not abstracted from history and actual institutional patterns of power and violence. I will use Wolin's account of realistic political education to fill in a more general framework offered by Raymond Geuss in his programmatic discussion of "real politics": evaluative understanding, imaginative orientation, and ideological critique.

EVALUATIVE UNDERSTANDING

Geuss argues that citizens should learn to recognize the way institutions constrain individual actions and what patterns these actions reveal over time. Pattern recognition is what citizens need to learn, whether it is patterns of climate change, patterns of aggressive behaviour, or patterns of economic development. "Understand how acting together in a given society actually works and explain why certain decisions are taken, why certain projects fail, and others succeed, or why social and political action exhibits the patterns it does. This requires understanding history, including the history of political theory."[14] Geuss's emphasis on pattern recognition is consistent with Wolin's approach to the history of political theory and politics. These patterns of "social and political action," according to Geuss, are the product of "real" institutional power, not mythic forces. While Wolin is careful not to divide politics into a real world and a fantasy world of non-existent myths, he would agree with Geuss that political myths don't play the same role in politics as "real" institutions. According to Wolin, "when myth begins to govern decision-makers in a world where ambiguity and stubborn facts abound, the result is a disconnect between the actors and reality."[15] In other words, political myths can "govern decision-makers" to the point where their actions are not connected as they should be to institutional reality, but obviously that doesn't mean myths never have real impact when they are believed and acted upon, especially by "decision-makers."

Then, according to Geuss, *evaluative* understanding requires pair-wise comparisons, and the grounds of the evaluation can vary. They may "include assessments of efficiency, simplicity, perspicuousness, aesthetic appeal, etc."[16] If we turn again to Wolin to flesh this out, we begin with the fact that the *demos* acquire evaluative political knowledge on the job, as it were, by participating locally. Wolin acknowledges that "demotic rationality is rooted in a provincialism where commonality is experienced as everyday reality and 'civic spirit' is unapologetic." However, this is not all that is needed, and Wolin suggests that the *demos* must include others who have the additional experience needed for evaluative understanding. "In that setting schools, businesses, law enforcement, the environment, the conduct of public officials, taxation all have an immediacy. That immediacy serves to chasten the actions of those entrusted with power, whether as council members, teachers, business-owners, police, or environmentalists."[17] Local participation may teach citizens the political arts of compromise and negotiation. But a realistic political education must also involve others at the local level who work side by side with industrial, manufacturing, and service sector workers. Wolin calls these other members of the *demos* a "counter-elite of democratic public servants."[18] I will return to this notion of counter-elite public servants within the *demos* and their role as agents and objects of a realistic political education in more detail below.

IMAGINATIVE ORIENTATION

A second element in Geuss's programmatic account of political realism is what he calls "orientation." Humans need a "surveyable image of their place in the world" so that they can locate themselves and their projects in some larger "imaginative structure" that gives them a sense of belonging in the world.[19] Wolin's account of inverted totalitarianism provides this kind of orientation. The history of Superpower and the evaluative language of fugitive democracy are embedded in a layered and shifting "political imaginary" consisting of two "bodies": a "constitutional imaginary" that limits the expansion of power and democratic inclusion and a "power imaginary" that encourages the outward and inward expansion of power as an engine of growth and security.

According to Wolin, the constitutional imaginary in the United States has defined the changing meaning of "We the People." The power imaginary has applied pressure on the frontiers. At times, the resulting "orientation" has been a settler-imaginary-facing "West." At other times it has been a New Deal imaginary oriented towards a more inclusive national community. Both a power imaginary and a constitutional imaginary are necessary elements in a realistic political theory. However, Wolin argues, the balance between the two has gradually been upset as a Cold War power imaginary has become dominant. "One consequence of the pursuit of an expansive power imaginary is the blurring of the lines separating truth telling from self-deception and lying. From within a Cold War imaginary, "power is not so much justified as sanctified, excused by the lofty ends it proclaims, ends that commonly are antithetical to the power legitimated by the constitutional imaginary."[20] This imaginative orientation of imperial benevolence is both fantasy and reality. Its promise of benevolence and harmony are fantasy. Its existence as a structure of power that those who benefit from it endorse as a benefit for all is a reality.

IDEOLOGY CRITIQUE

A third element in Geuss's account of realistic political theory is ideological critique. Realistic political theory should be able to discern how "Power can be used to indirectly shape opinions, attitudes, and desires, and thus to manufacture what looks like consent."[21] Realistic political theory should provide a critical understanding of structures of power and their history within an "imaginative structure" that can distinguish between truth and ideological falsehoods. According to Geuss, this kind of critical discernment will require some "conceptual innovation." Ideology critique goes beyond solving an existing problem; it requires identifying a problem or question that wasn't clearly visible before. For example, according to Geuss, "the State" was such a conceptual innovation. Its introduction required not merely a certain word but also a certain kind of theory, which has a strong normative component. "When they were introduced, concepts like 'the state' did not exactly mirror any fully preexisting reality, because using these concepts represented as much an aspiration as a description."[22]

Geuss, like Wolin, is adamant that applied ethics and liberal political philosophy are ahistorical and understate, at best, the patterns and dynamics of power. They both single out John Rawls for particularly harsh criticism. Geuss writes, "The 'original position' is obviously not at all a very good model for political deliberation or action, among other reasons because there is no discussion and no *Kairos* in it."[23] Wolin concurs. In the original position one abstracts from the supposed malfunctions of a free market, not taking into consideration their perennial existence. In Wolin's review of Rawls's later work, *Political Liberalism*, he objects to "the near invisibility of the [capitalist] economy, of its power relationships, and the interconnections between corporate and political powers."[24] This omission is exacerbated by the ahistorical nature of liberalism. "The most crucial omission from the original position is any recognition that a political society inevitably carries a historical burden as part of its identity, that it has committed past injustices whose reminders still define many of its members. Rawls, by contrast, gives a picture of an expiated community that has settled its injustices on terms that merely need to be recalled, as in the antislavery amendments to the constitution."[25] Guard rails, amendments, and recollections are not enough to address the presence of past injustices. The legacies of mass atrocities and oppression are not erased so easily. The history of Reconstruction after the Civil War in the United States is one example among many. This attempt to make American democracy more inclusive through the abolition of slavery quickly ran aground because of the deep-seated racist ideology that rationalized the economic interests of slave owners and others who benefited from this system.

For Wolin, this kind of philosophical device comes dangerously close to lying. He argues that "Lying goes to the heart of the never-ending questions, what is the world really like? what is in fact happening?"[26] Lying is not a matter of practical necessity in extraordinary circumstances, that is, the lesser of two evils. We are especially susceptible to buying into lies of abstraction because we have become conditioned by "a relentless culture of advertising and its exaggerations, false claims, and fantasies" produced and marketed at high speed. In this context, "Lying is more than deception ... At bottom, lying is the expression of a will to power."[27] The realist wants to know how what passes for reality actually has been foisted on us. That is, how ideology and propaganda present an apparent reality, which then can become actual reality when the propagandist takes office and can enact policies that make the world conform to his lies.

Superpowers' leaders do not win us over through charisma and rhetorical skill. Nor do they simply buy us off. They capitalize on a culture of branding; a politics of spectacle; a denial of history; and repeated, rapid-fire distraction.[28] In this matrix of fears, lies, and obfuscation, the very pace of change makes recognizing the patterns and dynamics of power and the presence of the past impossible for individuals. "Rapid change not only blunts the collective conscience but dims the collective memory ... Rapid change is not a neutral force, a natural phenomenon that exists independently of human will, or of considerations of power, comparative advantage and ideological biases. It is a 'reality' constructed from decisions arrived at within a certain framework – itself not accidental. We might call it the 'political economy of change.'"[29] The result is a Manichean universe in which information and knowledge are controlled by social media corporations and political leaders become their puppets.[30] In other words, we are on the doorstep of inverted totalitarianism. What can be done in practice to avoid succumbing?

Realistic Political Education in Practice

In his introduction to the collection of essays *Political Theory and Political Education*, published in 1980 as part of the Princeton Legacy Library, Melvin Richter noted that the essays originally were presented at an international meeting of the Conference for the Study of Political Thought. The purpose of the presentations was fairly straightforward: how did pre-eminent political theorists of the time think students of political theory should be educated? While the presentations were given in the early 1970s, by 1980 times had changed. The United States was falling into a deep recession, and institutions of higher education were beginning to reduce their investments in the humanities, including political theory.

One of the essays in *Political Theory and Political Education* was "Political Theory and Political Commentary" by Wolin. In it he described the responsibilities of the commentator in terms of political education, but in retrospect his argument is somewhat surprising, given his earlier writings in the 1960s on the student movement and the Vietnam War. In this essay he wrote that "Political education by commentary is not intended to galvanize the citizenry into action but to keep it gently oscillating between resignation and hope."[31] This should come naturally to the political theorist, according to Wolin.

However, Wolin was disappointed that most political commentary lacked even this much courage. Instead, commentary was striving to counsel those in power rather than help the *demos* see the familiar in an unfamiliar political light. Commentary on Watergate, he noted, turned the events into a criminal and constitutional problem, missing an important opportunity to illuminate a deeper political reality.[32]

In January 1981 the first issue of *democracy: A Journal of Political Renewal and Radical Change* was published under Wolin's editorship. He still believed that commentary should shift public conversation away from public policy and towards public goods, not divisible economic costs and benefits. However, working collaboratively with other scholars and activists, Wolin's own ambitions for political commentary was taking on a sharper focus. "Our aim," he wrote in the first issue, "will be to encourage the development of an historical and theoretical understanding around the concrete problems of the present. We cannot offer recipes or specific policies, but we can bring a critical approach that will illumine what is at stake for the future of democracy in current debates; how specific problems have come to have their present form; and what kinds of broad alternatives, consistent with democracy, are possible."[33]

Each issue of *democracy* was thematic, and the theme of the first issue was "The Current Crisis." Wolin wrote, "Policy questions are real and so are experts, but the fundamental questions provoked by a genuine crisis are not about policy and are not the monopoly of experts ... A crisis is not something that is but a condition that becomes. It is a gathering of the past and the present crystallized in opposing forces and ideas."[34] The crisis is explored in the first issue by one of the editorial board members, Lawrence Goodwyn, in his essay "Organizing Democracy: The Limits of Theory and Practice." An historian, Goodwyn retells the stories of three related cases of popular democratic resistance to economic injustice in order to explain how the past, when understood and evaluated realistically, can be a source of renewal in the present.[35]

None of these movements was successful by itself. But together, they illustrate how a crisis unfolds and what "alternatives, consistent with democracy, are possible." In his book devoted to this history of agrarian revolt in the United States, Goodwyn shows that before William Jennings Bryant emerged as the leader of the populist cause, populism was defined by concrete political programs designed to contest the power of private banks and the way in which agriculture was financed and insured.[36] Democratic movements, Goodwyn argues, should not be reduced to an abstract label (e.g., populism), let alone a single leader. He tells a similar story in the article in *democracy* about "Regulation" and the role that Samuel Adams played in Massachusetts at the time of the American Revolution. Goodwyn's point is that history and theory, when done with an eye on local power struggles, can reveal lines of continuity in democratic politics that are obscured by abstraction. Otherwise, "What we know – the intellectual content of modern sophistication – is a cover for modern resignation in the face of overwhelming centralized power."[37]

Political commentary was one way in which Wolin sought to imaginatively reorient the *demos* and evaluatively understand real power. While short-lived, *democracy* still has an important story to tell. The writers that Wolin recruited avoided abstract "modern sophistication" in order to understand and evaluate dominant structures of power, orient citizens towards the goods they held in common, and distinguish between reality and ideology (which is not the same as a democratic political imaginary). Goodwyn's commentary was designed to cast doubt on the ideological dismissal of populism as a form of irrational mass politics so that this reality could be addressed.

Wolin reserved some of his own strongest political commentary in *democracy* for the politics of higher education. In the second issue, "Democracy's State," he wrote about the history of higher education and how it reflected the social and economic class interests of society, culminating in proposals by the Reagan Administration to reduce funding for the humanities in favour of greater emphasis on science and technology. What will be left, Wolin argued, is another version of a two-tiered system of higher education, this time "advanced scientific education for the few, technical education for the many."[38] The primary audience for this essay was not administrators and politicians who favoured science and technology over the humanities, but faculty who were being told that in order to survive, education would have to be managed like a business. Faculty, Wolin feared, were the last line of defence and most vulnerable to ideological cooptation. Which leads us back to the role of counter-elite public servants in the *demos*.

The counter-elite includes teachers, but also security, health care, and social workers. Muralists, street theatre companies, graffiti artists, and poets also can play this role. Their contribution to the political education of the *demos* comes not only from their expert skills but from the way they collaborate within the *demos* in an education in power. One writer who described this kind of practice was Myles Horton. His work with labour organizers and civil rights workers at the Highlander Center illustrates how one can respect the knowledge of the *demos* by collaborating with them to reach a fuller understanding of their own history and the structures of power that they confront.[39]

For Wolin, real citizenship is grounded in human relationships. In an issue of *democracy* entitled "The Democratic Citizen," Wolin summarizes what it means to be a political being, not just an occasional voter or an enraged protester. The democratic citizen, he argues, rejects this abstract notion of participation in favour of what Geuss calls "locatedness" that draws its sustenance from circumscribed relationships. What makes this person a "political being" is participation in a network of relationships of power.

> These relationships are the sources from which political beings draw power – symbolic, material, and psychological – and that enable them to act together. For true political power involves not only acting so as to effect decisive changes; it also means the capacity to receive power, to be acted upon, force that is generated; it is experience, sensibility, wisdom, even melancholy distilled from the diverse relations and circles we move within. Democratic power, accordingly, bears the marks of its diverse origins – family, school, church, workplace, etc. – and, as a result, everything turns on an ability to establish practices whose form will not distort the manifold origins of power.[40]

These are the places and relationships in which counter-elite public servants can work side by side with other members of the *demos* as both agents and objects of realistic political education. It is how the *demos* prepares for what Wolin called "the long pull" and what Horton called the "long haul." In families and their penumbra consisting of social workers, daycare workers, public health workers, and neighbours, the parents and children learn to address the matrices of power that determine their ability to survive and sometimes flourish. In schools where students, parents, guardians, teachers, counselors, and coaches encounter and engage each other, decisions can be made more democratically that determine promotion, retention, reward, and punishment. In religious institutions congregants, choirs, and lay ministers struggle to respond collectively to the abuse of power in their midst. Finally, in the workplace, workers, shop stewards, safety inspectors, and security guards struggle to align the relations of production, the forces of production, and the means of communication to achieve greater human security.

The counter-elite public servants in these diverse groups are sometimes professionals with degrees in social work, school psychology, public health, and labour relations, but not always. By sharing these spaces with other members of the *demos*, together they are able to evaluatively understand what they are up against, imaginatively orient themselves to a meaningful world of their own making, and critically confront the ideological misrepresentation of existing structures of power. These complex and generative "demotic moments" are not sparks or angry outbursts. Participants are civil, as Wolin says, in two senses. They show radical poise and restraint in the face of violence and repression, and they can be the seeds of social movements.[41]

The Highlander Center provided a space for these generative "demotic moments" that can lead to sustained social movements. Now I want to describe a school with which I have had firsthand experience. It is the story of the creation and growth of a liberal arts and humanities program organized around a community engagement pedagogy located within a large public university. On 14 December 2006, I wrote to Wolin, describing the creation of a new residential college at Michigan State University that I had been chosen to lead.[42] I hoped that his experience at University of California Santa Cruz would enable him to offer me some advice.

Dear Sheldon,

… We are hiring new faculty right now – only two from MSU departments and the rest new to MSU – and we are recruiting a first-year class of students for fall 2007.

We have a new, well-equipped space and after some resistance we have moderate support from the departments of Theater, Art, Music (now a college), History, Philosophy, Linguistics, and some of the world language departments. The real challenge, I believe, will be hiring a group of faculty who are committed to this enterprise, can work collaboratively on it, and can press the curriculum into coherent shape. As we have begun to interview faculty, it is clear that we need people who have a great range (e.g., they can teach world history and cultural studies) and also a passion for their own particular area of expertise. We will also need people who have a knack for civic engagement projects and experiential learning, whether it is in a poetry, dance, or sculpture workshop or it is in a study abroad program in Costa Rica. Finding 16 faculty and 10 graduate fellows who fit this bill will be hard.

I was hoping that Wolin would recognize this as an institutional space in which counter-elite public servants could be developed and work effectively. Instead, he responded somewhat sceptically. Citing his Santa Cruz experience after he left UC Berkeley, he warned that indeed it is hard to find faculty who can flourish as scholars and teachers in this kind of residential environment. The best scholars will eventually move on, and the ones that do remain may not be strong enough to meet the tenure and promotion requirements of a Research I institution. I could see that some of our new hires were going to struggle in this way, but I also believed that the existing tenure and promotion criteria could be expanded to recognize participatory action research, community-based scholarship, and community-based arts activism. Time, I thought, was on our side, and by the time that our young faculty were reviewed for tenure and promotion, the Residential College in the Arts and Humanities (RCAH) would be in a position to make the case that most, not all, of them were doing the kind of engaged interdisciplinary scholarship and creative work that the university recognized. They would become counter-elite public servants.

What kept the faculty, students, and staff engaged, however, was not my administrative savvy. They were successful because of the particular way they combined the different talents and skills of all of the parties, especially our community partners and artists. The community artists proved to be catalysts who facilitated communication between counter-elite public servants and other members of the *demos*. One of our community partners served as a space for real political education and the development of counter-elite public servants through the collaborative and catalytic influence of RCAH faculty.[43]

For twelve years, students and faculty from RCAH have been working with Peckham employees and staff on several projects to empower the Peckham workers with disabilities, many of whom are refugees and immigrants. In 2013, one of the RCAH art faculty began working in the Peckham art studio with RCAH students paired up with Peckham employees. The employees began to paint and draw their stories as they recounted them to the RCAH students. Gradually their artwork was large enough to fill the 40'×200' factory shop floor wall.

The project was called Art@Work for two reasons.[44] The installation brought art to the workplace, giving it a more humane feeling. But it was also artists working in the workplace to transform relationships and create a common bond between students, faculty, and employees. The Art Wall became a mirror in which both students and employees could see themselves working together daily to produce a common good, the Art Wall. The catalyst in this case, the faculty artist, then worked with another group of students and many of the same Peckham employees to repopulate the Art Wall. Art@Work 2.0 will have more through lines, photographs, and visual depth. It will be connected to video animations in adjoining spaces. The goal is to share the stories more widely and make the space even more inclusive.

Photo by Stephen Esquith

Each panel told a story. Some were the journeys that the employees had taken to Lansing. Some were stories about their family life that they cherished most.

Photo by Becky Shink

There are many other counter-elite public servants working at Peckham, including the psychological counselling staff, other health care professionals, and career counsellors. But without the additional catalytic contribution of the RCAH artist, this extended demotic "moment" – five years and counting – would not have occurred and the greater sense of dignity and political consciousness would not have developed.

Conclusion

Each semester since we enrolled students in RCAH in fall 2007 and until I returned to the faculty in summer 2021, I wrote a "Dean's Message" on our college website in order to frame issues, prompt discussions, and address questions. It is not a blog; it is written for a very specific audience with no easy way to reply with comments online. The early instalments were written to tell students, faculty, staff, and parents what our mission was, to announce visiting artists, and rehearse the general values of a liberal arts education. The Art@Work project highlighting inclusion and integration was the subject of one message.

I intentionally avoided creating a blog, tweeting on social media, and generally holding forth on a daily or weekly basis on public issues such as freedom of speech, even when they had a direct relationship to RCAH's mission. On the few occasions when I expressed my views to a wider audience, it was through a more traditionally edited magazine or newspaper article. However, one could argue that messages posted once each semester are not much different, and because they don't afford a space for immediate responses and feedback the way social media do, they have little impact.

My answer is that while RCAH relies heavily on social media to recruit prospective students, the rapidity of this online discourse leaves little time for self-reflection, little time for seeing the familiar in a new light. It is a space in which likes, dislikes, and retweets are the measure of influence, but it has little to do with debate, discussion, and critical reflection. The *demos* may have to respond in a moment, but that should be the beginning of a process of reflection and practice. The role of counter-elite public servants in higher education is to think more slowly in order to actively listen to alternative points of view before acting, not to outscore opponents in a competitive race to the finish line.

One oft-mentioned candidate for this catalytic role is the public intellectual.[45] But what is needed is not an intellectual vanguard publishing radical calls to action in hopes of "creating a public." What is needed is a network of ordinary people, including counter-elite public servants, who can share the political responsibilities of everyday life, help repair historical injustices, and build more inclusive local institutions. How will realistic political education bring the *demos* together? The first thing to recognize is that the *demos* is not an undifferentiated mass, ignorant of the challenges they face and in need of enlightenment. What they need is to share their stories. Counter-elite public servants can help them do this in languages and genres that resonate across borders.

One such public servant, who moved primarily outside the spheres of official government but was not afraid to work within them when necessary, was the social worker, peace activist, and feminist Jane Addams. She wrote, "We are learning that a standard of social ethics is not attained by traveling a sequestered byway, but by mixing on the thronged and common road where all must turn out for one another, and at least see the size of one another's burdens."[46]

While not an artist herself, Addams viewed art, literature, and especially drama, if properly interpreted, as forms of democratic political education capable of motivating a transcultural and transnational political responsibility to reduce severe violence. Addams's term to describe democratic political education was acquaintanceship, and she hoped to cultivate this kind of politically informed companionship in Hull-House, but not only there. Among the many activities that occurred in and through Hull-House, theatre in particular was designed by Addams to bridge the gap between neighbourhood immigrant and poor women and children on one side and the middle- and upper-class residents and patrons of Hull-House on the other.[47]

While she did influence national and global debates, she remained rooted in the local concerns of ordinary persons. She was not an influencer in today's sense, paid by advertisers for the number of clicks on her website. Instead, she created a meaningful location, free of ideological misrepresentation, and built upon accurate information all the way down to public sanitation. In that space artists, among others, can voice the concerns of the *demos*, can visualize them, and can recall them in verse. Social workers, physician assistants, and classroom teachers have a political role to hear the public content in the concerns of the *demos*, see connections between local issues, and build networks from the ground up that can influence regional, national, and global political debates.

NOTES

1 Steven Levitsky and Daniel Ziblatt, *How Democracies Die* (New York: Crown, 2018); and Harry G. Frankfurt, *On Bullshit* (Princeton, NJ: Princeton University Press, 2005).

2 Sheldon S. Wolin, *Democracy Incorporated: Managed Democracy and the Specter of Inverted Totalitarianism*, new ed. (Princeton, NJ: Princeton University Press, 2017). Chris Hedges makes this point in his "Introduction to the 2017 Edition," xxvii. For a more equivocal reading of Wolin's interpretation of history and the history of political theory that treats it as a form of archaism, see Lucy Cane, "Sheldon Wolin and Democracy: Seeing Through Loss," *New Political Science*, Vol. 40, No. 2 (2018), 227–45.

3 Seyla Benhabib, *Perspectives on Politics*, Vol. 8, No. 1 (March 2010); and George Kateb, "Wolin as a Critic of Democracy," in *Democracy and Vision: Sheldon Wolin and the Vicissitudes of the Political,* ed. Aryeh Botwinick and William E. Connolly (Princeton, NJ: Princeton University Press, 2001), 44.

4 For a similar interpretation of Wolin's view of the "quotidian" dimension of democratic action, see Jason Frank, "Is Radical Democracy a Tradition?" *Contemporary Political Theory*, Vol. 16, No.1 (2017), 76–82.

5 Sheldon S. Wolin, *Politics and Vision: Continuity and Innovation in Western Political Thought,* expanded ed. (Princeton, NJ: Princeton University Press, 2004), 26.

6 Wolin, *Democracy Incorporated*, 61.

7 Wolin, *Democracy Incorporated*, 347–8.

8 W. Robert Connor, *Thucydides* (Princeton, NJ: Princeton University Press, 1984).

9 Sheldon S. Wolin, "The Destructive Sixties and Postmodern Conservatism," in *Fugitive Democracy and Other Essays*, ed. Nicholas Xenos (Princeton, NJ: Princeton University Press, 2016), 330–47.

10 *Sheldon S. Wolin and John H. Schaar, The Berkeley Rebellion and Beyond: Essays on Politics and Education in the Technological Society* (New York: New York Review of Books, 1970), 13.

11 Simone Weil, "The Iliad, Poem of Might," in *The Simone Weil Reader*, ed. George A. Panichas (New York: McKay Co., 1977), 153–83.

12 Wendy Brown, *Undoing the Demos: Neo-Liberalism's Stealth Revolution* (New York: Zone Books, 2015), 19. Also see Joan Tronto, "Political Theory: A Vocation for Democrats?" *Contemporary Political Theory*, Vol. 16, No. 1 (2017), 82–9.

13 Wolin, *Democracy Incorporated*, 249.

14 Raymond Geuss, *Philosophy and Real Politics* (Princeton, NJ: Princeton University Press, 2008), 38.

15 Wolin, *Democracy Incorporated*, 14.

16 Geuss, *Philosophy and Real Politics*, 39.

17 Wolin, *Democracy Incorporated*, 289.

18 Wolin, *Democracy Incorporated*, 291. For an opposing argument in favour of "unelected representatives," see John Keane, *Power and Humility: The Future of Monitory Democracy* (Cambridge: Cambridge University Press, 2018), 171–9.

19 Geuss, *Philosophy and Real Politics*, 40–2.

20 Wolin, *Democracy Incorporated*, 20.

21 Geuss, *Philosophy and Real Politics*, 51–3.

22 Geuss, *Philosophy and Real Politics*, 45.

23 Geuss, *Philosophy and Real Politics*, 72–3.

24 Sheldon S. Wolin, "The Liberal/Democratic Divide: On Rawls' Political Liberalism," *Political Theory*, Vol. 24, No. 1 (February 1996), 115.

25 Sheldon S. Wolin, "The Liberal/Democratic Divide," 116. See, for example, Eric Foner, *The Second Founding: How the Civil War and Reconstruction Remade the Constitution* (New York: W.W. Norton, 2019).

26 Wolin, *Democracy Incorporated*, 261.

27 Wolin, *Democracy Incorporated*, 263.

28 Wolin, *Democracy Incorporated*, 268. Also see Jason Stanley, *How Fascism Works: The Politics of Us and Them* (New York: Random House, 2018), xiv.

29 Wolin, *Democracy Incorporated*, 275.

30 Siva Vaidhyanathan, *Antisocial Media: How Facebook Disconnects Us and Undermines Democracy* (New York: Oxford University Press, 2018).

31 Sheldon S. Wolin, "Political Theory and Political Commentary," in *Political Theory and Political Education*, ed. Melvin Richter (Princeton, NJ: Princeton University Press, 1980), 196.

32 Wolin, "Political Theory and Political Commentary," 197.

33 Sheldon S. Wolin, "Editorial," *democracy*, Vol. 1, No. 1 (January 1981), 5.

34 Sheldon S. Wolin, "Theme Note," *democracy*, Vol. 1, No. 1 (January 1981), 8.

35 Lawrence Goodwyn, "Organizing Democracy: The Limits of Theory and Practice," *democracy*, Vol. 1, No. 1 (January 1981), 52.

36 Lawrence Goodwyn, *The Populist Moment: A Short History of the Agrarian Revolt in America* (New York: Oxford University Press, 1978).

37 Goodwyn, "Organizing Democracy," 60.

38 Sheldon S. Wolin, "Higher Education and the Politics of Knowledge," *democracy*, Vol. 1, No. 2 (April 1981), 52.

39 Myles Horton, *The Long Haul: An Autobiography*, with Judith Kohn and Herbert Kohl (New York: Teachers College Press, 1998).

40 Sheldon S. Wolin, "What Revolutionary Action Means Today," *democracy*, Vol. 2, No. 4 (Fall 1992), 26–7.

41 See, for example, David Graeber, *The Democracy Project: A History, A Crisis, A Movement* (New York: Spiegel and Grau, 2013).

42 http://rcah.msu.edu.

43 https://www.peckham.org/.

44 https://msutoday.msu.edu/news/2013/artwork-tells-stories-of-peckham-clients/.

45 Corey Robin, "How Intellectuals Create a Public," *Chronical of Higher Education*, 22 January 2016. https://www.chronicle.com/article/How-Intellectuals-Create-a/234984.

46 Jane Addams, *Democracy and Social Ethics* (Champaign: University of Illinois Press, 2002), 7. See, generally, Louise W. Knight, *Citizen: Jane Addams and the Struggle for Democracy* (Chicago: University of Chicago Press, 2005).

47 Jane Addams, *Twenty Years at Hull-House* (New York: New American Library, 1981).

7 Wolin and Said on Political Education, Vision, and Intellectual Tradition

LUCY CANE

Introduction and Overview

In this essay, I critically explore Sheldon Wolin's understanding of the relationship between political theory and political education by bringing his work into conversation with literary and cultural critic Edward Said.[1] Wolin sometimes uses the term "political education" broadly to include a range of institutionalized and non-institutionalized experiences, as when he refers to the sixties as "a decade of prolonged popular political education unique in recent American history."[2] However, his detailed discussions of political education tend to focus more specifically on the experiences available in four-year universities. He first analyses the possibilities for political education within the university in a series of articles in the *New York Review of Books* (1965–70). These articles, co-authored with John Schaar, closely engage with the ongoing student revolts on their campus at the University of California, Berkeley. Through Wolin's analysis of the educational crisis driving these revolts, he discloses an ideal of liberal arts education that would remain relatively consistent throughout his career: the liberal arts should provide a political education in the sense of preparing people for a life of citizenship. In order to preserve such a mission, he argues, universities must resist the prioritization of scientific over humanistic knowledge and the ever-increasing specialization of academic fields. A political education in the liberal arts also depends on cultivating meaningful interaction between faculty and students and on taking the latter seriously as agents of the educational process.

Wolin's work in the 1960s is notable not only for defending this general ideal of liberal arts education but also for advancing a particular understanding of the sub-discipline of political theory. My interest in this essay lies in exploring the possible disjuncture between a broad ideal of the liberal arts and this narrower understanding of political theory. *Politics and Vision* (1960) seeks to save political theory from marginalization amid the ascendency of behavioural political science. It does so by examining the visionary thinking of canonical theorists and suggesting that familiarity with this intellectual tradition is a key element of political education. After the frustrated activism of the late 1960s, Wolin offers a more high-flown account of his sub-discipline in the article "Political Theory as a Vocation" (1969). Here he claims that political theory is an "epic" enterprise that "seeks to reassemble the whole political world" and is uniquely capable of transforming political values.[3]

While Wolin's early formulation of the prescriptive task of political theory has been inspiring for subsequent generations of theorists, I argue that it sits uneasily with his broader ideal of political education in a couple of ways. For one thing, his understanding of the epic theorist, who attempts to comprehend and transform the entire world through their thinking, may not leave room for his more democratic impulse to allow students and other citizens to shape their own forms of life. For another, Wolin ties his notion of political theory to a relatively narrow Western canon. We might question whether the elevation of such an intellectual tradition accords with his criticism of specialization, as well as whether it prepares people for citizenship in a dynamic, pluralistic, and globalized society.

The potential drawbacks of Wolin's influential understanding of political theory are fruitfully illuminated through a comparison with Said. Wolin and Said worked within different disciplines and did not engage with each other's texts. However, their views of political education are in some ways quite alike, especially in their criticisms of academic specialization and their professed commitments to granting students agency in the educational process. These two thinkers are also both driven by an aspiration to offer broad, holistic perspectives on the world that maintain an emancipatory horizon. Finally, they share an abiding interest in studying the Western canon and are critical of some recent "postmodern" theoretical trends. Nevertheless, there are key differences between the ways that Wolin and Said negotiate their respective impulses to offer holistic perspectives on the world and to engage the canon, and these differences are generative for thinking through the possibilities for political education within the university more generally.

I argue that Said would always have looked sceptically on the potential chauvinism of epic political theory as Wolin defines it in "Political Theory as a Vocation." Over time, Wolin too distances himself from some of his epic aspirations. He comes to realize that a radically democratic theory must be more multifaceted and consciously incomplete than epic political theories of the past. Accordingly, in his later work, Wolin aspires to a holistic perspective only in a tentative and diagnostic sense, by advancing an overarching diagnosis of "inverted totalitarianism." Wolin and Said thus reach relatively similar conclusions about how to balance the value of a holistic perspective with an awareness of the potential chauvinism of totalizing theory.

I have found that more significant differences remain between the two thinkers regarding how they approach canonical intellectual traditions. While Said does defend his interest in the Western canon, he is always more critical than Wolin of the imperialist global contexts and the inadequacies of such intellectual traditions. Accordingly, Said has a far more expansive view of the archives that non-specialist academics ought to engage. I argue that a Wolinian approach to political theory could be brought closer to Wolin's own ideal of political education through an appreciation of Said's notions of counterpoint, exile, and worldliness.

Ideals of Political Education in Wolin and Said

The student revolts at Berkeley in the 1960s were driven in part by specific restrictions that the university had placed on student speech. However, Wolin and Schaar explain that the students were also reacting against the generally technocratic direction of the institution. The university was becoming "a mere research factory and training institution," as it focused increasingly on boosting research volume and providing students with training in various scientific, technological, and managerial fields.[4] Consequently, Berkeley was losing sight of its traditional, political purpose of preparing people for citizenship through a broad training in the liberal arts. To rediscover this purpose, Wolin and Schaar suggest, it would be necessary for the university to rethink its prioritization of scientific and technical over humanistic knowledge. It would also be necessary to lessen the "centrifugal tendencies of specialization" that deprive students of broad, integrative perspectives on the world.[5]

Relatedly, Wolin and Schaar worry that the Berkeley administration was elevating bureaucratic ideals of efficiency above values of teaching and learning, allowing for larger class sizes and more impersonal methods of instruction. These developments made it more difficult for faculty and students at Berkeley to engage with each other meaningfully. Students were being conceived as passive consumers of a relatively anonymous delivery of educational services, rather than as agents of their own education. In order to further promote the agency of students, Wolin and Schaar couple their defence of traditional liberal arts education with the radical suggestion that students should be incorporated into university decision-making and, within limits, actively shape curricula.[6]

Wolin's ideal of a political education in the liberal arts remains relatively consistent throughout his career. In the later essay "Higher Education and the Politics of Knowledge" (1981), he continues to worry about the prioritization of scientific and technical knowledge and the trend towards specialization.[7] In *The Presence of The Past* (1989), he defends his broad, humanistic ideal of education, bemoaning the neglect of "interpretive modes of inquiry."[8] Similarly, in his 1989 interview with Bill Moyers, Wolin argues that only "soft subjects," such as literature, philosophy, history, and "some of the softer social sciences," can empower students to interpret their world critically.[9] In his later work, Wolin focuses less on the eclipse of such subjects by scientific and technological knowledge and more on trends towards specialization and political irrelevance within humanistic disciplines themselves. In 2001, he dismisses dominant research trends in humanistic disciplines as promoting "theoretic theory" that is not responsive to events in the world and is removed from the goal of broadly preparing students for citizenship.[10]

While Said rarely tackles the plight of liberal arts education as explicitly as Wolin, we can glean from his texts some similar ideals of political education. Said too seeks to champion the role of a humanistic university education in preparing people for citizenship, and he regularly bemoans the threat posed to such an education by the trend towards specialization. In *The World, The Text, and the Critic* (1983), for instance, Said lambasts the "cult of professional expertise" and the "triumph of the ethic of professionalism" within the academy.[11] In *Culture and Imperialism* (1993), he condemns intellectuals who lionize "magic keys, special jargons and instruments, curtained-off practices."[12] Said also underscores the importance of student agency in the educational process. In an interview entitled "I've Always Learnt During the Class" (1997), he describes his dialogic teaching style and credits students with sparking many of his ideas.[13] For Said, as for Wolin, the humanistic intellectual should have a broad perspective on the world, take students seriously, and be passionately engaged not with policymakers but with the public at large.[14] These shared ideals provide a starting point for assessing how well Wolin and Said's understandings of their own scholarly activity cohere with their broader goal of political education.

The Vocation of Political Theory in Wolin's Early Work

As Wolin was co-authoring general-audience articles on the Berkeley unrest in the 1960s, he was also earning a reputation as a champion of the specific subdiscipline of political theory. From his perspective, the discipline of political science had been seduced in the post-war period by the general glorification of scientific over humanistic knowledge. This was expressed in the "behavioural revolution," through which political scientists sought to generate value-neutral, evidence-based knowledge about politics that could contribute to incremental policy reform. Compared to this supposedly scientific enterprise, political theory increasingly seemed outdated and ideological.

In response to the potential marginalization of political theory, Wolin surveys the work of canonical political theorists in *Politics and Vision* (1960) in order to demonstrate the ongoing relevance of the field. At the start of the book, he claims that political theory is distinguished from other forms of political knowledge by its efforts to grasp "what is 'common' to the whole community," to view society "in the round."[15] He explains, furthermore, that the comprehensive visions of political theorists are able to engage with urgent problems of the day and to imagine ways out of them. In order to perform this civic role, Wolin suggests, political theory ought to be relatively accessible. Accordingly, he insists that his study of canonical thinkers should be conceived "not so much an antiquarian venture as a form of political education."[16] Yet, because *Politics and Vision* is largely a survey of past thinkers, it leaves unclear what form new political visions might take. Wolin does not attempt here to outline his own prescriptive vision of the political beyond a vague call to embrace "citizenship."[17] The text might also leave us wondering whether the history of political theory, as Wolin defines it, is confined to the kind of Western canonical thinkers he surveys.

Wolin offers a more high-flown account of the enterprise of political theory in his influential article "Political Theory as a Vocation" (1969). In order to understand the special impact of this article, it is important to grasp some key aspects of the intellectual and political contexts in which it appeared. First, over the course of the 1960s, Wolin had perceived an increased antagonism between political theorists and political scientists.[18] Consequently, whereas *Politics and Vision* suggests simply that theory should be salvaged alongside more "scientific" approaches of politics, "Vocation" more combatively asserts the superiority of theory in the face of attacks from empirical colleagues. Second, Wolin's arguments in "Vocation" should be understood in their political context. He had grown frustrated with what he understood to be the descent of youth activism into factionalism and violence, and he attributed this deterioration in part to activists' failure to theorize what they were doing. In 1970, he asserts, "Over the course of its first ten years, the New Left failed to create the new radical theory beyond both liberalism and socialism which the Port Huron Statement had called for.... The anti-intellectualist strain which was present in the movement from the beginning has triumphed."[19] In light of this, "Vocation" seems to be recommending that political theorists step in where activists had failed and bring meaning and coherence to the movements of the preceding decade.

Wolin's argument in "Vocation" draws on Thomas Kuhn's *The Structure of Scientific Revolutions* (1962) to challenge behavioural political scientists' positivist understanding of their method. According to Kuhn, most "ordinary" scientists depend on established paradigms that set underlying assumptions and parameters for research.[20] While behaviouralists believe they are generating value-free, cumulative knowledge, Wolin suggests that they are merely applying the unspoken assumptions of a liberal-pluralist paradigm and thus validating the political status quo. In contrast, Wolin analogizes the political theorist to Kuhn's "extraordinary scientist," who perceives the limitations of an established paradigm and generates a radically new vision. To elaborate this transformative potential of political theory, Wolin formulates an ideal of "epic" political theory, which he claims has been exemplified by canonical thinkers such as Plato and Hobbes.[21] Epic theorists are distinguished by the unusual "magnitudes" of their theorizing, by their efforts to envision the social whole.[22] Their "distinguishing purpose or style" is their prioritization of public affairs over theoretical disputes, and their efforts to transform the world.[23] While *Politics and Vision* (1960) already advanced such a conception of political theory as holistic and politically engaged, "Vocation" (1969) conceives the prescriptive task of theory in more dramatic terms. Here, the epic theorist not only imagines paths out of our current predicaments but also "seeks to reassemble the whole political world."[24] Finally, Wolin demands that epic theorists embrace political theory as a spiritual commitment or "vocation," rather than a mere job.

"Political Theory as a Vocation" was an inspiring text for young political theorists. Harlan Wilson, a former Wolin student, recalls that it made him and others believe that "what we student-theorists were doing was not only intellectually important, but politically important work, in a way no other intellectual activity could equal."[25] However, some of Wolin's claims in this article sit uneasily with his broader ideals of political education.

First, Wolin's idealization of a theorist who "seeks to reassemble the whole political world" seems at odds with his wish to empower students and other citizens to shape their own forms of life. It is no coincidence that epic canonical thinkers were not democrats, and it remains unclear whether an epic political theory could complement a more egalitarian politics. Second, "Vocation" further reinforces Wolin's claim in *Politics and Vision* that political theory is best understood through a tradition of "acknowledged masters" who share a "continuity of preoccupations."[26] This relatively narrow understanding of the canon undermines Wolin's criticism of academic specialization, which would seem to call for a more expansive approach to the archives. Given that we now inhabit a dynamic, pluralistic, and globalized society, a narrow understanding of the canon also risks undermining Wolin's goal of preparing students for citizenship. For example, already in *Politics and Vision,* his articulation of the theoretical tradition leads him to characterize modern political thought as exemplified by the liberalism of John Locke. This obscures other dimensions of modern political cultures that are important for citizens to understand, especially nationalistic and imperialist visions of the political.[27] In the next section of this essay I will address the potential hubris of the epic theorist's ambition to "reassemble the whole political world" by examining Said's view of the value and risks of offering holistic, emancipatory perspectives on the world. I will then turn in the subsequent two sections to address the similarities and differences between Wolin and Said's approaches to canonical intellectual traditions.

Vision, Narrative, and the Value of a Relatively Holistic Perspective

Although Said shares with Wolin some fundamental ideals of political education, I believe that he would always have looked sceptically on the epic enterprise of political theory as it is characterized in "Political Theory as a Vocation." Consider, for instance, Said's discussion of "vision" in *Orientalism* (1978), the book that first established him not only as a literary critic but also as a major cultural critic and public intellectual. This text critically examines "orientalism," both as an academic field occupied by Western experts in "the orient," and as a more general tendency in Western culture to objectify and fetishize cultures deemed oriental. Said criticizes the academic orientalist's pretensions to comprehend the orient as a whole: "The Orientalist surveys the Orient from above, with the aim of getting hold of the whole sprawling panorama before him – culture, religion, mind, history, society. To do this he must see every detail through the device of a set of reductive categories (the Semites, the Muslim mind, the Orient, and so forth)."[28] "The Orientalist," he continues "is principally a kind of agent of such comprehensive visions."[29] His hubris leads to an assumption "that no Oriental can know himself the way an orientalist can."[30] And because the orientalist asserts his vision regardless of countervailing evidence, that vision has a "static" quality.[31] This description of the orientalist's vision is uncomfortably reminiscent of the panoramic vision of society that Wolin ascribes to the epic theorist. Indeed, Said extends his criticism of vision beyond studies of the Orient, stating, "The summational attitude of which I spoke earlier can be regarded as the Orientalist equivalent of attempts in the purely Western humanities to understand culture *as a whole*."[32]

Said contrasts vision with narrative, which he claims is better able to grasp the dynamic and multidimensional nature of social realities:

> Narrative is the specific form taken by written history to counter the permanence of vision.... Narrative asserts the power of men to be born, develop, and die, the tendency of institutions and actualities to change, the likelihood that modernity and contemporaneity will finally overtake "classical" civilizations; above all, it asserts that the domination of reality by vision is no more than a will to power, a will to truth and interpretation, and not an objective condition of history. Narrative, in short, introduces an opposing point of view, perspective, consciousness to the unitary web of vision; it violates the serene Apollonian fictions asserted by vision.[33]

When, after the 1960s, Wolin attempts to formulate his own prescriptive theory of democracy, he does move away from some of the more problematic, visionary elements of epic theory. His first attempt to formulate a democratic theory crystallizes in the early 1980s when he claims that Americans ought

to revive their radical tradition of local, participatory democracy and rediscover an associated "collective identity."[34] In the *Presence of the Past* (1989), he
describes this tradition of democracy as "archaic" and hopes that his account
of it will amount to a "coherent political theory."[35] At times, perhaps, Wolin's
archaic theory of democracy could be understood to reflect the theorist's epic
ambition to "reassemble the whole political world." In 1981, for instance, he
declares an ambition to transform society entirely by stating, "Nothing short of
a long revolution, aimed at deconstituting the present structure of power, makes
much sense."[36] Yet his theory of archaic democracy does not offer the kind of
comprehensive, structured vision of political power offered by epic theorists of
the past, such as Plato or Hobbes. In place of such a blueprint, Wolin offers only
general statements about the value of local power and reminders of exemplary
episodes of democratic participation from history. This "revolutionary," but less
structured, approach to democratic theory is more akin to what Said calls narrative than to vision. Instead of trying to survey, comprehend, and reassemble
the social whole from above, Wolin tells a story about America's democratic
past that is sensitive to historical development and the contingent actions of
individuals and groups. In Said's terms, archaic democracy seems to appreciate
"the power of men to be born, develop and die, the tendency of institutions and
actualities to change."

Nevertheless, while Said expresses a general preference for narrative over
vision, I believe he would still object to the formulation of archaic democracy
that Wolin offers in the 1980s. Wolin's narrative of America's radical democratic
past asserts a "collective identity" of the American people without adequately
engaging with the white and male supremacist aspects of the participatory traditions he invokes.[37] According to Said, such identity-based narratives always
risk eliding or re-inscribing historical exclusions. In the Afterword to *Orientalism* (1994) Said explains "The construction of identity ... involves the construction of opposites and 'others' whose actuality is always subject to the continuous
interpretation and re-interpretation of their differences from 'us.'"[38] Given this
exclusionary potential of identity-based narratives, he goes as far as to state
in *Culture and Imperialism* (1993) that "conventional narrative" is "central to
imperialism's appropriative and dominative attributes."[39] Moreover, in Said's
view, assertions of collective identity are not only exclusionary but also necessarily false. He explains, "cultures are hybrid and heterogeneous ... [they] are so
interrelated and interdependent as to beggar any unitary or simply delineated
description of their individuality."[40] Accordingly, he condemns those who offer
"falsely unifying rubrics like 'America,' 'the West,' or 'Islam' and invent collective identities for large numbers of individuals who are actually quite diverse."[41]

Certainly, Said insists on the right of colonized people to narrate their own
history, and he appreciates the important role that assertions of collective identity have played in the decolonization process. But, while he may find strategic

value in the assertion of national identity by colonized peoples, he is consistently wary of the risks of nationalism in any form. "To tell a simple national story," he argues, "is to repeat, extend, and also to engender new forms of imperialism."[42] Thus, despite Said's personal experience as a colonized subject and a Palestinian in exile, he generally resists any appeal to collective identity. After disclosing that "*Orientalism* is written out of an extremely concrete history of personal loss and national disintegration," he nevertheless repudiates a simple political program of "restored national identity resurgent nationalism" in Palestine.[43] Said most admires anti-colonial thinkers such as Frantz Fanon, whom he understands as appreciating the strategic importance of asserting national identity but whom ultimately "pull away from separatist nationalism toward a more integrative view of human community and human liberation."[44] According to Said, Fanon "wants somehow to bind the European as well as the native together in a new non-adversarial community of awareness and anti-imperialism."[45]

Despite all of Said's criticisms of "vision" and simplistic narratives of collective identity, I still find in his work an impulse to offer relatively broad, holistic perspectives on the world. The breadth of his perspective is evident, for instance, in his influential formulation of "orientalism" as a general phenomenon that is not only "manifest" in a specific academic field but is also "latent" in Western culture as a whole.[46] His ongoing interest in offering such broad diagnoses of social ills leads him in *Culture and Imperialism* to criticize Michel Foucault for moving "further and further away from serious consideration of social wholes."[47] Said also insists, like both visionary political theorists and advocates of collective liberation, that social criticism should maintain an emancipatory horizon. He therefore seems to stand for a kind of cautious humanism, which is reflective about the potential chauvinism of political visions and identity-based narratives, but which somehow still appreciates the value of holistic, emancipatory perspectives on the world.

Eventually, Wolin develops a comparable appreciation of the need to balance a broad, emancipatory perspective with reflexivity about the potential chauvinism of visions and assertions of collective identity. In the 1990s, he seems to accept that his "archaic" narrative of America's collective democratic identity is prone to re-inscribe antidemocratic social hierarchies such as race and gender. It is partly for this reason, I argue, that he shifts from a primarily backward-looking, localist conception of democracy to a conception of "fugitive democracy."[48] The latter incorporates a transgressive impulse that overturns inherited forms and identities in unpredictable ways. In his later work, Wolin also comes increasingly to accept that democratic action must move beyond local communities and engage with large-scale institutions. He thus reaches what I have elsewhere called a "polymorphous" understanding of democracy, consisting of several irreconcilable registers: local, transgressive, and institutional.[49] In other words, Wolin realizes that the meaning of democracy cannot be contained within either a unified vision or a narrative of collective identity, and so he thoroughly abandons the epic aspiration to transform the world in line with such a vision or narrative. The multifaceted, consciously incomplete theory of democracy that emerges from Wolin's later work seems to me more compatible with his ideal of a liberal arts education in which students have agency to formulate their own ways of life.

Although Wolin comes to see that a prescriptive theory of radical democracy cannot be epic in the way he had intended, he remains committed to offering a relatively holistic, emancipatory perspective on the world. He does so in the form of what he calls a "tentative, hypothetical" diagnosis of our contemporary condition of "inverted totalitarianism" in *Democracy Incorporated* (2008).[50] This diagnosis certainly has blind spots, especially concerning the centrality of white supremacy to American political culture. However, it succeeds in offering a relatively broad perspective on our political condition that maintains an emancipatory, democratic horizon without asserting a closed vision or narrative of collective identity. Wolin and Said can therefore be understood as reaching relatively similar conclusions about how to balance the value of a holistic perspective with an awareness of the potential chauvinism of totalizing theory.

The Canon and Postmodernism

More significant differences remain between Wolin and Said regarding how they engage with canonical intellectual traditions, and I believe that this comparison can serve as fruitful challenge to democratic theorists who want their work to contribute to "political education" broadly conceived. Whereas Wolin's sources are often narrowly canonical, Said generally insists on engaging with a wider range of sources in order to develop a broader perspective on the world. I have suggested that Wolin's reliance on the canon in *Politics and Vision* and "Political Theory as a Vocation" sits uneasily with his ideal of a political education that is non-specialized and which prepares students for citizenship. In the decades following these early texts, Wolin never wrote in detail about a feminist or scholar of colour. This persistent lack of interest in engaging a wider range of sources undermines his efforts to develop a more multifaceted perspective on democracy that unsettles the chauvinistic vision of Western humanities and the historical exclusions of American collective identity. When John Gunnell criticizes texts such as *Politics and Vision* for fabricating a "myth" of a coherent tradition of Western political thought, Wolin simply defends the breadth of his understanding of this tradition.[51]

Wolin's ongoing investment in the Western canon becomes especially clear in his critique of "postmodernism." In "On the Theory and Practice of Power" (1988), he takes aim at Foucault as a representative of the "postmodern" trend of understanding power as pervading all aspects of social life. In doing so,

Wolin alleges, Foucault decentres attention from the most important forms of power: the state and corporate capitalism. According to Wolin, Foucault "was not directly concerned with great tyranny but with smaller ones," such as hegemonic sexualities.[52] Moreover, because Foucault understands discourses of expert knowledge to be shot through with power relations, he is sceptical of the emancipatory metanarratives of the Western canon. In Wolin's view, this means that Foucault can assert no principle of legitimacy that might provide a ground for critique. Wolin alleges, "There is no exit because Foucault has closed off any possibility of a privileged theoretical vantage point that would not be infected by the power/knowledge syndrome and would not itself be the expression of a Nietzschean will-to-power."[53] Faced with the de-centring and nihilistic tendencies of such a "postmodern" approach to theorizing, Wolin urges us to revive a "classic" form of theory, which he associates with thinkers such as Plato, Hegel, and Marx.[54] Despite his growing awareness that a radically democratic theory cannot be epic in the manner of such canonical theories, he suggests that the tradition of classic theory continues to provide a privileged vantage point for tackling the major antidemocratic powers that we face. In his later work, Wolin's continues to label as "postmodern" any attempt to engage, practically or theoretically, with forms of power that are not centred on the state or capitalism."[55]

Wolin's critique of "postmodernism" is bound up with his concern about the increasing specialization and political detachment of some theoretical discourses. Whereas in the 1960s he worries about the marginalization of theory, by the turn of the twenty-first century he observes that theory has proliferated across the humanities with "a dizzying series of intellectual permutations – Marxism, critical theory, poststructuralism, deconstructionism, neopragmatism, etc."[56] He worries that the pace of these theoretical developments is out of sync with the slower pace that ought to guide "deliberations about political life."[57] This slower pace has been reflected in the sub-discipline of political theory in "the amount of labor, perhaps even affection, that accompanies its perpetuation of a canon."[58] According to Wolin, the fast pace of theoretical change today generates obscure "theoretic theory" that responds to trivial problems in other texts rather than to major problems in the world.[59]

While aspects of Wolin's critique of "postmodernism" and "theoretic theory" are compelling, I am unsettled by how he uses of this critique to defend his reliance on a relatively narrow Western canon. First, this seems at odds with his critique of academic specialization, which has been central to his understanding of political education since his analysis of the unrest at Berkeley in the 1960s. While Wolin might consider the Western canon to be more accessible than many contemporary permutations of theory, it is nevertheless specialized in the sense that it omits a much broader array of sources – speeches, manifestos, literature, anything non-white or non-Western – that a general scholar of political ideas might examine. Second, Wolin's efforts to shore up a canonical approach to theory conflicts with his goal of preparing people for citizenship in a dynamic, pluralistic, globalized society. I have suggested that Wolin's canonical understanding of modern political thought in *Politics and Vision* obscures the centrality of nationalist and imperialist political visions in modernity. His ongoing blind spot regarding the centrality of racialized power to American political culture in *Democracy Incorporated* may be similarly attributable to his relatively narrow range of sources.

To be sure, Said shares Wolin's abiding interest in studying the Western canon and is critical of some recent, "postmodern" theoretical trends. Said defends his focus on canonical sources in some of his work and denies that marginalized scholars should be cited simply because they are marginalized.[60] Because of this, he states: "in such matters as culture and scholarship I am often in reasonable sympathy with conservative attitudes."[61] Moreover, I have already noted that Said criticizes the postmodern Foucault for losing sight of "social wholes" and focusing on what Wolin calls "smaller tyrannies." Also like Wolin, Said condemns "postmodern" theorists for failing to offer emancipatory visions and thereby eschewing political responsibility. According to Said, "There is a kind of quietism that emerges at various points in Foucault's career: the sense that everything is historically determined, that ideas of justice, of good and evil, and so forth, have no innate significance, because they are constituted by whoever is using them."[62] Similarly, Said alleges, Jean-François Lyotard's dismissal of the "great narratives of emancipation and enlightenment" limits him to "local games and pastiches" and political "laziness."[63] Finally, like Wolin, Said associates postmodernism with the proliferation of specialized and political detached academic discourses. He bemoans the popularization of a kind of "textuality" that neglects the historical contexts of texts, observing, "American literary theory of the late seventies had retreated into the labyrinth of 'textuality'" characterized by "fixed special languages, many of them impenetrable, deliberately obscure, willfully illogical."[64]

However, more than Wolin, Said is deeply influenced by the postmodern insight that expert discourses are imbricated with relations of power. In particular, much of his work focuses on interrogating the ways in which Western intellectual traditions express a will to power over the colonized world. *Orientalism,* for instance, uncovers how the seemingly disinterested Western tradition of oriental studies is inseparable from imperial ambitions. Because of this work, Said maintains a generally critical perspective on the formation of canons and the authority that is claimed by experts in those canons. In *Orientalism* he writes, "Fields, of course, are made. They acquire coherence and integrity in time because scholars devote themselves in different ways to what seems to be a commonly agreed-upon subject matter. Yet it goes without saying that a field of study is rarely as simply defined as even its most committed partisans – usually scholars, professors, experts, and the like – claim it is."[65]

Said appreciates the way that the postmodern questioning of Western intellectual traditions opens space for an engagement with a previously neglected sources, what Foucault calls "subjugated knowledges."[66] With the advent of postmodernism, Said recalls, Europe and the West "were being asked to take the Other seriously."[67] Whereas Foucault focuses on marginalized voices within Western societies, Said is especially interested in texts from the colonized and post-colonial world. Unlike Wolin, then, Said does not believe that postmodern insights into the ubiquity of power inevitably lead to theoretical obscurantism or divert attention from capital and the state towards "smaller" tyrannies. While Foucault and Lyotard may have succumbed to such a fate, Said hopes that postmodern insights may instead enable us to grasp a wider range of global power dynamics and to integrate this awareness into a broader perspective on the world. He insists that the canon should still be read, but argues that it should be read alongside a wider range of material. For this reason, Said criticizes those who respond to the risks of postmodernism with the "effort to reassert old authorities and canons, the effort to reinstate ten or twenty or thirty essential Western books without which a Westerner would not be educated."[68] Instead, he argues, "The future of criticism or the critical function is ... in the traffic between cultures, discourses and disciplines, rather than in the appropriation, systematization, management, and professionalization of any one domain."[69] This open-minded and integrative attitude towards intellectual sources constitutes a more thoroughgoing response to the problem of academic specialization than a return to a relatively narrow canon, and it provides better preparation for citizenship in a dynamic, pluralistic, and globalized society.

Although Said finds in postmodernism a welcome scepticism towards canonical intellectual traditions and an openness to subjugated knowledges, he wishes to resist the "quietist" and "lazy" tendency of postmodern thinking to eschew an emancipatory horizon. He reminds us, "great antiauthoritarian uprisings made their earliest advances, not by denying the humanitarian and universalist claims of the general dominant culture but by attacking the adherents of that culture for failing to uphold their own declared standards, for failing to extend them to all, as opposed to a small fraction, of humanity."[70] He argues, furthermore, that intellectuals in a postmodern era still have the opportunity and responsibility to promote such "universal principles" of emancipation.[71] In other words, although Said accepts that knowledge is imbricated with power, he denies that this should compel us to withdraw from any theorization of resistance. Rather, he suggests that the intellectual should continue to advance general emancipatory principles, knowing that these principles are bound up with the operations of power and that they cannot offer the kind of privileged vantage point that Wolin seeks to salvage from "classic" theory.

Jeanne Morefield observes that this effort by Said to combine the insights of postmodernism with a stubborn humanism has led some critics to argue, "that his work is plagued throughout by a basic, unsettling irreconcilability."[72] Yet, like Morefield, I would argue that the politically responsible intellectual today has little choice but to maintain such a balancing act. Doing so is essential to the kind of non-specialized, civically engaged political education that both Wolin and Said value.

Counterpoint, Exile, and Worldliness

In order to explore further how Said's approach to intellectual traditions may enhance a Wolinian understanding of political theory and political education, I will now explore his notions of counterpoint, exile, and worldliness. Said explains his approach to canonical sources by drawing an analogy with the musical technique of "counterpoint." In music, counterpoint involves "various themes play[ing] off one another, with only a provisional privilege being given to any particular one; yet in the resulting polyphony there is concert and order, an organized interplay that derives from the themes, not from a rigorous melodic or formal principle outside the work."[73] To approach Western canonical texts "contrapuntally" is both to pay attention to the exclusions and imperialist ambitions of the cultures from which they emerge, and to read them alongside the non-canonical and non-Western sources to which they are implicitly connected. It is to maintain "a simultaneous awareness both of the metropolitan history that is narrated and of those other histories against which (and together with which) the dominating discourse acts."[74] For example, a contrapuntal reading of a nineteenth-century English novel may involve awareness "that a colonial sugar plantation is ... important to the process of maintaining a particular style of life in England."[75] At the same time, contrapuntal reading should be attentive to the way that the colonized culture is shaped through these processes of imperialism. Finally, in Foucauldian fashion, contrapuntal reading may also illuminate the relationship between canonical texts and what Said calls "minority and 'suppressed' voices within the metropolis itself: feminists, African-American writers, intellectuals, artists, among others."[76] In *Culture and Imperialism*, Said offers what he understands to be contrapuntal readings of canonical literary figures such as Albert Camus and W.B. Yeats, which underscore their often-neglected investments in imperialist and anti-imperialist politics, respectively.

Although contrapuntal reading may be especially aligned with Said's home discipline of comparative literature, "a field whose origin and purpose is to move beyond insularity and provincialism," it has something to teach political theorists as well.[77] It challenges them to shift how they read canonical texts as well as to broaden what they read to include non-canonical texts. For Wolin, a more contrapuntal approach to intellectual archives might have resulted, for instance, in a reading of Locke's liberalism that is more attentive to his investments in imperialism and specifically the North American slave trade. A contrapuntal approach might also have made Wolin more attentive to subjugated knowledges that fall outside his understanding of the tradition of Western political thought, and this might have enriched his diagnosis of inverted totalitarianism with a deeper appreciation of racial and gendered power.

Said's understanding of counterpoint is closely related to his application of the notion of "exile" to intellectual life. While he acknowledges that "exile is one of the saddest fates," he explains that his personal experience as a Palestinian in exile has also enabled him to understand both sides of imperial divide more easily.[78] For this reason he recommends that the intellectual embrace a kind of metaphysical exile: "Exile for the intellectual in this metaphysical sense is restlessness, movement, constantly being unsettled, and unsettling others. You cannot go back to some earlier and perhaps more stable condition of being at home; and, alas, you can never fully arrive, be at one with your new home or situation."[79] In other words, the intellectual in exile remains sensitive to what lies beyond her current purview, does not finally settle into any cultural or scholarly milieu, and so accepts a kind of continual discontent. Said distinguishes this generative metaphysical exile from what he calls "travelling theory." Theories "travel" when they "have been completely displaced – wrenched is the better word – from their contexts."[80] Intellectuals who engage with texts in this superficial way, revelling in the enjoyments of short-lived intellectual locations, divest texts of "some of their original power and rebelliousness."[81] Thus, according to Said, travelling theory is a kind of "trivialization" that is closely related to a dangerous trend in academia towards political detachment.[82] In contrast to the intellectual traveller, the intellectual in exile strives assiduously to understand the milieux they occupy, but never feels fully at home.

In the 1993 essay "Reason in Exile," Wolin criticizes Theodor Adorno for failing to offer a coherent political vision.[83] While Adorno offers compelling diagnoses of the political pathologies of modernity, Wolin alleges that he fails to develop a concrete strategy for emancipation in his new home of the United States and is resigned instead to mere escapism. In contrast, Said describes Adorno as "the quintessential intellectual" who is in "permanent exile."[84] Interestingly, when Wolin distances himself from his expectation that political theorists offer an epic vision or narrative of collective identity, and moves towards a more multifaceted and consciously incomplete approach to democracy, his attitude towards Adorno seems to shift. In "Political Theory: From Vocation to Invocation" (2000), Wolin praises Adorno for his suggestion that we continually strive to uncover from history "what might be called the waste products and blind spots ... cross-grained, opaque, unassimilated material."[85] Yet, despite this seeming appreciation of Adorno's intellectual exile, I have argued that Wolin's later work also exhibits an ongoing effort to make a home in a lovingly perpetuated canon and a defensiveness towards the efforts of "postmodern" thinkers to uncover subjugated knowledges.

According to Said, intellectuals who are committed to reading texts contrapuntally and who remain in metaphysical exile are better able to develop a "worldly" approach to scholarship and teaching. In Said's view, worldly intellectuals strive for an ever-broader appreciation of the global power dynamics that underlie texts and work to connect texts previously consigned to different disciplinary or regional silos. They do so while maintaining an emancipatory horizon for humanity as a whole. Said describes a worldly approach to marginalized texts in this way:

> By linking works to each other we bring them out of the neglect and secondariness to which for all kind of political and ideological reasons they had previously been condemned. What I am talking about therefore is the opposite of separatism, and also the reverse of exclusivism. It is only through the scrutiny of these works *as* literature, as style, as pleasure and illumination, that they can be brought in, so to speak, and kept in. Otherwise they will be regarded only as informative ethnographic specimens, suitable for the limited attention of experts and area specialists. *Worldliness* is therefore the restoration to such works and interpretations of their place in the global setting, a restoration that can only be accomplished by an appreciation not of some tiny, defensively constituted corner of the world, but of the large many-windowed house of human culture as a whole.[86]

A worldly humanism would thus radically resist academic specialization and prepare students for their roles as citizens not only of a nation-state but also of the world.

Conclusion

Amid ongoing threats to liberal arts education, Wolin and Said's shared ideal of a political education that is non-specialized, prepares people for citizenship, and grants students agency is as important as ever. I have argued that, in order to bring their own scholarly enterprises into line with this ideal, Wolin and Said both ultimately strive for a relatively holistic, emancipatory perspective that does not assert a closed vision or narrative of collective identity. Despite this similarity, Said is more attentive than Wolin to the imbrication of expert knowledge with power and, consequently, insists upon engaging with a broader range of sources. In contrast to Wolin, Said seeks to embrace the challenge that postmodernism poses to Western intellectual traditions, while still resisting the tendency of postmodern thinkers towards obscurantism and political irresponsibility.

I have argued that Said's more expansive and integrative view of intellectual archives, as exemplified by his notions of counterpoint, exile, and worldliness, could bring a broadly Wolinian approach to democratic theory further into line with Wolin's own ideals of political education. Certainly, Said's reluctance to elaborate the humanist principles that he embraces can imbue in his work what Morefield calls an "unfinished quality."[87] After *Orientalism*, Said does not really develop the kind of holistic, emancipatory diagnoses of our social ills that he claims to favour. This unfinished quality, along with Said's restless inter-disciplinarity, leads Morefield to describe his work as sometimes "exhausting," "deeply frustrating," "overwhelming," and "maddening."[88] Perhaps Wolin's "ten-tative, hypothetical" diagnosis of "inverted totalitarianism" better delivers on the promise of a relatively holistic, emancipatory diagnosis of our social ills. Yet there is no reason why democratic theorists could not strive to combine Wolin's willingness to formulate such broad diagnoses with Said's more expan-sive approach to intellectual sources.

NOTES

1 This essay develops themes that I first explored in chapter 5 of my book *Sheldon Wolin and Democracy: Seeing Through Loss* (New York: Routledge, 2020).

2 Sheldon S. Wolin, *Democracy Incorporated* (Princeton, NJ: Princeton University Press, 2008), 165.

3 Sheldon S. Wolin, "Political Theory as a Vocation," *American Political Science Review*, Vol. 63, No. 4 (1969), 1078.

4 Sheldon S. Wolin and John Schaar, "Berkeley and the Fate of the Multiversity," *The New York Review of Books* (11 March 1965), 7.

5 Sheldon S. Wolin and John Schaar, "Berkeley and the University Revolution," *The New York Review of Books* (9 February 1967), 10.

6 Wolin and Schaar, "Berkeley and the University Revolution," 10; Sheldon S. Wolin and John Schaar, "Is a New Politics Possible?" *The New York Review of Books* (3 September 1970), 1.

7 Sheldon S. Wolin. "Higher Education and the Politics of Knowledge," *democracy*, Vol. 1, No. 2 (1981), 38–52.

8 Sheldon S. Wolin, *The Presence of the Past* (Baltimore: Johns Hopkins University Press, 1989), 63.

9 Sheldon S. Wolin, "Interview with Bill Moyers," *The World of Ideas* (PBS), 14 June 1989.

10 Sheldon S. Wolin, "Political Theory: From Vocation to Invocation," in *Vocations of Political Theory*, ed. Jason Frank and John Tambornino (Minneapolis: University of Minnesota Press, 2000), 15.

11 Edward Said, *The World, the Text, and the Critic* (Cambridge, MA: Harvard University Press, 1983), 2, 4.

12 Edward Said, *Culture and Imperialism* (New York: Vintage Books, 1993), 312.

13 Edward Said, *Power, Politics, and Culture: Interviews with Edward Said*, ed. Gauri Viswanathan (New York: Pantheon Books, 2001), 280.

14 See also Edward Said, *Representations of the Intellectual* (New York: Vintage Books, 1994).

15 Sheldon S. Wolin, *Politics and Vision* (Princeton, NJ: Princeton University Press, 2004), 4, 31.

16 Ibid., 26.

17 Ibid., 389.

18 For evidence of this, see Sheldon S. Wolin, "Paradigms and Political Theories," in *Politics and Experience: Essays Presented to Professor Michael Oakeshott on the Occasion of His Retirement*, ed. Preston King and B.C. Parekh (Cambridge: Cambridge University Press, 1968), 125–52.

19 Sheldon S. Wolin and John Schaar, "Where We Are Now," *The New York Review of Books* (7 May 1970), 1–2.

20 Thomas Kuhn, *The Structure of Scientific Revolutions* (Chicago: University of Chicago Press, 1962).

21 See also Sheldon S. Wolin, *Hobbes and Epic Tradition of Political Theory* (Los Angeles: William Andrews Clark Memorial Library, 1970).

22 Wolin, "Political Theory as a Vocation," 1078.

23 Ibid.

24 Ibid.

25 Harlan Wilson, "From Oberlin to Berkeley and Beyond," *The Good Society*, Vol. 24, No 2 (2015), 205.

26 Wolin, *Politics and Vision*, 3, 5.

27 See Cane, *Sheldon Wolin and Democracy*, chapter 2.

28 Edward Said, *Orientalism* (New York: Vintage Books, 1979), 239.

29 Ibid.

30 Ibid.

31 Ibid.

32 Ibid., 258.

33 Ibid., 240.

34 Sheldon S. Wolin, "The People's Two Bodies," *democracy*, Vol. 1, No. 1 (1981), 9–24.

35 Wolin, *The Presence of the Past*, 1.

36 Wolin, "The People's Two Bodies," 24.

37 See Cane, *Sheldon Wolin and Democracy*, chapter 3.

38 Said, *Orientalism*, 331.

39 Said, *Culture and Imperialism*, 273.

40 Said, *Orientalism*, 347.

41 Ibid., xxviii.

42 Said, *Culture and Imperialism*, 273.

43 Said, *Orientalism*, 337.

44 Said, *Culture and Imperialism*, 216.

45 Ibid., 274.

46 Said, *Orientalism*, 206.

47 Said, *Culture and Imperialism,* 278.

48 Sheldon S. Wolin, "Fugitive Democracy," in *Democracy and Difference: Contesting the Boundaries of the Political,* ed. Seyla Benhabib (Princeton, NJ: Princeton University Press, 1996), 32–3; Sheldon S. Wolin, "Norm and Form: The Constitutionalizing of Democracy," in *Athenian Political Thought and the Reconstruction of American Democracy,* ed. J. Peter Euben, John R. Wallach, and Josiah Ober (Ithaca, NY: Cornell University Press, 1994) 50, 54–5.

49 See Cane, *Sheldon Wolin and Democracy,* chapter 4.

50 Wolin, *Democracy Incorporated,* xxiv.

51 John Gunnell, *Political Theory: Tradition and Interpretation* (Cambridge, MA: Winthrop, 1979); Sheldon S. Wolin, "History and Theory: Methodism *Redivivus,*" in *Tradition, Interpretation, and Science: Political Theory in the American Academy,* ed. John S. Nelson (Albany: State University of New York Press, 1986), 50.

52 Sheldon S. Wolin, "On the Theory and Practice of Power," in *After Foucault: Humanistic Knowledge, Postmodern Challenges,* ed. Jonathan Arac (New Brunswick, NJ: Rutgers University Press, 1988), 191.

53 Ibid., 186.

54 Ibid.

55 See, for example, Wolin's discussion of "postmodern cultural politics" in "Fugitive Democracy."

56 Wolin, "Political Theory: From Vocation to Invocation," 21.

57 Sheldon S. Wolin, "What Time Is It?" *Theory and Event,* Vol. 1, No. 1 (1997).

58 Ibid.

59 Wolin, "Political Theory: From Vocation to Invocation," 15.

60 Edward Said, *Reflections on Exile and Other Essays* (Cambridge, MA: Harvard University Press, 2000), 384.

61 Said, *The World, the Text, and the Critic,* 22.

62 Said, *Power, Politics, and Culture,* 53.

63 Said, *Reflections on Exile and Other Essays,* 383; Said, *Representations of the Intellectual,* 18.

64 Said, *The World, the Text, and the Critic,* 3, 292.

65 Said, *Orientalism,* 50.

66 Michel Foucault, *Society Must Be Defended* (London: Penguin Books, 2003), 7.

67 Said, *Reflections on Exile and Other Essays,* 313.

68 Said, *Culture and Imperialism,* 58.

69 Said, *Reflections on Exile and Other Essays,* 170.

70 Ibid., 385.

71 Said, *Representations of the Intellectual,* 11.

72 Jeanne Morefield, "Challenging Liberal Belief: Edward Said and the Critical Practice of History," in *Empire, Race, and Global Justice,* ed. Duncan Bell (Cambridge: Cambridge University Press, 2019), 199.

73 Said, *Culture and Imperialism,* 51.

74 Ibid.

75 Ibid., 66.

76 Ibid., 54.

77 Ibid., 43.

78 Said, *Representations of the Intellectual*, 47; Said, *Culture and Imperialism*, xxvii.

79 Said, *Representations of the Intellectual*, 53.

80 Said, *Culture and Imperialism*, 321.

81 Said, *Reflections on Exile and Other Essays*, 436.

82 Said, *Culture and Imperialism*, 321.

83 Sheldon S. Wolin, "Reason in Exile," in *Technology in the Western Political Tradition*, ed. Arthur M. Melzer and Jerry Weinberger (Ithaca, NY: Cornell University Press, 1993), 162–89.

84 Said, *Representations of the Intellectual*, 55–6.

85 Wolin, "Political Theory: From Vocation to Invocation," 4.

86 Said, *Reflections on Exile and Other Essays*, 382.

87 Jeanne Morefield, "Said and Political Theory," in *After Said*, ed. Bashir Abu-Manneh (Cambridge: Cambridge University Press, 2019), 112–28.

88 Ibid.

SECTION 4

Thinking with and beyond Wolin: Current Democratic Practices and Issues

8 Democracy between Reactionary Tribalism and the Megastate – Lessons from Italy and the UK

IAIN WEBB

I

The development of a condition and a logic of postmodernity was concomitant to a post-material turn that was afforded by the extended post-war boom and "golden age of capitalism." In such a "golden age," struggles over distribution or the structures of political power seemed to be, at least temporarily, solved and so this energy was instead harnessed by marginalized groups whose claims for recognition shook modern social theory but left unsettled the political-economic terrain of an ascendant liberal democratic capitalism. As such, questions about the consequences of an antagonism between liberal capitalism and democracy were deferred or rendered moot by new conceptions of the political that left little room for action outside of a closed, neoliberal system.[1] Postmodernity, then, as an advanced and by now mature expression of contestation *within* liberal capitalism, has at best an ambivalent relationship to democracy, or rather, to politics.[2] Theorists who, like Sheldon Wolin, hold a view of democracy as necessarily participatory and therefore stifled by constitutional or bureaucratic arrangements of representation are thus faced with a choice. They can either organize a theory of democracy that laments what is lost and seeks to reclaim it or reconceptualize postmodern social theory in order to re-articulate it to the political and to democracy.

The common critique of Wolin is that he was too much of the former. He was held to be too pre-occupied with the lament for a democracy that had become reduced to protean, sporadic, and fugitive disruptions. In his lament he therefore seemed to leave little theoretical guidance around which fellow radicals might conceptualize a persistent democratic resistance. This is at variance with other radical democrats, such as William Connolly, who consider the project of adapting democratic ideas to the increased speed and disintegrative logic of postmodernity to be a more feasible proposition than the nostalgic project of undoing or quarantining such logic entirely.[3] Connolly's inclusion of Wolin, "devotee of the community," in this critique might be a little bit one-sided, but only a little bit. Rather, it is the natural response to Wolin's body of work, a corpus which came to adopt a tone of ambivalence towards postmodernity but which skewed heavily towards the sceptical side of this ambivalence.

Wolin's sceptical but hopeful outlook on the democratic possibilities of post-modernity was provoked by the way in which he saw it initiate a fragmenta-tion of associational bases. The solid gemeinschafts of modernity were non-negotiable, given identities that derived substance from a temporality measured in generations and a geography bounded by the epochal materiality of moun-tains, rivers, or seas. Wolin saw collective identities escape this solidity and diffuse into more dispersed fragments, each of which reproduced the logics and pathologies of community but did so even as they followed the circuits of globalized capital in bypassing the proximate, local bonds that were heretofore the adhesives of such groups. Hence the ambivalence, hence the hope that was nonetheless couched in terms of mourning for something lost; modern associa-tion smashed and dispersed but, in their dispersal, also the potential bearers of "whatever remains of democratic possibilities."[4]

Hence also the withering remarks aimed at the kind of global counter-summits in Rio De Janeiro or Porto Alegre that sought to hold a mirror to the sleek corporate summits of the IMF, G8, or Davos. Indeed, the act of "shadowing" or mirroring the global summits of the capitalist elite merely reproduced a liberal model of interest group representation so that "the highest political expression of the postmodern ideal is of a Rio Conference where the representatives of boundary transcending special interests meet face-to-face with representatives of sovereign states."[5] Wolin's ire here was directed at the way in which the dif-ficult task of reconceptualizing democratic citizenship within and through the disjunctures and dislocations of postmodern plurality was elided. That instead there was the simple reproduction and extension of extant and democrati-cally moribund representation flowing along the border-straddling lineaments already carved out by the global extension of capital. We might recognize in this critique something of Carl Schmitt in its disdain for the global transposition of a liberal representationalism that talks over the people it purports to represent. It also exposes the anaemic remnants of a *homo politicus*, once embodied in English Levellers, French Jacobins, and American revolutionaries, that is now effaced and eroded by neoliberal reason such that, shiny as a marble, it slots neatly into the pathways of globalized neoliberal power. The vanquishing, as Wendy Brown has it, of *homo politicus* reflects not only the drive of neoliberal reason to grind the texture, autonomy, agonism. and individuality of human subjectivity and experience into an infinitely abstract "grey goo" of apolitical human capital, but also the postmodern aversion to potentially hegemonic dis-courses of political theory.[6] Michel Foucault's rejection of the classical canon of political philosophers, peddlers of "global systematic theory which holds everything in place" was in favour of a discursive conception of the political that was microscopic in its aperture and so looked past the larger concepts of political theory. In this way Foucault freed himself from what he saw as the totalizing domination of political theorists who "use thought to ground a political practice in truth," but in doing so did away with the subject of *homo politicus*.[7] As Wolin notes, Foucault paints a vision of a world in which we are all caught in a fine mesh of power fields, always discursively affirming and acting out the practices that constitute such a field. In this way *homo politicus*, the political, is disregarded as merely one more manifestation in a cacophony of discursive power-plays bouncing around the social system.[8] In such a system, as Wolin mentions in terms that are superficially similar to (but qualitatively different from) his own idea of fugitive democracy, political action can only ever be "an insurrectionary moment before power is reconstituted and action is redomesticated."[9] Wolin's conception of such an "insurrectionary moment" is different, however, because it rests on fundamentally different epistemological terrain. It reflects the appeal to a political democratic subject that has been rendered moribund by neoliberal reason but which is entirely absent in postmodern, discursive accounts of the political. It is different, therefore, for placing at its centre a subject whose absence is baked into an idea of the political that is not specifically *political*, or where, as Wolin put it, "politics becomes discourse and discourse politics."[10]

Wolin was criticized roundly for offering a sporadic, dispersed and amorphously vague account of what *his* fugitive democracy might entail and the kind of subject that might power it. In this way it has been compared to a kind of Sorelian myth, a stirring idea whose broad imprecision serves to animate and provoke to action diverse strata of society.[11] We might speculate, as George Kateb does, that this could have been a deliberate move. That it might be a way of eschewing any kind of prescriptive, doctrinaire "form" for his fugitive moments of demotic disruption so that all might be inspired to fill the gaps in different ways which nonetheless converge in their mutual opposition to the routinization and containment of democracy.[12] Nevertheless, though specific definitions of fugitive democracy and insights into the kind of ideal democratic subject are few and far between in Wolin's work, there are kernels scattered throughout. These are mere intimations, clues derived from his revelling in and enjoyment of the kind of demotic excess that so vexed the ancient critics of democracy. Kateb recognizes it in Wolin's admiration for a kind of wildness, or looseness, in the Athenian polis prior to its spasms of oligarchy and institutionalized democracy after the fourth century. Here the "rational disorganization" of rule by lottery led to an Isonomy in which citizens always simultaneously held within and among themselves both rulership and servitude. Consequently, as Hannah Arendt and later Sheldon Wolin were both to see, Athenian democracy was not a democracy per se but rather a state of no-rule,[13] the suffix -omy, as opposed to -cracy or -archy, indicating something that was less an Aristotelian constitution of power than a "dynamic and developing political culture."[14] Such a system places a significant burden on its citizens, each of which must be capable not just of the mere exercise of authority, as a manager might exercise authority over their employee, but rather be authoritative in their character so that they might be respected as *an* authority among authorities. For Aristotle this meant an apprenticeship of subjection, where one learned how to rule by labouring under the rulership of another. Wolin, rather, emphasized the productive and agonistic tensions of such an arrangement. Its hard to argue against Aristotle's injunction that to learn how to rule one must first be a good subject, but this begs the question as to why, in the context of isonomy, such a subject-ruler would ever feel compelled to defer to other subject-rulers in matters of policy in the assembly. With subjects that are each steeled by this radical equality and armoured by the kind of citizenship training advocated by Aristotle, isonomy becomes something not merely participatory, but innately rebellious. There is a sense that Wolin relished this kind of irreverence. We see this in the tone of smiling approval in his recounting of the demotic excess faced by Solon early in ancient Athens's democratic trajectory where a politely obstreperous gathering of citizens "besieged'" him in order to "deliver their opinions of his laws, to ask for detailed explanations and clarification, and to urge revisions." In the face of such a cantankerous demotic excess, Solon promptly "set sail after obtaining from the Athenians leave of absence for ten years," in the hopes that time might turn contentious reform into settled institution.[15]

Wolin's admiration for the unvarnished political culture of isonomy and its irreverent disregard of vertical hierarchy stands in stark contrast to the despairing way he described the kind of subject fit for neoliberal managed democracy in the context of American superpower. Here is a "citizen shrunk to the voter: periodically courted, warned, and confused but otherwise kept at a distance from actual decision-making and allowed to emerge only ephemerally in a cameo appearance according to a script composed by the opinion takers/makers."[16] What is crucial here is not that a hierarchy might emerge that would seek to dominate or contain a demos, the discontinuous history of democracy shows us that such a tendency is the norm, but that civic culture itself has been de-rendered and reconstituted in such a way as to do away with any political texture that might once have offered some friction to such a process.

Wolin's "imperial citizen" in this case is one that is "apolitical but not alienated," one who happily substitutes the difficult work of political participation with a lifestyle that conjoins and conflates rampant consumerism with fervent patriotism.[17] This apolitical but nevertheless engaged citizen represents the answer to the conundrum presented by the historically contemporaneous development of two contradictory aspects of bourgeoise liberation: democracy and capitalism. Democracy, and the sovereign citizen that was its subject, became the political bedrock upon which the capitalist edifice lay such that the concept of democracy became untouchable to a capitalism that simultaneously depended on democratic citizens to consume its product, even as it was at peril from them as bearers of the political and thus potential revolutionaries. The answer to this was to enfold the meaning of democratic participation into the capitalist logic of choice so that citizens might maintain something of a democratic connection to the modern, capitalist state even as they are shorn of the political imagination that might overturn it. Wolin summed up such a process when he observed that "popular sovereignty [became] absorbed into economic impotence and consumer sovereignty into political impotence."[18] In such a way does Wolin speak about an end of the political in postmodern capitalist democracy, where an aggregate mass of *homo oeconomici* ratify the state's choice of leaders in an economy of opposition in which the criteria for rule have become not a candidate's ideas, but their professed competence at overseeing the market economy. The product of this process is an inversion of the radical equality of isonomy. Where isonomy represents a particular kind of *political* culture, a no-rule of political equals that is excessive, inchoate, irreverent, but most importantly participatory, the neoliberal subject is caught in a kind of *Ophelomy*, a particular kind of *economic* culture in which the above values are disarticulated from their political meaning and transmuted into economic traits. The result is an evacuation of the space of the political and the heralding of what we might call the hollowed democracy of Wolin's inverted totalitarianism.[19]

Wolin was by no means alone in pointing to the progressively diminished space for the political, Ernesto Laclau and Chantal Mouffe diagnosed a similar malaise when speaking of "pure administration within a stable institutional framework." Here, the agonistic frontiers around which cluster the aggregations of "others" which fuel "appeals to new subjects of social change," are deferred and distended to such an extent that formerly antagonistic ideological cleavages, such as labour and capital, are dissolved and bought together. A closed economy of opposition melts away the distinctive incompatibility between them and reduces them to systemically compatible adversaries as opposed to diametrically opposed enemies.[20] For Mouffe the remnants of a real agonist friend/enemy distinction are those fundamentalist or traditionalist groups who, in explicitly rejecting the path of history towards individualized liberal democracy, are not amenable to cooptation and so are excised from the recognized sphere of legitimate (a)political engagement.[21] The project then becomes one of inaugurating a return to the political, of delivering a substantive, agonistic idea of democracy that revitalizes the Schmittian tension of equivalence and difference, free of the kind of ethnic and nationalist implications that Schmitt saw in it. While Mouffe and Laclau seek a return of the political from, or for, the left, this work looks critically at similar attempts from the far right. It posits that the far right has successfully leveraged postmodern social theory to ingratiate itself into liberal democracy's closed economy of opposition by strategically shedding those aspects of itself that had kept it firmly in exile. In so doing, this chapter relies heavily on the work of Sheldon Wolin, for, even as his eye was drawn mostly to the United States, his remarkable vision and the breadth and depth of his work means that his ideas are useful in helping to understand the theoretical and sociological movements underpinning the transition of the far right from twentieth-century extremism to twenty-first-century radicalism. This is particularly true of his idea of politics as a vocation, that political theory must have an affirmative and pro-active role in society, and his subsequent scepticism thereby that the centrifugal mix of disparate identities in postmodernity would, automatically, inaugurate a progressive and democratic outcome.

II

In parallel to this fusion of political and consumer sovereignty have been movements in the way in which political association, membership, and citizenship came to be understood. These involve the array of cultural innovations that were bought about by postmodernism. Firstly, a radical evacuation of the semiotic substance that gave meaning to the given determinations of modernity and the consequent floating of cultural signifiers from these semiotic anchorages. Secondly, the anti-universal assertions of difference and plurality that had previously been effaced and obscured by the totalizing social theory of liberal modernity. The unmooring of cultural signifiers, paired with the emergence of social theory that sought to raise difference in lieu of the modern liberal demand to obscure it in the name of commonality, pointed to a kind of "dismembering" effect on citizenship for Wolin. Under such conditions the notion of citizenship, for Wolin, becomes emptied of any over-arching significance, and, imbricated in the same logic of consumer choice that reconciled democracy with capitalism, becomes a status that is rendered into a "residual category useful merely for the rights and protections it affords," or a "sometime role with reservations attached"[22] that can be associated and disassociated with almost at will. The disavowal of the kind of theory, Marxism, Rawlsian justice, Kantian deontology, etc. that, in being blind to cultural difference became potential avenues of oppression against such difference, had the effect of opening the door to debates about the commensurability of different cultures. Wolin's concern was that the furthest logical extent of such anti-universalism is a pernicious particularism, which denies altogether the possibility of different cultural groups coexisting without some form of oppression or coercion to bring them together, and it is in capturing and weaponizing postmodern social theory at the coordinates of this extent that has fuelled the movement of the far-right from its exile. Nevertheless, the effects of this anti-universalism, the embrace and thinking through of new, anti-hegemonic perspectives that look to the local and the cultural, also power a dispersive current that runs counter to the centripetal, agglomerative tendencies of anti-democratic, corporate power for which those older appeals to wider, more abstract, and impersonal conceptions of association are amenable. This is the promise and the peril of postmodern identity politics, on the one hand (dis)membered and dispersed bases of solidarity, shorn of the heavy determinations of modernity, provide an accelerated and centrifugal cultural churn that exposes and mixes disparate "existential affirmations," inspiring people to affirm their own particular "existential faith" while simultaneously honouring its ultimate contestability in the face of another, equally valid "existential faith."[23] On the other hand, Wolin warns of the way in which each branch of this postmodern dispersal and fragmentation reproduces within itself the exclusionary pathologies of community. For Wolin, the eschewing of any theory with a whiff of the universal necessarily entails a following "in the footsteps of nationalism in insisting upon boundaries that establish differences," valorizing the particular over the universal such that there is a reproduction of nationalism's "absorption of the political into the pursuit of an homogenous identity" and so leading to pockets of nationalism, or nationalisms.[24] Quite apart from Connolly's rhizomatic vision, in which the ultimate uncertainty of all existential perspectives renders each porous to the other, inspiring fruitful experimentalism as subjects are forced to negotiate the gaps opening within and between their beliefs, Wolin warns of a patchwork of insular, discrete, and impermeable cultural niches.

This is the new appeal of the far right, an appeal that leverages the postmodern dispersal of the certainties of modernity in order to further its own discrete certainties, at once questioning postmodernity's implicit nihilism and appropriating from it to inaugurate a politicized variant, what Robert Antonio has identified as the post- to postmodernity: reactionary tribalism.[25] Antonio's is an elegant and rigorous account of the sociological movement of the New Right going into the twenty-first century, explaining it in terms of the postmodern exhaustion of the liberal sociocultural bases of post-war modernization, the convergence of this exhaustion from both the left and the right, and the revival thereby of the kind of total critiques of modernity seen in the interwar years of the twentieth century.

This account supplements the variety of other theses concerning the persistent appeal of the far right, a variety that, in their disparate disciplinary roots, reflect the slippery nature of the subject itself and led to a thicket of typologies and categories disputing the boundaries between different forms and coordinates of "the right." Cas Mudde has done much to clarify such a definitional morass, filtering down an impressive fifty-eight different identified features to a mere five upon which there is broad consensus (nationalism, racism, xenophobia, anti-democracy, and the strong state).[26] However, as Elisabeth Carter observed, Muddes's cataloguing of the most frequently identified definitional traits ultimately leads to a core of individually insufficient ideas that are all captured by a singular principle that is one rung higher on the ladder of abstraction: anti-democracy. To construct a useful typology from this, Carter worked at this higher level of abstraction in order to differentiate the idea of "extremeness" (anti-democracy) from "rightness" (inequality). In so doing she elaborated a typological template for the important distinction between extreme right groups and radical right groups, with the latter maintaining much of the extreme right but jettisoning that part of it that was necessarily extreme, i.e., a hostility to the democratic system as a whole.[27] This is important in so far as the movement of history into the twenty-first century, and the move from post-modernity to a period of reactionary tribalism, relies upon a movement from a pole of the far right predicated on its extremeness to one which can inject much of the sufficient but not necessary principles animating extreme-right parties into the mainstream political ecosystem through a transformation into less objectionable, "radical" right parties.

Complimenting the thesis of a move to a period of reactionary tribalism, Piero Ignazi has spoken of a "silent counter-revolution" to Ronald Inglehart's post-material "silent revolution."[28] Here, the societal changes noticed by Inglehart which would have threatened the world view of the conservative right at the time; the progressive liberation of previously oppressed or marginalized expressions of ethnic, sexual, and cultural identities, eventually become embraced by the far right as the entryway by which it can smuggle into legitimate politics the reassertion of its own exclusionary, cultural, and ethnic claims. Elsewhere, Matthew Goodwin and Rob Ford have identified a "left behind" generation,[29] while Hans Georg Betz offers his "losers of globalization" thesis.[30] Goodwin, Ford, and Betz each point to a generational disjuncture arising from a cohort whose lifetimes have overlapped awkwardly with the wholesale structural and cultural changes accompanying globalization and de-industrialization, born early enough to embed themselves fully in the industrial post-war economies but therefore also too old to be able to easily adapt to the shape of a new economy in which their skills were made redundant. Trained in the manual work that defined the post-war economies of the West, members of this cohort were left utterly ill equipped to flourish in the service-based economy after the 1980s. They were left behind not just economically but culturally too, in a social milieu that had become unrecognizable from the racially homogenous society they grew up in, a society in which normative discipline firmly upheld traditional models of the family, gender, sex, and marriage and in which the national identity was still inextricably linked to an idea of solitary empire and a consequent aloofness from the transnational institution building on the European mainland.[31] This generation, unacknowledged by mainstream parties that mill around a political centre defined by its consensus on neoliberal economic administration, then become a valuable electoral reservoir that outsider, populist political entrepreneurs like Nigel Farage, Marine Le Pen, and Donald Trump can tap into.

The movement from extremism to radicalism can be evinced by comparing the differing fortunes of groups in their adaptation to the post-materialist changes. If the temptation, when studying the far right, is to maintain an inoculating distance from the groups themselves and observe them as mere artefacts of a congruence of exogenous factors, appearing and disappearing as the salience of their issue priorities ebb and flow, then the impressive matrix of theories produced in this "externalist" manner would eventually be exceeded by the need for a more "internalist" perspective.[32] "Externalist" perspectives, with their grand, macro-economic and macro-social apertures, not only diminish the agency of the groups they examine in their preoccupation with the larger structures in which they operate, but in so doing render themselves inadequate to the task of explaining divergences within these larger social and economic changes. Theories that encompass the broad sweep of economic changes across nations as embedded liberalism made way for neoliberal globalization, and which might therefore predict similar fortunes for local far-right groups as the logic of globalized neoliberalism washed over the world, become less effective at explaining the divergent fortunes of specific far-right groups in nations that are all similarly enmeshed in such a process.

On the contrary, a more granular, qualitative, internalist perspective frees parties from their role as passive agents. Where before they are conceptualized in bondage to the determinations of a fortuna imposed upon them and so reduced to mere dependent variables within the broader political ecosystem, they are now reconceptualized as active agents that are reflexive and adaptable to such fortuna. The black-box artefacts of the far right, little monoliths in their obtuse reductions to passive, dependent variables, are opened and revealed to be intricate and multifarious in the attitudes, competencies, and experiences of their memberships and leaders. Thus, they become not merely passive in riding the waves of issue salience, but active participants in the generation of, and adaptation to, increased salience.

An excellent case in point for the kind of domestic adaptations that the broader, external perspective struggles to explain would be the radically different fortunes of specific far-right groups in Italy and the UK. For, while in Italy the political party with direct and indisputable (and unapologetic) lineage with its fascist heritage managed a kind of rebirth through which it was able to enter a governing coalition, their British equivalent signally failed to do so. Both parties, the Italian Social Movement and the British National Party (BNP), faced similar existential quandaries as post-material values gained traction during the golden age of capitalism and were increasingly normalized into the neoliberal late twentieth and early twenty-first centuries. The former, through a long and circuitous flirtation with liberal democratic "inserimento" and experiments in exotic, postmodern bricolages of anti-racist, anti-capitalist chauvinism, were able to persuasively jettison those toxic elements of its ideology that had become obsolete by the post-material revolution. The latter, on the other hand, presented with a "strategic window of opportunity" through which they might have made a similar manoeuvre, instead had such a window shut on it and the arc of its success terminated in 2010. This window opened for the BNP in 1997 when New Labour routed the Tories and took their place in the governing centre, establishing a political topography in which there was both a weakening of political polarization overall and a long-term retrenchment on the right as the Tories toiled in the political wilderness. Such a topography left space for extreme right groups like the BNP to build credibility in lieu of a dormant Conservative Party that had, for generations, siphoned support from them. The opening of space on the far right was contemporaneous with other aggravating factors, such as a broad political disillusionment and a marked increase in the political salience of immigration.[33] The closing of this window is marked by Carvalho as that point in which, having achieved an unusual (if still modest) level of political success in these favourable conditions, it signally failed to make the strategic and constitutional changes required to build upon it. It was then unable to defend the abundant political space it had been left in the wake of the Conservative Party's wilderness years.

For the BNP, there was an exoteric and superficial overhaul that did not well disguise the slim esoteric, substantive changes. These changes, superficial and slim as they were, nevertheless required a protracted and ill-tempered contestation with the weakening hegemony of John Tyndall's post-war, neo-Nazi wing before Nick Griffin's more politically astute, postmodern "racial nationalist" wing, dismissive of the former's "sub-mosleyite wackiness," could make its ascension. As a result, the BNP underwent a fraught, contested, but ultimately incomplete, transition to something that was hoped to approximate the national populism of the Italian Social Movement, or a more direct influence, the French National Front. Where formerly the electoral impact of Tyndall's (British) National Front and BNP had been predicated on the negative attention garnered through a strategy of "march and grow" extra-parliamentary militancy, Griffin's new-look BNP sought the positive attention gained through intense local engagement and a repackaging of its straightforward racism and xenophobia into a defence of the indigenous culture, identity, and ethnicity of "white Britain." Furthermore, Griffin's BNP sought to move from the antiquated leadership principle of John Tyndall's BNP towards a decentralized popular government, where a folkish common sense would prevail on matters of immigration, economy, and law and order and where international relations would be predicated upon a kind of pan-European fraternity that would develop among states through the mutual affirmation of each as impermeable, ethnically homogenous units. However, unwilling to definitively disavow the anti-democratic and racist principles that formed its ideological core, the BNP instead sought a form of historical revisionism that left those principles intact but merely obscured by a superficial and strategic modernist agenda, it underwent a "modernisation of its past for its future."[34]

This retroactive modernization allowed Griffin to affect an approximation of the kind of "baggage shedding" that the Italian Social Movement underwent throughout the 1970s and 1980s before climaxing in the 1990s (described below). However, rather than pack up and reconstitute a new populist nationalist party with a different name and different constitutive principles, Griffin attempted to offload its toxic baggage onto the legacy of its erstwhile leader John Tyndall and in so doing to create an image of a new BNP that was locally engaged and professional and which offered a clear distinction between its past life as an authoritarian, paramilitary, skinhead group that was now to be associated with the defeated Tyndall. In so doing it produced an alternative history in which one of Tyndall's compatriots and later rivals, John Bean, was proclaimed the ideological inspiration for this new-look BNP. This alternative history hinged on the strategic innovations that John Bean advocated for; intensive local engagement, a more positive attitude towards electoral participation, and a move from black boots and skinheads to suits and ties, but it remained silent on the many ways in which Bean was merely a continuation of the racialist and anti-Semitic extremism of Tyndall: his arrest for the obscene public provocations he instigated after the trial of Adolph Eichmann as well as his long list of anti-Semitic screeds.[35] Ultimately, the only thing separating John Tyndall and John Bean was that the latter could tactically subordinate his anti-Semitism to a broader animus against a globalization in which Jews and Gentiles both played a part. Bean saw that virulent anti-Semitism, of which he was a firm adherent, needed to be set aside in favour of an "ethnorealpolitik" which relativized the place of Jews as a foreign element to be purged so that they might be treated as "any other foreign people." The hope was that such a move would annul the pariah status that anti-Semitism conferred upon a political group and, rather ambitiously, that the door therefore be left open for an alliance with "good" Jews against the spectre of Islamification that Bean saw as the other great enemy of British culture.[36]

The BNP therefore underwent a purely strategic and superficial overhaul, its core principles remained not only unchanged but fundamentally unchallenged, merely repackaged in the language of postmodern identity politics and subsumed beneath an electoral calculation that required its hardliners to "hold their tongues" so that the presentable face of the party might instigate a semi-Gramscian strategy of embedding itself in local civil society and from there pragmatically ascend the ladder of what was politically possible.[37] This bottom-up, Gramscian political strategy was hobbled by the half-baked strategy of presentation that accompanied it, a presentation that strained to obscure a policy array whose only surrender to moderation was the softening of its long-standing commitment to involuntary repatriation towards a policy of incentivized, voluntary repatriation as part of a shift of emphasis away from race and towards "identity." The BNP's inability to embrace, in substance if not in strategy, a move towards a "new" right meant that Carvalho is quite correct to observe a window of opportunity slamming shut on it, as, in essence, the BNP doomed themselves to ebb and flow on the crests and troughs of "their" issue saliences. However, while the particular confluence of favourable electoral opportunities changed, the broader sociological and political economic movements that helped to open this window of opportunity persisted. Thus the decline of the BNP can be correlated almost precisely to the rise of UKIP, a party that provided the postmodern, radical right populism that a bolder or more flexible BNP might have been positioned to become.

The BNP's timidity in grasping the postmodern nettle can be contrasted sharply with the experience of the Italian Social Movement (MSI) in Italy. The MSI under Gianfranco Fini managed to thread the needle in plotting a course away from a proscribed adherence to revolutionary fascism, through a radical postmodern shift, towards a genuine and permanent constitutional adherence to the norms and values of liberal democracy and with it a place in government. The path that led there was contested and uneven, beginning with a policy of *inserimento* (insertion) that reached its apogee when the MSI wielded the parliamentary balance of power as kingmaker in propping up the minority Christian Democrat government in 1960, before almost immediately plunging to its nadir when violence at its National Congress, provoked by its own success in achieving such a powerful and prominent role, led to the whole government resigning anyway. Following this was an attempt to develop a broad, front-based group, the *destra nazionale*, from which the MSI sought to establish itself in a leadership position from the far right and appeal to more moderate groups. It did this with superficial ideological overhauls that were exposed by an increased focus on militant violence, purportedly as guarantee against the perceived threat from anti-fascist and communist violence against them. Indeed, this increased reliance on extra-parliamentary violence meant that, despite the attempts at moderating their ideological animus to liberal democracy, the *destra nazionale* only succeeded in scaring off moderate voters, even as it was successful enough in recapturing elements of the far right that had left it. Its failure in the election of 1976 prompted a reconsideration of these policies and led to a brief but redefining period of flirtation with the ideas of the *Nouvelle Droite*. During this period, the party attacked liberal democracy from the left and asserted a common ground between Italians and immigrants as mutual victims of a global system that impoverished nations economically and culturally. In so doing (and uniquely among parties of the extreme right), the MSI forcefully rejected racism and xenophobia.

Throughout its permutations, the MSI never questioned its core historical linkages to fascism; indeed the question of fascism for the MSI was always how best to develop a set of ancillary concepts amenable to the political success of fascism, or, as Piero Ignazi put it, "always on which tendencies of Fascism should the party pursue: *it never dealt with the hypothesis of abandoning the fascist ideal.*"[38] This ambivalent relationship to its heritage, an oscillation between determined "insertion" into liberal democratic political life and strong assertions around fascism's "eternal" and "untouchable" values was maintained even up to the MSI's convention in 1994.[39] Here, the MSI, in an extension of its earlier efforts towards establishing a "national right" was dissolved and its membership and apparatus, along with rogue conservative exiles from the mainstream Christian Democrat and Liberal parties, was reconstituted within a new National Alliance (AN).

Piero Ignazi is at pains to emphasize the continuities that persist with fascism even as the MSI was folded, pointing persuasively towards a persistent fidelity to a fascist intellectual heritage that included the likes of Julius Evola and Giovanni Gentile (even as they attempted to blunt this tradition by attesting an admiration for liberal democratic theorists like Alexis De Tocqueville), as well as to an attitudinal affinity for fascism that persisted among the rank and file even through the wholesale institutional transfer of the MSI into the AN.[40] However, while these points are indisputable, the "turning point at Fiuggi" still marks a watershed that can be described as an "end of fascism," in so far as it marks the culmination of a gradual absorption of fascist concepts into the broader purview of the liberal democratic right in general. This absorption was the result of factors both exogenous of and endogenous to the MSI/AN. It was propelled exogenously by a revisionist softening of Italian fascism's toxic reputation, something that was contemporaneous with a general diminishment in violence between neo-fascist fellow travellers of the MSI and their anti-fascist adversaries, all of which helped to normalize the idea of the MSI's participation in liberal democratic politics. The most important endogenous development was the earlier move towards a third-positionist, *nouvelle droite*–inspired identity politics that, while abortive, nonetheless acted to sever the MSI definitively and permanently from an association with the antediluvian politics of biological racism and anti-Semitism. This sincere and affirmative (as opposed to grudgingly concessionary) rejection of racism and anti-Semitism gave the MSI/AN credence when, at the Fiuggi conference, it sublated the concepts and intellectual history of fascism into a general right-wing orientation within liberal democracy, an orientation that "preceded fascism, had passed through it, and ... survived it,"[41] affirmed anti-fascism as a necessary force to save democracy from Italy's fascist episode, and unequivocally renounced revolutionary or anti-democratic ambitions to replace liberalism.[42] The "turning point at Fiuggi," then, was not so much a moment of spontaneous revisionism, but the culmination of a long process of entryism and ideological flexibility.

III

With an appropriation and politicization of postmodern theory's emphasis on the particular over an enlightenment impulse towards universality, the movement from a period of postmodernity to its politicized mutation in reactionary tribalism offers those on the far right an avenue by which they can be reintegrated into the broader "mainstream" political ecosystem. Fascism and the extreme right have, per Roger Griffin and Tamir Bar-On, historically sustained their own bespoke ideologies through the selective appropriation of disparate aspects of social theory; be it socialist or anarchist, monarchist or conservative, traditionalist or nationalist theories, and so on.[43] In so doing they pillage concepts adjacent to and peripheral with these ideological traditions and fuse them in a *bricolage* or *mazeway resynthesis* to their own core notions of xenophobia, chauvinism, anti-Semitism, national rebirth, etc. The wellspring of postmodern thought offers a veritable smorgasbord of material by which modern-day fascist equivalents on the radical right might initiate a twenty-first-century *mazeway resynthesis*, one that can embrace and appropriate the thought of such disparate thinkers as Antonio Gramsci, Julius Evola, Friedrich Nietzsche, Gilles Deleuze, Max Weber, and Giovanni Gentile. The experience of appropriating from postmodernism in this manner offers such far-right groups a developing theoretical guideline by which they can reconstitute and carry their programs into the sanctified space of the neoliberal political ecosystem, free of the appeals to straightforward racism that had kept them firmly in exile.

A party like the BNP, though it inherited the notoriety and prominence bequeathed it as direct heir to a political lineage that ran from Oswald Mosley's British Union of Fascists, through A.K. Chesterton and his League of Empire Loyalists to the fractious union of Chesterton, Colin Jordan, and John Tyndall in the National Front, nevertheless found itself reduced to an irrelevant and obscure political groupuscule, as it failed to make the necessary adaptations to reconstitute and repackage its xenophobic and racist principles in the light of postmodern reactionary tribalism. In the face of such failure the BNP found itself ideologically obsolete and was diminished as any kind of electoral force when competing radical right groups such as UKIP emerged and, post-2016, the newly inaugurated political hooligans of the Brexit party acted in concert with the European Research Group of Tory MPs to push the Tories towards a more radically anti-European, anti-immigration direction.

Reactionary tribalism, as a theoretical avenue through which far-right groups can reconstitute themselves as, or be replaced by, radical-right parties, thereby represents a dangerous sociological and political phenomenon. We see it in action in the laborious route that the Italian Social Movement took to eventual government, and in the inverse fortunes of the extremist BNP and the radical UKIP, but we also see it in the gradual colonization of both the Republican Party and from there the US government by the Tea Party, Trumpism, and radical nationalists like the Stevens Miller and Bannon. This danger was presciently observed by Wolin, who located remnants of the more traditional and, for him, more substantive associational bond at the local level and pinned democratic hopes on a fusion between the proximate bonds made at this level, and the centrifugal, if more dispersed and thereby weaker, bonds of postmodern association. The caveat when pinning democratic hopes on associational bonds forged at the local level is that such bonds are vulnerable to the pathology typically associated with this kind of tight-knit *gemeinschaft*: a suspicious and exclusionary chauvinism, or parochialism. This complicates hopes for a fusion of the local with the postmodern, stressing the importance of maintaining a balance of inclusivity while forging such proximate bonds, with the local typically being the arena of less desirable "anti-modern centrifugals": groups like the Ku Klux Klan, assorted militia groups, fundamentalist protestants and so on.[44] It is the job of theory to maintain this balance in transcending both "the autistic tendencies of localism and the self-centered pre-occupation of the postmodern individual."[45] That he issued such a warning about the potential spoiling of his slender democratic hopes shows us that he was aware of the way in which these anti-modern groups had already begun to take the initiative in such a fusion of the local with the postmodern. Indeed, in his pithy assertion about the kind of pinched, parochial perspective that drives certain conceptions of community and the similarly insular impulse behind strong-program postmodernism, he pointed precisely to the coordinates of reactionary tribalism, and to the kind of pathological demotic expression that might arise should there be no theoretical guide to ensure that these two tendencies are overcome. For if these tendencies are not overcome, then the reaction against the advance of a financialized *ophelemy*, one that subverts and absorbs the political equality of *isonomy* into the liberal "equality" of the market, is channelled towards an ethnic, racialized direction, where the return of the political becomes the return of ethnos.

In seeking to maintain a useful tension between the autistic extents of particularism and postmodernity, both William Connolly and Sheldon Wolin rely on the way in which a roiling and accelerating postmodern cultural churn can foment agonistic respect and tolerance for difference in exposing, and thereby reflecting, the mutual contestability of oblique creeds to one another. However, Connolly's advocacy of a gymnastic, fluid, and dynamic cultural churn that inexorably fosters such virtues begs the question, pointedly asked by David McIvor, as to why democratic virtues of tolerance and "agonistic respect" would, in and of themselves, necessarily overcome the myriad resentments, regressions, and retreats to a tribal, ethnic particularism that are similarly fostered by such a churn.[46] Connolly has faith that, suitably accelerated, postmodern pluralism will simply overwhelm regressive resistance from "anti-modern centrifugals," whose world views are presumed to be fatally eroded when exposed to the scouring winds of an ever-accelerating postmodern pluralism. Wolin, on the other hand, was less sanguine about the power of such a movement on its own to inculcate the kind of democratic ethos that would overcome reactionary tribalism, seeing in it simply another dimension of the kind of agglomerative corporate tendency that powers "inverted totalitarianism." This cultural effervescence is instead seen to be aligned to and captured within a broader centripetal superstructure, an economic homogeneity, in which we are all ceaselessly mobile but also always demobilized.[47] In swirling within the hollowed and inverted totalitarianism of Wolin's managed democracy, this cultural vitality is never truly *political*, for it represents merely the cultural and ethnic refractions of homo economicus. Thus, for Wolin, Connolly's self-propelling pluralism, his positive political resonance machine, can never affect a true return to the political, and certainly nothing in the manner of a reactionary tribalism that seeks to martial postmodernity towards a Schmittian "pluriverse" of discrete cultural and ethnic units.

Wolin's answer is indeed to find a way to resuscitate the lost subject of *homo politicus*, to anchor postmodern cultural vitality to the slower political vitality found in habits of democratic participation and engagement. If, for Wolin, Connolly's ideal of an ever-increasing political resonance machine is simply coopted by a corporate capital happy to encourage such discordance and revolution in the name of planned obsolescence, technological rents and the platform "gig" economy, then the political can only be sought in its inverse; the slower, more deliberate, and more proximate coordinates of local political action. For it is in the crucible of mundane local politics that homo politicus and the spirit of isonomy can carve a niche for themselves, addressing the granular peculiarities of local politics and in so doing forging a beachhead of "politicalness" wherein the attributes of democratic participation, engagement and isonomic, agonistic irreverence can be incubated. As McIvor notes, Wolin wished to subsume (but not eliminate) differences that would become bracketed in the collective pursuit of political ends. Such differences would still be recognized but would be temporarily de-centred in favour of episodic and discontinuous political endeavours that would forge a "commonality amid difference."[48] The pursuit of such common endeavours would reinvigorate the subject of homo politicus, re-introducing a civic subjectivity and sense of "politicalness" among the citizenry, a sense of "politicalness" which would then percolate upwards and outwards, inspiring a multifaceted engagement and participation at the edges of the apolitical, neoliberal mega-state. For McIvor this praxis of the "fast" pluralism of Connolly and the "slower" political engagement of Wolin is necessary for the full potential of Connolly's idea of pluralism to overcome the larger centripetal tendencies of the neoliberal mega-state; however, such a praxis is also the key to maintaining a useful tension between, and therefore overcoming, the radical extents of the exclusionary local and the insular postmodern. If reactionary tribalism has taught us anything it is that we cannot simply rely on the emergence of a postmodern sensibility that recognizes and relishes the differences between us to initiate on its own the unfolding of an attitude of agonistic respect between cultures and ethnicities. Left to its own devices, such an unfolding is far too vulnerable to folding back in on itself and, as Wolin observed, replicating the tendencies of chauvinistic nationalism. This is why the apolitical administration of the neoliberal mega-state is so dangerous and why the need to inculcate a new attitude of isonomy and multidimensional politicalness is so pressing; in maintaining the recognition of difference while subsuming it to the larger task of political contestation it encourages just the kind of agonistic respect in its pluralism that Connolly sees as vital to the project of positive political resonance.

Reactionary tribalism has had a seismic and disheartening effect on the manner of civic discourse and politics, and if we can recognize it in the coordinates of the local and the postmodern, we should take heart in recognizing the increasing "politicalness" of formerly apolitical citizenries who feel increasingly compelled to protest against its political results, be it the People's Vote demonstration in London or the Women's March immediately following Mr. Trump's inauguration, and also to engage with and participate in local politics. In so doing we should take heart in, but also act to make real, Wolin's assurance that the proper role of anti-modern centrifugals and their reactionary tribalism is as a spur to political awakening so that reactionary tribalism is not able to project its reactionary aspirations forward, but instead sit in our rear-view mirror as "provocateurs whose passionate commitments can arouse self-consciousness in the public, stimulating the latter to become aware of what they believe and of the mixed legacies that compose a collective inheritance."[49]

NOTES

1 Some scholars, such as David Harvey, Gerard Dumenil, Dominique Levy, and Andrew Glyn, consider the development of neoliberalism as the response, a "coup," of capital to a dwindling rate of profit growth. One that it faced as the yawning developmental disparities between nations that fuelled the golden age of capitalism after the Second World War narrowed and the consequent competition and inflationary pressures began to leave less room to accommodate both the level of profit that capital had become accustomed to, and the generous social policies that labour was used to. The economic policies that secured for capital the maintenance of its rate of profit: aggressive hiking of interest rates to break the back of labour, privatization of public infrastructure, the liberalization of foreign trade, massive expansions of finance, and above all, a singular fixation on maintaining low inflation, are the pillars of this idea of neoliberalism. While heavily indebted to the historical, economic, and theoretical scrutiny that such scholars have undertaken in the study

of neoliberalism, this paper instead follows Wendy Brown in adopting (or adapting) the Foucauldian conception of a neoliberal *reason*, one whose central tenet is *competition* and whose primary innovation is less the discrete bundle of economic policies outlined above, and more the over-arching rationale by which competition is to be secured, or rather, by which capital defines the conduct of conduct. Such reason assumes that there is no distinction between capital and labour, that labour is folded into capital in the conceptualization of the working individual as *homo oeconomicus*, one who strives to build up their own human capital to leverage it in a market in which everyone is the CEO of themselves as their own enterprise.

2 Postmodernity is, of course, a substantially over-determined term. When deploying the terms postmodernity, or postmodernism, this paper does so through the lens of Wolin's dialogue with what he saw as its central problematics. For Wolin these were the way in which postmodernity did away with any foundational grounding by which to legitimate power, as well as the way in which postmodern political theory decentred the state and so also, for Wolin, decentred and eradicated the possibility of revolutionary and radical politics, of the political, which stood arrayed against the state. This had implications for Wolin about the substance of association and commonality, the twin pillars of his conception of the political, and what it meant to "belong" to a citizenry, implications that have become ever timelier as the radical right has wielded postmodern social theory for its own exclusionary conceptions of membership and association.

3 Robert Antonio, "After Postmodernism: Reactionary Tribalism," *American Journal of Sociology*, Vol. 106, No. 1 (2000), 162.

4 Sheldon Wolin, *Politics and Vision: Continuity and Innovation in Western Political Thought*, expanded ed. (Princeton, NJ: Princeton University Press, 2004), 587.

5 Sheldon Wolin, "Fugitive Democracy," in *Fugitive Democracy and Other Essays*, ed. Nicholas Xenos (Princeton, NJ: Princeton University Press, 2016): 100–15, 104.

6 Wendy Brown, *Undoing the Demos: Neoliberalism's Stealth Revolution* (New York: Zone Books, 2015).

7 Sheldon Wolin, "On the Theory and Practice of Power," in *Fugitive Democracy and Other Essays*, ed. Nicholas Xenos (Princeton, NJ: Princeton University Press, 2016): 283–300, 285.

8 Ibid., 287.

9 Ibid., 284.

10 Ibid., 287.

11 Kateb, George. "Wolin as a Critic of Democracy," in *Democracy and Vision: Sheldon Wolin and the Viccissitudes of the Political*, ed. Aryeh Botwinick and William Connolly (Princeton, NJ: Princeton University Press, 2001), 39–58, 44.

12 Ibid., 44.

13 Hannah Arendt, *On Revolution* (London: Penguin Books, 1963), 30.

14 Sheldon Wolin, "Norm and Form: The Constitutionalizing of Democracy," in *Fugitive Democracy and Other Essays*, ed. Nicholas Xenos (Princeton, NJ: Princeton University Press, 2016), 77–100, 85.

15 Ibid., 80.
16 Wolin, *Politics and Vision*, 565.
17 Ibid., 565.
18 Ibid., 576.
19 In the manner of the irreverent and provocative approach to authority that he so admired of the demos, Wolin chose to put the name "inverted totalitarianism" to the constellation of pathologies he observed in the United States as the prerogatives of capital pushed against its political heritage. It is an *inverted* totalitarianism, as it is the product of just this evacuation of the political. Where the classical totalitarianisms of the twentieth century sprung from the political singularities of characters such as Hitler or Stalin whose power poured down to a ceaselessly mobilized citizenry, inverted totalitarianism has no particular fountainhead, no singularity. Instead the broader corporate-economic culture that is said to have captured democratic institutions produces its own, resolutely unremarkable, slate of leaders/CEOs who are legitimized by a de-mobilized consumer-citizenry. It is the capture of these institutions and processes, the denuding of their popular aspect, that accounts for the totalitarian bent of inverted totalitarianism, producing what Wolin termed an "economy of opposition," whereby democracy is managed and rendered safe for corporate capitalism in establishing the boundaries of acceptable contestation.
20 Ernesto Laclau, *On Populist Reason* (London: Verso, 2005).
21 Chantal Mouffe, *The Return of the Political* (London: Verso, 1993).
22 Wolin, *Politics and Vision*, 587.
23 William Connolly, *Neuropolitics* (Minneapolis: University of Minnesota Press, 2002).
24 Sheldon Wolin, "Fugitive Democracy," in *Fugitive Democracy and Other Essays*, ed. Nicholas Xenos (Princeton, NJ: Princeton University Press, 2016), 100–15, 101.
25 Antonio, "After Postmodernism," 40–87.
26 C. Mudde, "The War of Words: Defining the Extreme Right Party Family," *West European Politics* (1996), 225–48.
27 E. Carter, *The Extreme Right in Western Europe: Success or Failure* (Manchester: Manchester University Press, 2003).
28 Piero Ignazi, "The Silent Counter Revolution: Hypotheses on the Emergence of Extreme Right Parties in Europe," *European Journal of Public Research*, No. 22 (1992), 3–34.
29 Matt Goodwin and Rob Ford, "Understanding UKIP: Identity, Social Change and the Left Behind," *Political Quarterly*, Vol. 85, No. 3 (2014), 277–84.
30 Hans Georg Betz, *Radical Right Wing Populism in Western Europe* (London: Macmillan Press, 1994).
31 Goodwin and Ford, "Understanding UKIP," 277–84.
32 Matthew Goodwin, "The Rise and Faults of the Internalist Perspective in Extreme Right Studies," *Representation*, Vol. 42, No. 4 (2006), 347–64.

33 Joao Carvalho, "The End of a Strategic Opening? The BNP's Window of Opportunity in the 2000s and Its Closure in the 2010s," *Patterns of Prejudice*, Vol. 49, No. 3 (2015), 271–93.

34 Graham Macklin, "Modernizing the Past for the Future," in *The British National Party: Contemporary Perspectives*, ed. Graham Macklin and Nigel Copsey (Abingdon: Routledge, 2011), 19–37.

35 Ibid., 25.

36 Ibid., 27.

37 Nigel Copsey, "Changing Course or Changing Clothes? Reflections on the Ideological Evolution of the British National Party 1999–2006," *Patterns of Prejudice* (2007), 61–82, 70.

38 Piero Ignazi, "From Neo-Fascists to Post-Fascists? The Transformation of the MSI into the AN," *West European Politics*, Vol. 19, No. 4 (1996), 693–714, 704.

39 Ibid., 704.

40 Ibid.

41 Roger Griffin, "The 'Post-Fascism' of the Alleanza Nationale: A Case Study in Ideological Morphology," *Journal of Political Ideologies*, Vol. 1, No. 2 (1996), 123–45.

42 Ibid., 140.

43 See Roger Griffin, "Modernity, Modernism and Fascism. A 'Mazeway Resynthesis,'" *Modernism/Modernity* (2007), 9–24; and Tamir Bar-On, *Rethinking the French New Right: Alternatives to Modernity* (New York: Routledge, 2013).

44 Wolin, *Politics and Vision*, 604.

45 Wolin, "On the Theory and Practice of Power," 298.

46 David McIvor, "The Politics of Speed: Connolly, Wolin, and the Prospects for Democratic Citizenship in an Accelerated Polity," *Polity*, Vol. 43, No. 1 (2011), 58–83.

47 Ibid., 75.

48 Ibid., 76.

49 Wolin, *Politics and Vision*, 604.

9 The Fate of Fugitive Democracy Today

TERRY MALEY

In the closing pages of the expanded edition of *Politics and Vision* in 2004 Sheldon Wolin talks about a new configuration of power he called "inverted totalitarianism." This heuristic construct captured the totalizing nature of the American state after 9/11 and a new neoliberal/late modern merging of corporate and state power. Wolin was careful to argue that this was not German fascism of the 1930s, but rather a new historical mutation of totalitarianism characterized by the symbiotic alliance of the vast powers of the late modern state and capitalism. Personnel from Wall Street, regardless of party, move fluidly between the commanding heights of Wall Street and the upper reaches of the American state, while the citizen-consumers of Joseph Schumpeter's post–Second World War plural-elite model of liberal-democracy were largely excluded from the exercise of democratic power. Ordinary citizens were (and often still are) reduced to passively watching the machinations of the powerful while being subject to the vicissitudes of the globalized economy, ecologically wasteful mass consumerism, the surveillance of an enlarged security state and private tech behemoths Google, Apple, etc., along with the relentless propaganda of Fox News and the far-right conspiracy blogosphere. This new form of totalization was "inverted," more cultural, and did not need to rely on the overt (state and extra-judicial) violence and/or the biological racism/anti-Semitism of the Nazis. The anti-democratic implications of these developments are, for Wolin, profound.

Yet in 2004 the idea of "totalitarianism" in the United States seemed far-fetched to most observers. In the post–Second World War era it had been part of the (binary) American self-understanding that totalitarianism was something that Western liberal-democracies had fought against and overcome, first against the Nazis and then Soviet communism.[1] Yet already in the late 1970s the Canadian political theorist C.B. Macpherson speculated, in his widely read book *The Life and Times of Liberal-Democracy* (1977), that liberal-democracy might be finished. Macpherson thought that the plural-elite model of liberal-democracy, which had argued that citizens were consumers of packaged political goods/ programs produced by ruling elites, had run its course. Macpherson, who had become well-known in theory circles in the early 1960s (just after Wolin's *Politics and Vision* in 1960) for his groundbreaking critique of the "possessive individualism" of Hobbes's and Locke's early liberalism, argued that Anglo-American liberalism had two strands.[2] One, following from late nineteenth-century "ethical liberal-democrats" such as J.S. Mill, emphasized the freedom of citizens to fully develop their individual capacities. The other, more Lockean strand, focused on market-based freedoms and property rights. The problem, Macpherson argued, was that liberal-democracy had uneasily combined the two strands, but that market-based freedoms had won out over developmental freedoms.[3] The plural-elite model enshrined market-based freedoms (in favour of property owners) while limiting or marginalizing developmental freedoms for all (i.e., for the non-property-owning classes – everyone else).

The rise of neoliberalism since the 1980s has exacerbated this tension within liberal-democracies, driving the two strands of liberalism further apart.[4] We now need to be concerned (again) not only with the issues of corporate power that Wolin raised in *Democracy Inc.*, but as Wendy Brown and Lucy Cane note, with resurgent white supremacy/racism, misogyny/homo- and transphobia, and nationalism. In *In the Ruins of Neoliberalism ...* Brown argues that this is not only an economic, or class-based development. Neoliberalism has enabled older oppressions to re-emerge forcefully, "unleashing" them alongside deregulated corporate and state power. Like Macpherson at the time, Wolin was at the forefront of critical discussions about democracy that were important precursors to current commentators, such as Cornel West and Wendy Brown, who have incorporated many of Wolin's critical insights but also diagnosed and envisioned democracy beyond his work. Wolin and Macpherson both sought to map out the limits of the plural-elite model's self-understanding and to envision democracy beyond them. In his later work (in the expanded edition of *PV*, 2004, and *Democracy Inc.*, 2008) Wolin tenaciously explored the tensions between the increasing power of the modern institutions of the state and capitalism, and the diminished power of the *demos* under conditions of growing inequality. Here I argue that Wolin's work remains relevant today in an era of growing authoritarianism.

In his well-known article "Fugitive Democracy," Wolin argued that genuine democratic involvement in pursuit of public, common causes, or what he called the *political*, was seen to be only fleetingly (and more locally) possible outside of the institutions of the state and party system. Democratic participation is also fleeting because in liberal-democracies most wage-earning citizens do not have the leisure time to engage in sustained democratic activity.[5] Instead, the state for Wolin had essentially been captured by a tightly interwoven plutocracy of wealth and power. This assessment in Wolin's later work was the culmination of an ongoing critique, which he developed through the 1980s, 1990s, and 2000s, that critically challenged the Schumpetarian plural-elite model – and practices – of late modern liberal-democracy.[6]

In his last published work, *Democracy Inc.* in 2008, Wolin asked two very provocative questions that could not be more relevant today in the age of global populism: "What causes a democracy to change into some non- or anti-democratic system, and what kind of system is democracy likely to change into?"[7] These questions, which at the time of the publication of *Politics and Vision*, expanded edition, in 2004 might have seemed far-fetched have now acquired a palpable urgency. Since Donald Trump became president in 2016 there have been a flood of books and articles about the emergence of (variously) new forms of illiberal democracy, authoritarianism, tyranny, and despotism beyond but also within liberal-democracies of the Global North.[8] This gives Wolin's concern with democracy an ongoing relevance. At the same time, as Lucy Cane has rightly argued, we also need to be mindful of the blind spots in Wolin's work. To say his work is still timely is not to write it a blank check.[9]

Here I bring Wolin into conversation with other discussions (some in political theory, others in political economy) about what democracy means today. In doing so I want to ask whether Wolin's view that the *demos* has been reduced to a state of "fugitive democracy" makes sense now, in a (still-, post-?) Trumpist era of "reactionary tribalism" and authoritarian backsliding in which basic liberal-democratic rights and institutions need to be defended but also changed significantly in the fight against right-wing populism.[10] I argue that while Wolin's diagnosis of inverted totalitarianism still makes sense today, it can be complemented by the views of the interlocutors I engage. Green's view presents a "realist" challenge to Wolin without engaging his work directly. Others take up issues that Wolin did not engage in detail but that can supplement his view of inverted totalitarianism – social movements and horizontal leadership, for instance, or the political economy and social psychology that are integral to neoliberal "rationality." By looking at these discussions of democracy in the twenty-first century, I argue that Wolin's elusive term "fugitive democracy" is a necessary but not sufficient response to the issues identified by Keane, Brown, and others in the current moment of democratic peril. In his later work Wolin was concerned about what was happening to democracy under circumstances in which neoliberal dominance was being consolidated in the United States and globally. We now need to be concerned, as Brown and Cane note, with the toxic configuration that adds white supremacy, blatant misogyny/homo- and transphobia, and nationalism to Wolin's concerns about Superpower in *Democracy Inc.*[11]

After the financial crash of 2007–8 Jeffrey Green's first book, *In the Eyes of the People: Democracy in an Age of Spectatorship* (*Eyes* hereafter) offered a defence of a liberal-democratic realism inspired by Max Weber's view of plebiscitary leadership. In 2016 a sequel appeared in *The Shadow of Unfairness: A Plebeian Theory of Liberal Democracy* (*Shadow* hereafter). Green's arguments are symptomatic of the strains which the advanced democracies of the Global North are labouring under today. I think there is a difficult but fruitful dialogue to be had between Green, Wolin, and others in the historical moment that confronts liberal-democracies today. The other interlocutors I'll engage still believe – as Wolin would have as well – that we should not simply resign ourselves to liberal democracy's inherent "shadow of unfairness."

For Green, in *Eyes*, the idea that the voice of the people is sovereign is out of step with the hard realities of the plutocracy to which ordinary people must accommodate themselves if they (paradoxically?) want to recover any shred of dignity as citizens.[12] In *Eyes* Green argues that "Democracy hitherto has been conceived as an empowerment of the People's voice." But under the kind of popular powerlessness that was baked into representative democracy by post–Second World War plural-elite theorists (in a time of prosperity), and reinforced in a media-saturated world, Green issues "a call to consider the People's *eyes* as an organ that might more properly function as a site of popular empowerment."[13] The fact is that for most of us, our political voice is something we exercise rarely if at all. Green argues that the focus on the people's voice is, "by itself ... too narrow and too ... out of touch with the way politics is experienced by most people most of the time."[14]

By focusing on *spectatorship* Green seeks to redefine the liberal-democratic problem of political apathy that observers have long noted. For Green spectatorship is "a problem that indicates the distinctive difficulties besetting democratic life at the dawn of the twenty-first century." Mass communications technologies and television have turned the majority of citizens into a permanent spectator class. Taking the relationship between elite political agents and the mass of citizens-spectators as hierarchical and fixed, there is virtually no room in *Eyes* for the kind of engaged, participatory democratic decision-making practised by social movement and other engaged actors. For them, democracy is not a passive (as the saying goes) spectator sport.

Green's response to the "pathologies and dysfunctions ... of 20th century liberal-democracies is to revive 'a forgotten alternative within democratic theory: ... plebiscitary democracy.'"[15] Green argues that today a plebiscitary view of democracy inspired by Max Weber can "develop political principles that ... respect the everyday structure of political experience. Taking spectatorship seriously is a way of respecting the political lives of ordinary people." Green argues for an "ocular" model of democracy that "represents a new ethical paradigm that would reshape the way the moral meaning of democracy is approached."[16] The tough question Green asks is how modern democracies, which are governed by elites who control huge institutions and massive resources, can come to terms with the existing, low democratic capacities of ordinary citizens. The only realistic way of correcting this, Green suggests, is to shift the focus of what democracy means away from the people, who are not sovereign in any meaningful way, back to leaders. Green wants to revive a focus on plebiscitary leaders that Weber emphasized in his famous 1919 lecture, *The Profession and Vocation of Politics*.[17]

Green's proposal for correcting the defects of non-participation in liberal-democracies is to subject leaders to "ocular" scrutiny. He suggests that highly visible public spaces such as presidential debates are the appropriate venues for this spectator's check on elite power because party leaders are not in complete control of such events (i.e., the questions journalists can ask). By having leaders respond "spontaneously" in these settings the people will be able to decide on the credibility of leading party candidates. Green argues that this kind of surveillance will have a "disciplinary" effect on leaders, and that as a result they will behave with more "candor."[18] Green argues that Foucault's idea of the disciplinary surveillance of populations can be turned back onto political leaders, making them more accountable.[19] Green's "ocular" view accepts, somewhat paradoxically, political passivity as unchangeable while also accepting the autonomy of voting.

In *Shadow* (2016), Green argues that there will always be a certain unfairness built into liberal-democracy. He corrects, to a degree, for what critics had noted about *Eyes*, viz. that there had been no discussion of economic inequality, capitalism/corporate power, or the power of the "voices" of social/protest movements.[20] Green argues that inequalities of wealth and power, and the way they distort representative democracy, can never be eliminated. Given this state of affairs Green offers a "plebeian theory of democracy" in which he argues that there are ways in which ordinary citizens can make their views known to powerful elected officials. But only under the following limiting realities.

Green notes that plebeian democracy is defined by three factors that can never be significantly altered. One is Remove – the realization that ordinary citizens will never hold power in high offices. The second is Manyness – that in order to achieve political change ordinary citizens can only do so in large numbers, and not individually. And third, that liberal-democracies are actually run by plutocrats whose enormous wealth gives them great power that plebeians will never exercise. For all of these reasons plebeians are essentially second-class citizens in liberal-democracies.

Green's view in *Shadow* is that the dignity of ordinary working-class citizens can be restored only by resigning themselves to the shadow of unfairness. In *Shadow* Green suggests two things (among others) that can partially compensate for plebeian powerlessness. First, citizens can engage in expressions of "principled vulgarity" to let elected officials know that they are unhappy with given policies or arrangements – by interrupting meetings, publicly obstructing political events, etc. Second, Green proposes an inversion of Rawls's Difference Principle as a way of regulating the superrich and the insidious influence of big/dark money on representative democracy. As is well known Rawls's original version of the Difference Principle had proposed that inequalities should only be tolerated if they benefit the most disadvantaged. Green "inverts" this when he suggests that the political influence of the superrich should be tightly regulated by reform measures, such as strict campaign finance laws.[21] In the plutocratic context of unfairness Green outlines in *Shadow*, these might be necessary reforms, but they are insufficient; they will not save neoliberal democracy from itself.

In neither work does Green engage radical democrats, either because he does not want to confront their issues (to his left) head on (fearing they may have a point?), and/or because he thinks them too unrealistic. Radical democrats have engaged in significant discussions of collective and democratic agency, constituent power, "fugitive democracy" (Wolin), "insurgent democracy" (Miguel Abensour), and other issues amid severe social and economic inequalities.[22] Green chooses not to engage with those who seek more far-reaching changes to both the global political economy and the institutions of the liberal-democratic state.[23]

The implication of Green's sobering analysis is to provide a safety valve for the frustration of a precarious working class, consigned to powerlessness and second-class citizenship, within the frame of a constitutively flawed liberal-democracy characterized by new and extreme forms of disempowerment, political, social, and economic alienation. Green's gives us the plural-elite model updated for neoliberalism. But with the implicit assumption that the white, male breadwinner of the Second World War era has been de-centred. Gone is the post–Second World War prosperity and redistribution that had provided the political-economy backdrop for the plural-elite model. The kind of plebeian dignity that Green envisions might have been more realistic for relatively privileged plebeians in the welfare state era, where white working- and middle-class male workers (though not workers of colour, women, or marginalized communities) had unionized full-time jobs with benefits and pensions.

I think Green's argument is an attempt to both *contain and safely release the rage* of ordinary, powerless (white male) citizens of the neoliberal era in a way that would salvage their dignity (and liberal-democracy) so that working people do not embrace far-right populist demagogues like Trump. In *Shadow* I think Green wants to give plebeian citizens an outlet – principled plebeian vulgarity and regulation of the superrich – so that their anger can be contained, very much as Weber wanted to, within the frame of liberal-democracy. Affectively unleashed by neoliberalism and now Trumpism, those disaffected plebeians have veered sharply towards racist, sexist, homo- and transphobic, and conspiratorial "vulgarity" and have found "solace" in the far-right blogosphere – not the dignity Green's plebeian theory envisions. Many disaffected plebeians have turned to precisely the kind of centrifugal far-right eruptions of which Wolin warned at the end of *Politics and Vision* in 2004, and that Green's plebeian theory seeks to contain.[24] Under Trumpian populism Green's ameliorative proposals have not worked. Overall, Green's analysis might have had greater resonance in different registers had he engaged more critical interdisciplinary work, such as critical theory, political economy, feminist or critical race theory, or the now burgeoning literature on neoliberalism.[25]

Green's argument does not, I think, move us forward along a path to the alternative(s) he argues are missing on the left. One can't rescue liberal-democracy by grounding an ethical theory of plebeian democracy in the powerlessness of second-class plebeian citizens. While parts of his diagnosis in *Shadow* agree with a number of current views about the "pathologies" of liberal-democracy, Green's solutions share some of the same problems that Max Weber's view of plebiscitary democracy did under a different moment of crisis. Now, one hundred years after Weber's famous *Politics as a Vocation* lecture Green's attempt to call the kind of resignation on offer a way of recognizing the dignity of plebeian citizens reveals the limits of a spent liberalism in an era in which neoliberal Superpower has helped unleash authoritarian populism.[26]

But as we saw in the reactions to the brutal police murders of George Floyd, Breonna Taylor, and Rayshard Brooks in 2020, the anger of millions of ordinary citizens has not been contained. Nor has the dignity of millions of precarious plebeians – e.g., Black, Latino, and poor white citizens who have been marginalized under neoliberalism (a term that does not feature in Green's account), women in the Me Too movement who have been sexually assaulted by predatory men in positions of power – been restored. Green's plebeian theory of democracy tries to keep working-class citizens within the frame of a somewhat more regulated and accountable liberal-democracy. Whether it is possible to reform liberal-democracy (with a post-neoliberal/Picketty welfare state redux?), to save it from the raw, deregulated capitalism of the neoliberal era or the new authoritarianism to which it is now wedded, is an open question that seemed inconceivable only a decade ago.

Yet Green's issues remain vexing for both those who would like to reform liberal-democracies in social democratic directions or those who would like to see it replaced by arrangements and institutions that involve even more significant democratic change. We need to look elsewhere for answers to Wolin's two questions. In response to Green's point that the left has not offered a vision of the *political* based on new forms of commonality, I will use the rest of the paper to explore this concern in light of commentaries on the future of democracy more informed by the discourse of political economy: in particular, why Wolin's alternative to Green's plebeian "realism" is more helpful for practically envisioning democracy today, even though Green would likely dismiss these democratic theories as unrealistic.

There has been a good deal of frustration recently on the left about why the global social movements have not been able to bring about more far-reaching political change, even with their trenchant critiques of growing inequality, the concentration of wealth in the hands of the 1 per cent, and state-sponsored austerity.[27] This is so despite the fact that the movements have been highly visible, horizontally/democratically organized, tech/social media savvy, and at times very effective in drawing attention to their issues. This may seem to validate Green's argument, but political economists such as Martijn Konings beg to differ.

Konings offers this as context. He notes that on the left, "Explanations for why neoliberalism is still ... operational have tended to focus on the ability of financial elites to capture public discourses and institutions."[28] The corporate elites have mobilized to capture both the "commanding heights" of the global economy, states/governments, and the media. Since the 1980s the global corporate elites have pushed back aggressively against the redistributive policies of the welfare state by "occupying" state electoral offices and institutions, funding think tanks, and changing the rules of the political game in their favour whenever possible.[29]

For Konings the state capture view sees "the legitimating spirit of neoliberalism as an external ideological moment, portraying populists' loyalty to neoliberal discourses as a kind of cognitive impairment or moral failure."[30] Many radical democrats as well as mainstream liberals held this view of Trump's 2016 presidential election victory. Recall Hillary Clinton's now-infamous remark during the campaign about the "deplorables" who voted for Trump. The moral and intellectual deficiencies of the Trump regime and its supporters were nightly fodder on non–Fox News American cable networks such as CNN and MSNBC. There is a long history of conservatives, some liberals, and even social democrats seeing the working class as immature and unfit to govern.[31] The implication of this "cognitive impairment/moral failure" view is that any rational thinking person could not possibly have voted for a populist like Trump. And how could working people support a demagogue whose own politics of self-aggrandizement and division ran so directly against their own interests?

Yet Konings asks a very timely question. Referring to the political mood that followed the 2007–8 financial crash, after which the term "the 1%" entered the popular political vocabulary through the Occupy movement, he asks, "how elites could continue to access such tremendous material, institutional and symbolic resources even in a context where discontent with key neoliberal institutions was at an all-time high and the political air was thick with ... distrust towards bankers."[32] This ambivalent situation – in which Green's plebeians find themselves – is now the "new normal." Konings's answer has to do with two things that are intertwined under neoliberalism. One is affect, or the emotional connection people have to neoliberal values and institutions, to the self-reliant "legitimating spirit of neoliberalism." The other is the culture of risk. For Konings both are integral to the "logic" or rationality of neoliberalism.

Under neoliberalism, with the relative security of the welfare state reduced for the most vulnerable/racialized parts of the population and the former industrial working class (and now for sections of the middle class as well), the volatility of capitalist risk-taking without much state protection has become part of everyday life. Insecurity – the way that precarious, vulnerable populations take the brunt of market risk-taking and state-induced austerity – has become pervasive under neoliberalism. This economic insecurity leads to both fear (of Others as market and/or racialized competitors – the undocumented, Dreamers, Blacks and Hispanics, even legal immigrants) and to volatile and even desperate *need*, as a defining cultural experience of plebeian citizens. As Toronto Star columnist Rick Salutin notes, Trump loyalists "feel so disdained and patronized that when someone shows up who they believe really cares, an earthquake could not shake them, so great is their need."[33] Of course, as so many Black and Brown writers, activists, scholars, and politicians have noted for so many years, need, fear, and marginalization have been the experience of African Americans, people of colour, and Indigenous peoples for generations, centuries.[34]

Fear, volatility and need are janus-faced, complex political forces. They can either reinforce emotional attachments to whatever symbolic sources of (real or imagined) security that plebiscitary or demagogic leaders offer up, and/or they can lead to rebellions against the causes of that volatility. Wolin captured the complexity of this dynamic in his 1996 article "Fugitive Democracy": "The democratization of advanced industrial societies has come down to this: the labor, wealth, and psyches of the citizenry are simultaneously defended and exploited ... protected and extracted, rewarded and commanded."[35]

In the post–Second World War era this affective volatility was assuaged and contained by the social provisioning of the welfare state. Konings identifies this with Karl Polanyi's "double movement," in which the volatility of recurrent market crises was re-balanced by state social policy. In Polanyi's view, markets have historically been embedded in society. When economic crises dislodged markets from their social and historical embeddedness, causing social disintegration and political turmoil, a mix of popular/social pressure and government programs re-embedded them, returning a kind of balance to the relationship between markets and society. Konings notes that under neoliberalism this "re-embedding" has not occurred; a new, sustainable balance has not been restored. In the neoliberal era volatility, historically always part of modern market economies, has become perpetual. Wolin has pointed to the corollary of this. Not only have the financial markets in particular become virtually autonomous from society.[36] Over the past forty years the neoliberal state has also succeeded in further insulating/liberating itself to a significant degree from popular pressure or control from "below." The state's *capacity* to rebalance or re-embed the markets in society has, by serial acts of legislative self-limitation, been seriously and deliberately diminished. Thus, heightened risk and crises, at the intersection of the global political economy, the state, and the personal and work lives of plebeian citizens, have been normalized. Konings argues that what the left had previously thought were states of exception, deviations from what were thought to be liberal-democratic norms and the "normal" functioning of markets, are now simply part of the way neoliberalism works.

For Konings there is a specific dynamic to the way that neoliberalism produces widespread insecurity in the form of acclimatization to market precarity and risk, and an emotional and cultural reaction to insecurity that can result in a strong identification with charismatic authoritarian leaders by destabilized parts of the population. The normalization of crises has become part of what Wolin called managed democracy.[37] Thus, through a lens influenced by both Foucault (neoliberal rationality) and political economy, Konings sheds light on a different dimension of the plebeian experience that relates to Wolin's question of what democracy can become.[38]

One example of the kind of centrifugal forces cast off by what Wolin saw as postmodern fragmentation is the ecosystem of social media companies/platforms and far-right conspiracy blogs and podcasts, such as those of Alex Jones and Steve Bannon/Breitbart. The way in which these conspiracy theories, websites, and social media personalities have moved from the outer fringes of the blogosphere to the political mainstream, and in Bannon's case right into the heart of the White House, are symptomatic of new and extreme forms of disempowerment, dislocation, and alienation that are part of the "rationality" of neoliberalism. The disaffected base, with its virulent racism and xenophobia, that Jones delivered to Donald Trump in the 2016 election reflected this volatility and a deep sense of grievance and loss (of plebeian white, male privilege and power), as well as the unbridled greed of Wall Street.[39] Of course, the African American and Latino communities and women (particularly of colour) have been much more brutally and directly oppressed; they have experiencedf loss and trauma for decades, centuries. The sense of loss and anger expressed by

Trump supporters is the flip side (though not the equivalent – the Trumpist sense of loss is profoundly anti-democratic) of what Lucy Cane has argued is a deep sense of the loss of local democracy and a common, progressive *political* that infuses Wolin's thought. As Jason Frank has argued, for Wolin two "bodies" – one market based, the other democratic and participatory – have always existed in tension as part of the American political experiment.[40] The migration of far-right grievances onto widely popular social media platforms has effected a newly resurgent anti-democratic balance between these forces. In addition to helping the left – eco, feminist, BLM, and many other local, national, and international social justice groups – organize, social media has also facilitated the creation of a community of forces which are actively defining an anti-democratic *political* on the far right. This is part of the story of how neoliberalism has enabled or helped create the conditions under which liberal-democracy is morphing into something different, how democracy can become something else. It is the further development of Wolin's inverted totalitarianism.

This constellation of forces is behind John Keane's 2020 book *The New Despotism* (*Despotism* hereafter). In many ways Keane updates Wolin's more US-centric view in *Democracy Inc.*, broadening it into a global perspective. In *Despotism* Keane provides a comprehensive global survey of the wide range of Machiavellian strategies and tactics populist authoritarians are using to undermine both newer (post-1989) and established liberal-democracies. They have not merely enabled "state capture" by oligarchs. Keane also talks about the reverse, the capture of oligarchs and business elites by a new political class. The new despotisms, Keane argues, "are dominated by 'poligarchs,'" "rich government officials and business people who work together to stuff staggering amounts of wealth into their own pockets … and family dynasties they control." The new poligarchs "are state protected crony-capitalists who practice the dark arts of corruption."[41]

Picking up on recent discussions, Keane provides a further elaboration of the distinction between mid-twentieth-century totalitarianism and the new configuration of despotism. "Unlike twentieth century totalitarian systems, which cultivated the 'atomization and isolation of the individual', rendering people 'more easily manipulable by destroying civil society associations and replacing them with 'huge and undifferentiated mass organizations', the new despotisms thrive on privatized connections.… Many institutions, including government bureaucracies, parliaments, and the courts, are captured by these networks of patronage."[42] The newer forms of despotism are more nimble and electronically sophisticated than the plural-elite model of the post–Second World War generation could have imagined. As Keane says, "The new despotism are plutocracies, but their extreme concentrations of wealth are camouflaged by the deployment of scrambled political languages that have the tactical effect of enabling rulers to gaslight their subjects by being different things to different people at different times. The new despotism is a new form of state-regulated surveillance capitalism."[43]

They are, for Keane, "phantom democracies" which use "less spectacular, more complex and much cleverer" methods to gain popular assent. Keane sees this as a new "shape-shifting form of power whose protean qualities are harder to summarize, yet much more sophisticated in their ability to dissolve the spirit of democracy in the acids of voluntary servitude and popular quiescence to arbitrary power."[44] That quiescence also "depends on loyal middle classes who are prepared to trade some liberties for comfortable peace and quiet. Periodic elections and digital media storms offer a voice to subjects," along with selective "handouts, official talk of the need for legality and order, and the public camouflaging and privatization of violence."[45]

Keane's view incorporates elements of both Green's description of the plebeian experience and Wolin's analysis of managed democracy. Yet he also notes (and this is an important difference in emphasis from earlier analyses of neoliberalism such as David Harvey's) that this new configuration of power is not simply "the political expression of modern capitalism."[46] Phantom democracies certainly share some of neoliberalism's anti-democratic aspects, but the phenomena Keane outlines go beyond the economic. In this Wolin would have agreed.

Keane warns that lest we think the new despotisms are only to be found in Russia, Egypt, Singapore, India or Turkey – not in the West – they are not simply the polar opposites of Western liberal-democracies. His argument is that the line or distinction is no longer so clear. The issues he canvasses are already present in the liberal-democracies of the Global North in the early twenty-first century. Keane thus also details how democracies can turn into something undemocratic.

Yet in the closing pages, Keane argues that while these regimes and their self-dealing poligarchs go to great lengths to insulate themselves from popular dissent and accountability, "unplanned events ... can rock despotic power to its foundations ... Judges can speak against rulers. Investigative journalists risk ... their lives.... Digital mutinies and non-violent strikes by organized groups can give birth to a rebellious civil society. Established institutions may show signs of crumbling. Rigged elections can be lost. Big dramas can grow from small openings. Democratic openings can happen."[47] Or pandemics can happen, exposing deep inequalities in a new light, as well as the desperate attempts of poligarchs to cling to power by subverting established electoral, legal norms and institutions. Here Keane echoes the language of the global social/protest movements in the 2000s. Or Wolin, writing about fugitive democracy.

In the mid-1990s Wolin's provocative idea of "fugitive democracy" was grounded in the distinction between politics and the political. The search for a new political emerged in the 1990s in reaction to the argument that the realist or competitive-elitist model of democracy had reached its limits. By the 1990s, the capitalist democracies of the Global North were being transformed in neo-liberal directions. By calling democracy "fugitive," Wolin addressed profound changes in the meaning of liberal-democracy in the late twentieth century.

The distinction between "politics" and the "political" involves a critique of representation, the assumption that truth is fully present in existing empirical or historical realities (such as the modern liberal subject), and an implicit potential, in Wolin's work, for the *demos* to "transcend" or go beyond existing conditions.

In Wolin's view: "The *political* ... is an expression of the idea that a free society composed of diversities can nonetheless enjoy moments of commonality when, through public deliberations, collective power is used to promote or protect the well-being of a collectivity."[48] The political involves diverse attempts to create and articulate the constitutive moments of commonality, or the foundational ends of politics. Yet Wolin is acutely aware that any revival of the political takes place in a "disenchanted" world that has been shaped by the great modern powers of the state, bureaucracy, and capitalism, science and technology.[49] By contrast, *politics* for Wolin is the "legitimized public contestation ... by organized and unequal powers" over collective public resources. Everyday politics provides the institutional forms within which the political is reproduced, legitimized, and contained. Attempts to define the political always involve struggles over how democratic institutions work, but also struggles for the hearts and minds of the *demos*, its symbols, coalitions, and movements – all in attempts to either defend, reform, or contest the foundations upon which normal politics are based.

For Wolin, the key institution in which politics takes place is the state, or what in his later work he called Superpower. It encompasses what is, in the first decades of the twenty-first century, a "managed" democracy in which plutocratic elites seek to contain the *demos* and a selectively deregulated global capitalism buttressed by the vast technological and military resources of the state. This provides the context, for Wolin, of the paradoxical trajectory of widening social and economic inequality and diminished citizenship under the banner of liberal-democracy. The gap between ordinary citizens' capacity to govern themselves and the vast powers of Superpower and corporate capital has grown exponentially in the democracies of the Global North over the last forty years, even as those democracies partially fulfilled some of the promises of liberal modernity in the post–Second World War era. Some key progressive gains have been made via the ballot box and through the courts. The trajectory of neoliberalism has not been seamless or simply linear/totalizing; there are cracks and openings in the system at different levels and at different times; progressive gains are possible. But it continues to be a struggle; gay rights were won through decades-long battles in the same court system that ultimately ruled in favour of

Citizens United and that recently overturned *Roe v. Wade*. Both were examples of "the long march through the institutions."

For Wolin, the ability of the *demos* to realize common purposes was fleeting in the era of Superpower. People are caught between the complex mechanisms of democratic inclusion/exclusion created by the Superpower state on the one hand and the centrifugal and disaggregating forces of global capitalism and postmodern culture on the other. For Wolin, the tendencies of Superpower and global capitalism are "totalizing in the sense that they are obsessed with control, expansion, superiority and supremacy." The political economy behind this lies in the privatization of state/public resources and the deregulation of finance capital by the Superpower state that has enabled unbridled, global market expansion. Neoliberalism has unleashed "a structure for organized [and patriarchal, militarized] aggression."[50] Trump's policies (border separation, the use of unidentified federal troops on the streets of Portland and Washington, DC, voter suppression by trying to de-fund the US Postal Service) typify the unleashed aggression of the plutocratic elites *and* the frustration of precarious plebeians in an era in which the remaining – and still stubbornly persistent – aspects of a previously more unrestrained neoliberalism (deregulation, tax cuts for the rich, austerity for the rest, disciplinary policing of racialized people, growing social inequality) are now toxically mixed with nationalism, open racism/xenophobia.

In the current conjuncture in which the legitimacy of Superpower is often challenged, now partially de-legitimized, but still dominant, possibilities for democratic commonality are still fugitive, not revolutionary in the more traditional Marxian sense.[51] Already in the 1980s Wolin had said that they are "fugitive in the very specific sense of being non-scientific and non-institutionalized."[52] Wolin's critics have argued that his idea of fugitive democracy signalled a deep political despair.[53] Fundamentally dissatisfied with liberal democracy and capitalism, Wolin polemically argued that democracy can be something else: "Democracy is a project concerned with the political potentialities of ordinary citizens, that is, with their possibilities for becoming political beings through the self-discovery of common concerns and of modes of action for realizing them."[54] Provocatively, almost in tension with his own analysis of Superpower, Wolin insisted that "ordinary individuals are capable of creating new cultural patterns of commonality at any moment."[55] The *demos*, in Wolin's later work, can periodically refashion itself into political subjects.

The question that is left open-ended in Wolin's work is: each time a fugitive democratic event or movement occurs, does it contain within itself the *potentiality* (though not the necessity) to create a new kind of community; does it create a memory, or a "trace" of the political for the future?[56] These fugitive moments of resistance and revolt need not be revolutionary in a totalizing way. Fleeting but unifying moments that go beyond the fragments and congeal into constellations of commonly created yet diverse democratic experiences and possibly counter-institutions. These moments, possible pre-figurations of a new political, are created in different times and places, often unpredictably, by parts of the *demos*. In his essay "Norm and Form," on Ancient Greek democracy, Wolin celebrates the anarchic, rebellious nature of the *demos*, its refusal to be constrained by ruling oligarchic forms of power. He celebrates those fugitive moments in which "democracy is wayward, inchoate, unable to rule yet unwilling to be ruled. It does not naturally con*form*." Democracy "is inherently formless."[57]

In this respect Wolin prefigured ideas that subsequently appeared in the global movements, such as those in the following description by UK social movement observer and participant Hilary Wainwright. Wainwright notes that new forms of the political need not be organized under one unified theory, idea, party, or form of the state. With reference to movements such as UK Uncut (pre-Corbyn and pre-Momentum) Wainwright argued that they are "purposefully autonomous from political parties [and provide] an example of the decisive material impact of a new kind of multi-centered, molecular campaign, bringing together all kinds of social actors." Behind UK Uncut was "a story of a campaign that coordinated horizontally and rotated responsibilities, developing … a diffuse leadership through which capacities were developed and spread."[58] The movements created horizontal, new forms of knowledge and democratic power that rejected the top-down technocratic knowledge still thought necessary by all (including social democratic) parties which seek state power.[59] Wainwright noted that in the *Indignados* movement in Spain (that grew out of the 2007–8 financial crash) people participated, in local public squares, in "decision-making by the thousands, many of whom have never occupied anything." [60] This kind of democratic engagement both requires and produces what Robert Lifton has optimistically called a new, *protean self*.[61] This is not (only) the "flexible" self-managed gig worker of the neoliberal economy, but rather people who can access reservoirs of resilience and be open to the kinds of "diffuse" leadership and "new forms of knowledge and democratic power" to which Wainwright refers.

Wolin's later work sharply describes experiences/memories of suffering, oppression, and exclusion, as well as the resistance these can engender. Today these demotic moments are seen in struggles around race, BLM, Me Too, the ecology and Indigenous/Native rights to the land, culture, memory, and language that have, sporadically, galvanized parts of the *demos* globally. Against Superpower and global capital, Wolin sees local forms of community resistance and organizing as potential repositories of a more democratic political. These moments are not restricted to the organized working class, which Wolin does not see as the primary agent of social change. In this sense Wolin's idea of a new political that emerges in formative moments of fugitive democracy has affinities with – and itself prefigured – the eruption of the global social movements in the 2000s. That spirit, that "another world is possible," poignantly captures the experience of so many social movements of the last twenty years. Wolin echoes them when he argues that: "[Democracy] needs to be reconceived as something other than a form of government: as a mode of being that is conditioned by bitter experience, doomed to succeed only temporarily, but is a recurrent possibility as long as the memory of the political survives."[62]

Yet any revival of the political in the early decades of the twenty-first century is destined to take place under the shadow of the issues described by Konings, Brown, and Keane. In his restless search for intimations of a new (or lost sense of the) political, one could be left with the sense that Wolin thought that managed democracy and the Superpower state were beyond democratic engagement and redemption. But with the new despotism upon us globally, the fugitive self-fashioning of the demos ignores engagement with the state at its peril. Today a fragmented and at times particularistic, identity-driven *demos* needs to engage in *a dual strategy*, re-creating a shifting balance between recognition of histories, identities, and political memory in the diverse communities and movements outside of state-managed democracy, *and* still trying to change or re-shape existing institutional sites of state power, changing existing institutional structures from within and creating counter-institutions where possible. The two aspects – democratic engagement inside and outside the state – cannot be separated. As Wainwright has noted more recently, "It cannot be one or the other."[63] Holding poligarchs accountable is certainly necessary, but it is not enough. In her 2020 book Lucy Cane argues that in his last work, *Democracy Inc.*, Wolin saw "that a defense of constitutionalism is at least pragmatically necessary."[64] My reading of "at least pragmatically necessary" is that Wolin is suggesting a strategic, pragmatic defence of constitutions and institutions *for now*, and not simply a reversion to their neoliberal forms, or even older plural-elite versions. Yet these dual strategic interventions are necessary because the state is not as monolithic as Wolin's analysis of managed democracy suggests; there are, as Keane notes, gaps and openings. There can be interventions not only by the far right but by the broader left. This is not to deny what I see as Wolin's view of possibly totalizing "developmental tendencies." But the system is not completely closed. Along these lines, a few concluding observations.

It may be necessary for the social movement left to keep engaging in the kind of "insurgencies" that we saw in the US Democratic and UK Labour parties by Sanders in the United States and Corbyn (i.e., the Momentum movement) in the UK. Their campaigns pushed – admittedly with mixed success – more radical, previously "fugitive" issues into the centre-left/"third-way" mainstream parties. But their message was, that progressive, previously marginalized issues and voices need to – and can, in the alchemy that can emerge in the mix between spontaneous eruption, organization, and dogged persistence – find their way onto party agendas and into state policy wherever they can.

Anand Giridharadas, in his review of journalist Kurt Andersen's recent book *Evil Geniuses* (2020), notes that Andersen leaves us with two key messages for the mainstream left. One is that the left needs to focus on "the amassing of power, the building of institutions, networks … – the long game," employed patiently over decades by the far right. In his writings dealing with political education Wolin was also aware of the need to build democratic capacities in (local – and other) counter-institutions beyond fleeting eruptions.[65] It is what Erik Olin Wright explored in his "real utopias" series.

The second is that the left has been "too nice, … too pragmatic, too nuanced." They may, perhaps controversially at times, need to engage more in the kinds of tactics, media, and institutional strategies that the right has not shied away from (with all of the complications that might inevitably entail). I am deeply ambivalent about, but mindful of, this suggestion. Getting "dirty hands" is still a huge challenge for progressives who believe that one should not separate a more humane version of the political from a more humane, less aggressive way of *doing* politics. Perhaps Andersen's suggestion could still avoid the most unsavoury aspects of getting one's hands dirty when doing politics (in the way that, historically, both the Republicans and Democrats have engaged in). In light of Andersen's observations, the tough questions for the left are: can strong, resilient counter-visions and democratic practices contain or change the (very masculinist) "structures of organized aggression" that neoliberalism and now the populist turn to the right have helped unleash culturally and legitimize politically? How do marginalized, plebeian/working/racialized citizens, and social movements (like Me Too, BLM, or Idle No More and now Land Back in Canada), engage with and against determined, elite opponents who have enormous power over economic resources and state institutions?[66] John Keane, in an extension of his idea of "monitory democracy," provides an idea that can be seen as complimentary to Wolin's view of a "counter-elite of democratic public servants" with expertise who can help citizens raise issues (discussed by Stephen Esquith in this volume), pressure politicians, and build movements. For Keane, "unelected representatives" with a social media presence (my students often cite Rachel Maddow, or even Stephen Colbert. Of course, the same can be said for Fox News hosts) can use their celebrity to become political "influencers," reaching huge audiences in the way celebrity NBA players did by cancelling play-off games or taking a knee in the summer of 2020 in solidarity with BLM.[67]

The challenge to citizens and democratic theorists (radical and deliberative) at this point is paradoxical. Even the existing, flawed democratic state institutions of which Wolin was wary now need to be not only monitored but engaged, defended, and replenished. But they also need to be significantly changed from their current neoliberal form in order to stop their descent into a new despotism. Against the economic and cultural forces of neoliberal fragmentation that enabled Trumpism to emerge it is clear that democrats cannot leave the running of the state to populists and authoritarians or let democracy's "two bodies" be reduced to a cult of personality, or a "party of one."[68]

NOTES

I would like to thank John Wallach for his very insightful comments on an earlier draft of this chapter.

1 The "end of ideology" was first proclaimed by Daniel Bell in the early 1960s. The redux came after the fall of the Berlin Wall in 1989 when Frances Fukuyama heralded the global triumph of liberal-democracy. See Lucy Cane's recent book for a discussion of the binary opposition between Western liberalism and Soviet communism as the backdrop for the first version of Wolin's *Politics and Vision* (1960) in Lucy Cane, *Sheldon Wolin and Democracy: Seeing Through Loss* (New York: Routledge, 2020), ch. 2. Cane relies on Arendt's discussion of totalitarianism. It was only outside of and to the left of the mainstream of American liberal political and democratic theory – in the "western Marxism" of the first generation of émigré critical theorists (Horkheimer, Adorno, Marcuse) – that the idea of a kind of convergence between Western/American post–Second World War development and Soviet communism was kept alive during the Cold War. In *Soviet Marxism* (1957) Herbert Marcuse wrote that the American and Soviet systems resembled each other to a far greater degree than the Cold War American self-understanding acknowledged. Marcuse argued that the myth of the American Protestant work ethic and Soviet/socialist Man shared similarities of self-sacrifice to a larger system of top-down, Taylorist industrial-scale production in which the workers were not in democratic control of either the state or the production process (i.e., whether in private-sector hands or state controlled). And, of course, Marcuse's *One-Dimensional Man* argued that the American system of mass production and consumerism was culturally totalizing. See Herbert Marcuse, *One-Dimensional Man: Studies in the Ideology of Advanced Industrial Society* (Boston: Beacon Press, 1964); and Herbert Marcuse, *Soviet Marxism: A Critical Analysis* (New York: Columbia University Press, 1958).

2 In his book on Macpherson's political thought Philip Hansen has argued that Macpherson should be brought back into dialogue with political philosophy and critical theory. See Philip Hansen, *Reconsidering C.B. Macpherson: From Possessive Individualism to Democratic Theory and Beyond* (Toronto: University of Toronto Press, 2015). I first met Wolin as a new PhD student at a conference in honour of Macpherson

at the University of Toronto in 1989. The affinities between their work have not been explored and certainly bear further elaboration. To cite one example, Wolin's chapter on Locke, "Injustice and Collective Memory," in *The Presence of the Past: Essays on the State and the Constitution* (Baltimore: Johns Hopkins University Press, 1989), and Macpherson's critique of property in Locke share affinities and are complementary. Both were precursors in some ways to recent discussions, among feminist and post-colonial scholars, of colonial dispossession and property in Locke's view of the Americas. See Calvin Lincez's discussion in this volume of dispossession and collective memory in relation to Wolin through the lens of Indigenous Resurgence theory.

3 C.B. Macpherson, *The Life and Times of Liberal Democracy* (New York: Oxford University Press, 1977), 1.

4 I don't pause here to define neoliberalism more systematically, as many others have done. My shorthand below (1–10) is an amalgam that borrows from David Harvey, Wendy Brown, Martijn Konings, and others. In it, neoliberalism is defined by (1) its initial formulation, as a counter to communism and the New Deal in the 1950s, by Friedrich von Hayek, economist James Buchanan, and those who founded the Mont Pelerin Society, (2) then an attack on the welfare state beginning in the 1980s under Reagan and Thatcher, (3) deep cuts to social spending, (4) deep tax cuts for the wealthy justified (initially) by "trickle down" economics (Reaganomics), (5) the disciplining of marginal and "surplus" populations (mostly of colour), (6) deregulation, (7) privatization of public/state assets, (8) an ideology of individual self-reliance, (9) aggressive elite defence of private property and corporate rights, including the expansion of international trade and finance governed by democratically inaccessible international institutions such as the WTO, and (10) all brought about by a combination of "stealth" as well as more public, organized campaigns of state and institutional "capture."

5 As Wolin makes clear in his 2015 interview with Lucy Cane. See Cane, op. cit., 202. I take up Wolin's view of the *political* and its connection to "fugitive democracy" towards the end of this chapter.

6 And, of course, Rawlsian liberalism. See Wolin's unsparing critique of Rawls in "The Liberal/Democratic Divide: On Rawls's Political Liberalism," *Political Theory*, Vol. 24, No. 1 (February 1996), 97–119.

7 See Sheldon S. Wolin, *Democracy Incorporated: Managed Democracy and the Specter of Inverted Totalitarianism* (Princeton, NJ: Princeton University Press, 2008), xii.

8 See, among many others, Masha Gessen, *Surviving Autocracy* (New York: Riverhead Books, 2020); Tim Snyder, *The Road to Unfreedom: Russia, Europe, America* (New York: Tim Duggan Books, 2018); Anne Applebaum, *Twilight of Democracy: The Seductive Lure of Authoritarianism* (New York: Penguin Random House, 2020); Steven Levitsky and Daniel Ziblatt, *How Democracies Die* (New York: Broadway Books, 2019); and John Keane's *The New Despotism* (Cambridge, MA: Harvard University Press, 2020); Henry A. Giroux, "The Nightmare of Neoliberal

Fascism," *Truthout*, 10 June 2018; and Kurt Anderson, *Evil Geniuses: The Unmaking of America: A Recent His*tory (New York: Random House, 2020).

Wendy Brown notes in the Introduction to *In the Ruins of Neoliberalism: The Rise of Antidemocratic Politics in the West* (New York: Columbia University Press, 2019) that in the now wide range of liberal and left commentary on these matters there is no settled definition of what is happening, of whether these globally emergent phenomena constitute new forms of authoritarianism, tyranny, or despotism.

9 See the Introduction and chapter 2 of Lucy Cane's *Sheldon Wolin and Democratic Theory* for discussions of blind spots in Wolin's view of the *demos*, local historical traditions, and his critique of postmodernism.

10 The term "reactionary tribalism" is from the social theorist Robert Antonio, whose article "After Postmodernism: Reactionary Tribalism" (*American Journal of Sociology*, Vol. 106, No. 1 (2000), 40–87) was prescient in seeing how the current range of issues now associated with populism and authoritarianism were related to globalization and postmodern criticisms of political and intellectual "foundations." I address what I see as Wolin's sense of *strategically* needing to defend liberal-democratic constitutions and institutions at the end of this chapter.

11 See Cane, op. cit., for a discussion of these issues, and their omission, in Wolin's work.

12 The "people" have not actually been "sovereign" since Ancient Athens.

13 See Jeffrey Green, *The Eyes of the People: Democracy in an Age of Spectatorship* (New York: Oxford University Press, 2010), 3.

14 Ibid., 3–4.

15 Ibid., 5.

16 Ibid., 6–7.

17 See Max Weber, *The Vocation Lectures: Science as a Vocation and Politics as a Vocation*, ed. David Owen and Tracy B. Strong (Indianapolis: Hackett Publishing, 2004). Weber had argued that the working class (and its parliamentary "representative," the Social Democratic Party), needed to be included as "orderly" participants within a system of parliamentary democracy. At the same time Weber berated left political opponents such as Rosa Luxembourg and Karl Liebknecht, the revolutionaries of 1918, and those engaged in what he derisively called the "politics of the street," for being immature, childish, and "unrealistic." As an elite (but progressive) liberal in Germany who was fighting political opponents on both the far right and the far left, Weber was afraid that the newly enfranchised – and potentially unruly – working class could not be political leaders. The idea of including them in the parliamentary system was also, I have argued elsewhere, a strategy of *containment* – of the more revolutionary aspirations, ideologies (viz. Marxism), and left parties to which the working classes might be drawn. After all, post–First World War Germany combined great social instability with new-found electoral power. For the old monarchical system collapsed right after Germany's

defeat in the First World War, and Weber and others were engaged in intense debates over the new constitution for the Weimar Republic. Green's argument, coming from a similar place under different historical circumstances, echoes Weber's. There is a parallel between Weber's desire to include the working class in the parliamentary system and Green's desire to placate the powerless Many.

As Peter Breiner has noted, Weber's insistence on the character of leaders was already absent from Schumpeter's plural-elite model. See Peter Breiner, "The Origins of the Puritan Capitalist and the Vocational Politician – A Series of Just-So-Stories? Or Why Is Weber's Genealogy of the Vocational Politician So Uncontroversial?" *Max Weber Studies* Vol. 6, No. 1 (2005), 3–31.

I discuss Weber's view of leadership and how his realist view of liberal-democracy seeks to contain working class anger in Terry Maley, *Democracy and the Political in Max Weber's Thought* (Toronto: University of Toronto Press, 2011).

18 Greater public or ocular scrutiny did not make an authoritarian like Trump more accountable or "candid." But precisely because of the corruption and lying emanating from the Trump administration, this kind of scrutiny has become more important than ever. It reminds one of John Keane's view of "monitory democracy" (published a year after Green's *Eyes*) where citizen watchdog groups track political actors and government agencies to keep them publicly accountable. Since Green wrote *Eyes* citizen cell-camera surveillance and citizen journalism has become an important but still "fugitive" (unofficial) tool of public accountability – in the case of George Floyd and many others. On Max Weber's legacy as a democratic theorist in relation to Green's *Eyes*, see my pre-presidential American election view in Terry Maley, "The Relevance of Max Weber for Political Theory Today," in *The Anthem Companion to Max Weber*, ed. Alan Sica (New York: Anthem, 2016); and John Keane, *The Future of Representative Democracy* (Cambridge: Cambridge University Press, 2011).

19 Ibid., *Eyes*, 154.

20 See, for example, Paul Apostolidis, "*The Eyes of the People: Democracy in an Age of Spectatorship* by Jeffrey Edward Green," *Contemporary Political Theory*, Vol. 12, No. 1 (2013), e1–e4.

21 See Jeffrey Green, *Eyes*, 7–11, 110–19; and *Shadow* (New York: Oxford University Press, 2016), 72–7. Marx had already noted that the law reflects material and social conditions and is not independent from the larger political economy. For a discussion of Marx's view of the law, see Michael Mandel, "Marxism and the Rule of Law," *UNB Law Journal*, Vol. 35 (1986), 7–34. For an edited collection that engages in nuanced discussions of the complex relationship of neoliberalism to the law, see Honor Brabazon, ed., *Neoliberal Legality: Understanding the Role of Law in the Neoliberal Project* (New York: Routledge, 2016). Brabazon argues that changes in international law were integral to the establishment and consolidation of neoliberalism.

22 See, for example, Peter Niesen, "Reframing Civil Disobedience: Constituent Power as a Language of Transnational Protest," *Journal of International of Political*

Theory (2018), 1–18; Miguel Abensour, *Democracy against the State: Marx and the Machiavellian Moment*, trans. M. Blechman and M. Breaugh (Cambridge: Polity Press, 2012); and the collection *Radical Democracy: Politics between Abudance and Lack*, ed. Lars Toender and Lasse Thomassen (Manchester: Manchester University Press, 2005), from a more post-structural perspective.

23 Remarkably, Green only mentions Wolin in one short sentence in *Eyes* (73) and not at all in *Shadow*.

24 For a discussion of how centrifugal forces on the far-right have shaped democracy in the UK and Italy and how they have been shaped by neoliberalism, see Iain Webb's chapter in this volume.

25 To cite one example, Wendy Brown and Roslyn W. Bologh wrote pathbreaking feminist critiques of Max Weber's masculinist realism and power politics in the 1980s that were largely ignored by (mostly cis-gendered male) political and social theorists. See Wendy Brown, *Manhood and Politics: A Feminist Reading in Political Theory* (Lanham, MD: Rowan and Littlefield, 1988), and R.W. Bologh, *Love or Greatness: Max Weber and Masculine Thinking – A Feminist Inquiry* (London: Unwin Hyman, 1990). Much of the critical literature on neoliberalism (beginning in the 1990s) initially came from more left-leaning political economists (i.e., David Harvey).

26 As has become clear in my discussion, I do not prefer Green's view of plebeian democracy. I would rather recommend the view of Martin Breaugh in *The Plebeian Experience: A Discontinuous History of Freedom* (New York: Columbia University Press, 2013). Breaugh's view, inspired by Miguel Abensour's view of "insurgent democracy" has, from within a branch of French political philosophy, close affinities with Wolin's idea of fugitive democracy and the radical democratic tradition discussed in this volume by Jason Frank. Breaugh sees different historical iterations of the people – the Roman plebs, the sans-culottes or the English Jacobins – as capable of constituting themselves as political agents through acts of rebellion and insurgency. See also Martin Breaugh et al., eds., *Thinking Radical Democracy: The Return to Politics in Post-War France* (Toronto: University of Toronto Press, 2015).

27 There have been many analyses now of the growing economic and social inequality after the term 1 per cent (vs. the 99 per cent) made it into our political vocabulary after the Great Recession of 2007–9. The progressive think-tank the Canadian Centre for Policy Alternatives (CCPA) has for many years now, in the CCPA *Monitor*, published economic analyses of the growing wealth gap in Canada and produces the *CCPA Alternative Budget* every year. See also a recent Canadian example from a former Bay Street (the Canadian version of Wall Street) investment banker Jeff Rubin, "Why Give Tax Breaks to the Wealthiest?" (*Toronto Star*, Insight section, p. 3, 22 August 2020). Rubin notes that by far the greatest benefit of Canada's tax system (under what we have been calling neoliberalism) has gone to the top 1 per cent. And although income distribution is even more skewed towards the top 1% in the United States, it is a little-

publicized fact that Canada is the only OECD country that has no inheritance or estate tax.

28 Martijn Konings, "From Hayek to Trump: The Logic of Neoliberal Democracy," in *Rethinking Democracy: The Socialist Register*, ed. Leo Panitch and Greg Albo (London: Merlin Press/Fernwood, 2018), 50.

29 Examples were plentiful under the Trump administration but, of course, have a much longer history – from the gerrymandering of electoral districts by Republican lawmakers, to all manner of voter suppression tactics, to Trump's former Attorney General William Barr's flagrant abuses and suppression of investigative processes at the US Justice Department. And, of course, the history of race relations in the United States (and Canada) is marked by the use of arcane rules and regulations as discriminatory tools of white privilege and power. In her book *Democracy in Chains*, a study of the decades-long campaign against democracy, equality, New Deal policies, and civil rights by far-right libertarian economist James Buchanan and his billionaire backers (such as the Koch brothers), historian Nancy MacLean notes that Buchanan said that it is more important to change the rules, rather than the rulers, in order to resist changing racist, segregationist, or other unpopular, anti-democratic legislation and practices that were/are favoured by elites and not the majority of voters. See Nancy MacLean, *Democracy in Chains: The Deep History of the Radical Rights' Stealth Plan for America* (New York: Penguin Books, 2017).

30 Martijn Konings, op. cit., 48.

31 See my discussion in Maley, op. cit. (2011), and Hilary Wainwright, *A New Politics from the Left* (Cambridge: Polity Press, 2018).

32 Ibid., 50.

33 Rick Salutin, "How to Make It through the Stresses of Trumptime," *Toronto Star* (13 April 2018), A13.

34 See Wolin's former student Cornel West, *Race Matters* (Boston: Beacon Press, 1993/2017), as well as Toni Morrison, James Baldwin, and Leanne Betasamosake Simpson, among many others. See Leanne Betasamosake Simpson, *As We Have Always Done: Indigenous Freedom Through Radical Resistance* (Minneapolis: University of Minnesota Press, 2017).

35 Sheldon Wolin, "Fugitive Democracy," in *Democracy and Difference: Contesting the Boundaries of the Political*, ed. Seyla Benhabib (Princeton, NJ: Princeton University Press, 1996), 36.

36 Think of the vast, shadowy derivatives markets only brought to public awareness after the 2007–8 global financial crash. Jim Stanford, former chief economist for the (former – now UNIFOR after a two-union merger) Canadian Auto Workers union, has long documented and warned of the autonomy of stock markets from the real economy. See Jim Stanford, *Paper Boom: Why Real Prosperity Requires a New Approach to Canada's Economy* (Toronto: James Lorimer, 1999). Paul Krugman has noted this in his *New York Times* columns. It is now simply accepted as normal in the business press.

37 See Sheldon S. Wolin, *Democracy Incorporated: Managed Democracy and the Specter of Inverted Totalitarianism* (Princeton, NJ: Princeton University Press, 2008).

38 Wendy Brown, in *In the Ruins of Neoliberalism*, makes the key point that the resurgence of white male supremacy, racism, and nationalism/xenophobia were not directly caused by neoliberalism, but that in the now symbiotic relationship between these forces, neoliberalism has facilitated opening up the cultural and political spaces for these phenomena to flourish in the political mainstream. Brown draws on both Foucault (for how neoliberal rationality constitutes subjectivity) and Marx's political economy, arguing that both are complimentary when it comes to making sense of this new configuration of powers. Brown sees both analyses as necessary but insufficient on their own. I think Brown and Konings are right in not seeing neoliberalism as only economic in nature. And, as Wolfgang Streeck has argued in his two books, *How Capitalism Will End: Essays on a Failing System* (London: Verso, 2017) and *Buying Time: The Delayed Crisis of Democratic Capitalism* (London: Verso, 2017), unbridled neoliberalism is undermining itself and the social cohesion of liberal-democracies. His argument is complementary to Brown's and Konings'. As the deregulated market economy undercuts democratic agency, neoliberal democracies are in disarray. Neoliberal policies have unleashed a more unrestrained capitalism with myriad social pathologies, including the weakening of liberal-democratic institutions, ideological polarization, and the loosening of affective restraints in fearful populations. In Streeck's view we now live in world increasingly dis-integrated into what he calls the *Marktsvolk* (financiers and winners – the 1 per cent), and the *Staatsvolk* (the 99 per cent, the losers of globalization). And this is happening without the help of what Streeck sees as weak and dis-unified social movements that do not have a common plan for replacing neoliberal capitalism. For Streeck the global protest movements are in as much disarray as global capitalism and liberal-democracy. In the process neoliberalism has created the conditions for a potentially prolonged, destructive period of social and political disorder that could lead to neoliberal fascism.

39 The PBS Frontline documentary (July 2020) *United States of Conspiracy*, details how Jones delivered disaffected (mostly marginal white male) voters to Trump in the 2016 election.

40 See Jason Frank in this volume and Cornel West, *Democracy Matters: Winning the Fight Against Imperialism* (New York: Random House, 2005) and *Race Matters* (Boston: Beacon Press, 1993/2017).

41 John Keane, *The New Despotism*, 15.

42 Ibid., 37.

43 Ibid., 237.

44 Ibid., 17, 236.

45 Ibid., 237. These tactics were all deployed by the Trump administration. To cite one infamous example, recall Trump's blurring the lines and language by saying of the white supremacist rally in Charlottesville, "there were good people on both sides."

46 Ibid., 18. On this issue Keane would agree with Wendy Brown in *In the Ruins*.

47 Ibid., 253–4.

48 Wolin, "Fugitive Democracy," op. cit., 31. This is the challenge Streeck's critique presents to Wolin's view of the commonality of the *political*. For Streeck this commonality has been shattered under neoliberalism.

49 Lucy Cane notes that while Wolin was attuned to the postmodern powers of the state, capitalism, science, and technology, he was not as attuned, in his yearning for a lost commonality, to racism, nationalism, sexism, or the ecology – to the power of particularistic identities on the far right.

50 See Wolin, *Democracy Inc.*, op. cit., 38, 144; Brown, *Manhood and Politics*, op. cit.; and Wendy Brown, *In the Ruins of Neoliberalism: The Rise of Antidemocratic Politics in the West* (New York: Columbia University Press, 2019), 6; or what Brown notes Wolin had called an "'enraged' form of majority rule."

51 Perhaps *the* key question today that it is beginning to surface only now, as the COVID pandemic grinds on – forcing governments to take some significant re-allocative and market-restraining measures – is can the state step in to significantly change "the extreme globalization of the last 30 years"? (2); i.e., the global neoliberal policy regime to which the corporate sector wants to return as quickly as possible. A recent article in *Le Monde Diplomatique* (English edition, 20 May 2020, n. 2005) by Lori Wallach asks this critical question, suggesting that governments have now been compelled to "prioritize the needs of their citizens" (2). The byline to the article provocatively asks: "is the era of hyperglobalization at last over?" The elite response/pushback from the Canadian corporate community, who would very much like to maintain the neoliberal regime, restoring it from the momentary deviation/state spending of the COVID pandemic, can be summarized in the headline of an op ed piece by two former senior federal bureaucrats now working on Bay Street (the Canadian equivalent of Wall Street) – "Canadians risk becoming addicted to aid," by which the article means federal government COVID assistance. This is the business community argument that COVID relief is too generous and is providing a "disincentive" to get workers back to work (at their non-unionized, low-paying service-sector jobs). See Serge Dupont and Kevin Lynch, "Canadians Risk Becoming Addicted to Aid," *Globe and Mail* (21 August 2020), A13.

52 Sheldon Wolin, "Postmodern Politics and the Absence of Myth," *Social Research*, Vol. 52, No. 2 (Summer 1985), 218.

53 See George Kateb, "Wolin as a Critic of Democracy," in *Democracy and Vision: Sheldon Wolin and the Vicissitudes of the Political,* ed. Areyh Botwinick and William Connolly (Princeton, NJ: Princeton University Press, 2001); Ronald Beiner, "Review of *Democracy and Vision: Sheldon Wolin and the Vicissitudes of the Political* (Princeton, NJ: Princeton University Press, 2001)," *Bulletin of Science, Technology, and Society*, Vol. 24, No. 1 (February 2004); Mark Warren, "Review Article: *Politics and Vision: Continuity and Innovation in Western Political Thought*," *Political Theory*, Vol. 34, No. 5 (October 2006).

54 Wolin, "Fugitive Democracy," op. cit., 43.

55 Ibid. David McIvor cites this quote in the context of a larger – and very plausible – argument that while many commentators have interpreted fugitive democracy's fleeting nature in a way that resembles Rancierian eruptions, "Wolin was concerned with enduring democratic projects involving longer time horizons, instead of momentary eruptions of resistance." McIvor argues that we should not "miss or downplay Wolin's emphasis on the daily labors that can build democratic consciousness and a sense of political vocation," including the idea of the "multiple civic self." McIvor also recognizes that the two aspects of democratic engagement – eruptive and more sustained – are not mutually exclusive. This idea certainly has affinities with the dual strategy I argue is necessary in the current democratic moment and the "protean" self that is needed to pursue it. See David McIvor, "The Conscience of a Fugitive: Sheldon Wolin and the Prospects for Radical Democracy," *New Political Science*, Vol. 38, No. 3 (2016), 411–27, 412.

56 Martin Breaugh uses this evocative phrase in *The Plebeian Experience: A Discontinuous History of Freedom* (New York: Columbia University Press, 2013), 242.

57 Sheldon S. Wolin, "Norm and Form: The Constitutionalizing of Democracy," in *Athenian Political Thought and the Reconstruction of American Democracy*, ed. Peter Euben, John R. Wallach, and Josiah Ober (Ithaca, NY: Cornell University Press, 1994), 50. Wolin may have been influenced by John Dewey, who in *The Public and Its Problems* said that "the public, to form itself, must break existing forms" (31). And that, "By its very nature a state is ever something to be scrutinized, investigated, searched for. As soon as soon as its form is stabilized, it needs to be remade (31–2). See John Dewey, *The Public and Its Problems: An Essay in Political Inquiry*, ed. *Melvin Rogers* (Athens, OH: Swallow/University of Ohio Press, 2016 [1927]).

58 See Hilary Wainwright in *Beyond the Fragments: Feminism and the Making of Socialism* (London: Merlin Press, 2013), 60.

59 See Hilary Wainwright, *A New Politics from the Left* (Cambridge: Polity Press, 2018).

60 Hilary Wainwright, in *Beyond the Fragments*, op. cit., 46.

61 See Robert Jay Lifton, *The Protean Self: Human Resilience in an Age of Fragmentation* (Chicago: University of Chicago Press, 1995).

62 Wolin, "Fugitive Democracy," 31.

63 Wainwright later came to the view, with the Corbyn leadership of the Labour Party, that the movements also needed to engage with and try to transform the Labour Party, and not simply build democratic capacities in the movements outside of it. See Hilary Wainwright, "Radicalizing the Party-Movement Relationship: From Ralph Miliband to Jeremy Corbyn and Beyond," in *Rethinking Revolution: Socialist Register* (London: Merlin Press, 2017), 80–102, 83.

64 Cane, op. cit., 57, 39, 123–4, 134, and ch. 4, "Towards a Polymorphous Democracy." This is part of Cane's detailed discussion of Wolin's view of "polymorphous" democracy that is, in the spirit suggested by Hilary Wainwright, not reduceable to

one form and can include local deliberative forms, transgressive forms that break existing boundaries, insurgencies into political parties that I mention briefly below, and even engagement with large-scale institutions of the state – all democratic practices that are multifaceted, or "protean," in Robert Jay Lifton's suggestive phrase.

65 See Stephen Esquith's discussion in this volume of Wolin's idea of "counter-elite public servants" and their role in building counter-institutions. The contribution by Romand Coles and Lia Haro also addresses the building of Black counter-institutions historically. Both chapters provide compelling case studies. I have looked at similar issues in previous work on participatory budgeting in Porto Alegre, the EU, and Canada. See Terry Maley, "The Democratic Imagination in Ontario and Participatory Budgeting," in *Divided Province: Ontario Politics in the Age of Neoliberalism*, ed. Greg Albo and Bryan M. Evans (Montreal: McGill-Queen's University Press, 2018), 493–522. See also my comment in note 55.

66 The quotes are from Anand Giridharadas's review, "Hijacking America," *New York Times Book Review* (International edition), 29–30 August 2020, 9. Nancy MacLean's book *Democracy in Chains* outlines in chilling detail the way the "long game" was devised and funded, over decades, by the far-right libertarian economist James Buchanan (and his later backers such as the Koch brothers).

67 I see Keane's view of "unelected representatives" (celebrity or otherwise) as complementary to, and not a substitute for, the kind of long-haul, counter-institutions and organizing discussed by Esquith.

68 This is the title of Canadian journalist Michael Harris's book about the Canadian Conservative Party Prime Minister Stephen Harper (2006–15), and his Republican-style strategies and tactics that sought, dangerously for Canadian democracy, to hollow out and radically transform the institutions of the Canadian state. Harris's book – and some of its themes in a Canadian context – outlines distinct affinities with the "long game" of the far right discussed in Nancy MacLean's *Democracy in Chains*, referred to in notes 24 and 57. Harris's book is titled, *Stephen Harper and Canada's Radical Makeover: Party of One* (Toronto: Viking Press, 2014).

10 Transformative Sanctuary: Rethinking Fugitive Democracy and Black Fugitivity with Frontline Communities in the Underground Railroad

ROMAND COLES AND LIA HARO

Experts predict that climate change intersecting with violence, extreme poverty, and political breakdown will result in between 200 million and 700 million displaced people searching for shelter within and beyond national borders by 2050 – many "illegally."[1] High levels of crisis-driven human mobility for the foreseeable future are grave challenges confronting democracy today – as is already becoming evident around the world. Toni Morrison recently observed: "Excluding the height of the slave trade in the nineteenth century, the mass movement of peoples in the latter half of the twentieth century and the beginning of the twenty-first is greater than it has ever been. It is a movement of workers, intellectuals, refugees, and immigrants, crossing oceans and continents, through customs offices or in flimsy boats, speaking multiple languages of trade, of political intervention, of persecution, war, violence, and poverty."[2] What happens to democratic horizons when mass global displacement begins to overwhelm contemporary political practices and paradigms premised on greater stability – however thoroughly they are entangled in disavowed histories of massive displacement, slavery, and genocide?

At the same time, as growing numbers of people find themselves in physical flight and instability, democracy itself is also on the run.[3] Sheldon Wolin has argued that democracy, whereby citizens actively strive to co-create and sustain the well-being of complex commonwealth against incredible odds, has historically been confined to fugitive "democratic moments."[4] Much of Wolin's writing provides penetrating accounts of how corporate power has reinvented politics according to its own economistic logos, giving birth to a form of "Superpower" and "inverted totalitarianism" that depoliticizes and demobilizes publics, undoing the footholds achieved by democratic struggles in previous decades.[5] This "economic polity" magnifies inequality to unprecedented levels while shredding and reconstituting cultural traditions through which many cultivated some degree of power over their everyday lives. Since Wolin's writings, the antidemocratic constellation has become further infused with new intensities of xenophobic, racist, and sexist vitriol, all of which proliferate through contemporary communication technologies. These anti-democratic trends in conjunction with looming mass displacement that unhinges citizens and communities from stable associational life make the present prospects for democracy appear flickering, flightful, and fugitive at best.[6]

Such narratives of catastrophic urgency shed important critical light on the contemporary condition and are integral to mustering political reflection, vision, and action – particularly in relation to how conditions long-suffered by many are metastasizing in new ways that both increase the scope of those targeted and intensify dynamics of white supremacy and overall collapse. Yet, they can also perpetuate a mythic oblivion to how modernity has always been entangled with such catastrophes, beginning with the tens of millions of enslaved Africans and colonized peoples whose genocide and subjugation continues in myriad ways through the present. "Modern life begins in slavery" as Morrison writes.[7] A growing volume of contemporary political theory is devoted to rethinking terms of political discourse (e.g., freedom, justice, property) in relation to this fact and its disavowal by most mainstream thinkers.[8] Accounts that conceal the constitutive disasters of modernity also tend to efface the many histories of fugitive struggles for survival that have embodied transformative political visions, strategies, and even utopian aspirations. We believe the knowledge and experience manifest in these struggles can be indispensable for responding to the emergent catastrophes sweeping our own times.

In this context, we rethink Wolin's notion of fugitive democracy by attending to the lived theory of fugitives – in this case the Black communities that formed the front lines of the Underground Railroad – to disclose modes of cultivating transformative political power and community amid severe conditions. In reconsidering the concept of fugitive democracy, we join other recent theorists who are now emphasizing the importance of putting Wolin's concept in dialogue with the lived experiences and knowledges of fugitives themselves. Exemplary here is Neil Roberts's call to political theorists to tend more carefully to "what happens during the act of flight itself."[9] We take up that call here to build on Roberts's rich theorizing of marronage or fugitivity as a space of freedom. Juliet Hooker in *Race in the Americas* similarly emphasizes how "the experience of fugitive ex-slaves and the philosophical insights that have been culled from those experiences" reveal zones of the political to which Wolin was less attuned.[10]

Roberts argues that inattention to processes of flight has impoverished our political imagination and sustained a static binary between freedom and unfreedom. Focussing primarily on maroons – fugitive slaves who crafted autonomous communities in the margins of oppressive orders in the Caribbean – he conceives of spaces of marronage as "zones of refuge" (a term borrowed from James C. Scott) in which different political imaginaries and ideals of freedom emerge through specific struggles in "liminal transitional spaces" of both "flight and transformation."[11] Theorizing in relation to the work of Frederick Douglass, he demonstrates the rich plurality of experiences and political possibilities that inform a range of "comparative freedoms." Hooker also grounds her intervention significantly in the work of Douglass to underscore the extent to which democratic politics has always placed many people outside the polity and made their actions "unlawful" (for example, fugitive slaves and undocumented migrants). As such, Black fugitive democracy involves an ecology of practices that accent lawbreaking, concealment, secrecy, and flight as vital in the repertoire of democratic action.[12] She argues that fugitives' perpetual exposure to extreme risk not only intensified a sense of precarity but, relatedly, generated alternative theories of Black autonomy, democracy, and utopian horizons that "exceed or bypass the nation-state."[13]

Like Hooker and Roberts, we find compelling evidence in the Black front-line communities of the Underground Railroad for understanding fugitivity, and hence fugitive democracy, as much more than simple flight away from subjugative conditions. In this article, we contribute to this ongoing project by theorizing sanctuary as the generative twin of fugitivity. As we begin to show in this article, fugitives and the condition of fugitivity have, in the best cases, historically conjured up receptive counter-practices of refuge and hospitality for those in flight. By paying attention to the practices, expressions, and movements of sanctuary as elaborated by fugitives and those on the undersides of power in the Antebellum period, we cast light on the possibility of re-theorizing sanctuary as transformative harbour for democratic relationships and powers. This insight complexifies and shifts Wolin's insights on fugitive democracy. We suggest that integrating displacement and fugitivity into the heart of democratic theory and practice may enable the elaboration of nuanced understandings and political capacities for resisting anti-democratic dynamics and forging commonwealth. As such, we believe fugitivity and sanctuary illuminate a crucial political path for generating transformative power – especially as increased numbers of people are displaced, targeted, and rendered precarious.

Sanctuary as elaborated by Black front-line communities illuminates a powerful and complex modality of fugitivity that hinges upon a *creative oscillation* – where Hooker identifies a more contradictory relationship – between Black fugitivity's modes of concealment and lawbreaking, on the one hand, and Wolin's notion of democracy as public tending, on the other. This oscillation, we suggest, illuminates possibilities for more fruitfully entangling efforts to build community autonomy with efforts to create more widespread change in the broader polity of "white democracy."[14] Indeed, we venture that democratic struggles against barbarism, more generally, should take seriously the idea that building power stems significantly from creative dialectics between concealment and expansive publicity, autonomy, and proliferating coalitions, illegality, and changing laws – points underplayed by both Wolin's fugitive democracy and some theorists of Black fugitivity.[15] This reorientation is not only relevant in times of rapidly escalating displacement and neo-fascistic reactions to refugees worldwide. We think that the interlocking combination of fugitivity and sanctuary responses to it can reform our most elemental understandings and practices of democratic ethics and politics.

Reorienting fugitive democracy in this way beseeches a certain nimbleness that might be called fugitive theorizing. By this, we mean experimental modes that amplify creative aspects of historical moments, movements, and thinkers, unchaining them from dominant misappropriations and interpretive norms. Fugitive theory, as we practise it here, carefully attends to the lived theories and practices of those struggling to escape subjugation and move towards alternatives. Such theorizing itself seeks to function as a kind of sanctuary for the cast-off dimensions of theorists, concepts, and movements, insofar as sanctuaries are places of unwonted commingling in which people bring together parts of their lives torn from other contexts – for better and worse – to produce new processes and visions.

In our own efforts, we learn from Walter Benjamin as a practitioner of fugitive theory – who himself committed suicide as a fugitive without sanctuary. Benjamin articulated a philosophy of history that embraced, even in its fragments, all that was fugitive. In doing so, he strove to provide theoretical sanctuary in which those fragments or sparks might burn brighter as he cultivated solidaristic connections between them to resist the catastrophe of "progress" and illuminate alternatives obliterated by it. Because the catastrophe is often immanent in as well as external to fugitive struggles, Benjamin thought that efforts to align one's thinking with the fugitive require that we "brush history against the grain," seeking to separate more emancipatory tendencies – the "courage, humor, cunning, and fortitude" from their entanglements with other dimensions that were not so.[16] This *aufheben* involved taking liberties (sometimes with a "brush," sometimes with a "blast") to extract "a specific era out of the homogeneous course of history – blasting a specific life out of an era or a specific work out of the lifework."[17] An engagement with and among fragments might produce, however improbable, redemptive connections across time and space. For Benjamin, "thinking involves not only the flow of thoughts, but their arrest as well" so that we might form connections with exemplary "configuration[s] pregnant with tensions" that generate electrical shocks that open "past" and "present" beyond the "continuum of history."[18]

In this project, we seek to perform a kindred type of fugitive theory as we approach questions of fugitive democracy and sanctuary through historical excavation of traces that have been largely suppressed by the dominant forces of history. Our theorizing of the generative and transformative dimensions of fugitive sanctuary emerges as we gather textures of life and struggle in Black front-line communities as remnants of a far richer text never written down as such.[19] In accentuating generative aspects of a given movement or set of ideas, we intend neither to romanticize them nor their larger, more complicated contexts. Our aim is to gather such fragments into an inter-illuminating constellation that can shed light on and energize fugitive possibilities for sanctuary for democracy. The lived-theory of people fleeing *from* brutal forms of power were also flights *towards* and *into* alternative democratic possibilities and powers. We take this lived theory to be indispensable for theoretically articulating and pragmatically responding to "the fierce urgency of (every) now."[20]

Fugitive Democracy/Sanctuary

For Wolin, democracy all the way back to ancient Athens has been largely fugitive insofar as its proponents struggle on the undersides of power to transgress multiple registers of dominant inequality with comparatively little time and few resources, while under threat from all sorts of tyrants, elites, and anti-democratic tendencies. In modernity, democracy is fugitive, additionally, in the sense that constitutions have circumscribed more than they have promoted the demos. In his last writings, Wolin proposes what might rightly be called *hyper-fugitive democracy* as characteristic of the millennial moment. Democratic cultural forms of knowledge and lifeways that might (in part) nurture democratic capacities are perpetually ripped asunder by the "permanent revolution" of elites who have "self-consciously become the agents of discontinuity" in paradoxically totalizing economic, technological, political, and cultural processes of anti-democracy.[21] As such, not only can democracy no longer be a form of rule, but even its marginal manifestations tend to be ever more precarious – either flashing up in dramatic, quickly fading public protests or building extremely tenuous possibilities in shifting local pockets of associational life. It is always threatened by devitalizing anti-democratic modes of assimilation.[22]

Many have criticized Wolin's work on fugitive democracy for abandoning all hope for broader systemic change (and inadvertently contributing to hopelessness).[23] However, we think that reflectively dwelling with the severity of fugitivity can open windows onto unexplored potentials for political transformation, especially those embedded in the wisdom and power of past fugitive struggles.

To begin to excavate these potentials, we find it useful to brush parts of Wolin's definition of fugitive democracy against the grain, beginning with the profoundly emblematic selections from the *Oxford English Dictionary* that he uses to open his section on fugitive democracy in the second edition of *Politics and Vision*: "Fugitive: evanescent … one who flees from danger, an enemy, justice, or an owner … One who shifts about from place to place" (ellipses are Wolin's).[24] It is interesting to tarry with the punctuation in this epigraph as itself suggestive of certain subtle assumptions about fugitivity. In some ways, the first ellipses in the epigraph well evoke how democratic action in our time tends to spring forth and just as quickly disappear, while more pervasive dynamics grow stronger and keep democracy on the run. However, we observe that the colon after "Fugitive" and the ellipses that follow insinuate a certain definitional, fate-like impotence. This structure, framing the whole piece, tends more to suppress than call up reflection, imagination, and experimentation on how the evanescent flashings and modes of flight might be enacted such that the demos generates powers more capable of transformation and less destined to retreat.

Wolin's critique of anti-democratic tendencies in the contemporary world, in combination with his accurate sense that proponents of democracy always act under conditions of scarce time, money, and energy, led him to understand the "evanescence" of democracy in terms of surrounding adverse conditions much more than in relation to the internal modes, characteristics, and common sense of those practising democracy. Yet, if we linger in the ellipses, the disappearing tendencies of democratic action and power beseech us to ask: what may be the characteristics of democratic actions that make them particularly prone to dissipation? How might we dwell in the passages between the evanescent bubbling up and evaporation or flight such that they become opportunities for deliberately building and renewing democratic practices and powers? Fugitive might be reconceived in that context such that flight *from* morphs into flight *towards* and *into* alternatives.

The emphasis in Wolin's OED selections on *one* who flees, *one* who shifts, suggests an interesting relation between *specific* fugitives and the *generality* of democracy itself as fugitive. Wolin's selections imply that the general fugitivity of democracy is always entangled with specific people and groups targeted and driven into flight. Vitriolic assaults on specific peoples and ways of being both fuel and are fuelled by more general anti-democratic and anti-egalitarian dynamics. The entanglement of specific assaults with the more general dynamics undermining democracy suggests that we cannot fight either one without addressing the other. We cannot tend to the general fugitivity of democracy without cultivating solidaristic power among those who are most targeted (through deportation, disenfranchisement, discrimination, incarceration, dislocation, silencing, etc.). Moreover, such work can energize the broader movement for democracy by drawing it to the front line of action, which is well-recognized as the oxygen of transformative organizing. The flip side, equally important, is that linking specific struggles with the more general fugitivity of democracy can help draw attention to the collective co-creative aspirations and powers of each constituency. In today's context, naming democracy as a common fugitivity of contemporary movements can gather diverse groups towards challenging questions of possible egalitarian "with-ness" of the diverse struggles around race, climate justice, nationality, class, gender, sexuality, etc. Conjoining the specific with the general raises the potential of generating powerful energies and solidarities that may be as promising as the reverse dynamics of vitriolic anti-democracy are horrifying.

Tarrying with the figure of "one who flees danger" alongside democracy itself in such flight also illuminates something missing in Wolin's evocation of fugitivity. Historically, from biblical Cities of Refuge to the US Underground Railroad to recent responses to the perils of refugees and undocumented immigrants, fugitivity has repeatedly summoned forth practices and spaces of *sanctuary* harbouring those in flight. The enemies of fugitives and fugitivity have always known this. Indeed, as historian Cheryl LaRoche has recently pointed out in a new history of the Underground Railroad, the link between sanctuary and fugitivity is shown by the fact that even the earliest "legislation from the colonial period attempted to regulate two consistent responses to slavery – running away and harboring."[25]

Taking seriously this link between fugitivity and sanctuary can radicalize both concepts and open political horizons otherwise missed. By overemphasizing fugitivity as flight away from threats and destructive forces, some proponents of both fugitive democracy and Black fugitivity – for different reasons – miss the rich, generative, and transformative potentials of these activities as they emerge in modes of fugitive harbour. As we shall theorize in relation to Black front-line communities in the Underground Railroad, becoming democratic publics against the grain of an oppressive order involves complex and paradoxical negotiations of immanent relationships between concealment/publicity, autonomy/networked solidarities, and illegality/juridical transformation. These creative oscillations unfold within the broader space of sanctuary that is itself both protective of fugitives and also disruptive to the order that has rendered them such. We argue that understanding these interrelationships is pivotal to reconceiving and practising fugitive democracy as much more than hopeless flight even in the face of the worst anti-democratic forces. When we tend to these "other" modes of public tending exemplified by the Black front-line communities in the Underground Railroad (those involving concealment, illegality, and protective autonomy), fugitive democracy acquires dimensions that are at once profoundly challenging and also crucial to cultivating democratic power, survival, and flourishing. Those who miss the centrality of this highly tensional twinning of fugitive democracy and sanctuary fugitivity will likely embrace one or the other without realizing that each is a condition of the other's possibility and likely to be self-undermining on its own terms.

Womb of Sanctuary

Linking fugitive democracy with sanctuary may seem to surrender rather than intensify the transformative ambitions of grassroots democracy, substituting a politics of hiding in shelters. However, inspired by contemporary and historical sanctuary movements led by fugitives and those on the undersides of power, we believe that a sanctuary politics can generate deepening and widening democratic solidarities that enhance power for more radical change. An evocative organizing image provided by the contemporary New Sanctuary Movement of Philadelphia inspires our own line of flight towards sanctuary here. They conceive of sanctuary politics as "build[ing] bridges with different communities and join[ing] forces [to forge sanctuary] as an umbrella that covers us all from the storm and the womb to birth a new world."[26]

What practices might help catalyse such birthing? How might we shift the lines of flight of fugitivity and sanctuary such that protective actions against anti-democratic forces increasingly generate new possibilities and powers for creating better alternatives so that we are less and less fleeing *from* danger and increasingly fleeing *towards* and *into* alternative horizons and relationships with others that transform the status quo? How might we theorize this possibility? Oriented by our reading of fugitive democracy and Black fugitive thought, we turn to the less well-known activities of the Black front-line communities in the Underground Railroad, where we find the womb of sanctuary elaborated by fugitives themselves most illuminating of the generative possibilities for entangling fugitivity and sanctuary politics.

Most Americans have inherited a historically romanticized myth of "The Underground Railroad" born in the wake of the Civil War as a nostalgic structure of white benevolence.[27] The imaginary of fixed railroad lines, stations, and white conductors has long obscured Black agency and leadership, as well as the teeming, diverse multiplicity of actors, communities, and organizations that transgressed and undermined the dominant order of slavery.[28] However, in the last fifteen years, new histories have begun to provide fresh, provocative insights that collectively resignify the Underground Railroad as significantly a "multi-pronged vehicle for Black resistance," as LaRoche puts it in describing Black communities that formed on the borders between slavery and non-slavery territories.[29] Describing communities in the Ohio River Valley, historian Keith Griffler writes: "These women and men made their home on slavery's doorstep, endured the innumerable bounties placed on their heads, and at times paid the ultimate price for their activities. Joined by a small but dedicated group of white and Native American activists, they founded a genuinely interracial freedom movement, a practical experiment in American democracy."[30] Focussing on different locales, new histories each portray the Underground Railroad as a flexible, decentred, heterogeneous movement that consisted of an oscillating patchwork of myriad local initiatives, organizations, and communities, predominantly Black and some biracial, that *both* facilitated the work of practical abolition (assisting actual fugitives in escaping slavery) *and* actively reconfigured social forms, relationships, practices, and imaginations beyond the order of slavery and white supremacy.

In other words, what these new histories all show in everyday detail is that the fugitive is not only the OED's "one who flees from danger." Rather, the fugitive in the Antebellum United States was also one (and many) who fled *towards* alternative possibilities and *into* relationships and practices of bringing those alternatives to life in potent ways. These histories show that many fugitives did not evanescently pass through the North simply to escape beyond it. Many stayed in border zones to facilitate the freedom of others and practically resist the order of slavery in myriad ways that we will discuss here.

The Black front-line communities displayed a profound understanding of a distinctive kind of power that hinged upon nurturing a growing vortex of receptive tending and performative agency sufficiently magnetic to both *draw* fugitives northward and *hold* many who chose to stay and collaborate in the movement.[31] For example, LaRoche writes, "Brooklyn [Illinois]'s growth hinged on its ability to attract runaways. The town was a city of refuge."[32] Griffler notes, "success [of the front-line movement] wasn't measured by the numbers who made it to Canada, but by those who remained defiantly [in communities such as those] along the northern banks of the Ohio River."[33] The magnetism of these sanctuary communities is exemplified in the growth of the Black population in Detroit over two decades, from 193 in the 1840 census, to 587 in 1850 and 1,402 just before the Civil War.[34]

Local initiatives and modes of flight waxed and waned in improvisational dialogue with shifting conditions in a highly volatile political landscape. However, these new histories repeatedly demonstrate that Black communities and organizations constituted a vibrant "frontline of freedom" across different geographical locations and contexts. As they led the way in building durable communities as "frontline" structures of resistance and refuge for themselves and new arrivals, sanctuary became an ethico-political mode of being.[35] They intentionally crafted collective spaces and practices of harbour, built alternative community capacities, distinctive political imaginaries, and forged transformative power in the processes of self-organization as collective bodies that solicited, received, and facilitated the flights of others, resisting and disrupting the dominant order of white supremacy. Careful reading of these histories together begins to illuminate key practices and dispositions that characterize magnetic, transformative sanctuary politics as the vital twin of fugitivity and, by extension, fugitive democracy.

Tending in Fugitive Sanctuary

In *Presence of the Past*, Wolin distinguishes political tending from a politics of "intending," which subjugates the differences and irregularities of people and places to the power imperatives of nations, states, and corporations. Tending, he writes, "implies active care for things close at hand ... concern for objects whose nature requires that they be treated as historical and biographical beings ... [and] attentiveness to differences between beings." By this, he means that tending actively orients politics around "habits of competence or skill that are routinely required if things are to be taken care of ... habits of the heart ... and intimate political experience ... acquired in everyday life."[36] Tending is the existential infrastructural web weaving of a politics of responsiveness. Yet, Wolin's own account of tending focuses primarily on settled, rooted local communities.

The Black front-line communities, however, elaborated modes as a practice of care that opens receptively towards people and practices that are displaced and excluded from settlement, that arrive from elsewhere and may just pass through in addition to those people and practices that Wolin recognizes as constituting the history of a particular place. They show how a sanctuary politics of tending to alternative possibilities with and among the displaced and fugitives can be a powerful learning process that amplifies latent democratic possibilities – gathering fragmented legacies of mutualism and community governance towards the invention of new modes responsive to changing conditions.

The Black (and some biracial) communities that sprung up along the border between North and South, in ports of entry in the North, and the border with Canada were founded *as* communities of refuge and resistance based upon mutualist practices of responsive tending to those most threatened by the hegemonic order. Community institutions and organizations like churches and Vigilance Committees became vital networks of grassroots democratic web weaving oriented towards care for fugitives, collective well-being, and tender shoots of collective possibility in an extremely hostile and turbulent political terrain.

In northern urban areas, such as New York City; Boston; Philadelphia; Washington, DC; New Bedford; Detroit; and many more, Blacks led and organized Vigilance Committees to undertake the myriad activities that constituted "practical abolition." As historian Eric Foner puts it, "'Practical' meant that vigilance committees devoted themselves not simply to the dramatic escapes that have come to characterize our image of the underground railroad, but to day-to-day activities like organizing committees, raising funds, and political and legal action. Many of these activities took place in full public view, not 'underground.'"[37] Moreover, that daily activism went far beyond protection to also include campaigns for equal citizenship, the right to vote, access to public education, and economic opportunity.

The thirteen flourishing Black communities along the Ohio River as well as those in Cincinnati and Detroit were founded *as* communities of refuge and resistance centred around practices of responsive tending.[38] These multi-sectoral sanctuary communities effectively became large Vigilance Committees. As elaborate pragmatic webs of quotidian tending, these communities built multifaceted, flexible civic muscle that enabled them to mobilize effective and flexible sanctuary with little notice. For example, historian Roy Finkenbine writes

of a moment in 1846 when worshippers in two African American congregations in Detroit received warning that slave catchers were in the city. "*Within
minutes*, the city's Colored Vigilance Committee (CVC) mobilized its members,
most of whom were leaders in the two churches, alerting the entire local African
American community and 'scouring the lanes and streets' to identify and harass
the slave-catchers and to protect and assist the runaways they threatened."[39]

Such risky work and rapidly coordinated action emerged not out of thin air
but depended on a level of trust, shared knowledge and vision, voluntary agreements to cooperate, and pragmatic capacities that had evolved in a community
of people engaged daily with each other in myriad ways. Black churches were
often the first institutions in new communities and anchored these activities. As
one historian puts it, they served "the nucleus of African American social life."
Historian Adrienne Shaad explains:

> [T]he black church represented far more than a sanctuary of worship and a place
> to practice one's faith. It was always the first piece of communally owned real
> estate.... It was where leadership training took place. The church was the locus
> of community activism in general and antislavery activities, fugitive slave recep-
> tion in particular. And it was through the churches that previously unschooled
> ex-slaves received the first inklings of literacy, because both children and adults
> attended and learned to read and write in Sabbath Schools.[40]

Historians also describe organized societies entirely devoted to practices of
sanctuary tending to individual and collective well-being that extended far
beyond immediate fugitivity. Finkenbine writes, "A survey of the African
American community [in Detroit] in 1843 found some twenty benevolent and
improvement societies, all of which met in the churches."[41] Given the Black
population of Detroit at the time, this was an extraordinary level of associational density. Similarly, Shaad writes of "the creation of the True Band Society,
a self-help organization of black men and women who paid monthly dues into a
fund to help those truly in need, especially those who had recently arrived from
slavery and needed assistance to get on their feet."[42] Sanctuary, then, involved
myriad activities in which communities tended themselves into becoming a
powerful collective in everyday practices from shared worship to fundraising;
communicating; daily care and education of children; employment; collective
deliberation; formulation of strategies and tactics; and courageous actions to
hide, usher, and care for new arrivals.

These durable patterns of mutualistic care significantly distinguished Black
abolitionists from their white counterparts, who often provided very important
short-term assistance but not longer-term support to fugitives. Referring to white
abolitionist support in New Bedford, Massachusetts, for example, fugitive slave
George Teamoh wrote that "after a few weeks of indulgence ... you were 'free

indeed', and then thrown upon your own resources."[43] Kathryn Grover argues that there and elsewhere, "it was then that black abolitionists, who saw the situation through a different lens, stepped into the fugitive's life ... never separated themselves from the enslaved millions.... Thus assisting fugitives in the long term was as much a part of their lives" as supporting, finding work for, and protecting their own families.[44] Only occasionally do we find traces of this quotidian tending in the historical record. For example, Frederick Douglass praises the "noble hospitality" of Nathan Johnson, a Black abolitionist who taught him about the community, helped him find employment, loaned him necessary supplies and money, and provided ongoing support in navigating the new culture.[45] For the most part, however, Grover (who has poured through archives) notes that fine-grained accounts of these efforts "have gone unrecorded": "We know so comparatively little about them in large part because they assisted persons escaping slavery on an everyday level, that level of historical detail that generally eludes the public record."[46]

But, sanctuary tending was not only the nurturing care and community building that Wolin emphasizes. As Keith Griffler's account of the Cincinnati Black community makes vivid, tending to the survival and flourishing of fugitives, among fugitives, also involved taking a stand, sometimes with defensive violence, to ward off violence and recapture. For example, Griffler describes multiple instances of armed defence, including a fully organized and armed uprising against police and vigilante whites that successfully resulted in a decade of relatively peaceful coexistence and legal concessions in Cincinnati.[47] Indeed, unlike pacifist white abolitionists who often eschewed all forms of violence, many Blacks – having experienced the violence of the order – boldly affirmed acts of forcible resistance as part of a complex repertoire of sanctuary-tending practices. Indeed, in the case of New Bedford in Massachusetts, the Black community drew initially reluctant whites into a more complex ecology of sanctuary practices in which tending as care, protection, and community building also involved forcible resistance where necessary. For example, Kathryn Grover describes how, after the passage of the Fugitive Slave Act of 1850, Black leaders – leading by example and argument – gradually pushed white abolitionists to remove amendments in broader anti-slavery/slave-catching resolutions that proclaimed force would *not* be used.[48] Similarly, Foner shows that in many northern cities, the combination of terror from the Fugitive Slave Act and the leadership of militant Blacks in Vigilance Committees gradually persuaded both Blacks committed to respectability politics and many whites who had been committed to nonresistance, to abandon the rejection of defensive violence for fugitive slaves.[49] For fugitives, the solidaristic relationships and practices of tending on the one hand, and defensive action on the other, were conditions of each other's possibility. All of this suggests that the repertoire of practices in Wolin's account of tending needs to be expanded and transfigured in light of the challenges, arguments, and examples of fugitives.

Dramatic Sanctuary

Even as tending cultivated elemental community powers, it was only one dimension of transformative sanctuary action. Just as importantly, Black communities crafted fine improvisational arts of dramatic sanctuary. Facing overwhelmingly disproportionate modes of traditional power, these communities "improvised a kind of inspired street theatre" as an integral form of struggle, modulating modes of appearance and disappearance, often "hiding in plain sight."[50] Elaborate systems to detect the presence of slaveholders and slave catchers and coordinate responses involved a precarious mix of planning and wild improvisation – from hiding to mobbing the catchers and snatching people from their clutches to staging acts of confusion, subterfuge, and blockage that impeded pursuit. From one angle, this was strategic action under the direst circumstances. Yet, as such actions repeatedly unfurled, they produced (both unintentionally and intentionally) spectacles that, in turn, provoked significant changes in the sense of agency, intelligence, courage, power, and possibility among those who directly and indirectly witnessed them. We suspect that each time these sanctuary performances succeeded, they emboldened participants and witnesses to further heights of creative action just as an artist's or athlete's experience of a successful performance tends to enhance their capacities and confidence for the next one.

The work of providing refuge often involved myriad people engaging in complex performative ruses that distracted, confused, or deceived slave catchers. For example, people switched gender presentations to pass through public places unrecognized by those in pursuit. They powdered their skin to appear white. They hid fugitives in coffins, and whole congregations enacted fake funerals that enabled safe passage. They delayed entry by asking for papers while fugitives slipped out the back door. If nine people of a particular description were being chased, nine other people who looked sufficiently similar might appear in front of the slave catchers to provoke capture, only to gradually turn out to be the "wrong ones" – embarrassing the pursuers as the real fugitives got away.[51] Sometimes a succession of scenes was staged, requiring remarkable levels of coordination among different people: a pursued fugitive might be led through the woods to a "safe house" by the sound of a conch. Others would be ready there to stage a public commotion to distract slave catchers if they were able to stay on the fugitive's trail. Others still stood ready to assist in yet another flight to another shelter. At arrival points in port cities, individuals and vocal groups often enacted street sanctuary, swarming owners and physically accompanying slaves in getting away while others ensured necessary court protections.

While these performances strategically aimed to evade and discourage slave catchers, they simultaneously generated spectacles of creative, collective power *to* the Black communities who participated in and/or witnessed them.

Performances of sanctuary thus intensified vibrant experiences of agency denied by white supremacy – a sense of trickster capacities to break through walls and cages that the order strived to make impenetrable. In a variety of contexts, practical abolition involved intertwining shelter with performative dimensions that dramatized sanctuary in ways that re-constituted publics, publicness, and political imaginaries while contributing to transformative reconfigurations of the common sense of what the demos was and could become beyond the order of slavery.[52] This, in turn, ignited aspirations to project these emergent forms and qualities of public power outward to wider audiences. Thus, in the process of "giving birth to a new world" amid the toxic forces of the old, the traditionally interior aspect of the "womb of sanctuary" developed arts of strategic projection that slowly reconfigured the coordinates of possibility defining the milieu – inspiring Blacks and, in turn, many white abolitionists while creating despair in the enemy as increasingly bold spectacles appeared in mainstream forums.

Many Black abolitionists engaged in the strange and, at first glance, seemingly reckless practice of making public detailed accounts of their efforts in ushering people to freedom. Emblematic in this regard were the activities of Black abolitionist and former slave Jermain Loguen. Foner describes Loguen's activities in New York as "*flagrantly public*."[53] Loguen published annual reports of the numbers of people that had passed through the city on their way to freedom. He was even known to drive through the city with wagon loads of fugitives in open daylight. The New York Vigilance Committee held annual public meetings in which they announced how many fugitives had been assisted in the previous year.[54] Another common strategy was that "whenever an alleged fugitive appeared before a judge, large crowds of black New Yorkers ... from several hundred to nearly 2,000, gathered at the courthouse in lower Manhattan during the proceedings. Hundreds of blacks who could not gain admission paraded on Broadway, wearing hats bedecked with mottos such as 'No Slavery' and 'Down with Kidnapping.'"[55] In Boston, after passage of the Fugitive Slave Act, fifty Black men boldly entered a courtroom, disrupted the proceedings over a former slave who had been caught by his professed owner, and carried him to safety.[56] Newspapers were vital means of projecting performances of sanctuary and alternative publicness. Abolitionist newspapers regularly published detailed narratives describing, without names, who they had ushered to freedom and precisely how – broadcasting dramatic sanctuary actions across North America and the Atlantic.[57] In many places, dramatic declarations, displays of potentially violent mob capacities, and occasionally even actions of defensive violence, all played a crucial role in holding open spaces for these emergent publics.[58] Such dramatic activities did not merely happen *in* public. Rather, *flagrancy* – conspicuous "wrongness" and outlawry – formed and transformed *publicness itself* as the womb of sanctuary moved outward in strange ways that magnified and modulated capacities for political birthing and natality.

Of course, we are not claiming that flagrant publicness was the most pervasive form of practical abolition, nor that it was without incredible risks in the order of white supremacy. It was more akin to the tip of an iceberg, whose substance and conditions of appearance hinged on vast networks and practices of concealment, largely autonomous community formation, and creative lawbreaking. None of this is romantically to suggest that these publicly empowered practices meant fugitive Blacks in the North simply transcended the horrific vulnerability and terror associated with illegality and potential capture. Nevertheless, the many traces of dramatic harbour in the historical record suggest that this was a crucial aspect of the power, ecology of sensibilities, and transformative capacities of the abolitionist movement, one that is often overlooked in mainstream narratives and assumptions about the Underground Railroad. Tarrying seriously with these moments of flagrant publicity instead of dismissing them as episodic anomalies enables a much more complex understanding of Black fugitive sanctuary as a dynamic intertwinement of outward-turned publicness and inward-turned protection and arms-length autonomy. These entanglements simultaneously contribute to our reformed sense of fugitive democracy.

Not all abolitionists agreed with this mode of becoming public, including Frederick Douglass, who argued in 1857 in *My Bondage and My Freedom* that "the practice of publishing every new invention by which a slave is known to have escaped from slavery, has neither wisdom nor necessity to sustain it ... In publishing such accounts the anti-slavery man addresses the slaveholder, *not the slave*."[59] Yet, the historical record seems to suggest that practical abolition grew more – not less – effective in part by becoming public in ways that solicited and animated enslaved, fugitive, and free Blacks, swayed numerous whites that active resistance was legitimate, discouraged slave catchers, and contributed to the growth of front-line communities and large numbers of escapes to Canada. By becoming strange publics through dramatic forms of sanctuary solidarity, practical abolitionists constituted an imaginary of an alternative community – increasingly oppositional and biracial – a community that grew stronger in the lead-up to the Civil War. Douglass hoped that secrecy would strike the fear of violent death into the hearts of slave catchers. Yet, the spectacle of sanctuary also contributed favourably to this end.

What emerged with the dramatic sanctuary politics of the Black front lines of the Underground Railroad was a fugitive form of becoming public and generating power that is missed by most theories of the public sphere – whether Habermasian accounts of consensual deliberation, Arendtian divides between publicity and privateness, Scott's analysis of hidden versus public transcripts, or Warner's contrast between counter publics and publics.[60] Performative practices of dramatic sanctuary are intensifications and amplifications of publicness and power that hinge precisely upon a community's modulating between hiding and ruse on the one hand, and powerful appearances and disclosure on the other. Fugitive democratic power borne under duress is, on this reading, significantly cultivated through *arts of fluctuating* between public and private, manifestation and hiddenness, oppositional modes and consensual ones. By oscillating in these ways, fugitive democratic publics amplify the magnitude of their publicness. We might think of these increases and qualitative modulations as a comparative publicness that is analogous to Douglass's concept of comparative freedom. Precisely through these modulations, fugitive sanctuary shifts common sense and the sense of how democratic publicness may be enhanced under most dire circumstances. Neither Wolinian notions of fugitive democracy nor understandings of Black fugitivity as stepping back from efforts at transformative political engagement with broader publics and powers, fully grasp how this vital oscillating dynamic was integral to the movement and power of practical abolition – and, we suggest, important for empowering freedom movements today.

Disruptive Hospitality

By the 1840s, the well-known availability of refuge and assistance for fugitives had begun to significantly disrupt flows of commerce, threaten the profitability of slavery, and materially puncture holes in the totality of white supremacy.[61] We describe this as *disruptive hospitality* – harbouring practices and performances that disrupted the oppressive order. As we have begun to see, disruptive hospitality involved combining multiple dimensions of political action in reciprocally empowering ways – from tending to drama to creating change in formal systems of power.

For example, the city of New Bedford, Massachusetts, became infamous among slaveholders as a "den of negro thieves and fugitive protectors" as the port city regularly provided refuge for fugitives that repeatedly thwarted efforts at capture before and long after the Fugitive Slave Act of 1850.[62] Slave catchers complained that the population, police, courts, and city officials there were so well organized that they had to return empty-handed. At their practical abolitionist best, city officials intentionally lagged or did not respond at all to rendition requests while working supportively with churches and organized community members. One slave catcher, Major Hodson, wrote that "so generally was the manner bruited and so well posted was every citizen upon the subject" that rendition became impossible. He noted that despite attempts at secrecy, the arrival of his team was announced from the pulpits and bells were tolled throughout the city to let everyone know that a slave catcher had entered the city. Archival records in New Bedford show that this disruptive hospitality was grounded in everyday processes of grassroots democracy in which free and fugitive Blacks gathered frequently in large numbers, debated, voted, and charted paths for action.[63] These quotidian processes of tending to sanctuary capacities enabled rapid mobilization of democratic assemblies to craft responses to new threats. For example, after the passage of the Fugitive Slave Act, in response to rumours about the presence of slave catchers in New Bedford, 900 Black people were immediately mobilized to an assembly (involving nine-tenths of the Black community, which was over 5 per cent of the city's total population).

In conjunction with such sanctuary actions, Black and white abolitionists also conducted incessant battles in relation to municipal governance and the courts, as well as persistent legislative work at the state level – which formed the institutional dimensions of this broader ecology of disruptive hospitality. In many states, working in biracial coalitions, they succeeded in creating legal passage of the "freedom principle" that held that a slave brought by an owner into a free state immediately became free. Urged on by such actions as well as abolitionist campaigns of "moral suasion" that catalysed cultural shifts in the North, between 1842 and 1848, six states enacted sanctuary-like laws that barred public officials from taking jurisdiction in cases involving fugitive slaves or offering assistance to those seeking their recapture while also prohibiting the use of jails and other public buildings for detention of self-emancipated slaves. These emancipatory actions caused slave owners to lose income, whether through the immediate loss of the slave, by discouraging many slave owners from travelling north to conduct business, or by costs incurred in pursuing escaped slaves, paying slave catchers, etc. As successful sanctuary actions were publicized, growing numbers of the enslaved sought to flee, further disrupting the productive order. The disruptive hospitality of practical abolition eventually drove southern states to push for passage of the 1850 Fugitive Slave Law, an incredible expansion of federal power to override state and local law that effectively forced individuals and jurisdictions to cooperate in rendition. However, even as it sent fresh waves of terror into Black communities and many people responded by fleeing to Canada, by the late 1850s the law became virtually unenforceable as growing numbers of cities defended their rights to refuge and freedom.[64]

Disruptive hospitality highlights a third fruitful dynamic oscillation that complements those mentioned earlier: a modulating mix of informal political activity (including lawbreaking that exceeded civil disobedience, insofar as it focused on successful material harbour, bodily escape, and rendering the work of rendition inoperable) on the one hand, and investments in changing law and institutions on the other. For many Black abolitionists engaged in disruptive hospitality, the two were intertwined in mutually supportive ways, rather than mutually exclusive ideological options. This contrasts markedly with the purist pacifism of many Garrisonian abolitionists who advocated both non-resistance and non-participation in political institutions which they viewed as fundamentally and inexorably grounded in violence and slavery. As Foner shows, many Black abolitionists tended to work in ways that were far more plural, supple, dynamic, and expansive.[65] This included working in association with white abolitionists to change formal, institutional politics at all scales, from municipal to states to national; working across all branches, including legislative, judicial, and executive; and creatively organizing the interfaces between informal publics and formal political life, as Major Hodson was well aware. It appears that the aspirations of many engaged in disruptive hospitality were not, most fundamentally, oriented towards redeeming the promise of the nation, but towards hospitable visions of freedom, equality, and democracy. Political institutions were viewed as both integral to white supremacy thus far *and* as potential instruments towards emancipatory ends in the context of a much broader toolbox.

In this sense, those engaged in disruptive hospitality exemplified what Wolin called "democratic constitutionalism," by which he meant "the domination of democracy over constitution." He opposed this democratic constitutionalism to "constitutional democracy" as a form that he argued contained and neutered the demos. Integral to democratic constitutionalism is what Wolin called "rational disorganization" or the enactment of laws, institutions, and practices that block, impede, and disorganize designs for subjugation.[66] Midwifing – directly and indirectly – municipal and state legislative, judicial, and executive practices of intransigent non-compliance and contradiction with federal laws of rendition are a perfect case in point. When informed by the disruptive hospitality politics of fugitives, these examples disclose a perhaps more radical politics of disorganization than Wolin's discussions typically suggest.

Ethico-Political Negotiations in the Womb of Sanctuary

Of course, it would be a mistake to pretend that such multilayered sanctuary politics can somehow be exempt from inherited and emergent blindness, fear, and violence that so often plague political life. We began this section evoking the New Sanctuary Movement's metaphor of a "womb of sanctuary." Yet, as Saidiya Hartman poignantly theorizes, beginning in the slavery era, Black women's wombs were co-opted through the racist violence of rape and have continued, into the present, to transfer conditions of social death to subsequent generations, even as they give life.[67] This specific truth is also of general significance: the womb of sanctuary is itself complicated by legacies of subjugative power that remain at work – even as sanctuaries strive to function as umbrellas to shelter people from those storms. It is only insofar as we become ceaselessly vigilant about this complexity and its internal implications that sanctuary politics may become "wombs to birth a new world."

At best, receptive sanctuary politics provides resources for repeatedly addressing such problems. In this vein, it is important to keep in mind Jacques Derrida's warning that even the most well-meaning forms of hospitality can easily slide into "hosti-pitality" – the unacknowledged entanglements between welcoming hospitality and a hostility wherein the host maintains the power and privilege over his domain, leaving the guest hostage to the host's priorities.[68] Frederick Douglass was the first to provide an incisive critical analysis of such "hostipitality" when he described how white abolitionists and audiences welcomed him to speak about his travails as a slave but circumscribed the limits of how he could speak and what he could speak about. In his second autobiography, *My Bondage and My Freedom*, Douglass writes, "Let us have the facts, said the people ... who always wished to pin me down to my simple narrative. 'Give us the facts,' said Collins, 'we will take care of the philosophy.'"[69] The passage theorizes the double movement of hostipitality that can give space only according to the conditions and parameters of the host, remaining unreceptive to all that exceeds or challenges those limits. Derrida suggests that forms of hostipitality bar the newcomer (the foreigner, the fugitive, the other) from participating in fashioning the contours of coexistence and, as Douglass so vividly argues, hold the other hostage to the host's order and the host's sole arbitration of justice.

Democratic sanctuary requires that we become ever-attentive to the dangers of hostipitality by repeatedly placing power relations in question. For example, when middle-class white people offer sanctuary, their capacities to "host" are borne on legacies of colonialism, militarism, climate change, and global capitalism that have greatly contributed to the displacement of those in flight. Genuine hospitality in this context involves searching questions about the rights, powers, and prerogatives of "hosts" – in vulnerable dialogue that seeks to scramble the guest–host dichotomy. Derrida reminds us that "knowing not to know too well" is crucial for cultivating a politics of refuge that strives towards justice in relations of reciprocal learning and relearning what sanctuary and democracy might be(come).[70] Indeed, we would suggest that a politics of democracy *as* sanctuary would involve creating spaces and processes that midwife such receptive dialogue and learning, especially when the capacities are withering in the broader polity.

At stake in these questions of radical receptivity are not only questions of justice, but those of power. The purity and rigidity of Garrisonian abolitionists is well known to have diminished their capacity to form alliances across differences, think strategically, learn, and evolve with others – including Black practical abolitionists exercising militant sanctuary. Deliberate and ongoing care for fugitivity – in ourselves and others – helps keep us tuned to all that is deported, dislodged, and diminished both historically and in our own practices when we move too quickly towards problematic (hostipitable) commonalities. Little has undermined democratic power *from within* more than our tendencies to consider ourselves beyond these issues. In this context, we find the Philadelphia New Sanctuary Movement's insistence upon leadership by immigrants to be particularly promising, as are forms of multi-issue sanctuary emerging at the collaborative intersections among OCADA, Black Youth Project, and Mijente.[71]

Conclusion

The understanding of sanctuary power and responsibility elaborated by the Black front lines of the Underground Railroad did not necessarily end with the Civil War. For example, as Cheryl LaRoche writes, the AME church of Rocky Flat, Illinois, pledged after the Civil War to *"always be a refuge* against trouble and strife – and continues that tradition today."[72] At stake in that pledge is a weathered sense of the perennial trouble, strife, and torn-ness of the threads of humanity and also of the redemptive, potentially transformative power of continually offering sanctuary.

That pledge is a profound articulation of what Juliet Hooker describes as "ethical commitments fostered by fugitivity." In considering one such commitment, Hooker focuses on Douglass's affirmation – beginning during Reconstruction – of a "human right to migration" and a "politics of open borders" that would enable a conception of multiracial democratic citizenship not governed by state boundaries.[73] However, in important ways, the Rocky Flat community's commitment to refuge exceeds a "right to migration" by placing ongoing receptivity to all who are (and all that is) displaced, diminished, or threatened *at the heart* of what it means to be a community, citizen, and polity amid the strife of human existence. For those making that pledge, as we have seen, refuge was no mere abstract principle, but a textured, *quotidian activity* that they had lived. Surely, such a commitment would include what Douglass calls a "human right to migration." But the Rocky Flat pledge ethically speaks to the fact that human history incessantly produces its fugitives, its oppressive orders, and modes of displacement. It affirms the community's power, agency, and constitutive ethical obligation precisely there. Placing sanctuary at the heart of their ethical and political commitments, the Rocky Flat community staked out this zone as a much more powerful bulwark against all forms of oppression than mere flight or migration away from it. Rather, sanctuary is a movement towards and into a remarkably different form of power.

To our minds, the praxis and declaration of Rocky Flat, and the history of the Black front lines of the Underground Railroad more broadly, open onto a reconceptualization of democratic politics today. The Black front line communities have shown us that we might embrace the fugitivity of democracy itself as *both* flight away from anti-democratic forces *and* also, potentially, flight towards and into new modes of transformative sanctuary power. Theorizing and practising democracy on this ground of the Underground would mean committing, like the Rocky Flat community, to imagining and practising democracy as harbour by, with, and for all those who find themselves on the undersides of unjust power – whether by tyranny or simply majoritarian democracy. Proactively embracing fugitive democracy as a politics of harbour would involve deliberate receptive practices that seek to collaboratively build, maintain, and tend shelters that nurture alternatives to the dominant culture and order. Such sanctuary practices, as we have discussed, involve a complex ecology that generatively weaves together apparently opposed dynamics of tending as responsive collective nurture and defensive protective action, of dramatic receptivity that involves both cunning concealment and flagrant publicity, and of disruptive hospitality in which receptive practices block, puncture, and change the oppressive order.

The promise of fugitive democracy/sanctuary emerges (beyond ontologized hope or pessimism) from creatively staying with both the problems and unexpected possibilities that emerge in fugitive currents. It is in these currents and their inheritance that, in the most dismal times, people regenerate an active faith that "perversely and with no extraordinary power, reconstitute[s] the world."[74] In such currents, fugitive democracy/sanctuary might not only forge paths for survival in the face of new waves of fascism and the coming horrors of climate catastrophe, they can also foster forms of collective power and ethical heights that have thus far eluded us.

NOTES

1 See Christian Parenti, *Tropic of Chaos: Climate Change and the New Geography of Violence* (New York: Nation Books, 2011) for a good synthesis.

2 Toni Morrison, *The Origin of Others* (The Charles Eliot Norton Lectures) (Boston: Harvard University Press, 2017, Kindle edition), Kindle Location 794.

3 See, for example, Sheldon Wolin, *Democracy Incorporated: Managed Democracy and the Specter of Inverted Totalitarianism* (Princeton, NJ: Princeton University Press, 2008); Wendy Brown, *Undoing the Demos: Neoliberalism's Stealth Revolution* (New York: Zone Books, 2015); and William Connolly, *Aspirational Fascism: The Struggle for Multifaceted Democracy Under Trumpism* (Minneapolis: University of Minnesota Press, 2017).

4 Sheldon Wolin, "Fugitive Democracy," *Constellations*, Vol. 1, No. 1 (1994), 11–25.

5 See Sheldon Wolin, *The Presence of the Past: Essays on the State and Constitution* (Baltimore: Johns Hopkins University Press, 1990); Sheldon Wolin, *Politics and Vision,* expanded ed. (Princeton, NJ: Princeton University Press, 2004), chs. 16 and 17; and Wolin, *Democracy Incorporated.*

6 William Connolly, *Capitalism and Christianity, American Style* (Durham, NC: Duke University Press, 2008).

7 Quoted in Paul Gilroy, *Small Acts: Thoughts on the Politics of Black Cultures* (London: Serpant's Tail, 1993), 178.

8 See, for example, Barnor Hesse, "Escaping Liberty: Western Hegemony, Black Fugitivity," *Political Theory*, Vol. 42, No. 3 (2014), 288–313; Stephen Best and Saidiya Hartman, "Fugitive Justice," *Representations*, Vol. 92 (Fall 2005), 1–15.

9 Neil Roberts, *Freedom as Marronage* (Chicago: University of Chicago Press, 2015), 9.

10 Juliet Hooker, *Theorizing Race in the Americas: Douglass, Sarmiento, Du Bois, and Vasconcelos* (Oxford: Oxford University Press, 2017), 29. Lawrie Balfour reads Du Bois as a scholar of Black fugitivity and fugitive democracy in *Democracy's Reconstruction: Thinking Politically with W.E.B. Du Bois* (Oxford: Oxford University Press, 2011).

11 Roberts, *Freedom as Marronage*, 4–5; and James C. Scott, *The Art of Not Being Governed: An Anarchist History of Upland Southeast Asia* (New Haven, CT: Yale University Press, 2010).

12 Hooker, *Theorizing Race in the Americas*, 32.

13 Hooker, *Theorizing Race in the Americas*, 32–4 and 39.

14 Joel Olson, *The Abolition of White Democracy* (Minneapolis: University of Minnesota Press, 2004).

15 Our account has affinities with Stefano Harney and Fred Moten's lateral, vernacular, improvisational relationality in *The Undercommons: Fugitive Planning and Black Study* (New York: Minor Compositions, 2013). Yet precisely where they insist upon dichotomous anti-political contrasts, we suggest that Black front-line communities of the Underground Railroad brilliantly fashion generative entanglements that revolutionize democracy.

16 Walter Benjamin, "Theses on the Philosophy of History," in *Illuminations: Essays and Reflections,* ed. Hannah Arendt and trans. Harry Zohn (New York: Random House, 1968), 257 and 255.

17 Ibid., 263.

18 Ibid., 262.

19 Our approach is cognizant of Theodor Adorno's critique of Benjamin for underplaying careful, critical reflection and incorporates both modes. Theodor W. Adorno and Walter Benjamin, *The Complete Correspondence, 1928-1940,* ed. Henri Lonitz and trans. Nicholas Walker (Cambridge, MA: Harvard University Press, 2001).

20 Martin Luther King Jr., "I Have a Dream," 28 August 1963, in *A Testament of Hope: The Essential Writings and Speeches of Martin Luther King* (New York: Harper Collins, 1991), 218.

21 Wolin, *Politics and Vision*, 605.

22 Wendy Brown extends this motif in *Undoing the Demos: Neoliberalism's Stealth Revolution* (New York: Zone Books, 2015).

23 For an insightful overview of such criticisms of Wolin's notion of fugitive democracy, see David W. McIvor, "The Conscience of a Fugitive: Sheldon Wolin and the Prospects for Radical Democracy," *New Political Science*, Vol. 38, No. 3 (2016), 411–27.

24 Wolin, *Politics and Vision*, 601.

25 Cheryl Janifer LaRoche, *Free Black Communities and the Underground Railroad: The Geography of Resistance* (Urbana: University of Illinois Press, 2013), 3.

26 http://sanctuaryphiladelphia.org/who-we-are-new-sanctuary/2017-statement-sanctuary/, accessed 21 May 2018.

27 This myth was established by Wilbur H. Siebert, *The Underground Railroad from Slavery to Freedom: A Comprehensive History* (New York: MacMillan Press, 1898)

and was unchallenged until Larry Gara's definitive critique, *The Liberty Line: The Legend of the Underground Railroad* (Lexington: University of Kentucky Press, 1961), which foregrounded fugitives' active agency in their own escapes. His critique, however, focussed on escape to Canada and overlooked the ways that many fugitives stayed in border zones in the North where they joined free Black communities. For four decades, subsequent historians accepted Gara's narrative and treated the Underground Railroad largely as a figment of white imagination. Recent histories have begun to significantly complicate this myth, as we discuss.

28 Colson Whitehead's 2016 novel *The Underground Railroad* (New York: Penguin Random House, 2016) plays in interesting ways with this myth as well as its effacement of Black agency. The novel features a Black fugitive community, the Valentine Farm, as a sanctuary for Black flourishing and self-determination amid the barbarism of surrounding racism and systemic oppression. Nevertheless, his depiction of the sanctuary community as primarily turned inward and focussed on protection still largely misses many of ways actual Black communities also did central transformative work on the broader order while themselves being prime drivers and shapers of the flows of the Underground Railroad.

29 LaRoche, *Free Black Communities,* 41. In addition to LaRoche, these new histories include: Eric Foner, *Gateway to Freedom: The Hidden History of the Underground Railroad* (New York: W.W. Norton, 2015); Karolyn Smardz Frost and Veta Smith Tucker, eds., *A Fluid Frontier: Slavery, Resistance, and the Underground Railroad in the Detroit River Borderland* (Detroit: Wayne State University Press, 2016); Keith P. Griffler, *Front Line of Freedom: African Americans and the Forging of the Underground Railroad in the Ohio Valley* (Lexington: University of Kentucky Press, 2004); and Kathryn Grover, *The Fugitive's Gibraltar: Escaping Slaves and Abolitionism in New Bedford, Massachusetts* (Boston: University of Massachusetts Press, 2001).

30 Griffler, *Front Line of Freedom,* 11.

31 This point is resonant with Mamu Vimalassery's insight about "fugitive movement as transit against empire in the context of territorial dispossession of indigenous people and the enslavement of blacks," in "Fugitive Decolonization," *Theory & Event,* Vol. 19, No. 4 (2016), 1. https://muse.jhu.edu/, accessed 25 November 2018).

32 LaRoche, *Free Black Communities,* 36.

33 Griffler, *Front Line of Freedom.*

34 Finkenbine, "A Community Militant and Organized: The Colored Vigilant Committee of Detroit," in *Fluid Frontier,* Kindle Locations 4290–1.

35 See Griffler, *Front Line of Freedom*; LaRoche, *Free Black Communities*; and Frost and Tucker, *Fluid Frontier.*

36 Wolin, *Presence of the Past,* 89.

37 Foner, *Gateway to Freedom,* 20.

38 As LaRoche argues in *Free Black Communities,* many were formed as AME church encampments. The AME church was founded in resistance to white supremacy

and embraced a theology of responsive quotidian tending and sanctuary from the beginning.

39 Roy Finkenbine, "A Community Militant and Organized: The Colored Vigilant Committee of Detroit," in *A Fluid Frontier*, Kindle location 4277.

40 Adrienne Shad, "Extending the Right Hand of Fellowship: Sandwich Baptist Church, Amherstburg First Baptist, and the Amherstburg Baptist Association," in *A Fluid Frontier,* Kindle location 3427.

41 Finkenbine, "A Community Militant and Organized," Kindle location 4289.

42 Shad, "Extending," Kindle location 3573–5.

43 Cited in Grover, *The Fugitive's Gibraltar,* 287.

44 Grover, *The Fugitive's Gibraltar*, 287.

45 Frederick Douglass, *Life and Times of Frederick Douglass* (Radford, VA: Wilder Publications, 2008), 117.

46 Grover, *The Fugitive's Gibraltar*, 288.

47 Griffler, *The Frontline of Freedom.*

48 Grover, *Fugitives of Gibraltar.*

49 Foner, *Gateway to Freedom*, ch. 5.

50 Fergus Bordewich, *Bound for Canaan: The Epic Story of the Underground Railroad, America's First Civil Rights Movement* (New York: Harper Collins, 2005), 201.

51 Griffler, *Frontiers of* Freedom, ch. 3.

52 Jacques Ranciere, *Disagreement: Politics and Philosophy* (Minneapolis: University of Minnesota Press, 1999).

53 Foner, *Gateway to Freedom*, 180, our emphasis.

54 Foner, *Gateway to Freedom,* 9.

55 Ibid., 70

56 Grover, *The Fugitive's Gibraltar,* 222.

57 See the many accounts in Foner, *Gateway to Freedom.*

58 See Griffler, *Front Linesof Freedom*; Smardz and Tucker, *A Fluid Frontier*; and Grover, *The Fugitive's Gibraltar.*

59 Frederick Douglass, *Autobiographies* (New York: Library of America, 1994), 339–40.

60 E.g., Jurgen Habermas, *The Structural Transformation of the Public Sphere* (Cambridge, MA: MIT Press, 1991); Hannah Arendt, *The Human Condition* (Chicago: University of Chicago Press, 1958); James C. Scott, *Domination and the Arts of Resistance: Hidden Transcripts* (New Haven, CT: Yale University Press, 1990); and Michael Warner, *Publics and Counterpublics* (New York: Zone Books, 2002).

61 "Depredations to the amount of hundreds of thousands of dollars are committed upon the property of the people of the border slave states of this Union annually," stated one indignant senator from Missouri in congressional debates leading up to the Fugitive Slave Law, summing up the economic impact nicely, in Foner, *Gateway to Freedom,* 122.

62 Grover, *The Fugitive's Gibraltar*, 14.

63 Grover, *The Fugitive's Gibraltar*, 223.

64 Ibid., ch. 5.

65 Foner, *Gateway to Freedom*, especially chs. 3, 6, and 7.

66 Sheldon Wolin, "Norm and Form: The Constitutionalizing of Democracy," in *Athenian Political Thought and the Reconstruction of American Democracy,* ed. J. Peter Euben et al. (Ithaca, NY: Cornell University Press,1994), 37–9. See Romand Coles, "Democracy and the Radical Ordinary: Wolin and the Epical Emergence of Democratic Theory," *Christianity, Democracy and the Radical Ordinary: Conversations between a Radical Democrat and a Christian* (Eugene, OR: Wipf and Stock, 2008).

67 "The Belly of the World: A Note on Black Women's Labors," *Souls: A Critical Journal of Black Politics, Culture and Society*, Vol. 18, No. 1 (January–March 2016), 166–73.

68 Jacques Derrida, "Hostipitality," *Angelaki: Journal of Theoretical Humanities*, Vol. 5, No. 3 (2000), 6.

69 Douglass, *My Freedom, My Bondage*, 265–6, quoted in Roberts, *Freedom as Marronage*, 60.

70 See, for example, Jacques Derrida, *The Gift of Death* (Chicago: University of Chicago Press, 1995).

71 Abou Farman, "In Defense of Sanctuary," *The Baffler*, 6 April 2017. https:// thebaffler.com/latest/in-defense-of-sanctuary-farman, accessed 30 September 2018. Farman discusses, "the coalitions built in Chicago where groups like Mijente [intersectional pro-Latinx organization], OCADA [cultivating grassroots responses to drug abuse], and Black Youth Project [intersectional empowerment project] have joined in what they call expanded sanctuary in order to tackle not just immigration-related sanctuary policy but also policies related to issues like law enforcement, education, labor, gender, and economic justice."

72 LaRoche, *Free Black Communities*, 32.

73 Hooker, *Theorizing Race in the Americas,* 49–52.

74 Adrienne Rich, "Natural Resources," in *The Dream of a Common Language: Poems 1974–1977* (New York: W.W. Norton, 1978), 67.

11 Visioning Limits or Unlimited Vision? The Vocation of Political Theory in the Anthropocene

ANDREW BIRO

One reads past theories not because they are familiar and therefore confirmative, but because they are strange and therefore provocative.
— Sheldon Wolin, "Political Theory as a Vocation"[1]

In May 2019, a group of geological scientists designated as the Anthropocene Working Group (AWG) decided to recognize a new epoch in the planet's history: the mid-twentieth century marks the end of the Holocene and the beginning of the Anthropocene.[2] The Anthropocene (the "Age of Man") is so denoted as the time when human impacts became visible in the fossil geological record, or when "human activity now rivals geological forces in influencing the trajectory of the Earth System."[3] The decision of the AWG constitutes only one step (albeit a significant one) in a larger process, and official scientific ratification of the designation ultimately will be determined by the executive committee of the International Union of Geological Sciences (IUGS).[4] Whatever the IUGS decides, however, the term has taken off in broader academic and popular discourse, and certainly is reflective of contemporary concerns about the scale of human influence on, and disruption of, planetary systems. And more obviously than many other emergent and contested scientific concepts, the Anthropocene raises *political* questions.

This chapter will rehearse some of these questions, but is not so ambitious as to posit answers to them. Rather, it focuses on questions that this epoch/concept raises for political theorizing, in particular by discussing it in light of a key tension in Sheldon Wolin's thought, between limits and vision. More specifically, that tension is between, on the one hand, the imaginative work of political theorizing, understood as necessarily transcending the limits of the politics of the day, and on the other, the importance of seeking limits on institutionalized concentrations of political power. The chapter proceeds as follows: after briefly rehearsing a series of political questions that are raised by the Anthropocene concept, we will turn to Wolin's work, with a particular focus on the tension between vision and limits. This tension is explored initially through the evolution from the first (1960) to second (2004) editions of *Politics and Vision*,[5] and then somewhat more broadly by bringing in other Wolin texts, including "Political Theory as a Vocation."

The Anthropocene and Its Politics

The epoch/concept of the Anthropocene raises political questions. Its political character may be seen by noting that it has spread not only through popular discourse but also through scientific discourse, even prior to its scientific ratification. There are scientific journals (*Anthropocene*; *The Anthropocene Review*; *Elementa: Science of the Anthropocene*) devoted to an event ("the Anthropocene") whose existence has not yet been scientifically verified.[6] For this reason, I refer to the Anthropocene here as an "epoch/concept" in order to emphasize its constructed and contested character. The politics of science aside, we can see where some other political questions and fault lines occur.

The first question, a focus of debates among earth scientists themselves, is about where (when) the boundary between the Holocene (the period starting at the end of the last ice age, roughly 11,700 years ago) and Anthropocene is to be drawn. The AWG has recommended drawing the line at the mid-twentieth century. This conveniently conflates two contemporaneous but distinct social events: the beginnings of the "Atomic Age" and the "Great Acceleration." The former denotes the explosion of atomic bombs (including not only the two bombs dropped on Japan during the Second World War, but also the many "test" bombs exploded over the next two decades), which produced a distinctive, long-lasting radioactive geological signature. The latter denotes the explosive growth in human population, economic activity, and resource consumption in the post–Second World War period,[7] which is linked very tenuously, if at all, to the development of nuclear power, let alone weaponry. As described in Meera Subramanian's report on the AWG's decision in *Nature*: "the mid-twentieth century [was] when a rapidly rising human population accelerated the pace of industrial production, the use of agricultural chemicals and other human activities. At the same time, the first atomic-bomb blasts littered the globe with radioactive debris that became embedded in sediments and glacial ice, becoming part of the geologic record."[8] It is the developments of the Great Acceleration, noted in the first sentence of the passage just cited, that are more commonly referred to when describing contemporary human impacts on the environment. For example, here is artist-photographer Edward Burtynsky's description in his "Anthropocene Project": "Terraforming of the earth through mining, urbanization, industrialization and agriculture; the proliferation of dams and diverting of waterways; CO_2 and acidification of oceans due to climate change; the pervasive presence around the globe of plastics, concrete, and other techno-fossils; unprecedented rates of deforestation and extinction."[9] And yet, many of the above markers of global consumer capitalism and its detritus are less likely than atomic bomb radionuclides to leave a clear and significant mark on the "geologic record," where the question is not about the legacy that will be left a few generations or even centuries hence, but rather about the legacy that will be left for future – not necessarily human – geological examiners of our planet millions of years from now.[10]

On the other hand, it seems likely that the broader popularity of the Anthropocene concept is connected to its resonance with contemporary environmental challenges that are measured on human rather than geological timescales. Steffen et al. connect their analysis of the Great Acceleration to the Anthropocene: "Today, humankind has begun to match and even exceed some of the great forces of nature in changing the biosphere and impacting other facets of Earth System functioning," leading to a "human-dominated planet."[11] And if it is human timescales that are, in fact, the primary concern, then the boundary marking the beginning of the Anthropocene and end of the Holocene might plausibly be drawn at other points than the mid-twentieth century. For example, in one of the earliest essays on the Anthropocene concept, Paul Crutzen and Eugene Stoermer "propose the latter part of the 18th century" as a boundary point, when the invention of the steam engine begins the increase in greenhouse gases associated with climate change (with the associated changing atmospheric composition detectable in glacial ice cores).[12] They immediately follow this by saying that the timing is contestable, and further add a parenthetical comment that "some may even want to include the entire Holocene."[13]

This leads to a second question: that of responsibility or agency. Dating the start of the Anthropocene matters politically because it attributes responsibility. If the Anthropocene indicates a problem of (un)sustainability, then different dates will provide different answers to what must be jettisoned and what can be maintained if we are to live sustainably. Is the Anthropocene driven by consumerism, industrialization, capitalism, colonialism, the "civilization" of agricultural settlement, or human nature? Each of these would suggest a different start date for the epoch and thus also a different prescription for a way forward: a non-consumerist form of capitalism, a non-capitalist form of industrial society, deindustrialization, nomadism, or human extinctionism.

This question of responsibility is similarly found in a series of debates that criticize the "Anthropocene" label. John Meyer notes that as a concept, the Anthropocene is largely understood through a "universalizing rhetoric of technocratic management."[14] The so-called Age of Man glosses over a whole series of social structures that entrench deep inequalities between human beings. After all, the decision to develop and deploy atomic weapons was made by political elites in a handful of sovereign states, not by humanity in general. Even more, the very existence of warring sovereign states presumes division within the species rather than a common humanity (*Anthropos*). Similarly, the fruits of the Great Acceleration have been enjoyed disproportionately by a minority of humans. And decisions about what to accelerate, when, how quickly, and for how long, have rested in even fewer hands, or could be seen to be driven by structural forces (the growth imperative of capitalism) that are outside the control of any individuals but not reducible to "human nature." Like the Anthropocene itself, the *Anthropos*, that is, its presumptive subject, can be seen as constructed and contested. The dominant narrative of the Anthropocene, as the name suggests, presumes a homogeneous "man" as subject. But more critical accounts seek to resituate responsibility by suggesting that there are more appropriate names for our current epoch: capitalocene, plantationocene, chthulucene, urbanthropocene, manthropocene, and so on.[15] Or, as Potawatomi scholar Robin Wall Kimmerer suggests, from an Indigenous perspective, the label might simply be rejected: "I don't believe that we are entering the Anthropocene, but that we are living in a transient period of profoundly painful error and correction on our way to a humbler consideration of ourselves."[16]

These considerations in turn are then reflected in somewhat more practical questions of contemporary governance. For some, if human activity is transforming the planet, then governance structures need to be similarly rescaled, with calls for institutions of "Earth system governance"[17] or "planetary management"[18] or for political processes that are more fit for purpose for an era of unprecedented species power.[19] Others, however, are more wary of such demands, either because global-scaled ambitions are seen as impractical and hubristic, as the quotation from Kimmerer above suggests, or because of a general scepticism of the logic of sovereignty entailed in such calls for planetary governance.[20]

Finally, there is the question of whether the Anthropocene presents us with a crisis or, rather, an opportunity. To make sense of seeing the Anthropocene as an opportunity, we might begin with the observation that all forms of life reshape their environment to make it more hospitable for needs satisfaction. Humans seem to be relatively unique only in being conscious of this process, and in the Anthropocene (however defined), in conducting this transformation at a global scale. Thus self-described "ecomodernists" share "the conviction that knowledge and technology, applied with wisdom, might allow for a good, or even great, Anthropocene."[21] A more modest, Marxian version of this claim is found in Steven Vogel's argument for a more self-conscious and democratic process of environmental transformation.[22] From this perspective, the problem is not transformation in itself (again, all living beings do this), nor even necessarily the global scale of those transformations. Rather, and related to the point raised by critics of the Anthropocene label, above, the problem is that these transformations are not being pursued for the purposes of the needs satisfaction of the species, much less ecological integrity more generally, but rather for more narrow and short-sighted purposes, like capital accumulation and empire building. On the other hand, the ecomodernist view in particular is seen by many, including many Earth system scientists, as overly optimistic, as it ignores what Meyer describes as the Anthropocene's "inherently Janus-faced" nature. The Anthropocene both "highlights the impact of human *power*" and "draws attention to the *limits* of intentional human action."[23] We will return to this characterization of the Anthropocene as Janus-faced below.

The Anthropocene, by virtue of the *content* of the concept – that planetary systems are shaped by human actions and systems – inevitably raises these kinds of questions about power and restraint or limits and about who has voice in articulating and implementing a vision for a changed world. Writing in *Nature Climate Change*, Noel Castree et al. observe, "it is now widely recognized that the sciences of nature cannot furnish us with all the knowledge or insight humanity will need to inhabit a post-Holocene environment."[24] This "recognition" is perhaps as much hopeful declarative invocation as mere description: the extent to which the hegemony of the sciences of nature are being displaced remains questionable. But it is also worth noting that it comes a half-century after Hannah Arendt observed a similar problem, at the end of *The Human Condition*: "Without actually standing where Archimedes wished to stand, still bound to the earth through the human condition, we have found a way to act on the earth and within terrestrial nature, as though we dispose of it from outside."[25] For Arendt, writing at the onset of what the AWG now characterizes as the Anthropocene, it was scientists and their achievements that brought us – to the extent that the collective subject invoked by Arendt can rightly be presupposed – "to the point of extinguishing the time-honoured protective dividing line between nature and the human world."[26] Arendt laments the restricted scope for politics – a "*vita activa*" – in a scientized world. The problem is one that runs through the questions and dilemmas that we have just briefly rehearsed: what to do when human techno-scientific prowess appears to outstrip the capacity of a *zoon politikon*, the capacity to engage in the kind of considered collective action that was thought to define our species? Scale up political ambitions to match technical prowess or scale down activity to match governance capacity? Or to put it in more Wolinian terms: is the appropriate path forward to pursue a vision of moving the world or to respect the limits of a bounded political community?

Sheldon Wolin: Preserving the Political

Sheldon Wolin's *Politics and Vision: Continuity and Innovation in Western Political Thought*, as the subtitle suggests, grapples with the dialectic of change (moving the world) and stability (respecting limits) in the Western tradition of political philosophy from Plato into the twentieth century. On the one hand, political philosophy is a tradition – an "extended conversation" – stretching over many centuries, which casts a long shadow over the work of those who engage it. Making an intelligible intervention in this ongoing conversation requires acknowledging past speakers and accepting many of the conversation's postulates, terms, and generic conventions. "Of all the restraints upon the political philosopher's freedom to speculate," Wolin writes, "none has been so powerful as the tradition of political philosophy itself."[27] The terms, concepts, and insights of past thinkers – or what Wolin calls a "cultural legacy" – act as "conservatizing agencies within the theory of a particular philosopher."[28] Political philosophy, as a discursive structure, necessarily limits what can be thought in political terms.

On the other hand, however, the task of any particular political philosopher is to recast this cultural legacy to make it relevant for their contemporary concerns and thus to push against those limits. Political philosophy is concerned not just with continuity but also with innovation. Crucial to innovation for Wolin is the political philosopher's "vision," meaning not only the ability to accurately describe the political world but also the use of the *imaginative* faculty. "The imaginative faculty has played a role in political philosophy similar to that Coleridge assigned to imagination in poetry, an 'esemplastic' power that 'forms all into one graceful intelligent whole.'"[29] Imaginative vision is thus *integrative* (a key term, as we shall see momentarily), allowing for the creation of an abstract, systematized understanding of the political realm. At the same time, imaginative vision is also normative and innovative: imagination "has been the medium for expressing the fundamental values of the theorist; it has been the means by which the political theorist has sought to transcend history."[30] To continue to make the case for Wolin's relevance, we can note here that both "Anthropocene" and the various contending critical alternative labels mentioned above can be seen as descriptions that not only imaginatively integrate geological and human systems, but also are necessarily expressions of normative commitments. The assertion of a new geological epoch characterized by human influence (or the influence of capital, plantation agriculture, etc.) can thus be seen as a form of political theorizing.

One way that Wolin understands the "history" that is to be transcended through political theorizing is the particular political context in which the theorist lives. ("An architectonic vision is one wherein the political imagination attempts to mold the totality of political phenomena to accord with some vision of the Good that lies outside the political order."[31]) But, as is made clear just a couple of pages later (perhaps most strongly in the passage about restraints on the political philosopher, cited above), the dead hand of history that is to be shaken off may equally refer to the inherited traditions of political philosophy itself.

These dialectical interplays, between continuity and innovation, and between the rootedness of limits and imaginative vision as an escape from history, form the intellectual core particularly of the first (1960) edition of Wolin's text, and provide the metatheoretical scaffolding for some wonderfully insightful readings of canonical political theorists. As one review of the 2004 edition begins:

> When it first appeared in 1960, *Politics and Vision* had an extraordinarily important impact on the development of political philosophy in the United States.... Time has been kind to what is now Part One of *Politics and Vision*. Many years after having cribbed liberally from it for my first lectures, I find it retains the freshness, subtlety, and extraordinary wisdom I found in a book then already twenty-five years old.[32]

A significant thematic focus, on the other hand, is rooted in what Wolin understands to be the main problem with the political conditions of his own day. The final chapter of the 1960 edition is titled "The Age of Organization and the Sublimation of Politics." In it Wolin most clearly expresses his own normative commitments (or "fundamental values") and "architectonic vision." The "Age of Organization" is a time which is fundamentally defined by the problem of the masses, as he asserts: "The concept of the masses haunts modern social and political theory."[33] The shift from Marxism to Leninism clarifies the political stakes here, as it signals a shift from seeing the bulk of humanity as the proletariat that is a universal *subject* to seeing the same people as the masses who are *objects* of manipulation by strategic-thinking elites. Wolin initially describes Lenin as being among the first to grasp "the possibilities of organization as the action medium best suited to a mass age." He then says that "the central point of Lenin's argument" was a decisive break from Marx (and other nineteenth-century views), in asserting the primacy of the political over the economic. But in a mass age, the political is crucially understood here to be "absorb[ed] into organization."[34] The organization is an "action medium" (we can recall here Wolin's claim that the imagination is similarly a "medium" for expressing the normative commitments of the theorist), but its own imperatives soon displace any autonomous political impulses that might have emerged from the masses, who are now conceived of as object rather than subject. The medium becomes the message.

While Lenin is among the first to grasp these insights,[35] he is of course far from the last, as they are lessons absorbed by many others across the political spectrum concerned with the problem of the masses. The dominant political ideologies of the first half of the twentieth century – Leninism, organization theory, and fascism – all sought (in different ways, to be sure) to solve the problem of the masses. "The measure of Lenin's success is that his lessons have become the common property of the age; the irony is that his prescription for revolution has also been used to preserve giant capitalism."[36] For Wolin, one important consequence of this lies in its casting out of democratic impulses – across the board, rather than just in Leninist Russia:

> Lenin's emphasis on the "small, compact core" of professional revolutionaries as the vital cog of organization led him to the question of what kind of democracy, and how much, could be permitted. His answer established a framework of argument that was to be duplicated by later writers concerned with the same broad question. It was the procedure adopted by [Roberto] Michels in his famous study of the oligarchical and bureaucratic tendencies in professedly democratic parties; by Chester Barnard in his analysis of the contradiction between the requirements of administrative leadership and democratic practices; by students of organization concerned at the way mass society, with its penchant for "radical leveling," "prevents the emergence of social leadership." *What is important here is the way that the question is posed: how much democracy can organization endure? – never the reverse.*[37]

Of note here is the way that this can be mapped onto the Anthropocene epoch/concept. The dominant Anthropocene discourse names "humanity" as the subject of the Anthropocene, while maintaining an elite-driven, techno-managerial approach to planetary management. Even if some economic redistribution is on the table in some more liberal accounts, the redistribution of political power – democratization – is not. What is wanting, as Castree et al. put it, is "mature *deliberation* rather than short-circuiting it in the rush to inform the key *decisions* humanity must take as it negotiates GEC [Global Environmental Change]."[38] The ideological sleight of hand in naming "humanity" as the subject of the Anthropocene, but in fact seeking to render most humans as objects of environmental governance, parallels quite strikingly the shift from Marx to Lenin and can be seen as another iteration of trying to "solve the problem of the masses."

For Wolin, the subordination of democratic principles to organizational imperatives is also traceable in a broader trend in the evolution of political theory. The locus of what is termed "political" activity has gradually shifted from the body politic (or state) to organizations more generally, and this change carries with it important, if more difficult to see, consequences. The emphasis on "organization" broadens the scope of the political in the sense that it allows us to see power operating in a multitude of non-state institutions and networks ("governance without government" to use a more current formulation). But this broadening simultaneously distracts us from the political understood as "what is general to a society," or "the general responsibility for the welfare of the whole society."[39] "Localism" is Wolin's term for our tendential blindness to the political in this sense. He identifies localism's roots not only in the hegemony of the organizational imperative but also in the scientization of the discipline of political science: its increasing reliance on objective, to the exclusion of imaginative, vision. This diagnosis provides a crucial point of reference for understanding Wolin's architectonic vision, or how *Politics and Vision* itself can be seen as an attempt to "escape from history": "The chopping-up of political man is but part of a broader process which has been at work in political and social theory. During the past two centuries the vision of political theory has been a disintegrating one, consistently working to destroy the idea that society ought properly to be considered as a whole and that its general life was best expressed through political forms. One result of this kind of theorizing has been to flatten the traditional *majestas* of the political order."[40] Political concerns, at least as these had previously been understood, are therefore integrative (rather than disintegrative) ones, and ones that consider "society as a whole." And the course of modernity has involved a detrimental downplaying of these sorts of concerns, in favour of the "localism" encouraged by the organizational imperative. To be clear, Wolin is not arguing that politics disappears in the Age of Organization, "but rather [that there has been] the sublimation of the political into forms of association which earlier thought had believed to be non-political."[41]

The Anthropocene epoch/concept develops these trends in contradictory ways. If Wolin's complaint is that the Age of Organization has been dis-integrative, then the Anthropocene would appear to be a welcome move in the other direction. Notwithstanding Wolin's characterization of environmentalists as partisans of postmodern plurality,[42] it is easy enough to see the environmentalist dictum to "think global" even further intensified in the Anthropocene, with its explicit emphasis on interconnected planetary-scale systems. In this sense it is surely an integrative project, going beyond state-centric conceptions of "society as a whole" to a globalized nature-society. And while a concrete institution for organizing "humanity" and its mass production/consumption complexes at a global scale has yet to be developed, the impulse to "Earth systems governance" or "climate leviathan" is clear enough to discern.[43] On the other hand, we should also be mindful of how Wolin concludes his discussion of the Age of Organization. After lamenting the decline of a more integrative view of politics, Wolin notes that a potential objection is that resistance to this integrative vision is a necessary bulwark against totalitarianism. His response to this objection is to claim that totalitarianism itself may be a *response to* disintegration and that therefore a renewed focus on the integrative orientation of citizenship and the political (as classically understood) is required to avoid it. Seeing totalitarianism in this way highlights the premature closure or false identity that it seeks to impose. In seeking to impose a (false) totality, totalitarianism does not allow space for politics, in the sense of the legitimate(d) contestation of what is in the interest of society as a whole. Again, to the extent that the Anthropocene naively presumes an undifferentiated human subject as the agent of geological change, it continues the Age of Organization's foreclosure of the political.

To conclude this section, we can return to the conclusion of the lengthy passage cited above: in the Age of Organization, organizational imperatives consistently trump democratic ones. As Wolin says, "how much democracy can organization endure? – never the reverse." If organizations provide a medium for implementing a vision (by party elites or corporate CEOs), that vision remains "local" insofar as the organization is not identical to society as a whole. The vision remains limited. But that is only one half of the problem. The other is that, in generating and implementing a vision, it is also repressive of contending visions from within. People within the organization are conceived not as potential political agents or subjects (a demos) but as masses, an object to be manipulated. This is the danger of totalitarianism: a readiness to limit alternative visions and an inability to envision legitimate limits on its own power.

Vision 2004: Postmodern Power, Superpower, Inverted Totalitarianism

By the time Wolin publishes his expanded edition of *Politics and Vision* in 2004, the political context has changed in important ways. In the preface to the new edition, Wolin notes that the original 1960 edition had been published "midway between the Allies' victory over one totalitarian regime and the collapse of another."[44] Later, he observes that "the midpoint between the defeat of one totalitarianism and the disintegration of another was the high-water mark of American liberalism and the beginning of that ideology's evolution from "social conscience liberalism" to "neo-liberalism.""[45] This changed political context, in which "The new liberalism remained state-centered, but its state was now imperial," demanded a different response from the one formulated in 1960 – a different theorization of politics, a different architectonic vision – which Wolin characterizes on the first page of the new preface as the difference between "liberalism and democracy."[46] Our discussion of Wolin's understanding of the changed political context in this section will be fairly restricted, with a brief explication of the constellation of three key terms that, for Wolin, characterize the contemporary (in the 2000s) political conjuncture: postmodern power, Superpower, and inverted totalitarianism, and some brief consideration of how these are extended to the current time of writing (early 2020s), which is now as far from the collapse of the Soviet Union (and the formation of the Intergovernmental Panel on Climate Change) as those events were from the publication of the first edition of *Politics and Vision*. These terms will be helpful for elaborating the tension between limits and vision and its significance for the Anthropocene.

In his summary remarks in the preface, Wolin states: "In postmodern societies the coerciveness of power – its traditional threat of violence – is shadowed by abstract, non-physical power ... includ[ing] the generation, control, collection, and storage of information and its virtually instantaneous transmission."[47]

Information has become vital to *producing* a political reality, rather than merely *encountering* it. Previous political theorists were concerned with making a distinction between how politics appeared and its underlying reality: Plato, Machiavelli, and Marx provide three immediately obvious examples of thinkers, widely separated in time, whose contributions could be characterized as an ability to see through the world of political appearances. At the same time, for such thinkers, the reality that underlay the world of appearances imposed limits on political action. "For theorists of a postmodern era, however, the contrast between appearance and reality no longer holds."[48] While Foucault is not directly cited here, his characterization of power – as essentially "productive" – seems clearly similar to what Wolin has in mind.[49] If appearances constitute reality in some fundamental sense, then both the capacity for vision and the limits imposed by a largely invisible reality must be significantly transformed.

As noted above, by 2004 American liberalism for Wolin has passed its "high-water mark" and the American state has become more frankly imperial. At the same time, postmodern power is "simultaneously concentrated and disaggregated." Power is concentrated in multinational corporations and international financial institutions, but at the same disaggregated in "the market" and consumer politics. For this reason, the American state in some ways appears quite flaccid. Unlike earlier empires, characterized as "'command regime[s]' of domination.... Superpower is better understood as predominance, as ascendancy, preponderance of power, terms that suggest ... above all, an economy of power."[50]

This last phrase, of course, resonates with Wolin's famous characterization of Machiavelli, as a theorist who sought "to create an economy of violence, a science of the controlled application of force."[51] And indeed Wolin remarks in the book's second half (i.e., the 2004 edition) that "a contemporary economy of powerful multinational corporations resembles nothing so much as the warring city-states of sixteenth-century Italy."[52]

One of the unique features of Superpower is the impact of the disaggregation and concentration of power characteristic of postmodernity on the state itself. Wolin's use of the vaguer term "Superpower," like Hardt and Negri's "Empire,"[53] suggests the difficulty of locating a precise centre of power, when the largest multinational corporations control economies that are the size of many nation-states, and when state autonomy is constrained by globalized financial markets, free trade agreements, and institutions such as the World Bank and International Monetary Fund. What other observers have called a "market fundamentalism" underlies Wolin's observed shift from "social conscience liberalism" to "neo-liberalism" (or welfare state to Superpower).[54] But this cannot be identical with, for example, "American imperialism," because if the market is understood as fundamental, then political concerns are necessarily subordinated to economic doctrine. With the hegemony of neoliberalism, "the economy" becomes not only political but the dominant "public philosophy"; it "sets the norm for all practices concerned with significant stakes of power, wealth, and status."[55] In *Democracy Incorporated*, published a few years later, Wolin describes it as an "economic polity" which "subordinat[es] the political system to economic criteria – for example, being driven by the possible effects of a political decision on the sensibilities of 'financial markets.'"[56] The sentiment is depressingly prescient of contemporary demands to "open up" for the sake of the health of "the economy" during a pandemic.

Indeed, Wolin muses: "The twentieth century may have spawned some forms of totalitarianism without having exhausted the genus."[57] But this new species of totalitarianism is "inverted." The criticism of the subordination of the political to the economic is a familiar refrain of the final chapter of the 1960 edition. And in this sense, the current moment is perhaps better cast as "hypermodern" rather than "postmodern." While in the middle of the twentieth century the spectre was of politics (and democracy) being crushed under the weight of organizational imperatives, by the early twenty-first century, the emphasis lies on how the global market (and capitalist economics as ideology) constitutes a new totalizing form of power that is simultaneously concentrated and disaggregated.

While it is never quite stated as such, there is a sense that with the latest species of totalitarianism, history is repeating itself, but for the second time as farce.[58] While Wolin is careful to note that it is "far from absurd," nevertheless "Superpower, was inspired not by any ideology or theory but by a comic strip."[59] If there is farce that is to be found here (as Marx well understood), it lies not in any pleasantly humourous consequences, but rather in the absence of a sense of seriousness as the most dramatic of events unfold. And this appears to be just what Wolin apprehends: elections are now "lavish spectacles." "The political actuality of Superpower Democracy is of a continuous managed plebiscite, controlled excitement for the plebes: their Circus Maximus, their political Superbowl."[60] Thus at the same time that the economy is politicized in the important (Marxian) sense noted above, politics itself is also depoliticized, as a supersized spectacle substitutes for meaningful debate over contending architectonic visions.[61] Again, all this was observed by Wolin long before the Trump presidency took US politics as show business to its rationally irrational conclusion.

Contemporary totalitarianism is "inverted" because it combines a strong state – albeit one more inclined to use "soft" or postmodern forms of power – with an apparent flourishing of "liberal-democratic changes that appear to work against regimentation."[62] Just as postmodern theorizing, like Rawlsian liberalism, appears to celebrate difference without interrogating underlying economic structures, anti-discriminatory (i.e., identity) politics "may also contribute to splintering and fragmenting opposition."[63] The disaggregation of power provides the appearance of political pluralism and tolerance, while restricting the possibility of genuinely political debate – debate over the total constitution of society – and in particular limiting debate over the imperative of continuous economic growth.

Wolin reminds us that the earlier variant of totalitarianism was not completely inoculated from politics. Drawing on recent historians' descriptions of the Nazi regime, Wolin writes that:

> totalitarianism is consistent with a measure of competitiveness, disorder, rival centers of power, and competing loyalties.... It is not so much a refusal of politics as a practice of politics without any consistent ideological justification....
>
> If we substitute profit and exploitation for war and "dynamic" for "aggressive," then the postmodern economy begins to appear as a variant of the totalitarian in which "free competition" masks the dominance of small groups in intense rivalry with each other, a rivalry that in its own way is as expansive and aggressive as any practiced by the Nazis and Fascists.[64]

Finally, the inversion of what might be described as "classical" totalitarianism (i.e., fascism), occurs as the state no longer rests on mass mobilization, but rather on mass demobilization. The perceived connection between fascism and democracy (both in the sense that fascist regimes appeared to enjoy fairly broad popular support and in the sense that fascist regimes emerged out of mass democracies), meant that one of the "lessons" drawn by American social scientists from the experience of fascism was of the danger of "overpoliticizing civil society."[65] The "problem of the masses" needed to be solved in a non-fascist manner, but without contesting the nature of the problem itself. The result was that post-war liberal political science emphasized (explicitly or implicitly) the desirability of mass depoliticization, as "politics" devolved into an implicit "post-political" bargain aimed at "sustaining the unsustainable."[66]

This trend in social scientific thinking represents part of an ambitious (if "disaggregated") reconstitution of citizenship in the latter half of the twentieth century. Again, the parallels with the Leninist shift described earlier, of conceiving the masses as objects to be manipulated, are striking. While maintaining a democratic façade, the "problem of the masses" here is ultimately solved by dispersing the *demos* into individual consumers, slotted into the abstract and reified categories that dominate polling and marketing but do not correlate with lived or communicative communities (e.g., "soccer moms" or the post-2016 obsession with the "white working class"). "Without integrating them," elites "'target' [voters] with a 'message' [which] appeals to some broad 'value.'"[67] This view of mainstream social scientific thinking as complicit in rationalizing depoliticization in America was a significant focus throughout Wolin's work, as we will see when discussing his 1969 essay "Political Theory as a Vocation" below. In a section of *Politics and Vision*, titled "Faltering Vision," Wolin lays at least some of the blame for "uncollapsed" capitalism[68] at the feet of contemporary intellectuals who have rationalized the status quo rather than take up the vocation of political theory: "the disinclination of new millennial intellectuals to conceive of an alternative economic order that could support genuinely political forms of life represents either a failure of the theoretical imagination or the exhaustion of tradition – or both."[69] A "genuinely political form of life" must be at once oriented to a potential reconceptualization of "society as a whole" (visionary thinking) and at the same time admissive of dissenting views (self-consciously limiting).

Fugitive Democracy and the Politics of Limits

In *Politics and Vision*'s discussion of Machiavelli, the latter is described as a figure in which we find "a passionate commitment to the vocation of political theorist." Indeed, it is striking that only a handful of the book's indexed citations for "political theory" are not connected to Machiavelli. And if, as noted above, the contemporary political moment is in important ways analogical to the context in which Machiavelli found himself, we might say that *Politics and Vision* is in some sense Wolin's exhortation for liberation from the barbarians.

Wolin is of course more interested in rekindling a democratic impetus within society than in finding a prince who will reconstitute society from without. The development of postmodern societies, which provide an experience of perpetual change (technological and other), and which therefore tend to perpetuate expert and administrative rather than democratic rule, are "overwhelmingly, a revolution from above."[70] It is perhaps not for nothing that Wolin turns, in the book's final sentences, to Gramsci, who had sought to apply Machiavelli's insights to the mass age: "In the era of Fascism Gramsci had conceived the task to be one of arousing 'the civic consciousness of the nation.' In the era of Superpower the task is to nurture the civic conscience of society."[71]

In a sense, the task that Wolin sets is more modest than Gramsci's. Rather than mobilizing a counter-hegemonic bloc that might successfully challenge the power of capital, Wolin is concerned with protecting and producing resistances to Superpower and contemporary inverted totalitarianism. Democracy, for Wolin, is a "fugitive" experience of politics, rather than a settled form of government.[72] In *Democracy Incorporated*, Wolin names it "demotic politics," with the omission of the "-*kratia*" suffix emphasizing that it is not about "ruling" or "governing." It is the "political expression of the leisureless,"[73] or the episodic action of "those who lack leisure time" and thus for whom "dedication to a political life is hardly a conceivable vocation."[74] It is thus by its nature fleeting. But it is also rendered scarce by "the *inherently* anti-democratic structures and norms characteristic of the dominant institutions of so-called advanced societies, the contemporary corporation and the Superpower state."[75]

Demotic action is by its nature is difficult, if not impossible, to scale up. "What the economic polity renders scarce for its citizens is the direct experience of politics itself and the responsibilities of power. And that is the "renewable resource" unique to the political ecology of localism."[76] The connection between democracy and scale-limited, local politics is reiterated in *Democracy Incorporated*, where Wolin describes the collapse of democracy in ancient Athens: "the problem lay in the transformation of political identity from a city defined by circumscribed power to an identity unconfined and imperial."[77] Contemporary Superpower, similarly, constitutively presents itself as unlimited: "The *virtù* of that regime lies in its dynamic, its ceaseless reaching out. In its political economy form it is a furious drive for the innovations that promise greater rewards and expanded opportunities for exploitation. That drive is remarkable for its ability to keep extending the limits of the possible: the idea of limits becomes an incitement, new 'challenges.'"[78] Wolin's diagnosis of the problems faced by Athenian empire also fits well the Anthropocene and its domination of the non-human world. Part of what "the Anthropocene" represents is the *"limits* of intentional human action" as Meyer stated, above: "By its nature imperial conquest imposes a heavy, perhaps unbearable demand upon human rationality.... There are too many unknowns, contingencies, unpredictable consequences as well as a vast scale on which things can go wrong."[79]

By contrast with the "vast scale" of imperial ambitions, "A smaller political context is more congenial to nurturing democratic values.... [It] brings with it modest stakes and a consequent scaling down of power."[80] Notions of humility, restraint, and limits are crucial here in preserving space for democratic politics. For Wolin (as for E.F. Schumacher and countless ecological thinkers who have followed him), small is beautiful: "small scale is the only scale commensurate with the kind and amount of power that democracy is capable of mobilizing."[81] At the same time, because democracy is practiced by "ordinary citizens," lacking the leisure to engage in politics on a full-time basis, the modest scale of democratic political power is to be seen as a virtue, and is furthermore conveniently consonant with a long tradition in American political life.

There are two tensions worth noting here. The first is one that Wolin himself acknowledges explicitly, that "local" politics can be romanticized: local distinctiveness may also harbour and entrench oppressive forms of inequality.[82] Wolin does not romanticize the progressive *content* of contemporary local politics, acknowledging that "localism is typically the site of the 'anti-modern centrifugals' ... the Klan, militiamen and -women, neo-Nazis, Protestant fundamentalists, would-be censors of public and school libraries, champions of an 'original Constitution.'"[83] Rather, it is the *form* of local politics, the experience of political participation itself – which is most easily available at the local scale to the "ordinary citizens" with limited time for political engagement – that is valuable for rekindling the sense of citizenship and the possibility of collective action in the interest of society as a whole. Whether form and content can be neatly separated, however, is an open question. At the least, the persistence of "anti-modern centrifugals" in local politics disrupts any easy connection between local-scale political experience and a concern with societal rather than particular interests.

The second is whether the limited vision of the local scale has been rendered obsolete by the Anthropocene. Is an "anti-totality politics: small politics, small projects, small business, much improvisation"[84] adequate to a "human-dominated planet"? Here too, it is important not to overstate the extent to which Wolin might fetishize localism. After all, "localism" is also the intellectual orientation that afflicts the Age of Organization, its tendential inability to conceive of a general interest that is different than the sum of group interests: the "chopping up of political man" discussed earlier.[85] Rather than promote an inward orientation, the promise of local politics is that it can provide a space for the effective exercise of demotic action: engagement in (democratic) politics by those who, lacking sufficient leisure time, cannot be engaged in political life full time. Local politics serves as a sort of proving ground where engagement with "general" societal concerns is "most likely" to be cultivated.[86] At some points, Wolin argues that, at least in principle, it can and perhaps should be scaled up: "Democratic experience begins at the local level, but a democratic citizenry should not accept city limits as its political horizon."[87] Wolin cites the example of the response to Hurricane Katrina as an example of demotic action occurring at a national scale: a "spontaneous outpouring" that occurred even as the federal government "floundered." But Wolin is ambivalent on this even at a national scale, and whether or how it might work globally is even less clear. Wolin asks: "Does a demos have a future in the age of globalization, instant communication networks, and fluid borders?"[88] The basis of scaled-up demotic action in the case of Katrina was empathy: unmet "necessities of life … that ordinary Americans elsewhere could spontaneously understand."[89] To what extent would this "spontaneous understanding" obtain across the chasms of global inequality and cultural difference? Here it is worth noting the US-centrism of the arguments in *Democracy Incorporated*, particularly in light of what Wolin knows were the enormous efforts required to constitute "Americans" as a people (demos) in the first place.[90] As well, it is worth noting the character of Wolin's prescriptions, which are in some ways pointedly and explicitly conservative. The final chapter of *Democracy Incorporated* is titled "Democracy's Prospects: Looking Backwards," and in it Wolin prescribes a "different temporal perspective" that repeatedly invokes the past, self-consciously drawing on "unfashionable verbs – 'roll back,' 'revive,' and 'restore'" and concluding that: "Small 'd' democrats need to rediscover and rethink rather than mindlessly embrace 'the latest.'"[91] The kind of ecological thinking that this political vision endorses is also clearly articulated in the final paragraph of the 2004 edition of *Politics and Vision*: "The central challenge at this moment is … about nurturing a discordant democracy … discordant because, in being rooted in the ordinary, it affirms the value of limits."[92] The dialectic of the 2004 edition of *Politics and Vision* thus takes us from the political theorist's capacity for an architectonic vision that is innovative and imaginative – *unlimited vision* – to end with a call for *envisioning limits*.

The Vocation of Political Theory in the Anthropocene

With that in mind, let us turn finally to the text where Wolin considers the role of the political theorist most explicitly. In "Political Theory as a Vocation," Wolin suggests that major (the term he uses is "epic") political theorists are akin to the "extraordinary" scientists described by Thomas Kuhn, upending traditional ways of understanding the world through an innovative act of imaginative vision. However, he goes on to suggest that political theorists are also *unlike* those scientists in an important respect. Revolutions in scientific theory tend to occur, according to Kuhn, with the persistent appearance of "anomalies" which cannot be explained by the dominant theory. Scientific revolutions thus involve envisioning a new systematized understanding of the world (theory) in which the new, anomalous facts fit. But while scientific theories are descriptive, political theories inevitably have a normative dimension. Political theories involve the expression of "fundamental values" or a "vision of the Good."[93] And, the empirical facts that political theories describe are human creations, "organizations [that] are uniquely the product of mind."[94] Thus political theorizing involves an insistence on making the facts fit the theory rather than the other way around: "The shaping experience [for the political theorist] has been the recurrently problematic state of the world, not the problematic state of theories about that world."[95] The marking (or invention) of the epoch/concept of the Anthropocene is posited as a retrospective vision from the future. It is about how future geologists will read a geological record currently in formation. In this sense, it is less about how the Holocene as a conceptual category (theory) mis-describes the present, and more about the contemporary transformations of the earth systems and their (empirical and normative) implications for human and other forms of life.

This might provide a first line of defence against the accusation that Wolin is engaged in a romantic and ultimately untenable valourization of social forms and experiences being eclipsed by the epoch/concept of the Anthropocene. On this line of reasoning, to claim that Wolin's account of engaged political life is anachronistic or no longer feasible is to engage in the same kind of rationalization that smugly defends low voter turnout as a sign of satisfaction with the representative-democratic system. Key to Wolin's account of the vocation of political theory is the recognition that if, for example, capitalist modernity does not allow for the expression of our fundamental values, or for human beings to live the good life, then it is capitalist modernity, rather than our ideals and commitments, that ought to be jettisoned. But if it is possible (if only dimly) to imagine a human world in which capitalist modernity is a time period safely confined to history, the same is not so clearly true for the geological epoch of the Anthropocene. The Anthropocene turns out to force us to (re)consider: what is the normative basis for political theorizing?

Recall Meyer's observation that the Anthropocene is "Janus-faced." On the one hand, human power is planetary scaled, to the point that distinguishing between human and non-human systems is increasingly untenable. So, whether in the spirit of advocating planetary systems management or lamenting the "end of nature," responsibility cannot be evaded. And such responsibility now demands a global, if not unlimited, vision. A role for "epic" theory here seems clear. On the other hand, however, the Anthropocene discourse is also, for many, a story about "the *limits* of intentional human action." These limits are only partly described by the unanticipated consequences caused by lack of natural-scientific knowledge, or an inadequate scientific theory. Climate change is occurring not only because for some time we didn't understand the climatological consequences of burning fossil fuels. It is also occurring because, for example, entrenched fossil fuel interests have blocked a more rapid transition to other energy sources. Even more, the synoptic vision that appears to be demanded by the epoch/concept of the Anthropocene is itself an imposed framing (as the critics of the Anthropocene label discussed above have noted). It ignores "the perennial desire of some people to replace one socio-environmental regime with an entirely different one"[96] and presumes a societal consensus – a singular "Anthropos" – where it doesn't exist. And finally, in a world where "natural" and "social" systems are co-evolving and increasingly interpenetrated, if not logically indistinguishable, reserving "political" theorizing to a domain of "organizations [that] are uniquely the product of mind" seems increasingly untenable. In short, "epic" theorizing is increasingly urgent but also increasingly difficult.

It is difficult because the "totality" that is to be theorized is both vastly expanded in scope and also seriously fractured. Earth systems governance or planetary management seems only possible through the imposition of an elite-driven vision in the face of stark global inequalities. A more democratic form faces the enormous obstacle of constituting the global demos.[97] The democratic – or demotic – alternative, Wolin seems to suggest, is a more limited vision: a retreat, both temporally and in terms of political scale.

James Wiley suggests that Wolin had begun to reject epic theory as an "an elitist form of theory" as early as 1970 (in *Hobbes and the Epic Tradition of Political Theory*), or in other words almost immediately after it was fully articulated in "Political Theory as a Vocation."[98] Wolin's rejection of epic theory came out of a growing sense that it was "an immodest attempt to emulate the heroism of political action in thought by creating powerful and memorable theories that would make their authors 'immortal.'"[99] This drive for immortality can be seen as being of a piece with the ceaseless, totalizing drive for expansion that he identifies in Superpower, or that Mann and Wainwright describe as "Climate Leviathan." Instead, Wolin's democratic vision entails enabling the political participation of those "ordinary citizens" for whom political engagement is not the primary focus of their daily lives. On such a view, the role, or vocation, of the political theorist is perhaps no more than to articulate the call for "tending" to the institutions, cultural practices, and forms of life that might enable episodic outbursts of "fugitive" democracy.[100]

Might such fugitive democratic episodes congeal into something more sustainable? Rather than a new epic theory based on a putative unlimited vision, Wolin offers something different. Crucial to democratic practice is not only a limited spatial scale, but also a slower pace: democracy requires *time* for deliberation.[101] In practice, democratic deliberation not only serves the instrumental purpose of the expression and negotiation of needs, but also and at the same time (re)produces the social bonds of a political community. As for deliberation in theory: in an essay on Max Weber, Wolin notes that political "theorizing has been conceived as a performance ... intended as a model for a new form of politics."[102] For at least the last several decades, the profession (if not vocation) of the political theorist has rarely, if ever, involved epic theorizing, and far more routinely involves the staging of confrontations with "strange and therefore provocative" political theories of the past. Here, perhaps, a model of deliberation that neither endorses hubristic unlimited vision nor unnecessarily blinkered limits. Instead, a strange and provocative reminder that the path to a truly humane Age of Man lies through conversation with the past.

> When evening has come, I return to my house and go into my study.... I enter the ancient courts of ancient men, where, received by them lovingly, I feed on the food that alone is mine and that I was born for. There I am not ashamed to speak with them and to ask them the reason for their actions; and they in their humanity reply to me.[103]

NOTES

Thanks to Mark Brown, Terry Maley, John Meyer, Peter Stillman, Zev Trachtenberg, John Wallach, and Harlan Wilson for helpful comments on an earlier version of this chapter, and to Chris Sardo (via Twitter) for scanning and sending a publication during COVID lockdown.

1 Sheldon S. Wolin, "Political Theory as a Vocation," *American Political Science Review*, Vol. 63, No. 4 (December 1969). Hereafter cited as PTV.

2 Meera Subramanian, "Anthropocene Now: Influential Panel Votes to Recognize Earth's New Epoch," *Nature*, 21 May 2019.

3 Will Steffen et al., "Trajectories of the Earth System in the Anthropocene," *Proceedings of the National Academy of Science*, Vol. 115, No. 33 (14 August 2018), 8252.

4 Subramanian, "Anthropocene Now."

5 Sheldon S. Wolin, *Politics and Vision: Continuity and Innovation in Western Political Thought*, expanded ed. (Princeton, NJ: Princeton University Press, 2004). Hereafter cited as *PV*.

6 See, for example, the call for a special issue of the journal *Quaternary* on "What if the 'Anthropocene' is not formalized as a new geological epoch?" https://www .mdpi.com/journal/quaternary/special_issues/anthropocene_formalization, accessed 26 August 2022.

7 W. Steffen et al., *Global Change and the Earth System: A Planet Under Pressure* (Berlin: Springer, 2004).

8 Subramanian, "Anthropocene Now."

9 Edward Burtynsky, "The Anthropocene Project," https://www.edwardburtynsky .com/projects/the-anthropocene-project, accessed 26 August 2022.

10 Jan Zalasiewicz et al., "The Geological Cycle of Plastics and Their Use as a Stratigraphic Indicator of the Anthropocene," *Anthropocene*, Vol. 13 (2016), 4–17.

11 Steffen et al., *Global Change*, 81.

12 Paul J. Crutzen and Eugene F. Stoermer, "The 'Anthropocene,'" *Global Change Newsletter*, Vol. 41 (May 2000), 17.

13 Crutzen and Stoermer, "Anthropocene," 17. For a review of some of the contending dates, as well as an argument for equating the Anthropocene with the Holocene, see Bruce D. Smith and Melinda A. Zeder, "The Onset of the Anthropocene," *Anthropocene*, Vol. 4 (December 2013), 8–13. Not included in Smith and Zeder's review, although argued by others, is the European conquest of the Americas and the beginning of the Atlantic slave trade (variously dated between 1460 and 1619). See, for example, Katherine Yusoff, *A Billion Black Anthropocenes – Or None* (Minneapolis: University of Minnesota Press, 2018).

14 John M. Meyer, "The Politics of the 'Post-Political' Contesting the Diagnosis," *Democratization*, Vol. 27, No. 3 (2020), 417.

15 Jason W. Moore, *Capitalism in the Web of Life* (New York: Verso, 2015); Donna Haraway, "Anthropocene, Capitalocene, Plantationocene, Chthulucene: Making Kin," *Environmental Humanities*, Vol. 6 (2015), 159–65; Timothy W. Luke, "On the Politics of the Anthropocene" *Telos*, Vol. 172 (Fall 2015); Kate Raworth, "Must the Anthropocene be a Manthropocene?" *Guardian*, 20 October 2014; Damian F. White, "Critical Design, Hybrid Labor, Just Transitions: Moving beyond Technocratic Ecomodernisms and the It's-Too-Late-Ocene," in *Rethinking the Environment for the Anthropocene*, ed. Manuel Arias-Maldonado and Zev Trachtenberg (New York: Routledge, 2019).

16 Robin Kimmerer, "Returning the Gift," *Minding Nature*, Vol. 7, No. 2 (2014), 23.

17 Frank Biermann, *Earth System Governance: World Politics in the Anthropocene* (Cambridge, MA: MIT Press, 2014).

18 Vaclav Smil, *The Earth's Biosphere: Evolution, Dynamics, and Change* (Cambridge, MA: MIT Press, 2003).

19 John S. Dryzek and Jonathan Pickering, *The Politics of the Anthropocene* (Oxford: Oxford University Press, 2019). While more explicitly grounded in a "new materialist" perspective, and thus more sceptical of human exceptionalism, the recent work of William Connolly in some ways also fits here. See, for example, William E. Connolly, *Facing the Planetary: Entangled Humanism and the Politics of Swarming* (Durham, NC: Duke University Press, 2017).

20 Timothy W. Luke, "Political Critiques of the Anthropocene," *Telos*, Vol. 172 (Fall 2015); Geoff Mann and Joel Wainwright, *Climate Leviathan: A Political Theory of Our Planetary Future* (London: Verso, 2018); Mick Smith, "Against Ecological Sovereignty: Agamben, Politics, and Globalization," *Environmental Politics* (2009).

21 John Asafu-Adjaye et al., "An Ecomodernist Manifesto," http://www.ecomodernism .org/manifesto-english, accessed 26 August 2022.

22 Steven Vogel, *Thinking Like a Mall: Environmental Philosophy after the End of Nature* (Cambridge, MA: MIT Press, 2015).

23 John M. Meyer, "Vocations of (Environmental) Political Theory in the Anthropocene," in *Rethinking the Environment for the Anthropocene*, ed. Arias-Maldonado and Trachtenberg (New York: Routledge, 2019), emphases in original.

24 Noel Castree et al., "Changing the Intellectual Climate," *Nature Climate Change*, Vol. 4, No. 9 (2014), 763.

25 Hannah Arendt, *The Human Condition*, 2nd ed. (Chicago: University of Chicago Press, 1998 [1958]), 262.

26 Arendt, *The Human Condition*, 324.

27 Wolin, *PV*, 21.

28 Wolin, *PV*, 21–2.

29 Wolin, *PV*, 18.

30 Wolin, *PV*, 19.

31 Wolin, *PV*, 9.

32 Mark Warren, review of *Politics and Vision* in *Political Theory*, Vol. 34, No. 5 (2006), 667.

33 Wolin, *PV*, 377.

34 Wolin, PV, 378.

35 In a later essay, Wolin describes the late eighteenth-century discourse of the US "Founding Fathers" (federalists) as one of "organizationism." Sheldon S. Wolin, "Tending and Intending a Constitution: Bicentennial Misgivings," in *The Presence of the Past: Essays on the State and the Constitution* (Baltimore: Johns Hopkins University Press, 1989), 92.

36 Wolin, *PV*, 378.

37 Wolin, *PV*, 381, emphasis added.

38 Castree et al., "Changing the Intellectual Climate," 10, emphases in original.

39 Wolin, *PV*, 385.

40 Wolin, *PV*, 386.

41 Wolin, *PV*, 385.

42 Wolin, *PV*, xxi.

43 Mann and Wainwright, *Climate Leviathan*. See also Luke, "Political Critiques of the Anthropocene."

44 Wolin, *PV*, xvi.

45 Wolin, *PV*, 552.

46 Wolin, *PV*, xv. Wolin specifically refers to "the author's … journey from liberalism to democracy," although it should be clear that the journey is impelled by the tides of history as much as Wolin's independent thinking on the matter. Some of these ideas are further developed in Sheldon S. Wolin, *Democracy Incorporated: Managed Democracy and the Specter of Inverted Totalitarianism* (Princeton, NJ: Princeton University Press, 2008).

47 Wolin, *PV*, xx.

48 Wolin, *PV*, 395. A now-classic diagnosis of this postmodern collapsing of essence and appearance is in Fredric Jameson, *Postmodernism, or The Cultural Logic of Late Capitalism* (Durham, NC: Duke University Press, 1991).

49 See, for example, Michel Foucault, *Discipline and Punish: The Birth of the Prison*, trans. Alan Sheridan (New York: Vintage, 1979); and Michel Foucault, *The History of Sexuality, Volume 1*, trans. Robert Hurley (New York: Vintage, 1990).

50 Wolin, *PV*, xix. Wolin also emphasizes the extent to which the state's monopoly on the legitimate use of violence is now challenged by "decentered terrorism."

51 Wolin, *PV*, 198.

52 Wolin, *PV*, 564. The similarities between Wolin's reading of Machiavelli and his understanding of his own political project are at times quite striking and no doubt worthy of further comment. While a few others will be mentioned in passing below, a full treatment is beyond the scope of this essay.

53 Michael Hardt and Antonio Negri, *Empire* (Cambridge, MA: Harvard University Press, 2000).

54 Wolin, *PV*, 575–8.

55 Wolin, *PV*, 564.

56 Sheldon S. Wolin, *Democracy Incorporated: Managed Democracy and the Specter of Inverted Totalitarianism* (Princeton, NJ: Princeton University Press, 2008), 287.

57 Wolin, *PV*, 564.

58 This phrasing borrows from the famous opening passage of Marx's essay "The Eighteenth Brumaire of Louis-Napoleon Bonaparte." In an epilogue to a new edition of that essay that was being published in 1965, Herbert Marcuse observes that under fascism "the 'World-historical facts and persons' which occur 'as it were twice', no longer occur the second time as 'farce'. Or rather, the farce is more fearful than the tragedy it follows." Herbert Marcuse, "Epilogue to the New German Edition of Marx's 18th Brumaire of Louis Napoleon," *Radical America*, Vol. 3, No. 4

(July/August 1969), 55, https://www.marcuse.org/herbert/pubs/60spubs/65Marcus eEpilogMarx18thBrumaireEnglish.pdf, accessed 26 August 2022.

59 Wolin, *PV*, 553. The "comic strip" inspirations of Superpower are perhaps even more evident in the current moment, when superhero movies are such a dominant presence in popular culture.

60 Wolin, *PV*, 554.

61 The literature on a "post-political consensus" is critically analysed through a Wolinian lens in Meyer, "Politics of the Post-Political."

62 Wolin, *PV*, xvi.

63 Wolin, *PV*, xvi. On postmodernism, see Wolin, *PV*, 566–7; on Rawls, see Wolin, *PV*, 530–6.

64 Wolin, *PV*, 579.

65 Wolin, *PV*, 554.

66 Blühdorn, "Sustaining the Unsustainable," *Environmental Politics*, Vol. 16, No. 2 (2007). While Blühdorn sees this as a relatively recent phenomenon, Meyer puts it into a longer post–Second World War context: Meyer, "Politics of the Post-Political."

67 Wolin, *Democracy Incorporated*, 285.

68 Wolin, *PV*, 565–6.

69 Wolin, *PV*, 578.

70 Wolin, *PV*, 605.

71 Wolin, *PV*, 606. The Gramsci quotation is from *The Prison Notebooks*. See also Antonio Gramsci, "The Modern Prince: Essays on the Science of Politics in the Modern Age," in *The Modern Prince and Other Writings*, trans. Louis Marks (New York: International Publishers, 1957).

72 Wolin, *PV*, 601–6. See also Sheldon Wolin, "Fugitive Democracy," in *Democracy and Difference: Contesting the Boundaries of the Political*, ed. Seyla Benhabib (Princeton, NJ: Princeton University Press, 1996).

73 Wolin, *Democracy Incorporated*, 277.

74 Wolin, *Democracy Incorporated*, 255.

75 Wolin, *PV*, 604, emphasis in original.

76 Wolin, *PV*, 604.

77 Wolin, *Democracy Incorporated*, 244.

78 Wolin, *PV*, 595.

79 Wolin, *Democracy Incorporated*, 247. A similar point is made in Joel Alden Schlosser, *Herodotus in the Anthropocene* (Chicago: University of Chicago Press, 2020).

80 Wolin, *Democracy Incorporated*, 267.

81 Wolin, *PV*, 603. See also E.F. Schumacher, *Small Is Beautiful: A Study of Economics as if People Mattered* (New York: Vintage Books, 1973).

82 Mark Purcell, "Urban Democracy and the Local Trap," *Urban Studies*, Vol. 43, No. 11 (2006).

83 Wolin, *PV*, 604.

84 Wolin, *PV*, 603.

85 Wolin, *PV*, 85–6.

86 Wolin, *Democracy Incorporated*, 291.

87 Wolin, *Democracy Incorporated*, 291.

88 Wolin, *Democracy Incorporated*, 278.

89 Wolin, *Democracy Incorporated*, 288–9.

90 Wolin, "Tending and Intending a Constitution," esp. 87–8.

91 Wolin, *Democracy Incorporated*, 274.

92 Wolin, *PV*, 605–6.

93 Wolin, *PV*, 19, and see above.

94 Wolin, PTV, 1081.

95 Wolin, PTV, 1079.

96 Castree et al., "Changing the Intellectual Climate," 7. See also Meyer, "Politics of the Post-Political," 417–18.

97 The scale of the challenge is suggested, in different ways, in Mann and Wainwright, *Climate Leviathan*; and Mike Davis, "Who Will Build the Ark?" *New Left Review*, Vol. 61 (2010).

98 James Wiley, "Sheldon Wolin on Theory and the Political," *Polity*, Vol. 38, No. 2 (2006), 221–4.

99 Wiley, "Wolin," 221.

100 Wolin, "Tending and Intending"; Wolin, *Democratic Imagination*, 258, 267, and *passim*.

101 Wolin, *Democracy Incorporated*, 267.

102 Sheldon S. Wolin, "Max Weber: Legitimation, Method, and the Politics of Theory," *Political Theory*, Vol. 9, No. 3 (1981), 404.

103 Niccolò Machiavelli, "Niccolò Machiavelli to Francesco Vettori, Florence, December 10, 1513," in *The Prince*, 2nd ed., trans. Harvey C. Mansfield (Chicago: University of Chicago Press, 1998), 109–10.

Contributors

Terence Ball holds a PhD from UC Berkeley. Having taught for many years at the University of Minnesota, he moved in 1999 to Arizona State University, from which he retired in 2015. His special interests include the history of political theory, the history and philosophy of the social sciences, conceptual history, and green political theory. He is the author of several books, including *Transforming Political Discourse* and *Reappraising Political Theory* and over 100 scholarly articles and review-essays.

Andrew Biro is a professor in the Department of Politics at Acadia University, where he also teaches in the interdisciplinary programs in Environmental & Sustainability Studies and Social & Political Thought. His research focuses on the intersections of critical theory, environmental politics, political economy, and cultural studies. His most recent book, co-authored with Alice Cohen, is *Organizing Nature: Turning Canada's Ecosystems into Resources* (University of Toronto Press, 2023).

Lucy Cane teaches Politics at London Academy of Excellence Tottenham and Birkbeck, University of London. Her book, *Sheldon Wolin and Democracy: Seeing Through Loss* (Routledge, 2020), is the first full-length theory study of Wolin's work. Cane has published academic essays in outlets such as *Political Theory and New Political Science*, as well as journalism in outlets including *The Sydney Morning Herald* and *The Australian*. She has ongoing interests in the political cultures and democratic deficits of the United States, the United Kingdom, and Australia. For more information, visit www.lucycane.com.

Romand Coles was Professor of Political Theory at Duke University for two decades before becoming the MacAllister Chair and Director of the Program for Community, Culture and Environment at Northern Arizona University.

He is the author of many books and articles, including *Beyond Gated Politics: Reflections for the Possibility of Democracy* (University of Minnesota, 2005); *Christianity, Democracy and the Radical Ordinary: Conversations between a Radical Democrat and a Christian*, with Stanley Hauerwas (Wipf and Stock, 2008), which contains extensive engagement with the work of Sheldon Wolin; and *Visionary Pragmatism: Radical and Ecological Democracy in Neoliberal Times* (Duke University Press, 2016). He is currently an independent scholar and activist.

Ingrid Creppell is Associate Professor in the Department of Political Science and the Elliott School of International Affairs at the George Washington University. Her research interests have included the history of toleration, secularism, and threat, and currently focus on value-conflict, enmity, and identity. Among her books are *Toleration and Identity* (2003) and *Morality, Governance and Social Institutions: Reflections on Russell Hardin* (2018, co-edited with Thomas Christiano and Jack Knight). She has published in *Archives Européennes de Sociologie, International Theory, Political Theory*, and *Res Publica*, among other journals. She is writing a book on enmity as a political mindset.

Stephen L. Esquith teaches political theory, community engagement, and ethics in the Residential College in the Arts and Humanities, Michigan State University. He was a senior Fulbright scholar in Poland and then again in Mali in 2005–6. He has written on the rule of law, the problem of democratic political education, mass violence and reconciliation, and moral and political responsibility. He is the author of *Intimacy and Spectacle* (Cornell University Press, 1994), a critique of classical and modern liberal political philosophy, and *The Political Responsibilities of Everyday Bystanders* (Pennsylvania State University Press, 2010) on mass violence and democratic political education. He has been involved in numerous civic engagement projects in public schools and has led a study abroad program focusing on ethical issues in development in Mali in summer 2004, 2006, 2008, 2010, and 2014. He has co-edited a volume of critical essays on the human capabilities approach to development and has recently written on children's human rights, peacebuilding, the role of film in democratic political education, human security, and philosophy for children. He is currently working with Weloré Tamboura on several dialogue and reconciliation projects with internally displaced youth in Mali in collaboration with the Université des Lettres et des Sciences Humaines de Bamako, La Commission Vérité, Justice, et Réconciliation du Mali, and peace education projects for refugee youth in Michigan.

Jason Frank is the John L. Senior Professor of Government at Cornell University, where he teaches political theory. Frank's research is focused on historically situated approaches to democratic theory, with an emphasis on the modern history of popular sovereignty. He is the author of *Constituent Moments: Enacting the People in Postrevolutionary America* (Duke University Press, 2010), *Publius and Political Imagination* (Rowman and Littlefield, 2013), and most recently *The Democratic Sublime: On Aesthetics and Popular Assembly* (Oxford University Press, 2021). He is also the editor of *A Political Companion to Herman Melville* (University Press of Kentucky, 2013) and *Vocations of Political Theory* (University of Minnesota Press, 2000). His current book project is titled *Democracy at the End of the World*.

Lia Haro received her PhD in Cultural Anthropology at Duke University. She has worked as an independent scholar and activist in Africa, the United States, Latin America, and Australia. Her co-authored writings with Romand Coles have appeared in journals such as *Political Theory*, *Theory and Event*, and *Angelaki*, and they are currently completing a book titled *Revolutionary Love: The Politics of Receptive Power*.

Calvin Z.L. Lincez is an Omushkego Ininiw (Mushkegowuk Cree) of mixed descent and currently works with Indigenous organizations and their ENGO allies in the struggle to protect the land and mitigate the negative impacts of resource extraction on climate change and biodiversity loss in Canada's north. He holds a PhD in political science from York University, Canada. His academic research is conducted in the fields of political theory and critical Indigenous studies, with a focus on the intersection of radical democratic thought and Indigenous resurgence theory in the context of an analysis and critique of processes associated with the politics of reconciliation in settler-colonial contexts such as Canada.

Terry Maley teaches in the Politics Department and in the Graduate Social and Political Thought program at York University, Toronto, Canada. His published books include *Democracy and the Political in Max Weber's Thought* (Toronto, 2011). Edited books are: *Critical Theory in Dark Times* (Palgrave, 2022), co-edited with Peter Erwin-Jansen, Robert Kirsch, and Taylor Hines; *One-Dimensional Man 50 Years On: The Struggle Continues* (Fernwood, 2017); and *The Barbarism of Reason: Max Weber and the Twilight of Enlightenment* (Toronto, 1994), co-edited with Asher Horowitz. A recent article relating to Wolin and democracy appeared in the journal *Theory Culture and Society* (2021); book chapters on Weber's famous lecture, *Politics as a Vocation*, liberal-democracy, and authoritarianism/populism are in two volumes edited by Alan Sica (Anthem, 2016, and Routledge, 2022). Maley's recent work explores how the intersection between Wolin's thought and the first generation of Frankfurt School Critical Theorists can contribute to discussions of pressing issues facing democracy today – authoritarianism, far-right populism, and movements for democratic retrieval/renewal within and beyond the neoliberal state.

John R. Wallach has been a lecturer and visiting professor of political theory at Yale University and Vassar College, and (from 1991 to 2022) a professor of political science at Hunter College & the Graduate Center of the City University of New York. He has authored dozens of articles and reviews on contemporary political theory, ancient Greek political theory, American public law, democratic ethics, human rights, and the historical interpretation of political theory. His published books are *Democracy and Goodness: A Historicist Political Theory* (Cambridge University Press, 2018); *The Platonic Political Art: A Study of Critical Reason and Democracy* (Pennsylvania State University Press, 2001), and as co-editor with J. Peter Euben and Josiah Ober, *Athenian Political Thought and the Reconstruction of American Democracy* (Cornell University Press, 1994). He has received several grants from the National Endowment for the Humanities and was a Liberal Arts Fellow in Law and Political Science at Harvard Law School. He studied with Sheldon Wolin as an undergraduate at the University of California Santa Cruz and as a graduate student at Princeton University.

Iain Webb is a PhD candidate at York University in Toronto, Canada. His research focuses on theories of neoliberalism and the implications for democracy of its development. Broadly, his work seeks to extend and apply the democratic thought of Sheldon Wolin, as well as his critiques of emerging neoliberal apolitical administration, towards an examination of the post-war development of neoliberalism in the United Kingdom. More narrowly, Webb is currently examining the post-war history of radical and extreme right-wing groups in the United Kingdom and the ways in which their shifting political fortunes and ideological underpinnings have reflected the social changes that accompanied the turn to neoliberalism in the United Kingdom.

Milton Keynes UK
Ingram Content Group UK Ltd.
UKHW011114210424
441408UK00005B/172/J